The Legend of
CESSNA

These beautiful Cessna 165s, built in 1940, are flying over farms in Hutchinson, Kansas. The aircraft, also known as the Airmaster, is popular with aviation enthusiasts.

The Legend of CESSNA

Jeffrey L. Rodengen

For John Day...The nicest pilot I know.

Also by Jeff Rodengen

The Legend of Chris-Craft

IRON FIST: The Lives of Carl Kiekhaefer

Evinrude-Johnson and The Legend of OMC

Serving The Silent Service: The Legend of Electric Boat

The Legend of Dr Pepper/Seven-Up

The Legend of Honeywell

The Legend of Briggs & Stratton

The Legend of Ingersoll-Rand

The Legend of Stanley: 150 Years of The Stanley Works

The MicroAge Way

The Legend of Halliburton

The Legend of York International

The Legend of Nucor Corporation

The Legend of Goodyear: The First 100 Years

The Legend of AMP

Applied Materials: Pioneering the Information Age

The Legend of AMD

The Legend of Amdahl

The Legend of Echlin

The Legend of Pfizer

The Legend of Inter-Tel

The Legend of VF Corporation

The Legend of American Standard

The Legend of Rowan

The Legend of Ashland

The Legend of Federal-Mogul

Publisher's Cataloging in Publication

Rodengen, Jeffrey L.
The legend of Cessna /Jeffrey L. Rodengen.
p. cm.
Includes bibliographical references and index.
ISBN 0-945903-30-8

1. Cessna Aviation Company 2. Aircraft industry — United States. I. Title

HD9519.N8R64 1997 338.7'62913'0973
QBI97-40430

Write Stuff Enterprises, Inc.

1515 Southeast 4th Avenue • Fort Lauderdale, FL 33316
1-800-900-Book (1-800-900-2665) • (954) 462-6657

Library of Congress Catalog Card Number 97-60423
ISBN 0-945903-30-8

Completely produced in the United States of America
10 9 8 7 6 5 4 3 2 1

TABLE OF CONTENTS

FOREWORD

BY ARNOLD PALMER

WHEN I WAS a youngster growing up in Latrobe, a small industrial town east of Pittsburgh, one of my fascinations involved airplanes and aviation. Like so many other boys of that time, I built and crashed my share of balsa wood models.

I had other interests as well. When I was three years old, my father put a sawed-off golf club in my hands and showed me the right way to hold it. Since then, golf has been my passion. I lived with the game, especially since Pap was the professional and course superintendent at the Latrobe Country Club. I worked at it and played at it. But golf wasn't all-consuming.

When I was old enough and had the opportunity, I would spend time at the old terminal building at our nice little airport, barely a mile from my home on the perimeter of the course. I liked listening to the pilots trade stories about their planes and their adventures in the sky. Early on, a friend of a friend of my family who was an Army pilot took me for a ride in a Piper Cub. He did some things he probably shouldn't have done, and really gave me a scare. Though shaken, I was resolved that, just as soon as I could afford it, I would take lessons and become a flier. Little did I realize what an important part of my life — along with athletics, business and family — aviation would become in the years ahead.

I couldn't do anything about it at first, but my formative years on the pro tour solidified my determination to get my own plane — and for more than just the pleasure I knew I would get from the flying itself. Those arduous trips from tournament to tournament around the country were exhausting, and certainly didn't do my golfing any good. On some of the longer jumps between tournaments, particularly in the moves from the West to the East and South and vice versa, I practically climbed out of my car upon arriving in town and stepped onto the first tee.

As good things began to happen to me during the time I was on the tour, such as the birth of our daughters Peggy (1956) and Amy (1958), the highways became less and less a part of our lives. I began taking those flying lessons I had dreamed about as a kid. I learned to fly in Cessna 172s and 182s. After earning my private license, I rented small planes at first. Then in 1961 I acquired my first aircraft. I had met an unusually bright and talented young attorney named Russ Meyer who was working with a law firm in Cleveland. He helped me book exhibitions and negotiate the agreements for a variety of business relationships. Russ wrote the contract on my very first airplane, and he has written the contracts for every airplane I have

This tremendous saving of time, not to mention wear and tear on body and soul, through private flying has been even more evident during the last two decades when I have devoted more time and more of my non-tournament life to the design, construction and operation of golf courses throughout the country and abroad. We can usually fly into a small airport much closer to the job than an airliner can. The time saved enables me to get to one or two other sites hundreds of miles apart that same day. Weeks of travel translate into days because of my airplane.

I purchased my first of six Citation jets, a Citation I, in 1976 (see below). This began a relationship with Cessna which has lasted for more than twenty years. And, without question, my affiliation with Russ and Cessna was by far the best and most comfortable association that I ever had. I received the service that I needed on the airplane. I never experienced a breakdown in which I couldn't get to where I had to

owned. Russ and I became good friends, and we have remained very close friends ever since.

Aside from the decisions to marry Winnie and become a professional golfer, the choices I made that ultimately took me into private aviation were the smartest I could have made. To put it simply, I could never have accomplished even half as much as I have in my golf and business careers over the last four decades without owning my own airplanes, especially the business jets since 1966, and access to an excellent airport so close to home.

go. In each case, the maintenance, and the backup of Cessna, were impeccable.

After the Citation I, I went on to own and fly the Citations II, III, an improved version of the III, and the VII.

I anxiously awaited the Citation X, as did many people. I sat on the edge of my seat all the time during the Citation X development program. I saw it when it was starting to really take shape, and I was in the factory a lot when they were doing the planning in the very early stages. I saw it on its first flight. I was there enough to watch the people working on it to the point where I knew most of the people working on the airplane, and would talk to them about the various functions and systems. It was an exciting time watching the X come together.

When it rolled off the line, Russ Meyer and I, with our wives, took the number two airplane and flew it from Latrobe to Leuchers, a Royal Air Force Base just across the bay from St. Andrews in Scotland — a sort of holy ground for the game of golf. We flew it over there in five hours and 58

minutes nonstop, and in time for dinner! We got up the next morning and went to play golf with both the new and old Captain at the Royal and Ancient Golf Club, made a speech in the evening at dinner, and then flew back to Latrobe the following morning. The Citation X performed magnificently, naturally. The speeds and altitudes we attained, and the fact that we could fly nonstop and still have ample fuel for an instrument approach was just fantastic.

About a year later, I took delivery of Citation X number three in Latrobe. I remember the airplane coming over the golf course, and how pretty it was. All the excitement of taking delivery of the Citation X was thoroughly evident. Since I've had this beautiful aircraft — the first production airplane off the line — I've never failed to make a single trip. We have made every single engagement and commitment scheduled; believe me, with my schedule that's saying a lot!

Many people just don't realize how important a reliable aircraft is as a business asset. There is no way I could accomplish what I have without an aircraft. I build golf courses, I play tournaments, I do exhibitions, I do appearances, I make speeches, I do outings. For example, I recently visited nine golf courses in three days. On another occasion, I did a golf outing in Latrobe in the morning, and then played 18 holes on a golf course we're building in Reno, Nevada, the same day, and then entertained some customers that evening for dinner. That's the sort of thing the airplane has allowed me to do.

You give it the respect that it's due, and the X will do the job. As the fastest non-military jet in the world, except for the Concorde, it gets noticed. I recall an air traffic controller saying, "Arnie, we're going to have to slow you down. Those guys in front of you can't keep up and you're going to run over them. Do you want us to ask if you can play through?" The guys in front were running full speed in a 737.

I use my Citation X on short hops, even as short as 100 miles, from Latrobe to Wheeling or Columbus for a golf course job. On the other hand, I am planning to take it from Latrobe to Los Angeles, on to Hawaii, Guam and the Philippines, and do golf courses at each stop.

Russ Meyer and the whole team at Cessna won the 1996 Robert J. Collier Trophy for the Citation X. They have all just done a superb job. Russ has the ability to bring together the finest group of talent in the world that any manufacturer in any industry has been able to do, and

he is deeply thankful for the efforts which they have made.

Who knows what lies ahead with my aviation? I have every expectation of maintaining an intensive business and golfing schedule for quite a few years to come in my new Citation X and have no intention of changing my modus operandi very much. I log something like 30 hours a month in the air. Since 1966, that computes to around 5 million statute miles in the jets. I have more than 14,000 hours in my logbook.

On the occasion of the 70th anniversary of Cessna, and on the 25th anniversary of the Citation program, I wish Cessna and its dedicated employees continued success. I can't wait to see what's next!

INTRODUCTION

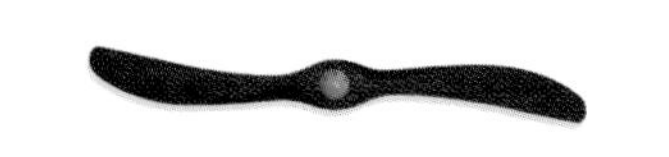

WHEN CLYDE CESSNA flew his beloved *Silver Wings* for the first time in 1911, flight itself was simply a novelty. Hundreds of people attended air shows to watch Cessna do little more than fly overhead and hope for a smooth landing. To people who had never seen an airplane, it was well worth the 50 cents of admission.

In less than 90 years, rapid advances in flight fundamentally changed the way we work, play and wage war. The Cessna Aircraft Company has helped pioneer the way. As the general aviation leader, Cessna provides the world's most popular business jets, as well as a host of other aircraft to serve a wide variety of needs, from the routine delivery of packages to medical evacuation.

Clyde Cessna, designer, manufacturer and pilot, started the company in 1927, setting Wichita, Kansas, on a course to become the "Air Capital of the World."

By 1927, more than 20 aviation-related companies were established in the thriving city.

But the Great Depression closed many of those early companies, Clyde's included. In 1931 he locked the doors to his plant. But in 1934, with the help of his nephews, Dwane and Dwight Wallace, he brought the business back to life. Resurgence in the face of challenge would prove to be a hallmark of the company.

In 1936, Clyde retired and Dwane Wallace became president of the company. He would remain at the company's helm until 1975, when Russell W. Meyer, Jr. took the top job. In Cessna's long history, these three men have been the only chief executives, providing the company with a Midwestern ethic and family atmosphere that has endured through good times and bad.

Dwane Wallace was a hands-on leader who infused his workers with the joys and challenges of manufacturing airplanes. During World War II, he convinced both the United States and Canadian militaries to use Cessna's T-50s to train fighter pilots. It was the first war to rely heavily on air power, and Cessna aircraft proved critical in training bomber pilots to fly multi-engine aircraft.

After the war, Wallace and other Cessna executives correctly predicted a surge in the popularity of aircraft, and began manufacturing planes that were exceptionally safe and easy to fly. These "family cars of the air" were used for both business and pleasure by pilots who had been trained in the war.

Cessna broke new ground again in 1972, when the company introduced the first Citation in what would become a flagship line of business jets. Quieter, simpler to operate and less expensive than other business jets on the market, it was ideal for corporate travelers. No longer did busy executives have to conform their schedules to the flight plans of major airlines. At a moment's notice, they could fly to airports large or small, conduct their business, and leave on their own timetables.

Another success story is the Caravan, a rugged utility aircraft introduced in 1985. The single-engine turboprop is used heavily by Federal Express as part of its sophisticated package delivery system.

Despite the success of these products, the eighties were a difficult decade for Cessna. Escalating interest rates and product liability premiums cost the company millions of dollars, and eroded the base of potential customers. By 1986, the company's workforce had dwindled from 18,000 employees to around 3,000.

But Cessna's legacy is one of survival. That year, the company was acquired by General Dynamics, a move that allowed Cessna to continue research and development at a time when other aviation companies languished. This favorable relationship lasted until 1992, when General Dynamics, responding to defense cutbacks at the end of the Cold War, sold Cessna to Textron. This relationship has also proved beneficial to Cessna, which today operates as a wholly owned subsidiary.

In 1986, the company was forced to halt production of piston-engine aircraft. While insurance rates had remained relatively constant over the years, product liability premiums for aircraft manufacturers had skyrocketed. A fight to change the liability law, led by Russ Meyer, resulted in the General Aviation Revitalization Act, approved in 1994.

During the legislative battle, Meyer promised to restore Cessna's piston-engine production if the law was enacted. In 1997, he kept his promise when Cessna opened a new, state-of-the-art assembly facility in Independence, Kansas.

It was no coincidence that Cessna's new plant was established in its home state of Kansas. Throughout its long history, the company has shown remarkable loyalty to its community. In 1989, for example, it started a model program called the 21st Street Project, which turned an abandoned supermarket — where crack cocaine vials could often be found — into a job-training site. The project spurred the revitalization of one of Wichita's most depressed areas. More importantly, however, Cessna created opportunity for disadvantaged persons who were previously considered unemployable.

Russ Meyer's — and Cessna's — affection for Kansas was shown in other ways. Following the passage of GARA, Russ Meyer only considered Kansas for the location the new piston-engine plant:

> *"We were committed to remaining in Kansas from the very start of this process. Cessna was founded in Kansas in 1927; we owe our worldwide leadership to the efforts of our employees here."*

In 1996, the company began deliveries of the crown jewel in its growing line of business jets, the Citation X. Able to travel at Mach .92, it is the fastest business jet in the world. Golf legend Arnold Palmer, an accomplished pilot and longtime Citation fan, was the first customer. Part of the fun of flying such a fast plane is the comments from air traffic controllers, he said, who let him pass slower planes with comments about letting him "play through." For its groundbreaking work on Citations, Cessna was twice honored with the prestigious Robert J. Collier Trophy.

Under consistently able leadership, Cessna has remained true to its roots even as it offers the latest technological marvels for the sky. "We have a leadership position in the world, and I think that says a lot about the company," Meyer said.

Noted Dean Humphrey, in charge of public relations from 1976 to 1993:

> *"Even though it's a large company and a leader in the industry, it's still a very small company in the way it conducts business, the way it treats employees, the way it stands behind its products."*

ACKNOWLEDGMENTS

RESEARCHING, WRITING AND publishing a book such as *The Legend of Cessna* would be impossible without the help of a great many individuals and institutions.

A large portion of the principal archival research was accomplished by two extremely talented and hard-working research assistants, Nola Brown Norfleet and Kenneth Hartsoe. Their thorough and careful work made it possible to publish much new and fascinating information about the origin and evolution of Cessna.

Nearly 100 people were interviewed for this book, providing valuable anecdotes and insights about the company. The author would particularly like to thank Russell W. Meyer, Jr., chairman and CEO of Cessna; Gary Hay, vice chairman of Cessna; Phil Michel, vice president, marketing; Roger Martin, manager, business development; Michael Shonka, senior vice president and chief financial officer; Milt Sills, senior vice president, product engineering; and Tom Wakefield, vice president and general counsel for taking time out of their busy schedules.

Velma Wallace shared many fond memories of her husband, Dwane, and his years at the helm of Cessna.

Bruce Peterman, retired senior vice president of aircraft development, was kind enough to read the first draft and provide valuable guidance.

The author was particularly honored to interview Bob Dole, the former Kansas senator and 1996 Republican presidential nominee, and Arnold Palmer, golf great and Citation owner. Special thanks goes to Palmer's executive assistant, Doc Giffin.

Wichita Mayor Bob Knight discussed the importance of Cessna in the city where it has always been headquartered, and Dorothy Cochran, curator, National Air and Space Museum, explained why a Citation will be the focal point of an upcoming exhibit.

Cessna executives who gave generously of their time include Ron Alberti, vice president, manufacturing; Dave Assard, president of Textron Lycoming; Arbery Barrett, vice president, aircraft completion; Pat Boyarski, general manager, single engine piston aircraft; LeRoy Burgess, project engineer; Steve Charles, director of product support; Ronald Chapman, vice president, customer service; Bob Conover, director, Caravan sales; John Daniel, product manager; John Hall, director of CitationJet and Bravo sales; Frank Harris, director, engineering services and product safety; W.C. "Bill" Hogan, manager, marketing support-propeller; Doug Hazelwood, director, flight test; Ursula Jarvis, vice president, administration; Charles Johnson, president and COO; Paul Kalberer, director, engineering projects; Bob Knebel, vice president, Citation domestic sales; J. Bruce Learmont, senior project engineer; Jim Lyle, project engineer for special projects and proposals; James Martin, vice president, materiel; John Moore, senior vice president, human resources; James Morgan, vice president, service facilities; Mark Paolucci, vice president, international sales; Peter Redman, president, Cessna Finance Corporation; Regene Prilliman, benefits supervisor; Marilyn Richwine, director, corporate affairs; Walt Thompson, project engineer; Donald Van Burkleo, vice president, total quality management, quality and reliability; Larry VanDyke, project engineer; Roger Whyte, senior vice president, sales and marketing; Doug Wood, director, government sales; and Michael Wright, leader, assembly-small parts.

For the chapter on the General Aviation Revitalization Act, insights were provided by many of the people who made the historic legislation possible, including Phil Boyer, president of the Aircraft Owners and Pilots Association; Dan Glickman, secretary of agriculture; and Ed Stimpson, president of the General Aviation Manufacturers Association.

Also providing valuable insights about Cessna's aviation contributions were Mark Blair, vice president of feeder operations for Federal Express; Richard Santulli, chairman, Executive Jet Aviation; and Al Ueltschi, president, FlightSafety.

The men and women who have retired from Cessna helped create a valuable portrait of a company that maintained its Midwestern values as it grew. Of particular help in this regard was Delbert L. Roskam, president of Cessna from 1964 to 1975 and Dean Humphrey, vice president of public relations from 1976 to 1993. Other retirees who contributed fond memories include Earl Biggs, machine shop supervisor; Gifford Booth, director of marketing communications; Karl Boyd, assembly foreman; Lucille Brunton, assistant manager for risk and insurance; Don Hammer, manager, credit and collections; Jay Landrum, an electroplater; welder Floyd Lundy; Dorothy Naylor, an employee relations representative; Dean Noble, manager of direct marketing; Don Powell, director of management resources; Treva West, a preflight inspector; Elsie Wilder, the company's first female production foreman; and Jack Zook, director of Marketing Administration.

Compiling the vast amounts of information and images for this volume would not have been possible without the cheerful assistance of many people. At Cessna, the long list of those deserving gratitude includes Edwin C. Parrish III, manager of marketing publications; Dolores D. Pankratz, secretary for marketing support; Steve Hines, manager of market research; Rene Sarver, executive secretary, public relations; Alice Helser, retired executive secretary, public relations; Deborah Drinkwater, executive assistant, office of the chairman; Russ Watson, manager, Air Age Education and CPC Sales; Dale Greenlee, manager, facilities engineering/maintenance; Tom Aniello, sales administrator, domestic sales-eastern division; Tillie Brin, secretary, marketing communications; Ronnie Robinson, coordinator, marketing communications; Bruce K. Garren, manager, finance systems and corporate procedures; Karen Nestelroad, administrator, legal department; Tom Zwemke, director, communication programs; Mark Shepherd, manager, client relations; Clair McColl, retired controller, Completion Division; Todd Duhnke, manager, regional sales, Caravan; Sharon K. King, supervisor, employee communications; Jim Shultz, supervisor, photo lab; Matt Amsden, manager, Caravan marketing communications; George L. Stathis, supervisor, engineering reproduction; Mike Fuhrman, director, marketing support; Bob Carnahan, section chief for Excel/Bravo; and Robert A. White, supervisor, air safety inspector and legal support. Special thanks goes to *Air Force Magazine*, which thoughtfully provided a number of hard-to-find images.

Also providing valuable assistance were Martha Gregg, local historian at the Wichita Public Library; Leslie Cade of the Kansas Historical Society; Mary Jane Townsend, former librarian at the Kansas Aviation Museum; Ailene Phelps, administrative assistant in the Kingman Schools Superintendent's Offices; Mike Kelly, curator of Special Collections, Ablah Library, Wichita State University; Shauna Payne, student assistant, special collections, Ablah Library, Wichita State University; Leta Mitchell, Kingman Carnegie Library; Byron and June Walker, Kingman County Historical Museum; Roger Wilson, Wichita Chamber of Commerce; Glen McIntyre, curator, Museum of the Cherokee Strip; Wilbur Dunkelberger, former neighbor of Clyde Cessna in Rago, Kansas; Greg Setter, production manager, Sullivan, Higdon and Sink, Inc.; Bill Peppard, sales representative, Printing Incorporated; Pat Rowley, Rowley Communications; DeAnna Peter, legal assistant to the Governor of Kansas; David Williamson, National Computer Resources, Inc.; Darren McGuire, associate director, Kansas Aviation Museum; and volunteers at the Kansas Aviation Museum.

Finally, a very special word of thanks to the hard-working staff at Write Stuff Enterprises, who put in many extra hours to make sure this book met our high standards, despite an unusually tight deadline. Proofreader Bryan Henry and transcriptionist Mary Aaron worked quickly and efficiently. Particular thanks goes to Executive Editor Karen Nitkin; Associate Editor Alex Lieber; Art Directors Sandy Cruz, Kyle Newton and Jill Apolinario; Fred Moll, production manager; Jill Thomas, assistant to the author; Marianne Roberts, office manager; Christopher Frosch, marketing and sales manager; Rafael Santiago, logistics specialist; and Karine Rodengen, product coordinator.

During the early years of aviation, air shows and exhibitions gave the public a chance to see flying machines that were little more than novelties.

A WING AND A PRAYER: AVIATION ATTEMPTS BEFORE 1908

"The desire to fly like a bird is inborn in our race, and we can no more be expected to abandon the idea than the ancient mathematician could have been expected to give up the problem of squaring the circle."

— Scientist Simon Newcomb, 1901[1]

CLYDE VERNON CESSNA is one of the world's best-known aviation pioneers, but his accomplishments would not have been possible if not for the work of many men before him. Cessna forms another link in a long chain of visionaries who looked toward the skies and saw challenge and opportunity.

Folklore, fable and mythology have long told of man's efforts to propel himself into the skies. Tales of genies on flying carpets and witches that travel by broom remain popular today. The Greek myth of Daedalus and his son, Icarus, is one of the earliest of such stories. Father and son were imprisoned by King Minos on the island of Crete, but managed to escape by making wings of wax and feathers. With these, they flew all the way to Naples. But Icarus was so excited by this new experience that he ignored his father's warnings and flew too close to the sun, melting his wings of wax, and plummeted to his death in the sea.[2]

Perhaps inspired by the myth, or enticed by the challenge, men have attempted to fly by methods as crude as strapping feathered wings to their arms and flapping them in the wind. One such account is that of a 17th century Turk named Hezarfen Celebi. According to legend, he jumped from a tower in Galata, near the shores of Bosporus and traveled several kilometers through the air before landing, unscathed, in the marketplace at Scutari, Turkey. Many others have made similar attempts, often with fatal results.[3]

More serious contributions to flight were made by engineer and artist Leonardo da Vinci, whose inventions included the airscrew (propeller) and the parachute. The flying machine that he designed was aerodynamically sound, but the materials to build the aircraft and the source of power to drive it were unavailable in his time.[4]

In 1783, brothers Joseph and Jacques Montgolfier invented the hot-air balloon. On November 21, 1783, Pilatre de Rozier and Marquis d' Arlandes became the first men to travel through the air in a balloon, near Paris, France.[5]

The Wright Brothers

In September 1901, one of the most important magazines in the nation, *McClure's*, published an article by respected mathematician Simon Newcomb. The article was titled "Is the Airplane Coming?" and Newcomb's answer was a resounding "no."

A sketch by Leonardo da Vinci, who invented both the propeller and the parachute.

The military advantage of flight was recognized long before practical methods were invented. This undated artist's conception (probably circa 18th century) depicts an invasion from both air and sea. *(Photo courtesy of Goodyear.)*

"No builder of air castles for the amusement and benefit of humanity could have failed to include a flying-machine among the productions of his imagination. The desire to fly like a bird is inborn in our race, and we can no more be expected to abandon the idea than the ancient mathematician could have been expected to give up the problem of squaring the circle. ... As the case stands, the first successful flyer will be the handiwork of a watchmaker and will carry nothing heavier than an insect."[6]

Newcomb's view confirmed the common-sense beliefs of many people. It simply didn't seem possible that a vehicle could actually lift humans and carry them safely through the skies. This pessimism seemed to be confirmed by the exploits of astronomer and physicist Dr. Samuel Pierpont Langley. Langley, secretary of the renowned Smithsonian Institution, constructed the world's first heavier-than-air machine capable of sustained flight. His conveyance, built with the backing of the U.S. War Department, contained a 52.4-horsepower engine that weighed 124 pounds.

Amid much fanfare, Langley twice launched his aircraft from a houseboat on the Potomac River in 1903. Both attempts failed and the pilot, Charles M. Manly, became temporarily trapped in the icy waters beneath the wreckage.[7] "It was a day of triumph for every faithful

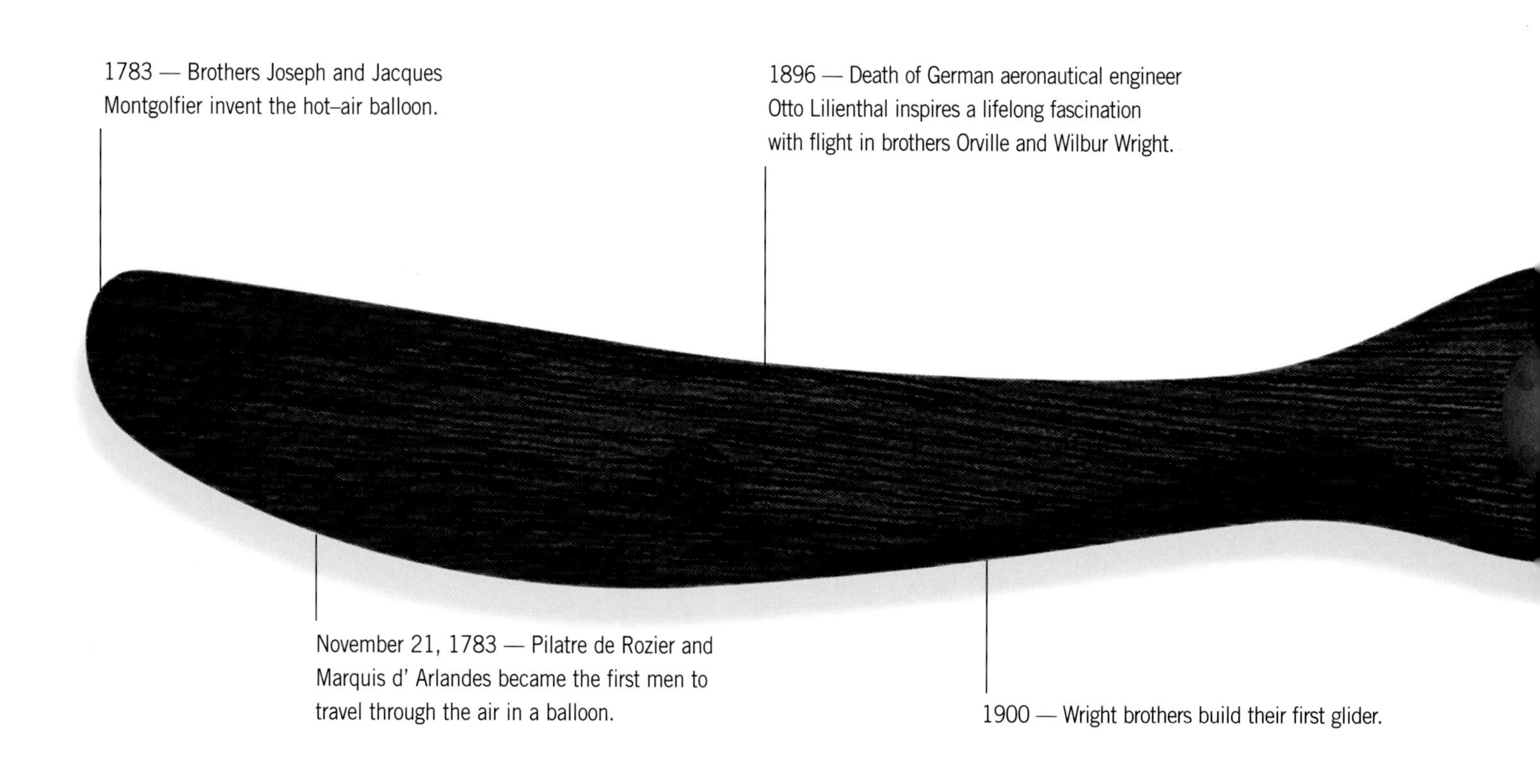

1783 — Brothers Joseph and Jacques Montgolfier invent the hot-air balloon.

November 21, 1783 — Pilatre de Rozier and Marquis d' Arlandes became the first men to travel through the air in a balloon.

1896 — Death of German aeronautical engineer Otto Lilienthal inspires a lifelong fascination with flight in brothers Orville and Wilbur Wright.

1900 — Wright brothers build their first glider.

defender of the immutability of what is," historian Mark Sullivan wrote in 1926. "Practically every headline and news story seemed to reflect smug satisfaction in the proof that man's conviction about the impossibility of human flight was still sound and right."[8]

Meanwhile, two brothers in Dayton, Ohio, owners of a modest bicycle repair shop, were putting the finishing touches on a machine that would put the naysayers to rest once and for all. Nine short days after Manly's second plunge into the Potomac, brothers Wilbur and Orville Wright made the first powered airplane flight in history.

Wilbur Wright was born in Milville, Indiana, on April 16, 1867, and his brother Orville was born in Dayton, Ohio, on August 19, 1871. Their father was a clergyman, and when the boys were young he returned from a church-related trip with a small flying toy. This novelty may well have sparked the creative genius that led the brothers to invent and fly the first practical airplane.[9]

The brothers were unusually close. Neither one married, and throughout their lives, they both worked together and lived together. Both dropped out of high school, and Orville opened a printing press, where Wilbur worked. In 1888, the two, who had always enjoyed tinkering with mechanical things, designed and constructed a large printing press and began publication of the *West Side News*, which Wilbur edited. In 1892, the brothers opened a bicycle repair shop, and three years later they began assembling their own bicycles, using tools they had created themselves.[10]

In 1896, Wilbur read a newspaper account of the death of Otto Lilienthal, a German aeronautical engineer and pioneer in the emerging field of gliders. Lilienthal, who had taken more than 2,000 flights during his lifetime, had plunged to his death in a crash-landing.[11]

Wilbur showed the article to his brother, who was recuperating from typhoid fever at the time. The brothers both became fascinated with flight, and read everything they could find on the emerging subject. By August 1900, the brothers built their first glider. After considerable research, they chose a coastal sand dune area near Kitty Hawk, North Carolina, as the site of the first launching because it was hilly and had consistent winds of high velocity. The first attempts were disappointing but valuable. Initially able to fly their unmanned glider like a kite, they reached the important con-

1903 — Dr. Samuel Pierpont Langley constructs the first heavier-than-air machine capable of sustained flight, but two test flights fail.

May 7, 1908 — *The New York Herald* alerts the world to the Wright brothers and their amazing flying machine.

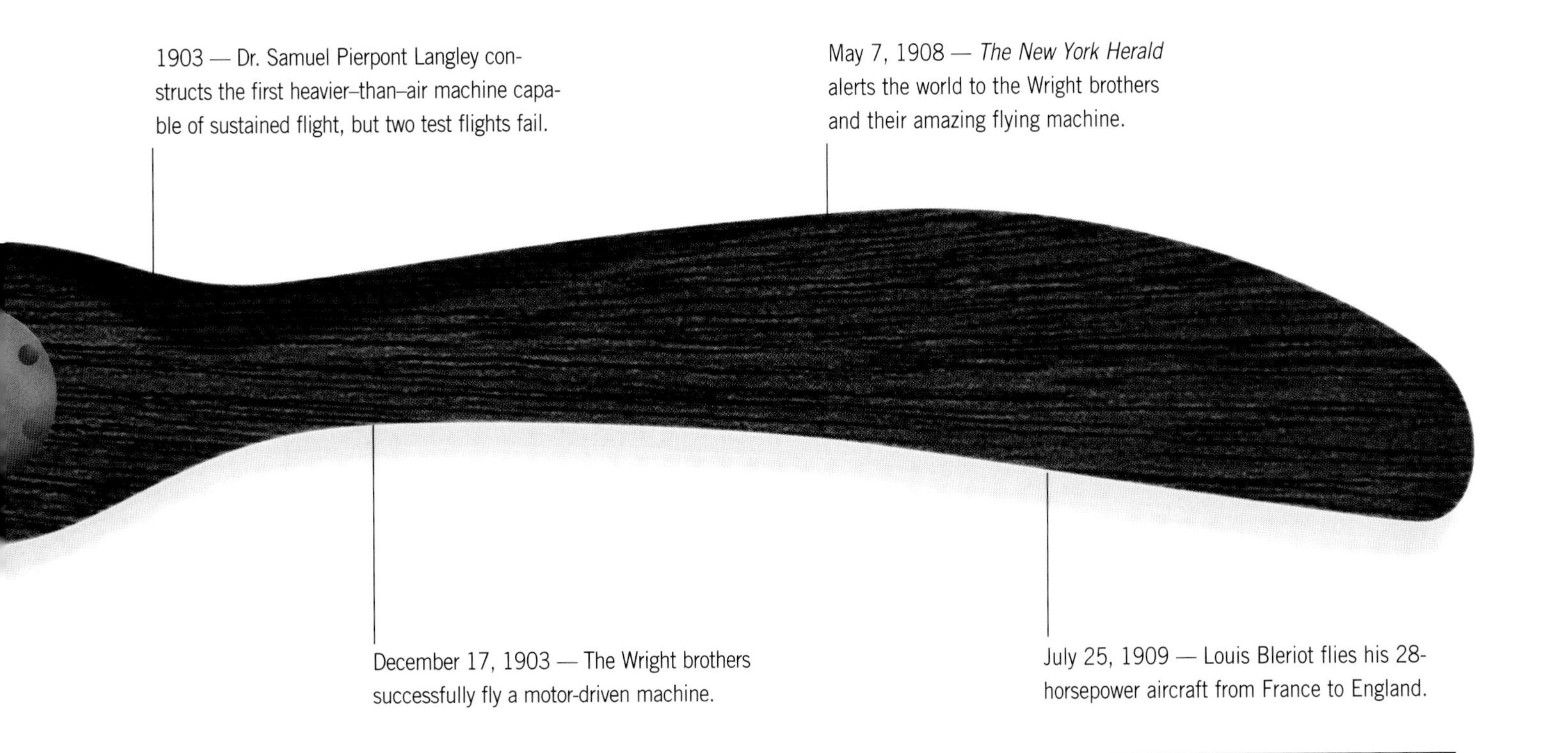

December 17, 1903 — The Wright brothers successfully fly a motor-driven machine.

July 25, 1909 — Louis Bleriot flies his 28-horsepower aircraft from France to England.

clusion that previously published information about wind pressure was incorrect. Over the next year, they tested the effects of air pressure on more than 200 wing surfaces, and in 1902, they set a manned gliding record of 620 feet.[12]

Elated, the brothers returned to Dayton and began developing a propeller and engine. They were determined to make their next flight in a motor-driven flying machine. Aviation history was made when they succeeded on December 17, 1903. Wilbur had tried to fly the machine first but was unsuccessful. With a flip of a coin, it was decided that Orville would next pilot the aircraft. At 10:35 a.m., he took to the air for 12 seconds, traveling 120 feet. The following is Orville Wright's account of what happened the day of that first flight:

> *"Wilbur ran at the side, holding the wing to balance it on the track. The machine, facing a 27-mile wind, started very slowly. Wilbur was able to stay with it till it lifted from the track after a 40-foot run.*
>
> *"The course of the flight up and down was extremely erratic. The control of the front rudder was difficult. As a result, the machine would rise suddenly to about 10 feet, and then as suddenly dart for the ground. A sudden dart when a little over 120 feet from the point at which it rose into the air ended the flight. This flight lasted only 12 seconds, but it was nevertheless the first in the history of the world in which a machine carrying a man had raised itself by its own power into the air in full flight, had sailed forward without reduction of speed, and had finally landed at a point as high as that from which it had started."*[13]

The historic accomplishment of the Wright brothers went unnoticed. It didn't become public until 1908, when a newspaper freelancer was

Orville Wright pilots the plane while Wilbur looks on during this historic flight at Kitty Hawk, North Carolina on December 17, 1903.

EDITION SPECIALE

Vingt-Sixième Année. — N° 9280

Dimanche 25 Juillet 1909

Le Matin

Stéphane LAUZANNE, Rédacteur en chef

SEUL JOURNAL FRANÇAIS RELIANT PAR SES FILS SPÉCIAUX LES QUATRE PREMIÈRES CAPITALES DU GLOBE

Jules MADELINE, Président

LE FRANÇAIS BLÉRIOT VIENT DE TRAVERSER LA MANCHE EN AEROPLANE

C'EST L'ENVOYÉ SPÉCIAL du "MATIN" qui l'a accueilli SUR LA TERRE ANGLAISE et qui EN ELEVANT LE DRAPEAU FRANÇAIS lui a fait le signal de l'atterrissement

FRANCE

strolling the beach of North Carolina looking for a story. On May 7, 1908, the *New York Herald* printed the first story of Orville and Wilbur Wright and their amazing flying machine.[14]

Once the miracle of flying was accepted, the public's thirst for new aviation feats seemed insatiable. In October 1908, the *London Daily Mail* offered a prize of 500 pounds for the first airplane crossing of the English Channel. The prize was not claimed that year, so it was doubled the following year.[15] On July 25, 1909, monoplane designer Louis Bleriot of France, in his handmade 28-horsepower aircraft, made the journey and collected the prize, covering the 25 miles from Calais to the Dover cliffs in 37 minutes.[16] This flight drew much attention because it bridged the gap between England and France, creating the possibility of fast and efficient travel between the countries. Overnight, the world seemed to have shrunk. The airplane Bleriot flew during this journey would become Clyde Cessna's future fixation.

Top: A special edition of *Le Matin* announces that Louis Bleriot had successfully crossed the English Channel in a monoplane.

Above: Louis Bleriot, whose flight would inspire Clyde Cessna's interest in aviation.

The Cessna family coat of arms. The Cessna name was derived from the French name DeCessna.

Clyde Vernon Cessna

1879-1911

"She skidded off and dropped down with a smack. By the time the crowd had come up I was sitting up beginning to take notice of things. They said I bounced like a rubber ball, but there were no bones broken. The plane looked just like it had been put through a thrashing machine. But I knew that day I could fly."

— Clyde Cessna, 1926[1]

CLYDE VERNON CESSNA was born on December 5, 1879 in Hawthorne, Iowa, the second child of James William and Mary Vandora Skates Cessna.[2] In early 1881, the Cessna family, including Clyde's brother Roy Clarence, two years his senior, loaded themselves and their belongings onto a train and moved to Kansas, where the government was offering land grants to those willing to stake their claims.[3]

James Cessna and his friend John Burchfield already laid their claims in Canton Township, having traveled there previously aboard covered wagons. The families built sod homes in a town that would become known as Rago two years later, when a trading post was established there.[4]

While in Kansas, five more children were born to the Cessna family: Pearl William, Noel Miles, Bert David, Hazel Dell and Grace Opal.[5] All would contribute to the difficult task of turning the virgin Kansas landscape into a thriving family farm.

Like many rural Americans at the time, Clyde was educated only through the fifth grade, attending a one-room schoolhouse in nearby Raymond, Kansas. Yet his knack for fixing things was astounding. Clyde's father put him to work repairing the farm's assorted and often makeshift machinery, and soon neighbors were asking the boy for help with their broken machinery, noted Gerald Deneau in *An Eye To The Sky, Cessna.*

"Clyde was 15 or 16 years old when a neighbor became distressed because the knotter on his self-binder had gone out of whack. The knotter was the most intricate device on the farm in those days. It took a sheaf of wheat or other small grain, ran a piece of twine around it, then tied a knot to hold the sheaf securely. When the knotter finished tying the knot, a knife cut the twine and an ejector kicked the sheaf out of the machine where it would be picked up and put in a shock.

"Mr. Cessna sent Clyde to see if he could repair the knotter. As Clyde came riding up to his neighbor on a pony, he was confronted with the greatest torrent of profanity he had ever heard. It was imperative that the wheat be put in the shock that afternoon! A majestic thunderhead was rising in the northwest, threatening thunder, hail and rain. In a jiffy, Clyde had the knotter fixed. The farmer mounted his seat and before the downpour began, five or six hours later, the farmer had his wheat safely in the shock."[6]

Clyde Vernon Cessna at age two.

When Clyde was 26, he met and fell in love with a local schoolteacher named Europa Elizabeth Dotzour. She had attended McPherson College and in 1900, at the age of 18, began her teaching career in Kingman County.[7]

The couple married on June 6, 1905 and moved to Clyde's 40 acres, north of the original family farm. With the responsibility of a new wife, Clyde decided that farming was not profitable enough. He began searching for a new way to make a living. The answer came in the form of a novelty known as a horseless carriage.

In 1907, both Clyde and Roy purchased vehicles. Roy's was a four-horsepower buckboard with solid rubber tires and springs made of hickory wood. Clyde's was an eight-horsepower Reo automobile.[8] It didn't take Clyde long to figure out the simple mechanics of the early automobile, designed by the famous Ransom Eli Olds, builder of the venerable Oldsmobile. With the knowledge in hand, Clyde went to work for the Overland Farm dealership in Harper. According to one account, the dealer recruited Clyde, who was fixing equipment for local farmers at no charge, so he wouldn't lose any more business to the young mechanic.[9] This career change was good timing, because on May 5, 1907, Clyde and Europa had their first child, Eldon Wayne.[10]

A 1941 photo of Europa Cessna, Clyde's wife.

The dealership had recently added automobiles to its sales line, and Clyde found himself repairing both automobiles and farm equipment. He soon found he had a knack for selling cars as well as fixing them.

"One afternoon, the dealer drove away to call on prospective car buyers. While he was gone, a man entered the shop to tell Clyde that he wanted to see an Overland, but did not intend buying until he had seen all the makes sold in Harper and Anthony. Then he would buy the one he felt was best. Clyde mopped the grease from his hands with a rag and told the prospect about the car and showed how the engine and other parts operated. To hear Clyde tell it, the Overland was

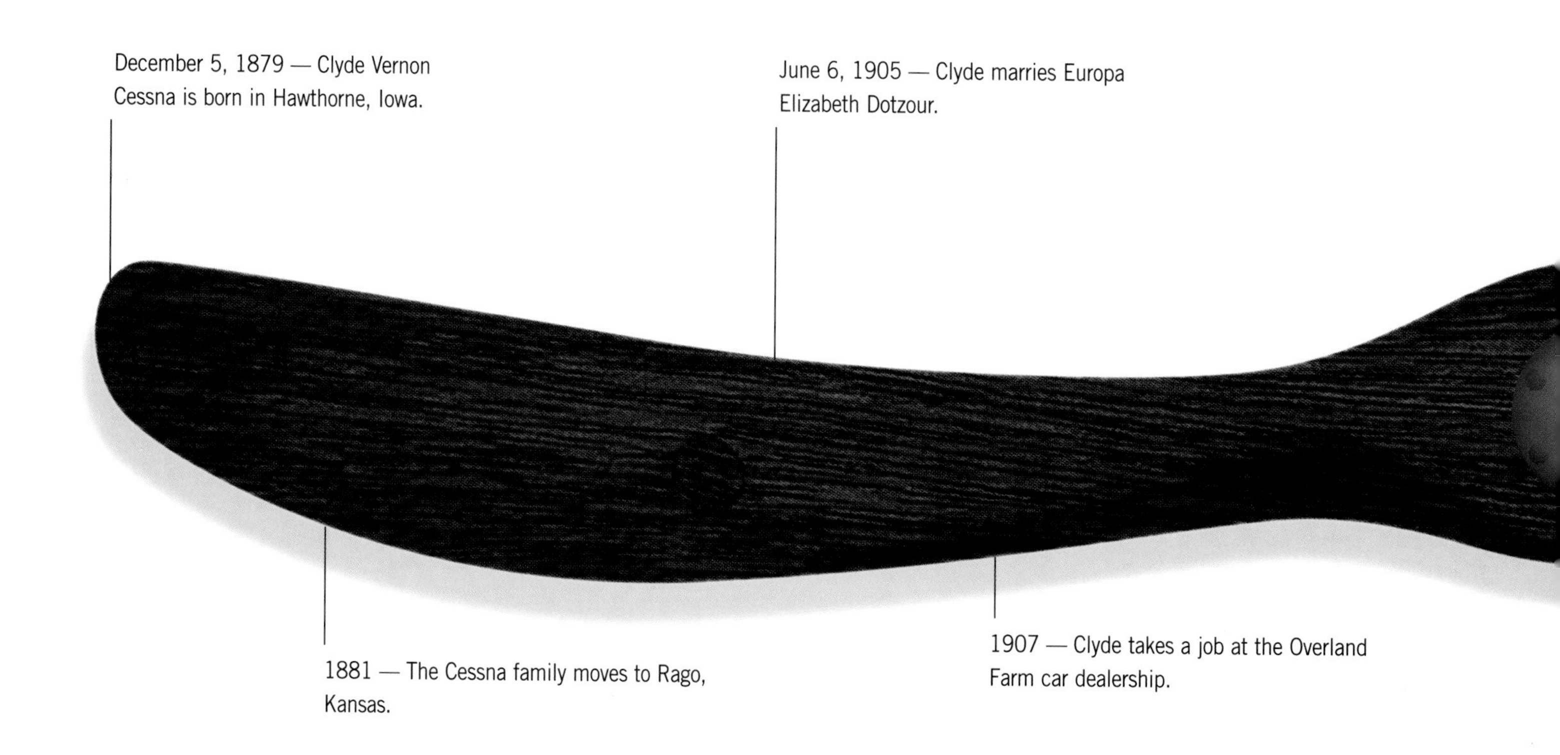

the best car made. The prospect suddenly lost all interest in calling on other car dealers. He wrote a check and drove an Overland away. From that day, the boss relied more and more on Clyde to handle sales."[11]

After the Harper dealership closed in 1908, Clyde moved his family to Enid, Oklahoma, where he became a partner with J. Watson in the Overland dealership there and reportedly sold more than 100 automobiles his first year. He soon became general manager of the enterprise, which was renamed the Cessna Automobile Company.[12] The same year, 1909, the Cessnas had their second child, Wanda Dolores.[13]

The famous Reo automobile, designed by Ransom E. Olds, similar to the one purchased by Clyde Cessna in 1907.

From Automobiles to Aircraft

There was no hint that Clyde would ever do anything other than sell cars. The course of his life changed, however, when he read of Louis Bleriot's epic crossing of the English Channel. Almost overnight, Clyde's interests turned from automobiles to aircraft. With the self-confidence exhibited by a natural-born mechanic, Clyde decided he would build an airplane like Bleriot's. His older brother Roy, however, was a little more practical. He reminded Clyde that he should probably learn to fly before building a flying machine.[14]

Clyde was 31 and still working at his Enid car dealership when he picked up the local newspaper and read about an air circus in Oklahoma City sponsored by the Moisant International Aviators. The event, scheduled for January 14, 1911, would allow

1908 — The Cessna family moves to Enid, Oklahoma, where Clyde becomes a partner in another Overland dealership.

1911 — Clyde purchases and assembles his first plane, *Silver Wings*.

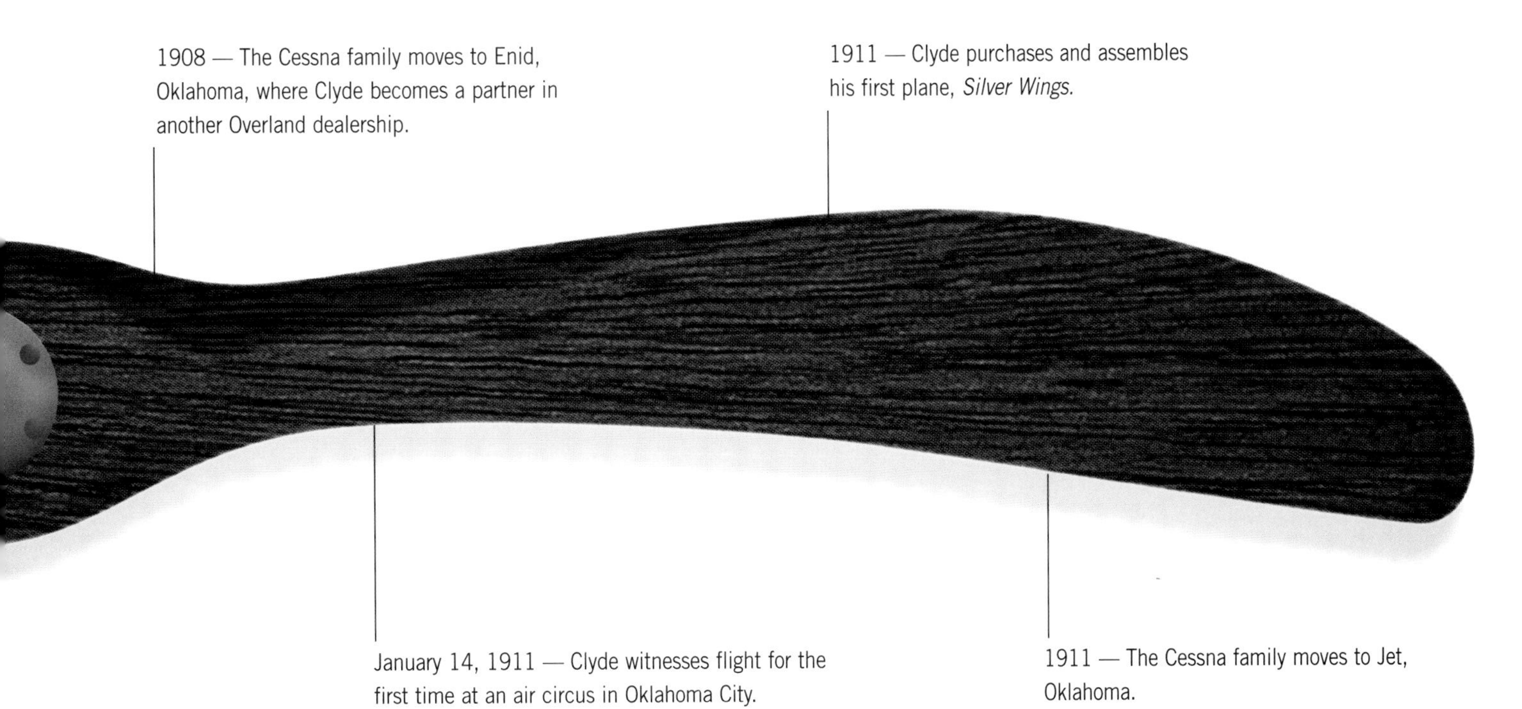

January 14, 1911 — Clyde witnesses flight for the first time at an air circus in Oklahoma City.

1911 — The Cessna family moves to Jet, Oklahoma.

Clyde to witness flight for the very first time. He grew even more excited when he learned that Bleriot monoplanes would fly at the show.[15] Clyde arrived early and stayed late. In 1926, he recalled the exhilaration of that day for an article in the *Wichita Eagle Sunday Magazine.*

> *"There were three machines and they were shipped from one place to the next by train. The flyers traveled by train. On that Sunday afternoon they stepped out and held up a red silk handkerchief to get the direction and force of the wind. Then they pointed one of the machines to the wind while about twenty men were called out to hold on while the engine was warmed up. For half an hour they fooled around and tinkered with this and that and tuned up the engine. Finally the pilot climbed aboard, gave her the gas and everybody gave him a shove. In those days a flight was successful if the ship completed a circle and landed where it started. That's what this one did. Everybody watched it circle around and land. That's all there was to it. The Frenchmen got $10,000 for the exhibition."*[16]

A born businessman, Clyde could practically hear the cling of a cash register when he learned how much the pilots were making. "Ten thousand dollars," he exclaimed to a friend, "think of it — ten thousand for that! Let someone else sell the Overlands."[17]

Clyde lingered after the show, watching as the aviators took their planes apart and loaded them on railway cars. Fascinated with the Bleriot monoplane, he took detailed notes and asked many questions. In particular, Clyde questioned pilot Roland Garros, asking where he could purchase a Bleriot Type XI. During this discussion he probably learned of the Queen Aeroplane Company of New York City, founded in the fall of 1910 by Willis McCormick, a successful stockbroker and aviation enthusiast. It was one of the first in America to build replicas of the Bleriot Type XI.[18]

Filled with excitement, Clyde returned to Enid, gathered up his life's savings and traveled east to New York City. There, he spent several weeks working on the monoplane assembly line at the Queen Aeroplane Company. He absorbed

Clyde Cessna's first airplane, the Bleriot, which Clyde named *Silver Wings.*

everything he could about airplane construction and even spent some time in the air with experienced pilots.[19]

Silver Wings

While in New York, Clyde purchased a copy of a Bleriot airplane for $7,500 and shipped it to Enid by rail.[20] The airplane, which Clyde dubbed *Silver Wings* because of its color, had been custom-built for John B. Moisant, who died in a crash before construction was complete.[21]

To keep costs down, Clyde did not purchase the Gnome or Indian rotary engines that were standard for Queen ships.[22] Instead, he opted for a V-type engine that he purchased from St. Louis, Missouri. The engine was to be shipped separately and would be accompanied by a mechanic.[23]

Clyde Cessna (above) encouraged spectators to marvel — for free — at the novelty of manned flight. Ads such as this one promoting the Sand Springs demonstration would appear in local newspapers weeks prior to the scheduled flight.

Clyde returned to Enid and awaited the arrival of his airplane. Flying was still a novelty and the people of Enid were eager to see *Silver Wings* take to the skies. Fred E. Botkin, the sales manager at Clyde's car dealership, took a particular interest in the whole affair. Although Botkin had no experience flying airplanes, he had been studying the problems of flight and engines, and he convinced Clyde that 11 years as an automobile driver qualified him to pilot *Silver Wings*.[24]

On February 20, 1911, Botkin announced that he and Cessna had reached an agreement with the Chamber of Commerce for Botkin to fly at the upcoming Garfield County stock show. The exhibition would attract thousands of people from Enid and the outlying areas, and was sure to net a profit for the Chamber.[25]

Silver Wings arrived in Enid on February 28. The date of the first flight was set for March 5. The monoplane was packed in crates and loaded on a special freight car. Cessna and Botkin retrieved the much-awaited plane from the train station and transported it directly to an exhibition tent that had been set up at the fair grounds. The pair, along with Clyde's brother, Roy, went to work assembling the machine.[26]

When the stock show opened, Clyde charged a small fee to spectators eager to see the monoplane. Although the tent was always crowded, Clyde had another concern. March 5 was fast approaching and the engine for his airplane had not arrived. The engine still had not arrived by March 8, so Clyde, at the Chamber's request, suspended the admission fee. The Enid-based *Oklahoma Events* trumpeted the news the following day under the headline, "Monoplane Exhibited Free, Big Flying Machine Now Can Be Seen By All Visitors of Stock Show."

"The monster Bleriot monoplane recently purchased in New York by C.V. Cessna of the Cessna Auto company is now on exhibition free at the stock pavilion. An admission fee has been charged heretofore but yesterday Mr. Cessna decided to place it on exhibition free as an inducement for the people to visit the show. The large tent in which it is kept was thronged all day yesterday with interested spectators who asked hundreds of questions about the big machine.

"The monoplane complete cost $7,500 and is said to be one of the largest of its type ever constructed. The machine is of especial interest because of the fact that it was designed and constructed expressly for the famous aviator Moisant who was killed at New Orleans the last of December. It is the only one of its particular kind ever constructed. The very latest ideas of construction of heavier than air machines obtained by Moisant through his long experience in flying are embodied in the construction of the machine.

"It was originally intended to give daily flights at the show but the failure of the engine and propeller to arrive in time have made that part of the program of the show an impossibility. However, if the engine arrives before the close of the show every effort will be made to make the flights."[27]

When the show closed in mid-March, the engine was still missing, and the much-anticipated flight never took place. The engine finally arrived in late March or early April, but without the mechanic who was supposed to help install it. Clyde retrieved the engine from the railroad station and took it to his Enid home at 520 South Buchanan. But after hours of puttering with the device, he was not able to make it run smoothly. In addition, his neighbors were starting to complain about the noises emitting from his garage all hours of the day and night.[28] Meanwhile, the propeller arrived. Clyde saw that it had been damaged during transport, and shipped it back to New York City for replacement.[29]

The Elbridge Aero Special, guaranteed to maintain 80 horsepower for an all-day run.

Finally, Clyde called upon an acquaintance in Waynoka, Oklahoma for advice about the engine. W.D. Lindsley had a biplane on the Salt Plains near Jet, Oklahoma, which he was preparing for trial flights. Cessna purchased an Elbridge Aero Special engine from his friend that April. The two agreed to make flights together, figuring two heads were better than one in the relatively unexplored field of aviation.[30]

The Great Salt Plains

On May 12, 1911, members of the Cessna family packed their belongings in a car, hitched *Silver Wings* to a trailer, and relocated to Jet (not named after the engine type of the same name), about 40 miles northwest of Enid.[31]

"I bought me a fifty-foot circle tent for a camp and assembly plant and I set up on the Salt Plains where there was a great big area as flat as a table. I know now it was a fool place to learn how to fly, because the glare is so dazzling from that white surface that a man can't see anything, and there is nothing on it to give a man a judge of distance."[32]

Shortly after the move, a new propeller arrived. Clyde and Roy installed it on the V-type engine, saving the Elbridge for later. The Cessnas were, at last, ready to try out their new wings. Although Clyde had flown with other pilots, it would be his first time at the controls. There were no books available to coach a potential pilot. He was literally forced to take a "crash course" in flying.[33]

"[Clyde] climbed into the pilot's seat and Roy whirled the propeller. The engine responded with a loud purr. Clyde taxied across the plains until the engine was running at top speed. But before he could get it into the air, it ground-looped and

burrowed its nose in the salt earth. Clyde was jarred, but he paid no attention to a few bruises. It took a week of time and $100 of new materials to repair the damage."[34]

Clyde blamed the unsuccessful flight on the lack of horsepower put out by the V-type engine. He told reporters that it produced only 30 horsepower, a far cry from the 80 horsepower promised.[35] The Cessna boys, as they were affectionately known, decided to replace the V-type engine with the Elbridge powerplant they had purchased from Lindsley.[36]

With the new engine, Clyde made several short flights. "I think I was never more happy in my life than I was the day my plane actually lifted itself free of the ground," he later said. "I was afraid to fly more than a few feet, but I was learning to fly. In a day or two, I got up courage to make a longer flight. I remember how proud I was when I stepped the distance and found I had actually flown a hundred yards. From that time I learned rapidly."[37]

Clyde endured 12 crashes before he had mastered his wings. With each mishap, it cost him about $100 in repairs and required about a week to get the machine back into running condition. But with each experience he learned more about his beloved aircraft. In particular, *Silver Wings* tended to overheat. Top airspeeds of 45 miles per hour simply didn't provide enough airflow to cool the water for the water-cooled engine.[38]

Despite the problems, Clyde continued to taxi his plane out on the Salt Plains runway and make trial flights. He even learned to make partial turns.[39]

"The first time I tried to turn the ship in the air I had the worst crackup I have ever had in

Left: A 1911 illustration of Cessna's first aircraft.

Below: The *Silver Wings* dazzles spectators simply by flying over a farm. In 1911, few people had ever seen a motorized flying machine.

Airship Flight a Failure

Quite a number from here went to Cherokee Saturday to see the air ship go sailing but all state that it was a complete failure. Two of the men received injuries while the start was being made thus leaving Mr. Cessna to ride. Mr. Beech, who had intended making the flight, fell from the machine accidently before it left the ground. Mr. Cessna, who started the engine, also received injuries.

A short flight was made by C.V. Cessna, but the machine was lowered before going a hundred yards, a number of telephone wires obstructing the pathway.

all my experience with airplanes. I was flying about 80 feet above the ground and made too sharp a turn, which resulted in my losing control of the ship and we landed head on. The plane was a total wreck. I was badly shaken up, but I guess no bones were broken and I did not go to a hospital. However, I was unable to do anything for several weeks."[40]

Off and on, spectators would come to witness the Cessna brothers' progress. They would usually leave scoffing at the pair, having only seen two men repairing a damaged airplane.[41] Clyde soon realized that his get-rich-quick scheme of flying in exhibitions was about as realistic as most other get-rich-quick schemes. "It was just the other way round — I went broke," he later told a Wichita reporter.[42]

"By that time, my money was gone and my spirit was gone, too, I don't mind telling any man. I would have quit then but I didn't dare. I made up my mind I would stick till I was starved out. I used to make flapjacks for breakfast and salt 'em

Upper left: Clyde's first attempts to demonstrate flying were somewhat less than successful. In this case, both Clyde and a passenger were hurt before they even left the ground.

Right: Roy (left) and Clyde pose with one of their homemade propellers.

with the salt right there on the plains under my feet. ... One day I had some luck.

"There was a nice breeze, so my brother, Roy, and I towed the old tub out a mile and I started once more. There used to be quite a crowd of folks who came out to see us. They thought I was half crazy, I guess. But that day everything went fine. I got up about 75 feet. I was sailing along so pretty I decided I wouldn't land at the camp. I kept right on going. Then I decided to make the turn. That was the trick in those days — if you could turn out of the wind and land you had made a flight. I turned, all right. She skidded off and dropped down with a smack. By the time the crowd had come up I was sitting up beginning to take notice of things. They said I bounced like a rubber ball, but there were no bones broken. The plane looked just like it had been put through a thrashing machine. But I knew that day I could fly."[43]

The crack-up had smashed *Silver Wings*' propeller, and it would cost $65 to replace. Depleted of funds, he reluctantly returned to Enid to sell automobiles. Clyde had become acquainted with Carl E. Evans of Wichita, a sales manager for the Arnold Motor company. One day, Clyde asked Evans if his employer, J.J. Jones would help him buy a new propeller. To Clyde's surprise, Jones gave Clyde the money. The pair then accompanied Clyde to the Salt Plains to help him tune the motor and install the new propeller.[44] The experience made a lasting impression on Evans.

"I shall never forget a minute we spent in the Cessna camp. ... Clyde had a tent pitched on the plains. His 'yard' was littered with oil cans and tools. Out front was the miracle machine, with the two-by-four for the engine rest. In three days, we had things in shape and I got in to run the motor a bit. The plane took off. I was actually off the ground two feet and scared stiff. I had wanted to fly. I about changed my mind that day. Before the sun went down, Cessna had been up, and had covered a mile or more in the plane. Everything was revolutionized before me there."[45]

To reduce the expense of replacing broken propellers, the Cessna boys eventually constructed their own wooden prop and proudly installed it on their great bird.[46]

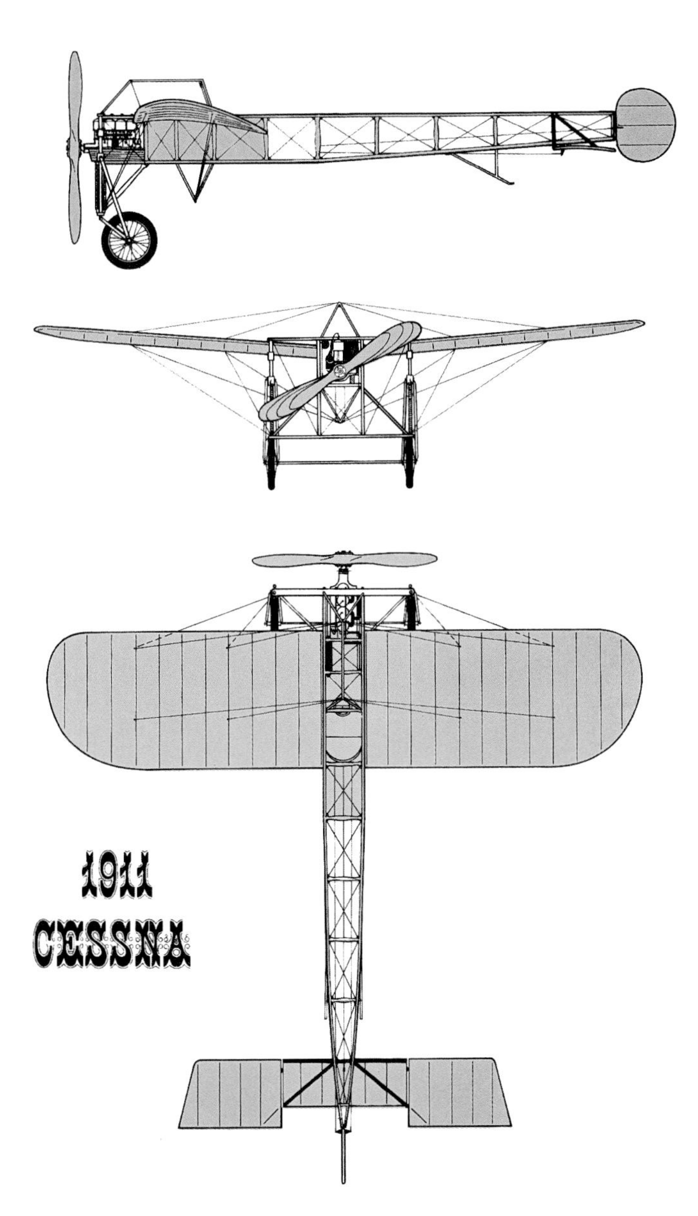

Drawings of Clyde Cessna's 1911 monoplane, showing the wooden propeller created and installed by Clyde and his brother Roy.

The remains of *Silver Wings* after it crashed on the Great Salt Plains in 1911. The identity of the onlooker is not known.

YEARS ON THE GREAT SALT PLAINS

1911-1916

> *"Elder Jenkins was in the midst of a powerful prayer. He was calling upon the angelic hosts to unfold their wings and hover about when a mighty whirring of wings was heard and a huge bird-like apparition was seen sweeping down from the sky, headed straight for Adams circuit meeting house. It was only Cessna coming to church, but it nearly broke up the meeting."*
>
> — *Topeka Capital*, 1915[1]

CLYDE CESSNA'S first flight without a crash landing took place in June 1911. Gerald Deneau wrote about the milestone in his book *An Eye to The Sky, Cessna.*

> *"Roy twirled the propeller and the engine purred. The wheels left the ground and Clyde soared higher. The airplane responded to his controls and turned at his bidding. After a well controlled flight, he landed and taxied up to the smiling Roy. Clyde was smiling, too. 'It flies,' he exalted. 'Like a hawk,' answered Roy."*[2]

Although Clyde had never made a public flight, he and Roy felt they were ready for an exhibition. The brothers wrote to Enid City Railway Manager Clarence Kline and asked to fly at Lakewood Park as part of the Independence Day celebration. Kline accepted.[3] The Enid newspaper, *Oklahoma Events*, wrote about the pending event under the headline "Cessna Will Fly At Lakewood, All Arrangements Made for Local Birdman to Aviate July 4."

> *"The flight will take place at 3 o'clock in the afternoon. Mr. Cessna has proven beyond a doubt that he can manipulate the machine and the only possible thing that would prevent the flight will be unfavorable weather conditions which always plays a prominent part in aerial exhibitions. The largest crowd ever seen at the park is expected to witness the flight, and already, Superintendent Kline is arranging to accommodate the large number of spectators who are expected from Enid as well as adjoining towns."*[4]

With a 50-cent admission fee, the Cessna boys figured the flight would help them recoup the money they had spent on repairs to *Silver Wings*. In addition, they set up a tent to exhibit some of the airplane's more mangled parts, and provided a narrative explaining how each part had sustained the damage.[5] But the flight never took place. Only $40 had been collected at the gate. Clyde told reporters, "We will go right on. But there is nothing in flying that justifies a flight unless we get the money back that we have spent."[6]

The pair returned to the Salt Plains and continued to fly. Their activity continued to attract attention. In August, experienced aviator A.C. Beech paid the men a visit and even made several flights in *Silver Wings*. Tulsa airman

Part of the six-cylinder Anzani engine that Clyde Cessna would use in his 1913 monoplane.

Clyde flying *Silver Wings*, 1912.

Herman Dvry, the first Oklahoman to build and fly an airplane, also joined the Cessnas.

Cosmopolitan Aviators

In August 1911, the Cessna boys joined with Beech and Dvry to form the Cosmopolitan Aviators. They planned to fly as many engagements as they could book.[7] Their first show, on August 19 at Cherokee, Oklahoma, was far from triumphant. Although Clyde could fly as far as two miles, the *Visitor* of Jet, Oklahoma, gave this account of the show:

"Quite a number from here went to Cherokee Saturday to see the airship go sailing, but all state that it was a complete failure. Two of the men received injuries while the start was being made, thus leaving Mr. Cessna to ride. Mr. Beech, who had intended making the flight fell from the machine accidentally before it left the ground. Mr. Cessna, who started the engine also received injuries.

"A short flight was made by C.V. Cessna, but the machine was lowered before going a hundred yards, a number of telephone wires obstructing the pathway."[8]

August 1911 — Cosmopolitan Aviators is formed.

November, 1911 — Clyde completely renovates *Silver Wings*, boosting its horsepower 25 percent in the process.

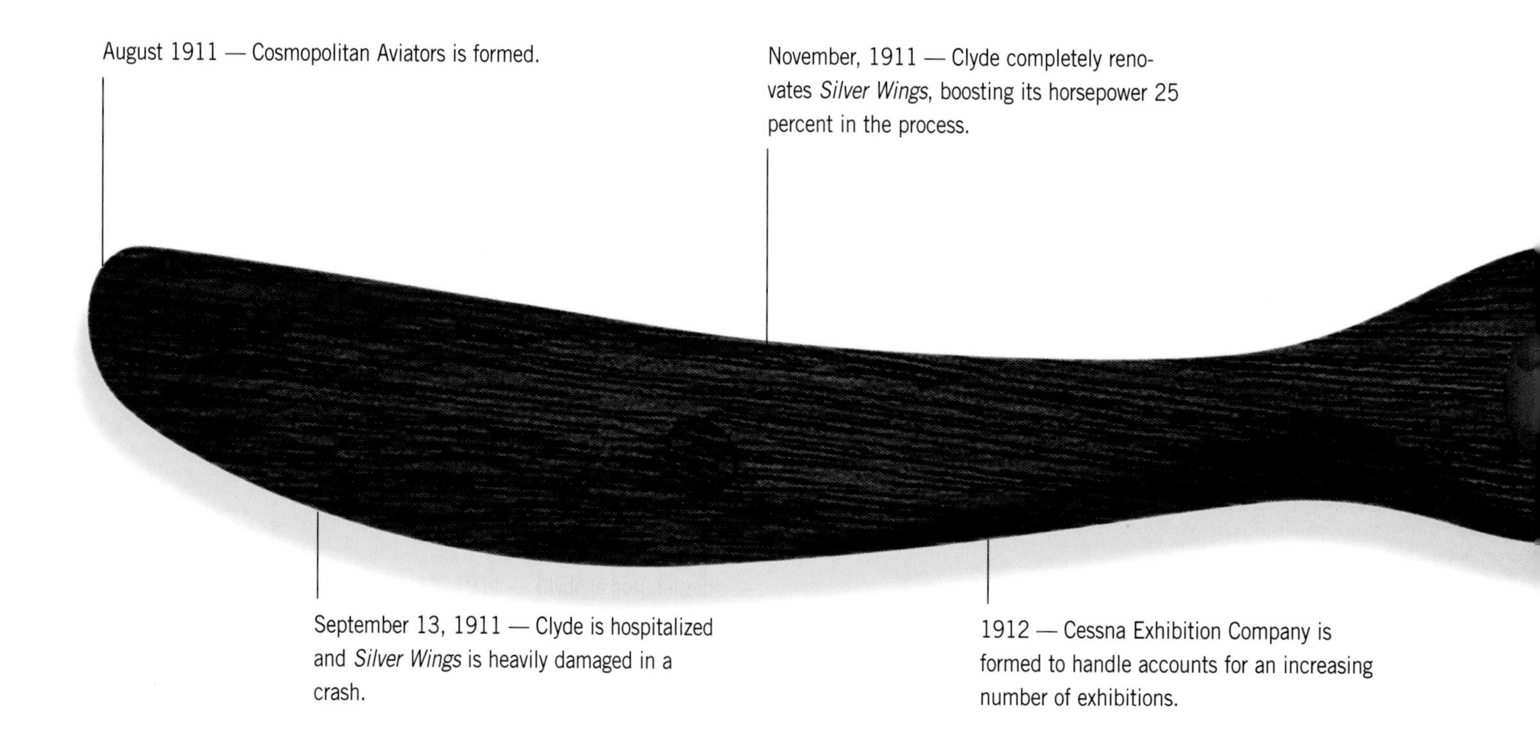

September 13, 1911 — Clyde is hospitalized and *Silver Wings* is heavily damaged in a crash.

1912 — Cessna Exhibition Company is formed to handle accounts for an increasing number of exhibitions.

Clyde built this barn on his Rago, Kansas, farm in 1913. He moved his family into the loft so he could use the ground floor to build his 1914 plane.

Despite this disappointment, Clyde accepted $300 to do an aerial demonstration at the state fair at Jet, Oklahoma. The early September demonstration was a huge success, winning over many of those who had earlier scoffed at the Cessna boys and their flying machine. The brothers booked more exhibitions in the Enid area that fall, collecting money for each. They continued to invite spectators to their camp in the Salt Plains to observe their flights.[9]

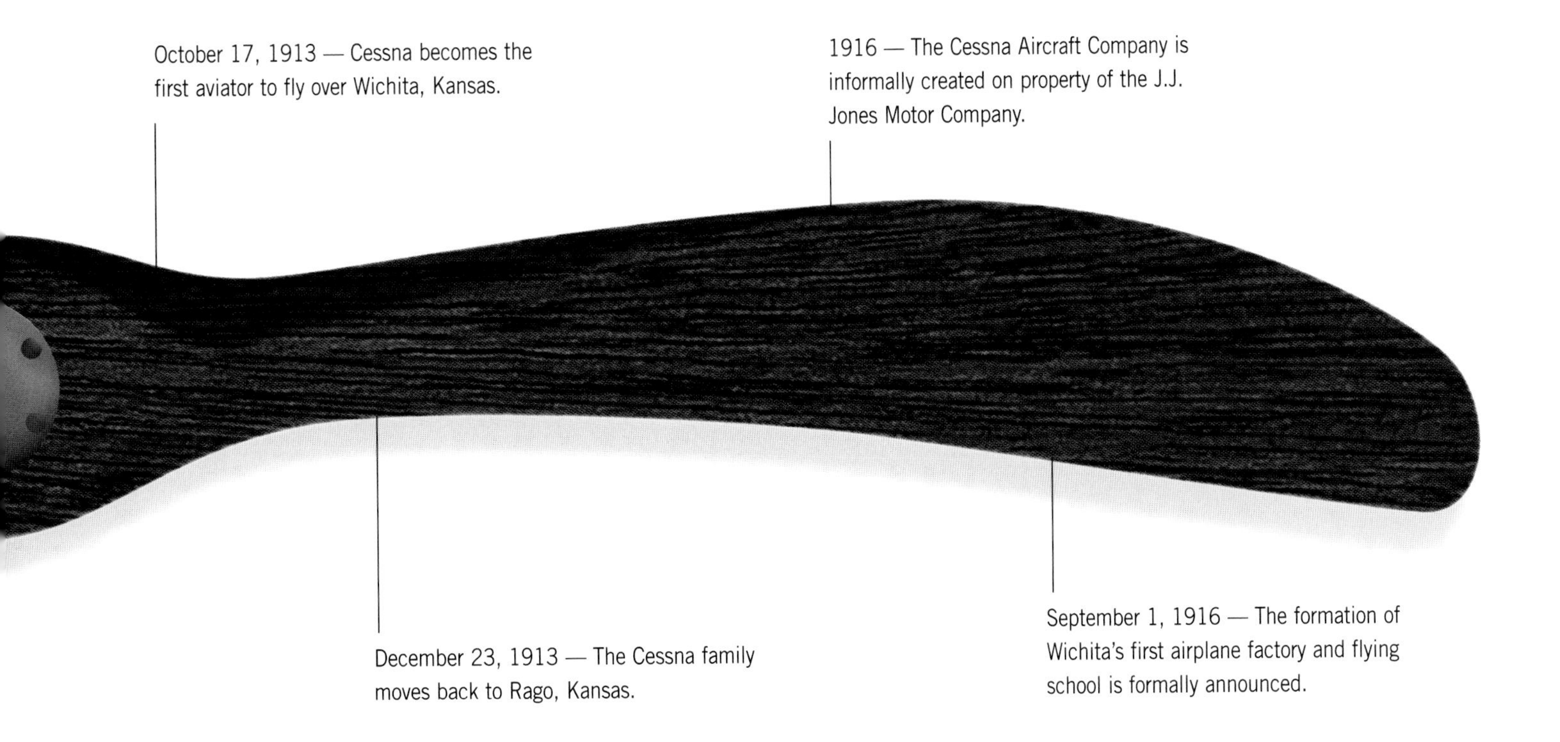

On September 13, 1911, Clyde had been out making short hops in *Silver Wings* when he decided to attempt a three–mile flight with a course reversal at the 1½-mile mark. The wind was sharp but Clyde was confident he could safely handle the airplane. He left the salty runway. As the wind jolted *Silver Wings*, Clyde made adjustments, concentrating on the upcoming turn. When he reached the turning point, Clyde realized he had a problem. The right wing was warped down much more than it should have been. The nose of the craft began to drop. Clyde made all the adjustments he could think of, but the ground was creeping up on him fast. Unable to control the plane, Clyde jumped from the cockpit. The airplane crashed into the flats of the Salt Plains, landing on its back.[10]

"Clyde slowly picked himself up. Dazed and in great pain, he moved lethargically toward his machine, gazing upon the wreckage, glad to be alive. It wasn't just the loss of an expensive airplane, but the loss of nearly $4,000 in booked exhibitions that hurt the most.

"Clyde was hospitalized and his injuries diagnosed. He wouldn't be flying for a month or more, the doctors said."[11]

The New *Silver Wings*

Silver Wings, with only the aft fuselage and empennage intact, required a complete overhaul. On September 16, the Cessna boys hauled the remains of the monoplane back to Enid, where they planned to build a new airship from the remains of *Silver Wings*. The people of Jet were sympathetic to the brothers' plight and 26 people donated a total of $30.50 to the cost of repair.[12]

Despite these contributions, Clyde's funds were very low. He decided to return to his farm in Rago, Kansas, where he remodeled his barn, converting the loft to a living quarters for the family and transforming the ground floor into a workshop. There, he and Roy completely rebuilt the airplane, making it lighter than the original model.[13] The wings and fuselage were fixed and the landing gear was completely redesigned.[14] The plane's Elbridge engine had sustained both external and internal damage. By the time the Cessnas finished their repairs, they had boosted its horsepower by 25 percent.[15]

In November, the Cessnas moved their flying operations to Val Johnson's farm south of the Enid baseball park. Johnson, a well-known rancher and personal friend of the Cessnas, had a large wheat field on his farm that he offered to the men for their flying needs. From that field, the new *Silver Wings* made its first successful flight Sunday, December 17, 1911.

"[Clyde] whirled the large propeller once, then twice. On the third pull, smoke belched from the engine's exhaust ports and the monoplane shuddered.

"Clyde quickly ran to the cockpit, climbed in and was off. For 100 yards the monoplane bounced and jinked, struggling to gain airspeed. Then it was airborne.

Crowds gather in Ford, Kansas, to watch Clyde Cessna fly his 1914 monoplane June 12, 1914.

Instead of driving, Clyde made a dramatic entrance when he flew to the Old Settlers Picnic in Kinsley, Kansas, June 9, 1914.

"Climbing out to the east, 200 feet of altitude was attained and a turn made to the west. People on the ground were awed by the smooth, graceful arc described by the airplane. Even from two miles away they could clearly see the aircraft, trailing its ever-present black plume of exhaust smoke.

"Clyde turned the machine back toward the field. As he approached to land, the crowd of about 100 people cheered him on. Men waved their hats. Ladies gave conservative gestures that belied their true excitement.

"At 50 feet altitude, Cessna cut the ignition. The propeller coasted to a stop. Only the subtle tremor of the wind in the wires could be heard as the aviator glided downward. In a few moments the airplane landed and rolled to a stop."[16]

In seven sweet minutes, Clyde had taken off, flown five miles and landed where he had departed, without damage to either himself or his airplane.

During the winter months of 1912, Clyde tinkered with his plane. By the time spring arrived, he had booked a number of exhibitions. He had become such a successful pilot that he found it necessary to form The Cessna Aeroplane Exhibition Company to handle accounts and contracts.[17] In 1912, Clyde made flights of varying success at Oklahoma communities such as Pond Creek, Kremlin, Jet and Cherokee. He capped off the year with a spectacular Christmas Day flight over Enid. Taking off at 5 p.m., he flew 10 miles in 20 minutes, describing a large circle over the

Above: Clyde, center, stands by his 1914 monoplane after an exhibition in Burdett, Kansas. The wooden extension behind the propeller was added to save the propeller from breaking if the aircraft nosed over during takeoff or landing.

southwestern section of the city. Thousands of people witnessed the flight.[18]

He continued to barnstorm in *Silver Wings*, but began contracting his exhibitions instead of flying for gate receipts.[19] After a flight at Kingman, Kansas on March 3, 1913, Clyde disassembled the ship and sent it to Enid by rail. The Cessna family also boarded a train for Enid where they would make their home once again.[20] After settling in, Clyde reassembled *Silver Wings* and flew the "old tub," as he called her, one last time before retiring her. He was already at work on a new monoplane.[21]

CESSNA IN HIS MONOPLANE
In Which he Will Give Three Exhibition flights
FRIDAY, SATURDAY and SUNDAY
At WALNUT GROVE PARK
On The Interurban
2 CASH PRIZES If you catch one of the foot-balls that he will drop from his Aeroplane you get $5.00, and if not caught $2.50 to the first person gaining possession of it. The scramble will be worth the price of admission.
3 CASH PRIZES Save the Numbered Coupon Given you at the Gate For it $5.00, $2.00, $1.00.
May Win From One to Five Dollars.
Cessna will start his first flight promptly at 4 P. M. each Day.
THE ARKANSAS VALLEY INTERURBAN
will give 15 minute service direct to the grounds, commencing at 3 P. M.
FARE 10 CENTS EACH WAY. ADMISSION TO GROUNDS 25c.
REMEMBER: This is the first appearance of a Monoplane in Wichita. All Great World's Records are Made by Monoplane Flyers

Left: A poster advertising Clyde's 1913 exhibition in Wichita, in which he became the first aviator to fly over the city that would later become the Air Capital of the World.

Designing his own Airplanes

Clyde Cessna's 1913 model featured many improvements over *Silver Wings*. It featured a simpler landing gear and a larger rudder. A small vertical stabilizer was installed in the empennage assembly. Clyde covered the extended fuselage with fabric woven by his wife, Europa.[22]

Despite these improvements, the first flight, on June 6, 1913, did not go well. The monoplane crashed when Clyde tried to avoid some telephone poles and high wires. He quickly repaired the plane and was back on the barnstorming circuit within days, cashing in on his new wings.[23]

On October 14, 1913, Clyde, Roy and an assistant traveled to Wichita, searching for a site where they could build airplanes and train pilots. To make some money on the trip, the Cessnas had scheduled exhibitions for October 17 through 19. To drum up publicity for the events, the brothers took to the streets delivering handbills.[24]

"[Clyde] hadn't gone far when J.A. Blair, superintendent of street cleaning, arrested him. The charge: unlawful distribution of handbills on city streets.

"Hauled into court, Cessna explained that he wasn't aware of the law and asked that the charge be dropped. Judge W.D. Jochens disagreed, levied a $1 fine and suggested dropping handbills from the airplanes next time. There was no ordinance against that."[25]

Despite his run-in with the law, Clyde's exhibition continued on schedule, and he flew above Wichita for the first time on October 17, 1913. During the 16-minute flight, he attained an altitude of 4,000 feet and became the first known aviator to fly across the downtown district.[26] Clyde was turning into quite the showman. The next day he dropped a football from 1,000 feet, promising $5 to anyone who could catch it. No one did.[27]

On Thanksgiving Day, Clyde made his final flight in the 1913 monoplane. Two days before Christmas, the Cessna family and airplanes traveled back to the Rago farm, where Clyde would build his 1914 model plane.[28]

This model had a windshield, a feature that dramatically enhanced the comfort of the pilot and would appear on all of Clyde's future airplanes.[29] It also had a more powerful engine. With his 1913 earnings, Clyde had finally been able to purchase the 60-horsepower Anzani engine which had been beyond his financial reach.[30]

His first flight in the new machine was in June 1914. Flying from his farm to Adams, Kansas, he reached a speed of nearly 90 miles per hour.[31] Later that month, Clyde and his new plane made an appearance at the grand opening of a new bank at Adams.

"Clyde Cessna, farmer-aviator, looped the loop, made a figure eight over Adams today and glided gracefully down to the front door of the new State Bank of Adams.

"Then he stepped from the machine, doffed his cap to the astonished onlookers, walked into the bank and made the first deposit in the new institution.

"The opening of the bank was made for a gala day there. Three thousand persons had left their waving wheat fields for a day to attend the celebration, and the coming of the monoplane added a thrill they weren't expecting."[32]

Cessna made more than 25 exhibition flights in the summer of 1914. To attract even more attention, Cessna used the plane for such routine errands as shopping and going to church, as a 1915 newspaper article described.

"One Sunday morning ... Cessna spruced up, started his machine and flew to church at the Adams circuit meeting house. Elder Jenkins was in the midst of a powerful prayer. He was calling upon the angelic hosts to unfold their wings and hover about when a mighty whirring of wings was heard and a huge bird-like apparition was seen sweeping down from the sky, headed straight for Adams circuit meeting house. It was only Cessna coming to church, but it nearly broke up the meeting.

Clyde with the Anzani motor that he was finally able to afford in 1914.

"But that was before the folks really became monoplane-broke. Now they are accustomed to seeing Cessna skimming across the sky."[33]

Between 1915 and 1917, Clyde continued to build monoplanes for himself in the winters, and hedgehop in the summers. He also did odd jobs for extra money as he continued to dream of a facility where he could build his airplanes for the public and teach aviation enthusiasts how to fly.

The Cessna Aircraft Company

In 1916, George Sherwood, production manager for the J.J. Jones Motor Company, visited Clyde at his home. Sherwood represented a small group of prominent Wichita businessmen who were interested in aviation.[34] Most of the men in the group belonged to the local Aero Club, which could claim only a hot-air balloon as its flying machine.[35]

Sherwood offered Clyde factory space at the Jones Motor Car plant in Wichita if Clyde would build an airplane there. Financial support, the use of Jones' woodworking tools and 73 acres adjacent to the plant to serve as a flying field would also be thrown into the package.[36]

Clyde knew Sherwood from his friendship with Jones, the automobile distributor who, six years earlier, had put Clyde in charge of the Enid Overland Agency.[37] Jones was now manufacturing a car of his own, called the Jones Light Six, and he wanted the car's name painted on the underside of the new airplane's wings.[38] Jones believed that if Clyde built an airplane in his shop it would draw attention to both the plane and his new automobiles.[39]

To Clyde, it was a dream come true. He would live in Wichita during the week and fly home to the Rago farm on the weekends.[40] So, with the shake of a hand, Clyde set up shop in the I building of the Jones plant. As the first airplane manufacturer in Wichita, he set the city on a course to becoming the "Air Capital of the World."

Below: Beaver Booster club members stand in front of Clyde's plane in Beaver, Oklahoma.

Above: The Cessna factory at the J.J. Jones Motor Company.

At first, the Cessna Aircraft Company had no stockholders, no incorporation and no capital investment. The business was funded solely by a handful of businessmen and some profit from the Cessna Aeroplane Exhibition Company. Clyde and Roy continued to book and fly exhibitions for additional cash.[41]

The Jones plant, a series of red brick buildings, had been built in the 1880s as the Burton Car Works, a manufacturer of railroad sleeping cars. This spot, north of Wichita, is now the location of the Coleman Company's north Wichita plant at 3600 North Hydraulic.[42]

At a luncheon held in honor of the Cessna brothers on September 1, 1916, the Aero Club formally announced the formation of Wichita's first airplane factory and flying school. Approximately 40 individuals came forward as prospective students, although Clyde predicted it would take nearly six months to organize the school. Among those interested was Jack Turner, a well–known businessman who approached Clyde and Roy with the prospect of building a monoplane for his own use.[43]

The doors of the new aircraft factory were opened for spectators on October 5. While Clyde stood outside with his monoplane answering questions, his brothers Noel and Roy gave tours of the plant.[44]

World War I had erupted in July 1914 and the presence of aircraft in that conflict had increased each year. Because of the public's heightened interest in airplanes and flying, Clyde expected the 1917 exhibition season to be the most profitable yet. To gain even more publicity for his new factory, Clyde planned a spring or summer flight from Wichita to New York City. To make the 18-hour flight, he would need a new and more powerful airship.[45] He decided to build a one-seater for exhibitions and a more powerful two-seater for the trip to New York.

By Thanksgiving Day, the final pieces of machinery had been installed in building I. As the weather grew colder, exhibition opportunities became more scarce and the Cessna boys set to work constructing Wichita's first airplanes.[46]

The first class of Clyde's Cessna Flying School, which opened in 1917. The school closed within the year.

Aviation Pioneer

1917–1927

"His new plane is of a fast monoplane type, constructed entirely with his own hands and plans with exception of the motor and wheels. Any person who understands something about the flying game can realize how complex a task Mr. Cessna undertakes when he builds a plane that will perform like his new machine does."

— *Wichita Eagle*, 1917, on Clyde Cessna's *Comet*[1]

CONSTRUCTION of the Cessna Aircraft Company's first two monoplanes began in December 1916. Clyde was already booking exhibitions for the 1917 season, and enthusiasm was high for the planned flight to New York. The slogan around the factory became, "From Wichita to New York," but the marathon flight was reluctantly grounded due to a lack of funds.[2]

In February, Clyde moved his production line to the larger building H of the Jones plant, and a month later the single-seat exhibition monoplane, powered by the 60-horsepower Anzani engine, was complete. The two-seater, named the *Comet*, was finished in June. Because of the extra seat — intended for a paying passenger — the ship was somewhat larger than the single-seater. Also powered by an Anzani engine, it featured one window on either side, extending aft from the engine to the open cockpit so that it enclosed most of the passenger compartment. It also had larger wheels and tires, and a newly designed propeller eight feet in diameter. After flying the airship for the first time on June 24, Clyde declared it his favorite.[3]

The first flight school class commenced June 4, 1917 with five students — W.E. True, Joseph J. Smitheisler, Edgar B. Smith, Marion McHugh and E.F. Rickabaugh.[4] Paying $400 for six to eight weeks of lessons, they learned to fly in Clyde's 1913 monoplane.

"To teach the mechanics of flying, the 1913 monoplane with its Elbridge engine was suspended by block and tackle from the rafters of the factory building. One at a time, the would-be aviators ascended a ladder, clambered into the cramped cockpit and moved the controls in accordance with their mentor's instructions.

"After the rudiments of control were learned, the airplane was moved outside to teach the students how to start the engine, taxi and begin the takeoff roll. Cessna observed his charges with a trained eye and evaluated each one for his potential as a pilot. He was planning to select the two best students as pilots for his exhibition company, which already had bookings for more than 30 flights during the upcoming autumn season."[5]

Although three of the students had soloed by July, the lessons were abruptly terminated in August. Busy with his strenuous exhibition schedule, Clyde simply neglected his teaching duties. Angrily, the five students filed suit against him for breach of contract. The suit never went to trial and there are no records indicating whether

Clyde Cessna and the *Comet* monoplane. (*Bob Pickett Collection/Kansas Aviation Museum.*)

the case was settled out of court or dropped. But the flying school was dissolved.[6]

A Nationwide Speed Record

Clyde found flying his *Comet* more exhilarating than teaching others about aviation. On July 5, 1917, he set a United States speed record in the machine. The triumph was detailed in the *Wichita Eagle* the following day.

"Traveling at the rate of 124.62 mph, Clyde V. Cessna, noted Wichita aviator, flew from Blackwell, Oklahoma, to Wichita early yesterday morning and thereby established a speed record not only for this vicinity but also for the United States. About 5:30 yesterday morning, Mr. Cessna rose over Blackwell and, after warming his motor for several minutes, flew over the town with a wide open throttle at exactly 5:46.

"At 6:22:35 he flew over the Jones Motor Car factory in North Wichita, having made a record flight of 76 miles in 36 minutes, 35 seconds.

"Cessna gave two flights at Blackwell on July 4. He generally ships his machine to the place of his exhibitions but he flew to Blackwell and back because he wanted to try out his new plane and determine its maximum cross-country speed. He flew to Blackwell in 41 minutes and thought that was making pretty good time. Returning, he flew with a light wind and, with a perfect working

The *Comet* was Clyde's first attempt at enclosing the cockpit. Note the pulley for wing warping at the top of the kingpost. (*Bob Pickett Collection/Kansas Aviation Museum.*)

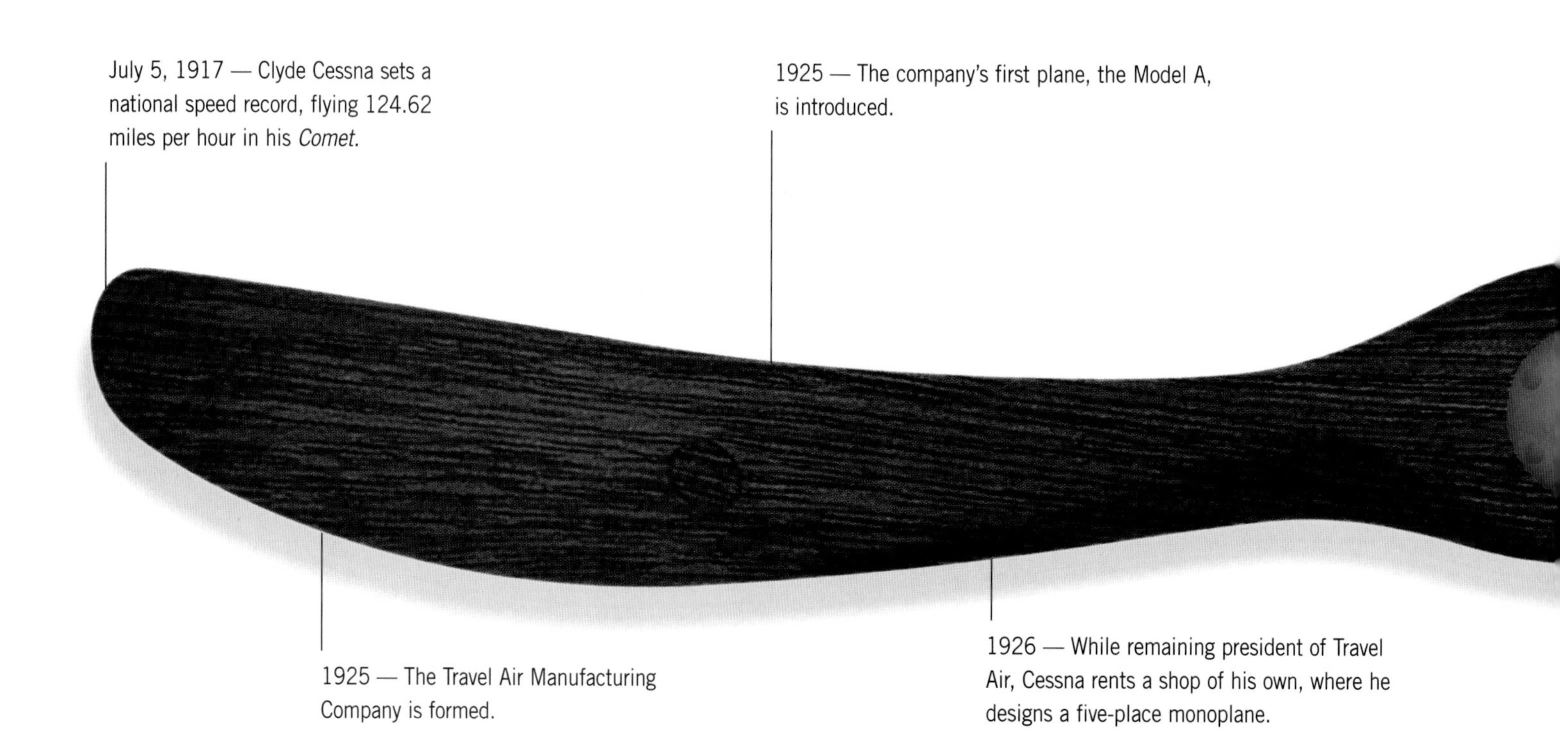

July 5, 1917 — Clyde Cessna sets a national speed record, flying 124.62 miles per hour in his *Comet.*

1925 — The Travel Air Manufacturing Company is formed.

1925 — The company's first plane, the Model A, is introduced.

1926 — While remaining president of Travel Air, Cessna rents a shop of his own, where he designs a five-place monoplane.

motor made a record that will stand in this section of the country for some time to come.

"His new plane is of a fast monoplane type, constructed entirely with his own hands and plans with exception of the motor and wheels. Any person who understands something about the flying game can realize how complex a task Mr. Cessna undertakes when he builds a plane that will perform like his new machine does.

"Cessna made a decided hit at Blackwell. He flew in the morning before a small crowd and, at 7:30 in the evening, he performed before an enthusiastic crowd of 11,000 people. Dipping, twisting, volplaning (gliding) down from 1,000 feet in the air, with his motor shut off, then starting it within a few inches of the ground and flying so close over the heads of people that they ducked and tried to get out of the way, Cessna put on an exhibition that was decidedly thrilling in every way. Twice he banked his machine so steep that the wings of the machine were almost vertical with the earth. After landing, Cessna said that on account of the heavy wind it was the most dangerous flight of his career."[7]

In the fall of 1917 the Cessna brothers moved their company from the Jones factory to a small field a quarter-mile north of present-day Wichita State University. They continued to store their airplanes at the Jones location.[8]

Between August and October, Clyde implemented several improvements to the *Comet*, including the installation of a new 70-horsepower Anzani engine. Clyde was so proud of his updated ship that he decided to stage a race.[9] Through the press, he challenged Louis Gertson, who had flown at the 1917 Wheat Exposition, to a speed match in the sky. He offered Gertson $1,000 if his biplane could beat the *Comet* in a race from Wichita to Hutchinson, Kansas. But Clyde never received a response to his challenge.[10]

World War I

Meanwhile, World War I was gathering intensity in Europe. Despite President Woodrow Wilson's vehement efforts to keep the United States from becoming involved, Congress approved a declaration of war against the Central Powers, and America entered the conflagration on April 6, 1917.

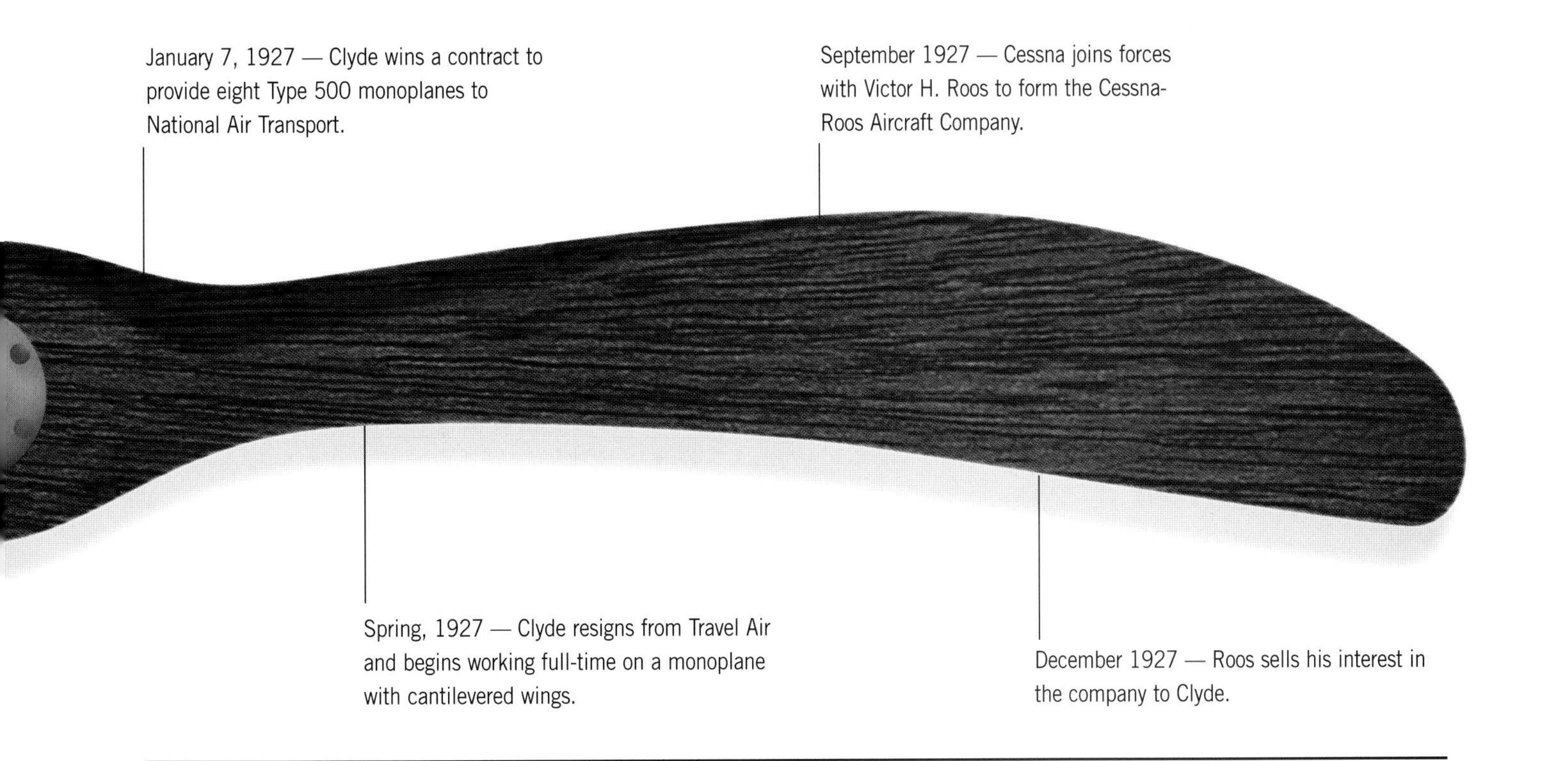

January 7, 1927 — Clyde wins a contract to provide eight Type 500 monoplanes to National Air Transport.

September 1927 — Cessna joins forces with Victor H. Roos to form the Cessna-Roos Aircraft Company.

Spring, 1927 — Clyde resigns from Travel Air and begins working full-time on a monoplane with cantilevered wings.

December 1927 — Roos sells his interest in the company to Clyde.

For the first time, airplanes dueled over battlefields, adding a new dimension to warfare. At the war's onset, enemy pilots merely waved as they passed each other to observe troop movements. At some point a pilot thought to bring along a rifle or small explosive. By 1918, full-scale dogfights occurred between pilots whose aircraft were equipped with machine guns.

Clyde was too old to enlist for active duty, but to show his support of the American troops he wired the Defense Department, offering his two airplanes for their disposal. He also assured government officials that his factory was ready to produce as many as one airplane a week if they desired to enter into a production contract.[11]

AIRCRAFT IN WAR

CLYDE CESSNA GENEROUSLY offered to provide the U.S. military with aircraft for use in World War I, but the military was still experimenting with how to deploy the novel flying machines for military purposes. The Army preferred to use French-built planes while it experimented with the aircraft's role in war.

Throughout the history of warfare, wise commanders preferred to attack or defend from the "high ground," so they could observe the enemy's movements from above. Soldiers screaming down from the heights carried a psychological advantage as well.

It was the ability to observe troop movements that first encouraged the military to take to the skies. In 1794, the French army stationed artillery officers aboard balloons to direct fire against Austrian positions.[1] During World War I, Germany used airships for both reconnaissance and aerial bombing of both troops and civilians.

But lighter-than-air craft were slow, easy targets for troops on the ground, and were simply massacred when attacked by propeller-driven airplanes. The airplane was first used as a weapon during the Italo-Turkish War in 1911. Soldiers attached to the Italian Air Flotilla flew a Bleriot monoplane from Tripoli to Azizia, in North Africa, to observe troop movements. The first bombs dropped in war fell on Turkish soldiers during this conflict.[2]

The use of planes in warfare was hampered because no one had figured out a way to fire a cockpit-mounted machine gun without shooting off the propeller. One solution was to armor-plate the propeller, so some of the bullets bounced off the blades while the rest went through to the target. The Fokker airplane, designed by Dutchman Anthony Fokker for the German army, introduced the true concept of the fighter plane when he invented a timing mechanism that fired bullets between the spinning blades. German aircraft almost owned the skies until the Allies developed the same mechanism. From 1916 on, aircraft engaged in what became known as "dogfights." Legendary aces — pilots who shot down five or more aircraft — emerged, such as Germany's famous Baron von Richthofen, also known as the Red Baron, and America's first ace, Eddie Rickenbacker.

Except for reconnaissance purposes, the aircraft-as-weapon was not pivotal in World War I. However, the war spurred new roles and tactics. By World War II, warplanes would become decisive weapons for all sides.

In an April 24 telegram to Kansas Congressman William A. Ayeres, Clyde requested assistance in lobbying Capitol Hill for equipment, vehicles and airplanes that could be used to train pilots. Clyde had read about America's lack of trained airmen and was ready, with the assistance of his brothers, to give flight instructions to students before they applied for formal army training. The government declined his offers.[12]

Putting this rejection aside, Clyde busied himself with plans for flying nearly 60 exhibitions during the late summer and fall of 1917. His barnstorming activities were abruptly suspended, however, due to growing restrictions on fuel allocations for civilian flying, under rules set down by the War Industries Board. Clyde closed down his shop and returned to his Rago farm in late 1917, where he cultivated the land and operated a profitable custom threshing business until 1925.[13]

The E.M. Laird Airplane Company

Little is known of Clyde's activities outside of farming between 1917 and 1925, but the aviation industry in Wichita continued to grow without his involvement. By the time the war ended in late 1918, more than 10,000 men had been trained to fly in the air services. Many of these former soldiers were eager to purchase airplanes of their own and enter the barnstorming business. Wichita became a mecca for aviators, spurred on by the Chamber of Commerce, which recognized the potential economic benefits of the aviation industry. In early 1919, the Chamber's aviation committee began promoting a landing field owned by J.J. Jones as the ideal site for demonstrations and other airborne events. Nearby provisions for fuel and repairs were also promoted.[14]

Once the airfield opened, several companies emerged, offering services ranging from a local air taxi service to the sale of aircraft. One of these was the E.M. Laird Airplane Company.

In 1920, Emil Matthew "Matty" Laird moved his Laird Aviation Company out of Chicago and — along with Wichita oil man Jacob Melvin "Jake" Moellendick and Okmulgee, Oklahoma, car dealer William Burke — established the E.M. Laird Airplane Company at the corner of Wichita and English Streets. This factory produced the 1920 Swallow, marketed to aviators who wanted something better than a war-surplus Jenny. In its first year of production, more than 25 Swallows were ordered.[15]

The company soon hired Lloyd Stearman, a Kansas State Agricultural College architecture student, to draw up aircraft plans. Aviators Walter Beech and Buck Weaver also joined the company as salesmen. A new factory opened in 1921. But in 1923, following a disagreement with Moellendick, Laird left the company and returned to Chicago.[16] The E.M. Laird Airplane Company was reorganized and became the Swallow Airplane Manufacturing Company.[17] Shortly after Laird's departure, Weaver left as well. Beech and Stearman left the company in 1924 after they failed to convince Moellendick that it was time to switch from the old wood design airframes to metal.[18] Ken Weyand, in a *Pilot News* article, described the events that led to the departure of Moellendick's colleagues.

"All went well until September 1923. A minor matter triggered a violent argument between Matty and Jake. Jake, who had been known for settling disputes with his fists, threatened Matty. Matty walked out, taking two airplanes and $1,500 with him. He returned to his native Chicago and began building Laird Commercials, the beginning of a long and successful aircraft business.

"Jake changed the company name to the Swallow Airplane Manufacturing Company, and went back to work. The no-longer-hapless Walter Beech was promoted to chief test pilot and Stearman became chief engineer. Lloyd Stearman's brother, Waverly, was brought on board Moellendick's payroll and things began to calm.

"Jake still ran things with an iron hand and seldom took advice. Fanatic about flying, he flew whenever possible and whenever the Wichita Eagle *or* Beacon *would cite barnstormer crashes, Jake would rage and curse. He even had a large sign painted on the airport fence stating: NO STUNT FLYING HERE. Whenever a pilot so much as banked too steeply around the plant, Jake would boil over. Jake was known to punch out pilots who strayed too far from the stunt-flying edict. After each model was sold off Jake's pro-*

duction line, he would go into hysterics of jubilation and begin an 'orgy of planning' which generally ended in a scrap with his executives. Everyone at the factory knew not to confront Jake directly. They rather rode out the storm, hoping the matter would be forgotten. It was not the most efficient way of running an aircraft business.

"Early in 1924, Lloyd redesigned the Swallow. The new single-bay New Swallow would later prove itself by winning the Admiral Fullam Derby Race in St. Louis with Walter Beech at the controls. But the New Swallow was the cause of another schism in the Moellendick firm. Stearman and Beech decided the fuselage should be constructed of tubular steel instead of the traditional wood. Jake would have none of it and there was little use in arguing with Jake — no one wanted to be punched in the nose by the burly Jake. Discouraged, Stearman and Beech walked out."[19]

The Travel Air Company

Determined to build their steel-frame aircraft but short on resources, Beech and Stearman, in early 1925, flew one of their Swallow airplanes to Clyde's Rago farm and talked him into joining them in business.[20] The trio proceeded to seek out Wichita investor Walter Innes Jr. With the backing of Innes, the group formed the Travel Air Manufacturing Company on February 5, 1925.[21]

Beech put up $5,000 while Stearman offered $700 and his plans for a new biplane featuring a steel fuselage. Clyde contributed $25,000. Although the amount provided by Innes is not known, it must have been substantial because he became the first president and treasurer.[22] Clyde was made vice president, Beech became secretary, and Stearman was installed as chief engineer.[23]

The partners set up shop in a small rented building that was part of the Kansas Planning Mill, at 471 West First Street in downtown Wichita.[24] By the end of the year, Innes had stepped out of the picture. Clyde became president, Beech became vice president, and Stearman was elected treasurer.[25]

The company's first Travel Air biplane, designated Model A, was powered by an OX-5 engine and sold for $3,500.[26] The company had found success with this model and by the end of the year, 19 planes had been built and sold. In 1926, 46 were built.[27]

Although the company was doing well, Clyde was not satisfied. He strongly felt the monoplane design was much better than the biplanes, with all their struts and wires. His partners preferred biplanes. Both sides refused to see the other

The Type 5000, built in 1927 for the National Air Transport Company, was Travel Air's first monoplane.

National Air Transport bought eight Type 500 aircraft, which were modified and named Type 5000. This one was used on the Chicago-Dallas airmail route.

point of view, and in 1926, Clyde rented a shop west of the Arkansas River on West Douglas Avenue. After completing a days' work at the Travel Air Company, he would go to his private shop and, with the help of Guy Winstead, a veteran Wichita pilot and skilled craftsman, worked on the design of a five-seater cabin monoplane. Edward H. Phillips described this monoplane in detail in *A Master's Expression.*

"It featured a completely enclosed cabin for five occupants, surrounded by a generous window area. A 300-pound, semi-cantilever wing, spanning 44 feet, was mounted above the fuselage, with dual lift struts on each side.

"Entry/exit from the ship was through a large door installed on the left side, complete with a viewing window. The wicker chairs could quickly be removed to convert the aircraft into a flying ambulance, with only five minutes required to make the change.

"Seated up front, the pilot had excellent all-around visibility. Landing gear was of conventional design with shock cord in tension on versicle strut assemblies. Powered with 110 horsepower, 10-cylinder, air cooled Anzani static radial, the monoplane could carry 1,000 pounds and land at only 45 miles per hour."[28]

As with all of Clyde's monoplanes, the rudder cable configuration was reversed from that of other airships. Clyde's close friend from his early flying days, Carl Evans, said Clyde built his airplanes this way because he feared patent lawsuits if he copied the conventional design. Clyde, however, contended that everyone else flew airplanes with rudder cables connected incorrectly.[29]

The Type 500 monoplane was completed in May, and Clyde showed it to Walter Beech, who liked the design. The pair knew of a company that needed a cabin plane that could carry mail from Chicago to Dallas during all hours of the day and night. The National Air Transport was holding a contest to find the best airplane for this purpose. On December 20, 1926, Beech agreed to fly to Kansas City with Clyde in the new plane. The pair won the contest and, on January 7, 1927, was rewarded with a contract worth $128,676. NAT wanted eight of the monoplanes, with a few modifications.[30]

An uncovered prototype of the Cessna "A" series cantilever wing, shown here in 1927.

In early 1927, the Travel Air Company moved to East Central Avenue, where Raytheon Aircraft is now located. By that time, 80 biplanes had been delivered, and production had begun on the NAT contract.[31]

With the promise of big sales, Beech decided that manufacturing monoplanes wasn't such a bad idea after all. The first Travel Air monoplane was an updated version of Clyde's original design and became known as the Type 5000. The Cessna tail was replaced with one designed by Travel Air, and a Wright Whirlwind engine of 224 horsepower was used instead of an Anzani engine.[32]

The new Travel Air monoplane was very successful and it wasn't long before several historic transpacific flight records had been established in them. On July 14, 1927, Earnest Smith and Emery Bronte flew a Travel Air monoplane named *City of Oakland* from Oakland, California to Hawaii. The *Woolarc*, flown by Arthur Goebel and William Davis, won the first Transoceanic Air Race on August 16 and 17. They flew from Oakland, California, to Wheeler Field, Hawaii, in 26 hours, 17 minutes and 33 seconds to win a first prize of $25,000.[33]

Cantilevered Wings

In the spring of 1927, Clyde approached Beech with the prospect of building a monoplane with fully cantilevered wings, meaning they would not be supported by struts or anchors. Most aviation experts at the time did not think a full-cantilever design was possible. Travel Air Company had always produced strut-braced wings, which were then conventional. Beech was not inclined to depart from the standard design, but he encouraged his friend to pursue his interest. Clyde took Beech's advice and resigned from Travel Air, selling his 179 shares of stock to three Wichita businessmen for $90 a share.[34]

Working with employee Guy Winstead out of his West Douglas workshop, Clyde was determined to be the first in America to build a full-cantilever plane. To doubters, he said: "The Creator made the limbs of a tree without struts, and He gave the bird cantilever wings. I'm going to try it."[35]

On April 19, 1927, Clyde, with his one employee, two airplanes and layouts for two cantilever-winged ships, unofficially began the Cessna Aircraft Company.[36]

The first layout was for a three-seater monoplane, informally known as the Cessna All Purpose, which would have a wingspan of 36 feet.[37] The second layout was for a monoplane called the Cessna Common. With a wingspan of

47 feet and powered by a 200-horsepower Wright J-4 engine, it would transport five people.[38]

A larger facility would be needed to construct these two monoplanes, and at the end of April the Cessna Aircraft Company moved to a more spacious workshop at 1520 West Douglas Avenue. The building had been the former home of Johnson's Poultry, Egg and Feed Company.[39] Three more men were added to the workforce. Clyde, Winstead, Johnny Heibert and Bob Phelps comprised the assembly line, while Romer G. Weyant became the first Cessna test pilot.[40]

Construction on the Cessna Common began May 1, 1927. By that time, strict government regulations governed the construction and strength of aircraft. In order to receive an Approved Type Certificate, a complete stress analysis was required on the entire plane. Since this was the first full-cantilever airplane in existence, Clyde knew particular attention would be paid to the wings. He paid Joe Newell, a professor of aeronautical engineering at the Massachusetts Institute of Technology, $800 to make the stress tests for federal approval.[41] Because the aircraft was so novel, Newell had to come up with some unusual testing methods, as an article in *Wichita* magazine later noted.

"The cantilever wing was such a revolutionary thing that the engineer had no other way to prove stress than by loading sandbags on the wings. They turned the plane on its back and elevated the fuselage two feet above the floor so that the wings stood straight out. They loaded on each wing 3,700 pounds of bags filled with sand. That gave a wide factor of safety and the wings were in perfect condition.

"Then Cessna exclaimed, 'Let's see what it'll take.' They loaded on 10, 20, 30 sacks of sand, each sack weighing 100 pounds. They added still more. Then Cessna had his six men stand on the wings until there was a total of 15,752 pounds on the two wings, or more than double the load required to prove safety. The wings sagged a little, but did not crack."[42]

On Saturday, August 13, 1927, Weyant taxied the first full-cantilever winged monoplane across a makeshift airfield at Hydraulic Avenue and 13th Street, eased the throttle forward and lifted the ship into the air for the very first time. The All Purpose reached nearly 100 miles per hour during that flight.[43]

Pleased with the airship's performance, Clyde renamed it the Phantom and decided to put it into production. However, he would need a new building in which to produce the plane. To raise funds, he organized a company and sold stock.

Cessna built the first cantilever-winged aircraft. Below, the weight of 28 men demonstrate just how strong this new type of wing is. Clyde's son is seventh from the right. Clyde is 12th from the right.

Above: This is the second of 12 Phantoms built. Clyde is pictured left in the same monoplane, which was painted red. Pilot George Myers was supposed to race in this aircraft, but dirt got into the fuel system and stalled the engine.

Below left: Test pilot Romer Weyant in a prototype Phantom.
Background: Architect's sketch of the new Cessna-Roos Aircraft Factory.

The Cessna-Roos Aircraft Company

During the summer of 1927, Victor H. Roos, a motorcycle dealer from Omaha, Nebraska, became interested in the Phantom. He invested in Clyde's new company, and on September 7, 1927, the name was changed to the Cessna-Roos Aircraft Company. With this infusion of capital, a new building was constructed at 1812 West Second Street (Second Street and Glenn Avenue), where a 10-acre grass plot served as a landing field.[44] Clyde and Roos each received salaries of $50 a week.[45]

While the factory was under construction, Clyde rebuilt the Phantom prototype, powering it with a 225-horsepower Wright J-5 Whirlwind engine. He also added a second door in the fuselage and fully enclosed the cockpit for the pilot. This plane, with its top speed of 150 miles per hour, became a successful racer.[46] Clyde continued to tinker with the model, which became known as the A series. He added more windows to the cabin for passenger visibility and reinstalled the Anzani engine. Orders began pouring in and Cessna airplanes were beginning to show up everywhere.[47]

Although business was good, tension grew between Roos and the company's board members, George H. Siedhoff, C.A. McCorkle and J.D. Fair. During the November 15, 1927 board meeting, the topic arose of changing the company's name to Cessna Aircraft Company. Roos vehemently objected to this proposal and the discussion was discontinued until the November 22 meeting. Once again Roos objected, claiming a name change "would be detrimental to the firm just when production was about to begin in earnest and was also an injustice to him personally."

Roos announced that he would be entitled to remuneration if the directors voted to change the name of the company. The board voted for the change anyway, and Roos subsequently tendered his resignation.[48] In December 1927, he received an offer to become general manager of the Swallow Airplane Company. He sold his interest in the Cessna-Roos Aircraft Company to Clyde, and the two men parted ways.[49]

Cessna's chief pilot, Earl Rowland, sits in the left seat, at the controls of this 1929 AW monoplane.

THE RISE & FALL OF THE CESSNA AIRCRAFT COMPANY

1927–1931

"I packed my belongings. I gave the keys to Mr. Sanders, and I did not even look back at the building that was no longer mine."

— Clyde Cessna, 1952[1]

BY 1927, WICHITA had become the nation's aviation mecca with more than 20 airplane companies within the borders of the growing city. The nation's enthusiasm for air travel escalated sharply after Charles Lindbergh successfully completed the world's first nonstop transatlantic solo flight. On May 20, 1927, the boyishly handsome 25-year-old boarded his single-engine monoplane, *Spirit of St. Louis*, and left New York City's Roosevelt Field at 7:52 a.m. He flew for 33 hours and 32 minutes, landing at Le Bourget Airport near Paris. Lindbergh's prize: $25,000 put up by the Franco-American philanthropist Raymond B. Orteig of New York City. Lindbergh seemed to make the world smaller by proving transcontinental flight was possible, and he was hailed as a hero around the world.[2]

The young pilot had originally negotiated for a Travel Air plane for the record-breaking flight, but according to Walter Beech, the volume of business and back orders at the time made it impossible to fill the request.[3] With no hard feelings, Lindbergh later returned to Wichita and was photographed behind the controls of a Swallow airplane on August 18, 1927.[4]

Wichita had become a pivotal stop for pilots on tour, but the entire industry was marred by crashes that took the lives of many pilots. A few such incidents were related in *Borne on the South Wind* by Frank Joseph Rowe and Craig Miner.

> *"A Wichita car salesman and his Texas pilot were killed in 1923 in a plane borrowed from William Lassen when the salesman became frightened during a flight, put his foot on the rudder guide, and froze. A Stearman salesman, Fred Hoyt, was lost in a forced landing over Utah and found frozen to death. A Wichita businessman was cut down by the prop of a taxiing airplane in front of his family."*[5]

Public confidence in aviation was critical, especially if Wichita planned to continue as a hub for the industry. In an attempt to show the public that airplanes were dependable vehicles, the Edsel Ford Reliability Tour was established and held annually from 1925 to 1931. Long-distance flight demonstrations were organized and carried out, and the construction of modern airports was promoted. The publicity to be gained from placing in the tour was the best sort of advertising. Travel

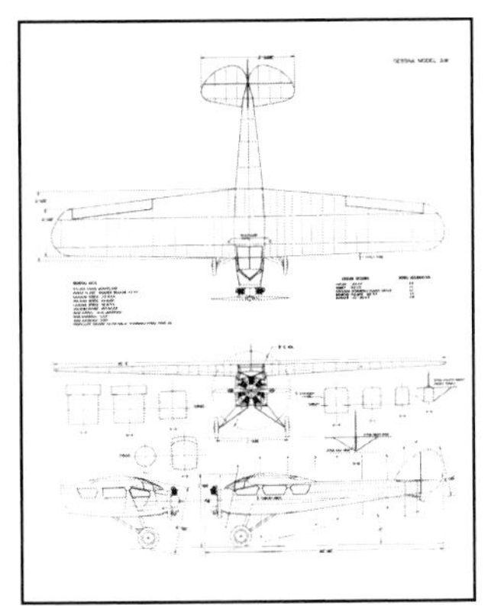

Specifications for the Model AW series airplane. The AW series, with the American-made Warner engine, became popular racing planes.

The Model AC used a Comet 130-horsepower engine.

Air won first through third place in the first tour, and a Swallow plane took fifth place that year.[6]

The Cessna Aircraft Company

Amidst all the activity, Clyde Cessna formally established his own aircraft company. On December 22, 1927, the Charter Board of the State of Kansas approved a corporate name change from the Cessna-Roos Aircraft Company to The Cessna Aircraft Company. A new factory had been built earlier in the month on 11 acres at First Street and Glenn Avenue. The production facility itself was 100 by 50 feet; for safety purposes the paint shop was detached from the main structure.[7]

Clyde and his 20 employees manufactured A Series monoplanes patterned after the original Phantom. It was the first production airplane for the company, although delivery got off to a rough

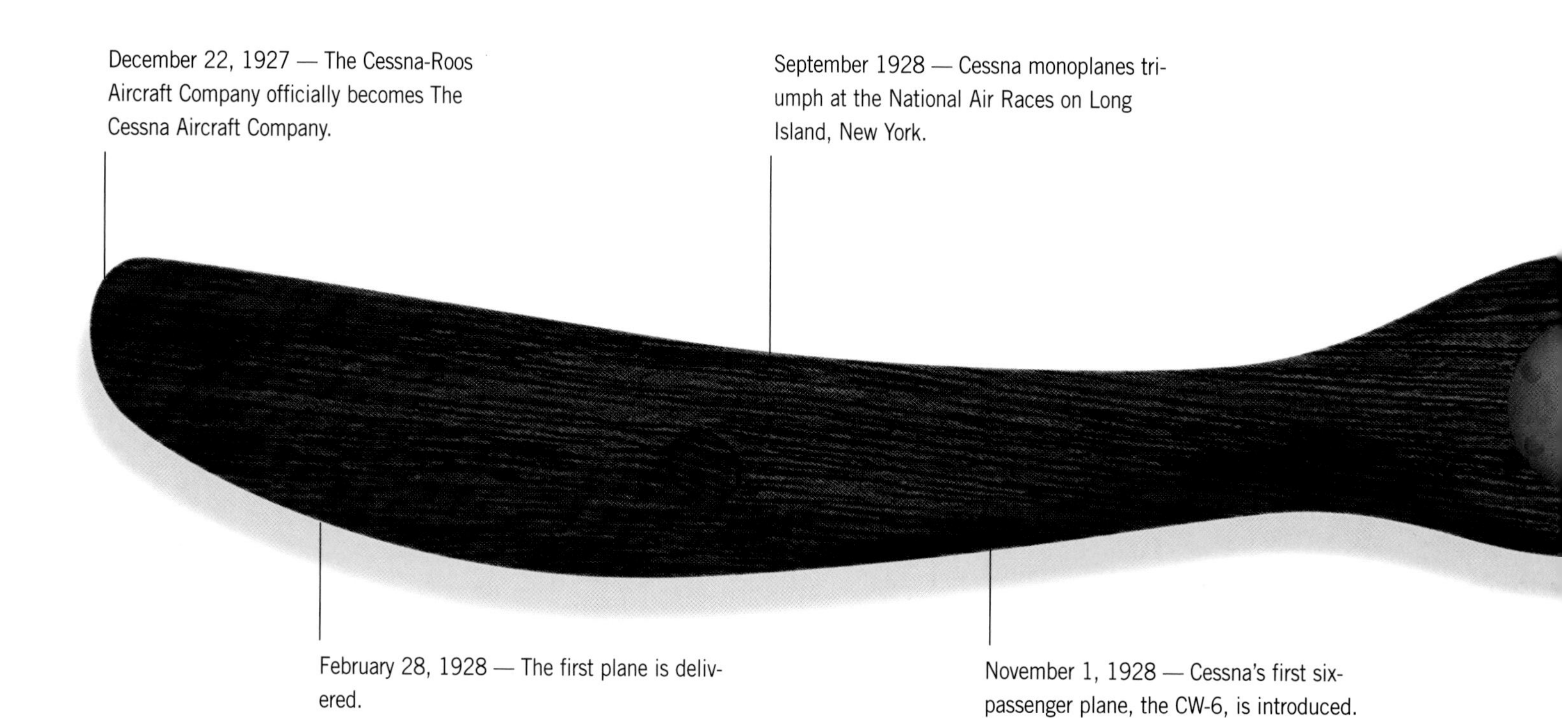

December 22, 1927 — The Cessna-Roos Aircraft Company officially becomes The Cessna Aircraft Company.

February 28, 1928 — The first plane is delivered.

September 1928 — Cessna monoplanes triumph at the National Air Races on Long Island, New York.

November 1, 1928 — Cessna's first six-passenger plane, the CW-6, is introduced.

Three AF Model monoplanes were built during 1928, using the 150-horsepower Floco engine.

start. By early February 1928, the Wright J-5 engines were still on back order. Not willing to wait, the resourceful Clyde modified his stock of French Anzani radial engines and used them instead. The first Cessna Aircraft Company plane was delivered February 28, 1928 to Edwin A. Link of Pittsburgh, Pennsylvania, who paid $6,500.[8]

Cessna A Series Monoplanes

Because of the shortage of Wright J-5s, the Cessna A was produced with a choice of five radial engines: Anzani 120-horsepower, Warner 125-horsepower, Siemans-Halske 125-horsepower, Comet 130-horsepower and Floco 150-horsepower. To differentiate between the models, a two-letter designation system was developed. The first letter represented the airplane series and the second designated the engine type. These were the AA (Anzani), AW (Warner), AS (Siemans-Halske), AC (Comet) and AF (Floco). A total of 69 A Series monoplanes were built between 1928 and 1930, of which 48 were model AWs, which became popular racing planes. The Warner was the only American-built engine of the five.[9]

On August 27, 1928, after much correspondence and a redesign of landing gear, the all-important Type Certification of the Model AA was granted. All the A Series aircraft produced previously were modified to comply with the required changes. Customers were able to take delivery of their aircraft and operate them without restrictions.[10]

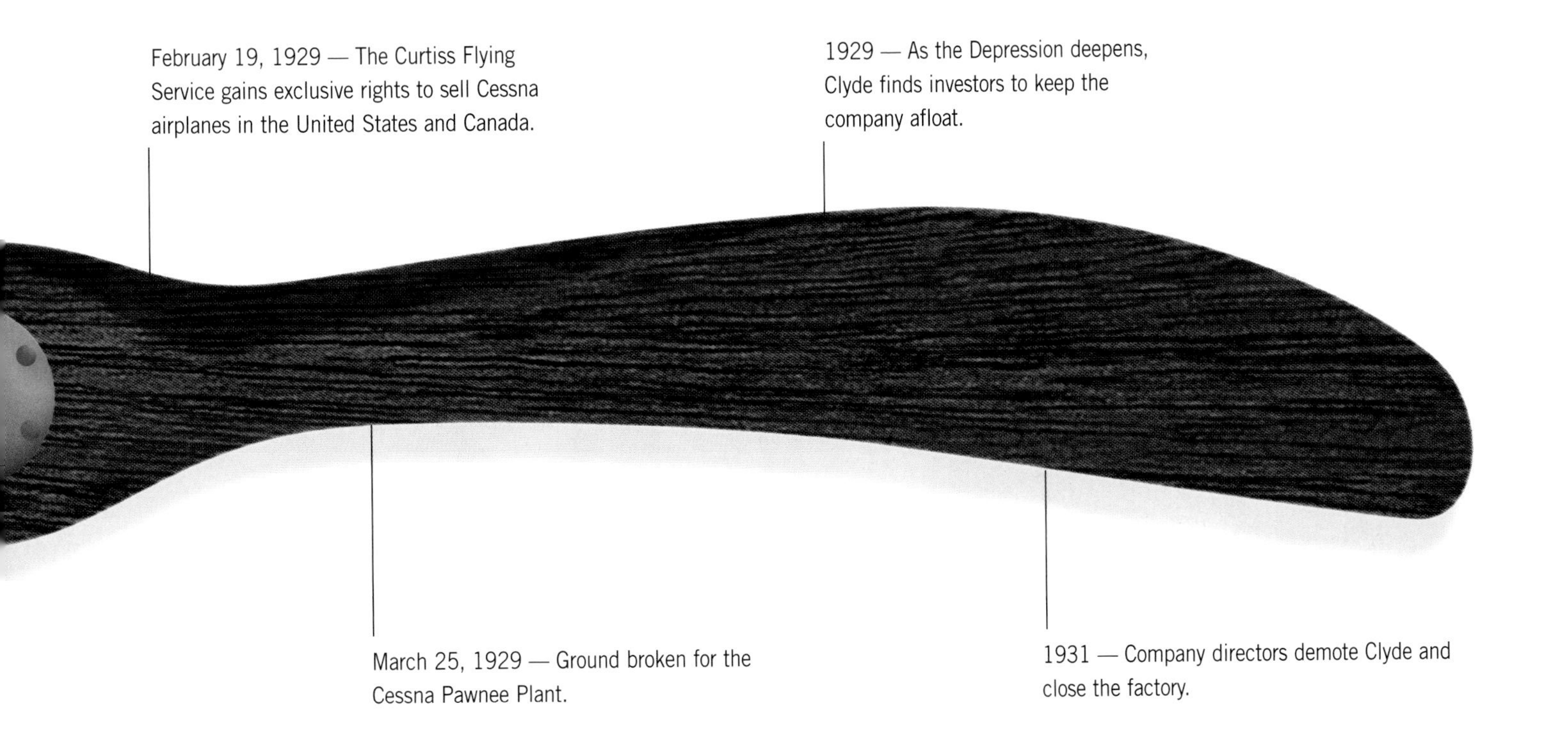

The Souped-Up BW

In addition to the A Series produced from 1928 to 1930, Cessna designed and manufactured a BW (B Series, Wright engine) model in 1928 and 1929. In essence, the ship was little more than a souped-up A with a 220-horsepower Wright J-5 engine. Weighing 2,435 pounds and selling for $9,800, it could sail through the skies at 150 miles per hour.[11]

The first BW rolled off the assembly line on March 28, 1928, and was sold with Type Certification pending. Clyde had even more difficulty getting approval on the BW than on the A Series. On August 27, 1928, the Department of Commerce said the BW could not be licensed to seat four unless the gross weight was increased, thus requiring a new set of stress-analysis tests. Clyde did not want to fall behind on production while submitting the new data, so he reluctantly removed one seat.[12]

Still, officials at the Department of Commerce were not satisfied. They worried about aileron flutter, a phenomenon that affected other aircraft of the era. Air flow streaming over the wings often caused the ailerons on the wings to flutter, creating a turbulent motion and, in extreme cases, loss of control. Ignoring the fact that several BW ships were already flying — without showing any tendency to flutter — officials decided the BW would also experience this problem at high speeds, and turned down the Type Certification.[13]

Clyde redesigned the aileron control system. On February 27, 1929, the BWs that had been sold were finally approved.[14]

Despite all the effort, however, only 13 BWs were produced. Clyde decided that without a higher gross weight the planes would not receive full benefit of the large engine.[15]

Above: The forward cabin view of the 1929 Cessna Model AW.

Below: Though the BW model flew just fine, the Department of Commerce kept delaying certification, forcing the redesign of the entire aileron control system. Only 13 were sold.

The Air Derby

The early days of flight tended to attract daredevils, because few pilots could resist the challenge of racing their beloved aircraft against others. By 1928, these races were gaining a degree of formality, and Clyde knew they offered cash prizes and invaluable publicity to the winners. A natural showman, he decided to enter only races which he had a better-than-average chance of winning.[16]

Along with his board of directors, Clyde decided to enter the National Air Race on Long Island, New York, in September 1928. It featured four cross-country dashes to Los Angeles, California, including a nonstop transcontinental Speed Dash. The Class A Division was open to all airplanes with engine displacement not exceeding 510 cubic inches. Cessna test pilot Earl Rowland would fly a model AW plane in this class. In Class B, open to all airplanes with displacement between 510 and 800 cubic inches, Cessna entered five B Series monoplanes with 220-horsepower Wright J-5 engines. Flying these would be Cessna test pilot Francis "Chief" Bowhan, Cessna distributors F.J. Grace, J. Warren Smith, Jay Sadowski, and pilot Edward G. Schultz. Also in Class B was a model AA piloted by Clyde himself and Curtis Quick, and a model BW flown by Owen Haugland. The company did not participate in C Division for airplanes with displacement exceeding 800 cubic inches.[17]

All eight Cessna monoplanes and nine pilots met at Roosevelt Field on September 2 for pre-race inspections. Edward H. Phillips, in the wonderfully anecdotal book, *A Master's Expression*, described the morning activities on the first day.

> *"September 5, 1928 dawned overcast and chilly. It was the morning 47 pilots had anxiously awaited for more than 30 days: the start of the New York to Los Angeles Air Derby.*
>
> *"By 4 a.m., the flight line at Roosevelt Field, Long Island, was bustling with activity. With $57,500 in total prize money up for grabs, pilots and sponsors double-checked their airplanes, mechanics ran up engines, changed spark plugs and adjusted carburetors for peak performance. Fuel trucks scurried from ship to ship, pumping in gasoline and topping off oil tanks."*[18]

Clyde and his airmen gathered for a brainstorming session, discussing flight plans, fuel capacities and throttle set-

Earl Rowland with his Warner-powered aircraft, and the winning trophy (inset) from the 1928 National Air Race.

Above and right: The Model BW was a beefed up "A," with a 220-horsepower Wright J-5 engine. The model shown above was flown by Edward Schultz in the 1928 Transcontinental Air Race, winning fourth place in the B Division.

Below: Cessna's popularity grew with each victory, the greatest being Earl Rowland's triumph in the 1928 derby.

tings. Sixteen stopover points were established, five of which were overnight; the rest allotted just 30 minutes to refuel and perform minor repairs.[19] Clyde was especially hopeful for victory in the Class A race, because Rowland would be piloting a fuel-efficient racehorse of a plane: the C7107, powered by a Warner engine.[20] The most serious challenge was expected from Robert Dake, an experienced and well-respected pilot of an American Moth monoplane.

As the pilots readied for takeoff, a dispute erupted between the Class B racers and the race committee. According to the rules, only stock aircraft built before August 1, 1928, were eligible to enter. The pilots argued that a Waco CTO and two Laird LC-RJ-200 biplanes had been modified and therefore should not be allowed to compete.[21] According to Phillips, Clyde called these planes "ringers ... a term echoing back to the horse racing days when a fast horse was entered under a new name."[22] But Stephen Day, chairman of the starting committee, informed the Class B pilots that the committee had decided to allow the three planes to compete, and welcomed those not happy with the decision to withdraw.[23] Chief Bowhan did so, but the rest of the Cessna team went ahead.

The remaining pilots took off at precisely 5:43:45 a.m. on Wednesday, September 5. Technical problems caused Cessna's B Series plane, piloted by J. Warren Smith, to drop out.[24]

Rowland took the early lead in the Class A division. When he landed his model AW in Fort Worth, Texas, he was more than a half-hour ahead of Dake. The flight over Texas, however, took its toll on both man and machine, as Phillips relates:

> *"Mercury readings in the high 90s and low 100s caused cylinder head and oil temperatures to soar above design limits and landing fields were infested with cactus thorns. Many tires and tubes burst on takeoff. ... Chapped lips and facial blisters plagued the airmen, with the usual skin balms giving little relief to the cracked, burning flesh. Eating was a painful ordeal, suffered only because of necessity."*[25]

Rowland's engine developed trouble after he took off from Fort Worth. By the time he landed in El Paso, he had lost eight precious minutes of his lead. A malfunction occurred in the ignition system, and after that was repaired, a tire went flat. But both were made right, and Rowland was ready for the last leg, to begin the following day at 5 a.m.[26]

He was the third to land at the next control point at Yuma, Arizona. Dake in his American Moth, and Clyde and Quick in their Model AA were already on the ground. Nevertheless, Rowland had gained back seven minutes and 50 seconds he had previously lost, thus remaining in the lead.[27]

Rowland captured the Class A title September 10 when he landed at Mines Field in Los Angeles. Second place went to Dake, third to William Emery, fourth to Theodore Kenyon and fifth to Tex Rankin. They won cash rewards of $5,000, $2,500, $700, $500 and $300 respectively. In addition, Rowland received two checks for $2,000 each from Richfield Oil Company and Kendall Oil Company. He also won $1,910 for having the lowest elapsed times between certain control points. Altogether, the race earnings for himself and The Cessna Aircraft Company totaled $10,910.[28] In the Class B Division, Cessna airplanes placed fourth and eighth. Clyde and Quick came in last.[29]

In the other race, Cessna did not fare as well. But then, virtually no one did. Owen Haugland, Cessna's only entry in the transcontinental Speed Dash, dropped out in St. Louis after his landing gear collapsed. He was consoled by the fact that nobody won the first-place prize of $12,500. The only pilot to cross the finish line in Los Angeles was Art Goebel flying *Yankee Doodle*. However, he was disqualified because he had previously landed for fuel.[30]

Cessna's decision to participate in the air derby was well rewarded. His planes, with their cantilevered wings, had proven their worth in national competition. New designs were put into production to capitalize on the company's growing popularity.

The Model CW-6

On November 1, 1928, Cessna's first six-passenger plane rolled out. It had a gross weight of 3,950 pounds and was painted a gleaming white.

Above: This Cessna AW was modified by Eldon Cessna to be used for racing.

Below: Clyde stands in the center of this 1928 photo of his 47 employees at The Cessna Aircraft Company.

The three-door aircraft, designated the CW-6 (C for the third Cessna model, W for the Wright engine and 6 for six passengers), was equipped with a 225-horsepower Wright J-5 engine. It could be purchased for $14,500.[31] In 1997 dollars, this would be $134,541.

The CW-6 was the center of attention at the 1929 automobile show, where it was painted with bright red trim and suspended from the ceiling of the Wichita Forum. In early December, Clyde flew with his son, 17-year-old Eldon, and Rowland to the Chicago International Aeronautics Show, where the CW-6 was to be displayed along with a Cessna Model AW. The three made the flight in five hours and 52 minutes, with an average speed of 121 miles per hour. The plane never went into production, though it did achieve fame of a different sort.[32]

Mexico

In 1929, the export market for airplanes was virtually untouched, and Clyde Cessna decided to see if he could sell some in nearby Mexico. In March, Clyde sent Rowland and salesman W.C. Vail to Mexico City in the CW-6 for a demonstration that might generate interest. While refueling in Texas, they agreed to return passenger J.S. Joffre to Mexico City as a favor to a local pilot, who was experiencing engine trouble.

Mexico was in the throes of revolution, during which the nation was slowly and violently moving toward agricultural, political and social reforms. The men landed in the tiny town of San Luis Potosi for fueling and damaged a wheel. The men were soon met by an armed guard and placed under arrest by the area governor, but were given "free run of the town," wrote author Edward Phillips.

"Their only restriction was a mandatory check-in every morning with officials. For almost a week the three men had one of the grandest times of their lives, being treated like heroes by the local population.

"Finally, Federales arrived and repairs were made to the landing gear, using an improvised wooden wheel (without brakes). An officer named Colonel Fierro then demanded that Rowland fly him to Mexico City, which he did, along with Vail and Joffre.

"Upon arrival, the colonel wanted Rowland to land at a military field, but Earl flatly refused and put the ship down on the commercial airport, Valbuena Field, knowing that to do so would constitute surrender of the ship.

This Cessna Model CW-6 was confiscated by the Mexican government during the Mexican Revolution, and used to drop bombs on the rebels. Mexico eventually paid for the aircraft.

"The Wright J-5 barely cooled off from its exciting adventure before Rowland was informed that the CW-6 was being pressed into military service for the government. There was nothing Earl could do to stop the confiscation, and U.S. Ambassador Morrow concurred. Fierro had the CW-6 towed to the military airport and within 30 minutes gave Earl a receipt for the monoplane and told him the government would pay for it later.

"Confiscation was a quick and easy method employed by the Mexicans to boost their small and pitifully inadequate air force, and Rowland wasn't alone in losing his airplane."[33]

The Mexican government kept its word and eventually paid The Cessna Aircraft Company for the airplane. A lieutenant colonel in the Mexican Army Air Force reportedly used it to drop bombs on the rebels.[34] However, Cessna's plans to drum up business in Mexico were put on hold for the immediate future.

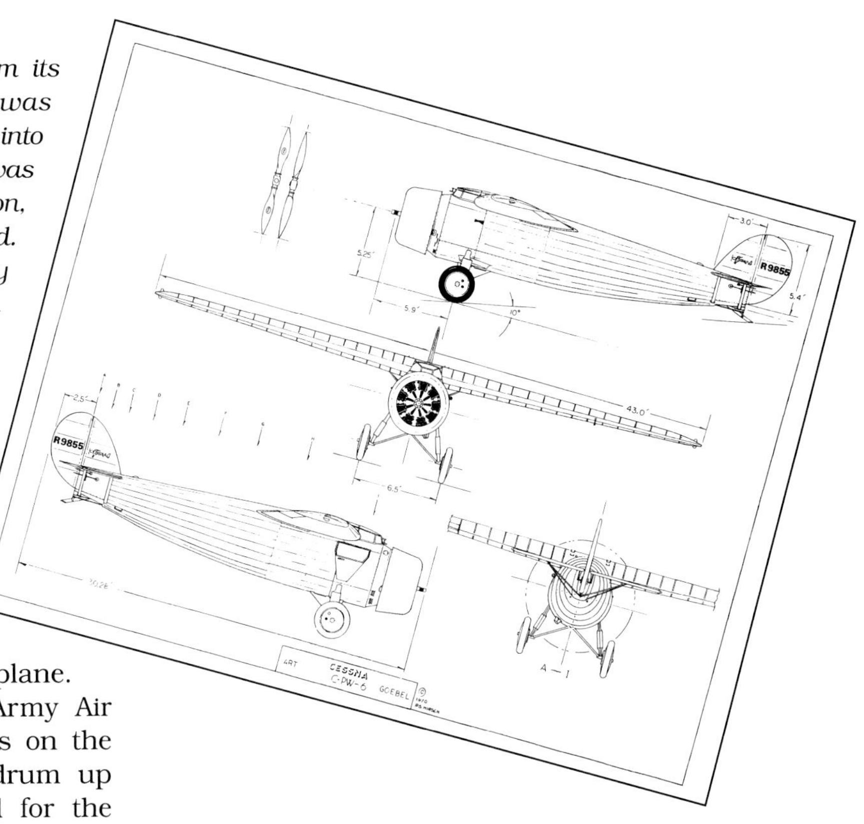

Schematic drawings for the CPW-6, known as the Goebel Special.

The CPW-6

In the early summer of 1929, racing pilot Art Goebel requested a modified CW-6 to use as a two-seater endurance racer. In accordance with his wishes, the ship was converted to accept a 420-horsepower Pratt & Whitney engine. The landing gear and ailerons were strengthened, and a clock, a bank indicator and an instrument to measure rates of climb and turn were added to the instrument panel. The enhanced vehicle could exceed speeds of 160 miles per hour, even while carrying 600 gallons of fuel. Officially designated CPW-6, the machine was widely known as the Goebel Special. Goebel planned to enter the ship in a nonstop race from Los Angeles to Cleveland in early September. During his flight to Los Angeles, however, he experienced fuel tank leaks and worried if the plane would be able to safely climb over the Rocky Mountains. He withdrew from the race.[35]

As 1928 drew to a close, The Cessna Aircraft Company could look back on a very impressive first year, with 46 airplanes already built and backlog orders for 96 more.[36] The existing facilities, which could produce two and a half airplanes a week, could not keep up with demand.

Plans were already under way to add a new production facility and increase the number of employees when, on February 19, the well-known Curtiss Flying Service of New York State signed a contract with Cessna, giving the service exclusive rights to sell Cessna airplanes in Canada and the United States. The service immediately placed an order for 39 monoplanes and said it could sell as many as 50 a month if Cessna could speed up production to meet the demand. This was a tremendous benefit for Cessna, which had no dealers at the time.[37]

Recognizing the deal's potential, the board of directors put its factory construction plans into high gear. To raise money for the expansion, the company issued 50,000 new shares of stock and sold them on the open market. (This was a very significant event. Until that time, Clyde held the most stock in the company, giving him the upper hand in negotiations. After the stock issue, he

CESSNA
AIRPLANES
CESSNA
AIRPLANES

remained the largest stockholder, but he no longer held enough to control the company.) Eighty acres were purchased at East Pawnee Road and Franklin Road — the current site of the Cessna Pawnee Plant — and a groundbreaking ceremony was held March 25.

Construction was rapid for six brick-and-steel buildings totaling 55,000 square feet of space, a 37,000-square-foot increase over the Glenn Avenue location.[38] Unit A would be used for experimental work, Unit B would be for the metal-working department, Unit C would house the woodworking area, Unit D would house all dope and painting operations, and Unit E was reserved for final assembly. The new plant was completed by midsummer and all operations were immediately moved to the new location.[39] Employment jumped from 50 workers in July to 80 workers in December 1929.[40]

The DC Series

The final model to be built at the Glenn Avenue location was the DC-6, equipped with a 170-horsepower R-600 Curtiss Challenger engine. The D line would consist of five models, of which the subsequent four were equipped with 225-horsepower Wright J-6 engines. Designated DC-6Bs and known as Scouts, these ships sold for $10,000. They cruised at 120 miles per hour and could reach speeds of 146 miles per hour. After test-flying the aircraft, however, company officials decided to make them even more powerful. Replacing the Wright J-6 engines with 300-horsepower Wright R-975 Whirlwinds, they created the DC-6A, known as the Chief, which reached a cruise speed of 130 miles per hour and topped out at 161 miles per hour. These aircraft sold for $11,500.[41]

Production of the DC series was in full swing by late summer and certification was obtained in August for the DC-6. The DC-6A and DC-6B earned certification on October 29, 1929 — the day of the infamous stock market collapse that heralded the start of the Great Depression.[42]

The Great Depression would consume the livelihoods, dreams and dignity of millions of American workers and families with a voracious and cancerous attrition in the months and years to follow. On that terrifying Tuesday, stocks plunged 43 points. By the end of October, the New York Stock Exchange as a whole declined an average of 37 percent.[43]

The Depression Takes its Toll

Airplanes, which had been potent symbols of American freedom and ingenuity during the Jazz Age, became unaffordable luxuries as the nation's economy worsened. The Curtiss Flying Service, which was then called the Curtiss-Wright Flying Service, after merging with Wright that summer, went bankrupt. Suddenly, The Cessna Aircraft Company was saddled with a new factory, a tremendous debt and a greatly diminished market for its products.[44]

At first, Clyde gave orders to continue building airplanes. But the company was forced to quit normal production when it could no longer meet payroll or sell the stocks it had counted on to help pay for the new building. Things got so bad that bats had begun to roost in the unsold airplanes in the plant.[45]

Clyde soon found assistance in the form of eight men from the East Coast who agreed to become Cessna franchise owners. In the November 23, 1929 issue of *Aviation* magazine, Cessna printed its "most important message of

Above: Clyde in front of the Cessna factory at First Street and Glenn Avenue during the spring of 1929.

Left: An inside view of the wing assembly line.

THE WEATHER
KANSAS—Rain, changing to snow; colder, windy; Wednesday slightly warmer.
OKLAHOMA—Cloudy, probably rain, colder; Wednesday, partly cloudy, colder in east.

The Wichita Eagle

SPORTS
On Pages 9 and 11

VOLUME LXXXVIII | PRICE: In the City 3c; Outside City, 5c | WICHITA, KANSAS, TUESDAY MORNING, OCTOBER 29, 1929 | SIXTEEN PAGES | NUMBER 132

STOCK MARKET COLLAPSES

BROTHER IS SOUGHT IN 2 KILLINGS

Harry Jones, Texan, Is Wanted in Dual Murder at Ark City

THREE OTHER KIN HELD

Father of Farmer and Two More Relatives Produce Alibis

ARKANSAS CITY, KAN., Oct. 28.—(AP)—Interest in the double murder of Carl Jones and his step-daughter, Elizabeth Walworth, Saturday night at Jones' farm four miles northwest of here, centered tonight in the search for Harry Jones, brother of the slain man, whose home is in McCamey, Tex.

John Phelan Jones, father of the murdered man, Neil Jones, his brother, and Clarence Walworth, brother of the dead girl, are being held for investigation.

Tires as Fugitive

LOS ANGELES, Oct. 28.—(AP)—Tony Cornero, once the alleged head of an international liquor smuggling ring, walked into the United States marshal's office and surrendered, ending a three-year search.

Cornero admitted he was "tired" of eluding federal agents. He was indicted in 1926 with six other men for the operation of Consolidated Importers, Ltd. Bmn., a concern charged with smuggling liquor to American ports from Europe. His bail was set for $10,000.

BINGHAM IS FACING CENSURE

Norris to Offer Resolution Today Condemning Action of Senator

WASHINGTON, Oct. 28.—(AP)—The dire promise of a resolution proposing censure for Senator Bingham, Connecticut, stilled a savage verbal exchange in the senate today between the Connecticut senator and his accusers of the lobby investigating com-

STOCKS IN ANOTHER COLLAPSE

More Intense Than Panic of Last Week, but Sales Are Less

BANKERS ARE CALM

Crash Regarded as Climax to Five-year Speculative Orgy

By STANLEY W. PRENOSIL
Associated Press Financial Editor

NEW YORK, Oct. 28.—(AP)—A further collapse in stock prices, exceeding in intensity last Thursday's demoralizing session, took place today as Wall Street continued to weed out its weakened speculative accounts and place its house in order after the wild orgy of speculation for the advance which has taken place in the last five years.

Net declines in many of the active issues ran from $10 to $60 a share.

THE EDITOR SPEAKING:

When the big bankers do not support the market against the attacks of the bears, it seems clear that there is always room at the bottom also.

IMPORTANT TRENDS IN THE STOCK MARKET

(By the Associated Press)
The following table gives the year's high, last Thursday's low, today's close and the net declines in some of the leading stocks.

Stock	Year's	Thursday's Low	Today's Close	Net Loss
American Can	184¼	137	136	17½
Anaconda Copper	140	92	92½	10
Bethlehem Steel	140⅜	92½	94½	9¾
Chrysler	135	43	40	5
General Electric	403	283	250	47½
General Motors	91⅜	49	47⅛	6¾
Johns Manville	242¾	140	132	28½
Montgomery Ward	156⅞	50	58¼	16
Natl. Cash Register	148¾	79	75	19
Radio Corp. America	114¾	44½	40¼	18⅝
S. O. of N. J.	83	61⅝	64⅝	8
Union Carbide	140	90⅝	84	20
U. S. Steel	261¾	192½	186	17½
Woolworth	103⅞	82	80	7
Atchison	298⅝	253¼	251	11⅝
Baltimore & Ohio	145⅞	117¼	115¾	⅞
Canadian Pacific	265¼	200	203	9
Erie Common	93½	60	55	11⅛
New York Central	256½	197	186	22⅝
Northern Pacific	118⅞	91½	93	5
Union Pacific	297⅝	250	240	16
American & Foreign Power	199¼	88	77½	29
American Telephone	310½	245	232	34
American Water Works	199	93	80	24
Columbia Gas & Elec.	140	80	70¾	22
Consolidated Gas	183¼	108½	97¼	20
General Gas & Elec.	112	84	77¾	12¼
International Tel	149¼	79	87	15
North American	186¾	99	97¾	18½
Public Service N. J.	137¾	89	87½	9⅝
Standard Gas & Elec.	243¾	134¼	105½	40½
United Corporation	75½	31½	33½	8¾
Western Union	272¼	220	191	39½

SHOCK KILLS PATIENT TAKING CURE FOR COLD

FOUR SOVIET FLIERS WELCOMED BY FORD

SEEK VOICE OF HOOVER ON TARIFF

Senators Argue Whether or Not Bill Now Is Acceptable to President

FORESEES A DEADLOCK

Reed Says Measure Is Dead and Predicts House Will Reject It

WASHINGTON, Oct. 28.—(AP)—A pronouncement of ultimate death was read over the tariff bill in the senate today by one of its sponsors, Senator Reed, Republican, Pennsylvania, and the post mortems that quickly ensued found leaders of all factions passing the blame around.

The assertion, a repetition of a statement by Senator Reed in a speech in Philadelphia over the week-end, led to a free for all political discussion which saw Republican regulars and independents quarreling over the attitude of President Hoover

Inconsiderate Thief

KANSAS CITY, Oct. 28.—(AP)—A diamond cluster ring, containing 42 stones, including three large stones taken from a ring worn by her husband before his death, was stolen late this afternoon from Mrs. Mabel Parkinson. The ring was valued at $1,150.

Mrs. Parkinson, employed by a physician here, had just returned from a month's vacation. She was preparing to leave the office when the robber entered. Articles valued at $100 were also taken from the office.

LINER LOST WITH FIVE ON BOARD

Western Air Express Ship Is Down, Presumably Near Mount Taylor

WINSLOW, ARIZ., Oct. 28.—(AP)—L. C. McGill, manager of Transcontinental Air Transport's field here, announced tonight that A. A. T.'s schedules temporarily had been halted because of bad flying conditions after the westbound T. A. T. plane had arrived here from

OHIO LOSES A SENATOR BY DEATH

Burton, Active Figure in G. O. P. Politics, Dies in Washington

RECEIVES SACRAMENT

Methodist Bishop Is Among Last to Visit Bedside of Solon

WASHINGTON, Oct. 28.—(AP)—Senator Theodore E. Burton of Ohio died tonight after an illness of several months.

Word of Burton's death grieved official Washington from President Hoover down. From time to time the president had called on the 77-year-old legislator to keep in close personal touch with his condition.

Among the last visitors to the bedside were Senator Fess of Ohio and Bishop William T. MacDowell, of the Methodist Episcopal church. Mrs. Grace Burton, a niece of the senator, and a nephew, William Burton, were with him through the last hours. He

Aircraft became unaffordable extravagances during the Depression. Clyde Cessna tried one idea after another to keep the company afloat.

the year." The article said the company was financially strong and was being led by men with vast experience in the aviation industry. In fact, it promised, the company was ready to do more business than ever before.[46]

It was an overly optimistic prediction. December wreaked financial havoc on the company. Stock that sold for more than $100 a share after the 1928 air derby victory had plunged to only $12 a share. In an attempt to remain solvent, Cessna sold the First Street and Glenn Avenue factory for approximately $50,000.[47]

Cessna Aircraft pinned its hopes for survival on a prototype glider designed by Eldon Cessna, who had played a substantial role in the engineering and certification of the DC-6 series. By the end of December, two CG-1s (Cessna Glider, Model 1) had been built and Clyde had convinced company directors there was a market for the aircraft. Glider clubs had begun to form all across the country and Clyde believed his ability to sell the simple flying machines would bring the company through the Depression. Production began on a revised glider, the CG-2, which had a wingspan of 35 feet and was used primarily as a training glider.[48] The CG-2, at 120 pounds, had a flying speed of 25 miles per hour and a landing speed of 15 miles per hour.[49] On January 1, 1930, Clyde added the title of general manager to his responsibilities as president of the company when the former general manager, Howard Wehrle, left to work as a military consultant.[50] The company continued to focus on the CG-2 Gliders. During 1930, Cessna produced 300 of these single-seat gliders and sold them for $398 each.[51] In addition to the CG-2s, a few DC-6As and DC-6Bs were also produced. But airplane sales had dropped substantially. Cessna, like numerous other Wichita airplane companies, was forced to lay off workers.[52]

Clyde would do whatever he must to save the company. He decided to enter as many air races as possible in hopes of winning cash prizes and free publicity. For the Miami All-American Air Meet, held January 13 through 15, 1930, he sent company pilot Jack Bridges in a DC-6B, ordering him to enter every event for which the airplane qualified. Bridges won first place in both 15-mile races for cabin ships with cubic inch displacement of 800. He brought home hundreds of dollars for his efforts.[53]

To prepare for a new capitalization effort, company officers were elected on February 6, 1930. Clyde retained the presidency, Hugo Kenyon was made vice president, Eldon Cessna became secretary and William B. Harrison was elected treasurer. James P. Verts was to assist the secretary and treasurer. The board of directors decided to raise money through a company reorganization. Charles Yankey, a Wichita attorney, and M.L. Arnold, operator of the Wichita Arnold Motor Company, offered Clyde $50,000 for capitalization, and the company's 50,000 shares of stock was doubled.[54]

Meanwhile, improvements to Eldon's glider continued. In April 1930, the CPG-1 glider, fitted with a 10-horsepower Cleone engine, was built from the basic design of the CG-2. A CS-1 (Cessna Sailplane) with fully cantilevered wings was also developed as an attempt to get a marketable product in the air during the Depression, but only one was ever built. Perhaps Eldon's most noted design was the FC-1, or Baby Cessna. Eldon enclosed the fuselage of a CG-2, making a small cabin and added a 25-horsepower Cleone engine, landing gear and 35-foot cantilever wings. Although it was marketed as "every man's airplane," the Baby Cessna never saw production.[55]

The Baby Cessna was the company's last hope. Designed with a 25-horsepower engine, it never saw production.

Losing Control

On January 7, 1931, the board of directors met to elect new officers and determine the company's future course. The men were tired of trying one idea after another to keep the company afloat, only to see each new venture fail. They decided upon a radical action.

At the meeting, Clyde was made vice president and Thad Carver, president of a local bank, became the new president of Cessna. "Mr. Carver and Mr. Cessna have been associated in the aviation business for many years, since they and Walter Beech were working together in the upbuilding of the Travel Air Company," noted the *Wichita Eagle*.[56] Initial reports were optimistic.

> *"A definite program of development will be worked out in the immediate future and new Cessna models will be brought out shortly, it was announced. Mr. Carver has been in Wichita for the past two days. He is a prominent figure in state banking circles and is exceptionally well known in the aviation industry in Wichita. ... Expressing himself as pleased with the new arrangement, Mr. Cessna said he had great faith in the men with whom he now will be associated."*[57]

Perhaps it wasn't the right time for optimism. In short order, Andrew S. Swenson, Roscoe Vaughn and A.B. Sanders formed a committee to determine the best way to close down the The Cessna Aircraft Company's production facility, effectively shutting down the company.[58]

Clyde pleaded with the directors to keep the plant open and even offered to work for free if that would help. But his pleas were ignored.[59] Clyde was heartbroken. The company he had founded was being closed and he was being turned out.[60] "I packed my belongings," said Clyde. "I gave the keys to Mr. Sanders, and I did not even look back at the building that was no longer mine."[61]

Dwane Wallace (right) with his uncle Clyde Cessna. Dwane, who became president in 1936, would lead the company for nearly 40 years. *(Photo courtesy of the Kingman County Historical Museum.)*

THE PHOENIX RISES

1931–1938

"I am sure you realize that our stock is practically worthless today. A complete liquidation would pay only a very small percent back on our original investments, while if you cooperate with me, The Cessna Aircraft Company will again be doing a good business and our stock on the market will rise accordingly."

— Letter from Clyde Cessna to shareholders, 1933[1]

MARCH 1931 WAS perhaps the most difficult month in Clyde Cessna's life. He was not only forced to walk away from the company he had worked so hard to build, but he also laid his father, James W. Cessna, to rest.

James, who had moved his family from Iowa to Kansas in 1880, died at his family homestead at age 74. Along with his brothers Roy, Noel and Bert, Clyde prepared their father's body for internment. The sons dug the grave themselves, served as pallbearers, and even helped preside over the simple funeral service. Apparently the elder Cessna had been ill for some time and had prepared his family for his death, telling them exactly how he wanted things arranged. The family granted each of his requests.[2]

Meanwhile, The Cessna Aircraft Company was boarded up and the buildings put up for rent in the hope of accumulating a little income and avoiding bankruptcy. All of the assets were sold. The only airplane Clyde was able to keep was a DC-6A from the Experimental Department, and that only because he personally paid all outstanding debts on it before removing it from storage.[3]

Clyde and his son Eldon decided to attack the Depression from a different angle. The two owned a model AW, renowned as one of the best racing planes of the time. With a few more races scheduled before the close of 1931, the pair intended to compete in each as if it were the last. Eldon entered a 25-mile race at Shenandoah, Iowa, on August 15, 1931, but didn't fare well. However, it was good practice for the upcoming Transcontinental Handicap Air Derby from Santa Monica, California, to Cleveland, Ohio, at the end of August. And although Eldon didn't win the $3,000 first prize, he took home a respectable third place ribbon and $1,200. He also won Event #36A, a speed and efficiency race for single-engine craft. That paid $750, plus a seven-foot-high grandfather clock with a built-in radio.[4] Eldon returned from the races with a reputation as a tough and able competitor.

C.V. Cessna Aircraft Company

In December 1931, Eldon married Helen Parcells of Hiawatha, Kansas. Now that he had a wife, the fact that he didn't earn a steady income weighed heavily on his mind.[5] He and his father decided to enter the airplane business once

The DeSilva Argentine Trophy won by Dwane Wallace at the 1936 Miami All America Air Races. *(Photo courtesy of the Kansas Aviation Museum.)*

again. The two were forbidden by the board of directors to build airplanes at the still closed Pawnee Plant,[6] so they formed the C.V. Cessna Aircraft Company with the help of a couple of supporters. The small building they rented at 3301 South Oliver Street was only a mile away from the closed plant.[7] Garland Peed was hired as the company's engineer and sole employee, and the three began work on the first of four racers to be built under the C.V. Cessna Aircraft Company name — the CR-1 Racer.[8]

This was Cessna's first airplane with landing gear designed to retract up and in until it fit snugly into the wheel wells on the underside of the fuselage. A handle on the instrument panel was used to manipulate the landing gear.[9] Powered by a 125-horsepower Warner radial engine, the craft was 14.5 feet long and had a full-cantilever wingspan of 18.5 feet.[10] The plane was named *Miss Wanda* after Clyde's daughter, who had served as his secretary until the closing of the Pawnee Plant in 1931.[11] *Miss Wanda* would attract a great deal of fanfare, but would also be at the center of a tragedy destined to change Clyde's life.

During the Depression, good news about the aviation industry was scarce, so the local press was excited when Clyde announced the debut of the new airplane in January 1932. *The Wichita Morning Eagle* wrote:

> *"Bumpy weather was expected to render conditions unusually exacting today for final flight tests on Clyde V. Cessna's new 220-mile-an-hour plane, which he hopes to make into the sensation of the nation's air races at Miami Thursday, Friday and Saturday of this week.*
>
> *"The ship, designed and built behind locked doors, has been seen only by its designer, his assistants and a very few favored friends. Its tests today will be kept as secret as possible. Eldon Cessna, son of the designer and one of the best racing pilots in the country, will put the ship through its tests. Only two close friends of Cessna have been invited to see the racer's maiden flight, and only they, besides Cessna and his assistants, know where that flight will take place.*
>
> *"Although he has not shown the ship to the public, Cessna describes it as a monoplane of metal and fabric, strongly streamlined, with a retractable landing gear among other features to decrease air resistance. Its 125-*

1931 — Clyde and Eldon Cessna begin the C.V. Cessna Aircraft Company.

1933 — The CR-2A crashes during the International Air Races, killing pilot Roy Liggett.

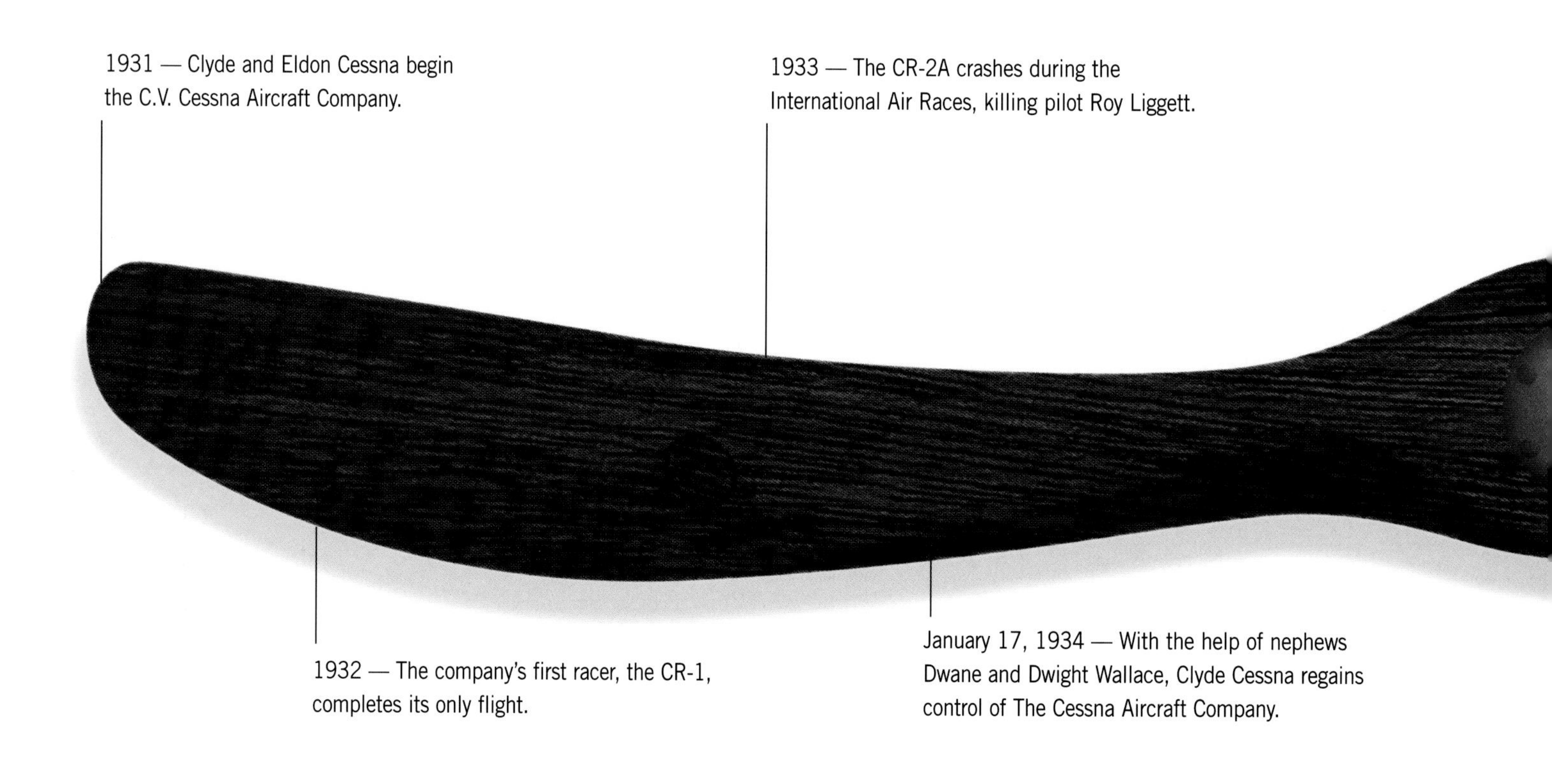

1932 — The company's first racer, the CR-1, completes its only flight.

January 17, 1934 — With the help of nephews Dwane and Dwight Wallace, Clyde Cessna regains control of The Cessna Aircraft Company.

horsepower motor is specially fitted to increase the speed.

"Young Cessna will take to the air in the racing ship Wednesday morning and will arrive in Miami Thursday to enter several events. Despite his youth, he is a veteran of several national races and last year placed first in the men's division of the national handicap derby."[12]

The much-publicized maiden flight of the CR-1 was canceled due to bad weather and delays in the production schedule, and the ship's entry into the Florida air race was also canceled because of delays.

With Eldon at the controls, the monoplane was finally ready on January 18, 1932.[13] Edward H. Phillips described the racer's dramatic flight — which also turned out to be its last.

"Hauled out to the California Section (an early runway in Wichita), Eldon donned his parachute and squeezed into the open cockpit. The Scarab was fired up, engine parameters checked, and then it was time to go.

"The Warner roared as Eldon fed in full throttle and the ship accelerated quickly, bouncing across the rough ground as full right rudder was applied to counter the Scarab's torque. Air speed increased rapidly to almost 80 miles per hour, but the ship was still ground-bound as its short, semi-elliptical wings strained to produce enough lift for flight.

"Back pressure on the stick produced no reaction, and the grass field's perimeter was getting closer every second. Back pressure on the stick at 100 miles per hour went unrewarded. Then the airplane struck a small dirt mound and finally bounced into the air.

"Eldon, who thought the takeoff roll was enough excitement for one day, now faced an even more serious challenge from his mount as he fought to keep the racer in a straight and level attitude. Longitudinal control was extremely sensitive, with the least stick movement provoking a nasty reaction that was immediately reversed when a correction was applied.

"Realizing that the airplane was only marginally controllable, Eldon elected to set the beast down as soon as possible, carefully making a turn around the field while keeping the airspeed high. Coming in at what was estimated to be 130 miles per hour on final approach, the CR-1 landed and rolled to a stop.

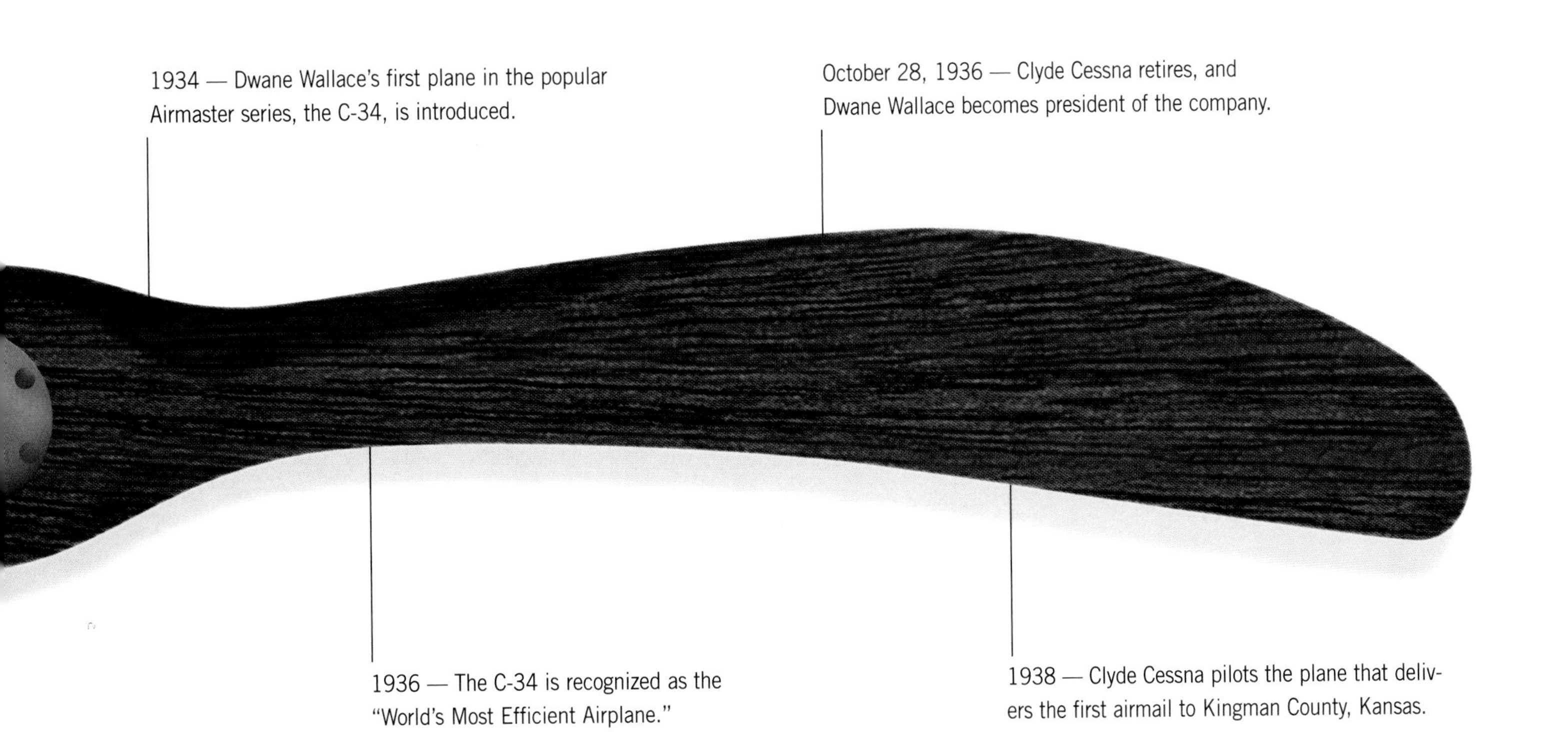

1934 — Dwane Wallace's first plane in the popular Airmaster series, the C-34, is introduced.

October 28, 1936 — Clyde Cessna retires, and Dwane Wallace becomes president of the company.

1936 — The C-34 is recognized as the "World's Most Efficient Airplane."

1938 — Clyde Cessna pilots the plane that delivers the first airmail to Kingman County, Kansas.

"He was helped from the cockpit and felt a little shaky for a minute or two, but Clyde Cessna was greatly relieved to have his son and his airplane back in one piece. So ended the one and only known flight of the CR-1.

"In Eldon's opinion, the monoplane definitely needed revamping aimed at taming some of its bad habits, particularly control sensitivity in pitch and the very high takeoff and landing speed. During the next three and one-half months the ship was rebuilt into the CR-2."[14]

The conversion required lengthening the fuselage to 17 feet, increasing the size of the empennage, and replacing the engine with a 145-horsepower Warner.[15] In June 1932, *Miss Wanda* was among five Cessna airplanes smashed by a tornado that whipped through the municipal hangar at the local airport. The storm, which lasted less than one minute, ripped the roof off the administration building and destroyed the radio station and other equipment.[16]

The rebuilt plane was entered in the 1933 Miami Air Races. Piloted by Clyde's dear friend Roy Liggett, it won the Col. Green Cup Race and placed second in the Unlimited Free-For-All, clocking 194.46 miles per hour.[17] At the American Air Race in Chicago on July 3, *Miss Wanda* placed second, with pilot Art Davis flying an average of 202.88 miles per hour. First place was grabbed by another Cessna that flew an incredible 204.54 miles per hour and clocked 213.40 in the fifth lap. Flown by Johnny Livingston, the plane had been specially built by Clyde and Eldon.[18]

The Tragedy that Changed Clyde's Life

The CR-2 was later sold to R.O. Herman and modified, becoming the CR-2A. These modifications included lengthening the pilot's headrest, enclosing the cockpit with a throw-over canopy, and the addition of a tight-fitting engine cowl with streamlined bumps to clear the rocker boxes (similar to valve covers in cars). This last modifi-

Pilot Roy Liggett stands next to *Miss Wanda* at the Miami Air Races in January 1933. *(Photo courtesy of the Kansas Aviation Museum.)*

Pilot Johnny Livingston with his custom-built CR-3. *(Photo courtesy of the Kansas Aviation Museum.)*

cation proved deadly at the 1933 International Air Races on September 2 in Chicago, when it came loose at 300 feet during a high-speed run and tore off the left wing. The plane went into a spiral and plunged to the ground, killing pilot Roy Liggett.[19] Gerald Deneau described the crash in *An Eye to The Sky, Cessna:*

> *"Liggett placed second in the first 500 cubic-inch event, clocking 191.1 miles per hour. It was during the Shell Speed dashes that the CR-2A came to its final end. Liggett had dived from 2,500 feet. Leveling off at 300 feet, he flashed across the field on his speed run. As the CR-2A approached the center of the field, the engine cowl tore loose, striking the left wing root. The left wing ripped from the fuselage and the ship buried itself in the ground in front of the shocked crowd, killing Roy Liggett. This was the end of a speedy racing plane and a famous pilot."*[20]

The airplane's steel structure clenched Liggett's corpse with such force that a special saw had to be used to disentangle it. Clyde, who witnessed the horror, was grief-stricken and guilty, since he had built the machine that killed one of his closest friends. Clyde's passion for aviation left him, and from that point forward he would fly only with deep reluctance.[21]

The CR-3

In 1933, racing pilot Johnny Livingston ordered a specially designed CR-3 equipped with the 145-horsepower Warner engine he had used in his famous Short-Wing Coupe.[22] The 17-foot-long, bullet-shape CR-3 made its first flight on June 11, 1933, and it soon became the fastest and most famous Cessna racer ever built.[23] Weighing in at only 750 pounds, it reached top speed at 255 miles per hour. Livingston had requested that its cantilevered wings, which spanned 18.5 feet, be raised from a mid-wing design to a shoulder position to improve its aerodynamics.[24] Though the CR-3 had a life span of only two months, during that time it won every race it entered.[25]

Among them was the 1933 American Air Race in Chicago, in which Livingston won the

Baby Ruth Aero Digest Trophy Races with an average speed of 201.42 and 204.54 miles per hour respectively around the pylons.

Livingston later established a new world's speed record for aircraft with engines of less than 500-cubic-inch displacement, flying four laps at an average speed of 237.4 miles per hour. The fastest of the four, at 242.35 miles per hour, broke the previous world record of 213.8 miles an hour established by Benny Howard in 1932.

The CR-3 met an appropriately dramatic demise on August 1, 1933, while the pilot survived in an equally dramatic way. While trying to land in Columbus, Ohio, Livingston was unable to lower the landing gear. (Had he tried to land with the gear still retracted, he would have surely crashed and died.) Realizing this, the veteran pilot flew north of the city and bailed out over open country. The plane flew pilotless for a few moments before plunging into a field.[26]

Another plane manufactured by Cessna was the C-3, built for Walter Anderson, founder of the White Castle hamburger chain.[27] Basically it was a modified Model AA equipped with a 125-horsepower Warner engine. Weighing 2,280 pounds, it had a wider four-seat cabin and an adjustable propeller. In later years, it would be owned by Marcellus Murdock, publisher of the *Wichita Eagle*.[28]

Dwight and Dwane Wallace

Clyde's enthusiasm for aviation may have diminished, but it burned within his nephews, Dwight and Dwane Wallace. Together, all three would revitalize the company.

Dwight and Dwane were sons of Clyde's youngest sister, Grace Opal Wallace and her physician husband, Dr. Eugene Wallace. There was also a younger brother named Deane. The Wallace boys grew up idolizing their uncle C.V., as they called him, and took their first airplane ride in January 1924 in a New Swallow biplane owned and built in part by Clyde.

Dwight was the older of the three brothers, born June 19, 1909. He had graduated from law school at the University of Kansas and ran his own law practice in Wichita in 1933.[29]

Dwane was born October 29, 1911. His affiliation with his famous uncle and his own interest in flying led him to enroll in the aeronautical engineering program at Wichita University. While in school, Dwane took lessons from Cessna test pilot George Harte. In the spring of 1930, he piloted a few Cessna gliders, and it was he who had suggested that the wing configuration of the CR-2 be changed as part of the transformation into the CR-3. He soloed for the first time after only three lessons, a total of one hour and 45 minutes.

In May 1933, he and three others graduated from Wichita University with aeronautical-engineering degrees. Dwane wanted to work for his uncle, but the Cessna plant was still closed, so the young man sought employment elsewhere. He was turned away from the Stearman Aircraft Company, where he placed his first application, so

Dwane Wallace's brother, Dwight, a Wichita attorney who became Cessna's secretary/treasurer in 1934.

he submitted his résumé to Beech Aircraft, which at the time rented space at the closed Cessna plant. In May, after several tries, Dwane finally was hired by Beech as third engineer. He worked on models B17L and A17F, but working daily in the old Cessna factory made him yearn to revive his uncle's company.

At the end of the year, Beech Aircraft purchased the old Travel Air plant and moved out of the Cessna buildings, once again leaving them empty and idle. But together, the two brothers began working to revive the padlocked plant.[30]

The Resurrection of The Cessna Aircraft Company

Dwane approached his uncle about reopening the plant. Clyde told his nephews he would help if he could return as president.[31]

A stockholder's meeting was scheduled for January 17, 1934. Charles G. Yankey, who had succeeded Thad Carver as president of Cessna in January 1933, wanted to sell off the remaining assets, disperse the funds among stockholders, and put the company out of business. Since Cessna stock had virtually no value, attendance was expected to be sparse, and Yankey's plan was expected to be approved without delay.

But Dwane suggested another course of action. At his urging, Clyde sent a letter with the proxy ballots, asking each stockholder to vote for an alternate plan, which would put him once again in charge. When there was no response, Clyde wrote a second letter:[32]

"Dear Sir:

"A short time ago, I mailed you a letter enclosing a proxy, which no doubt gave you a good idea of what has been going on at the Cessna plant for the past three years under its present management.

"I feel that I should write you more in detail of what I intend to do after I'm back in control of our company. There is no doubt but that the airplane industry could be a paying one today if handled properly. Good examples of which are represented by the Waco, Monocoupe, Douglas and Northrop airplane companies, as well as various others.

"Through the fact that I have been engaged in the airplane business for the past two decades and having always been recognized as one of the pilgrims in the airplane industry, I have made many valuable contacts in the field of aviation in the last three years with various companies and large distributing agents for airplanes, and with these connections I am sure that I can sell a large number of planes.

"I intend to re-design and develop the 4-place Warner ship to such an extent that it will develop a speed of approximately 185 mph and yet keep its present stability, airworthiness and other grand features that made it so popular. This ship will have many wonderful selling points, such as the low cost of maintenance and operation, upkeep and high cruising speed.

"I am sure you realize that our stock is practically worthless today. A complete liquidation would pay only a very small percent back on our original investments, while if you cooperate with me, The Cessna Aircraft Company will again be doing a good business and our stock on the market will rise accordingly.

A photograph of Dwane Wallace taken shortly after he graduated from Wichita University.

"I am enclosing another proxy in case you did not receive or have misplaced the other one, and I will appreciate your executing the same and returning it to me in the self-addressed envelope which is enclosed.

Very Truly Yours,

Clyde V. Cessna"[33]

When this letter also received no response, Dwane and Dwight decided that the best course of action would be to visit each stockholder in person. Clyde agreed this might work, and Dwight was sent to Massachusetts and New York to call on stockholders there, with a warning from Clyde to pinch every penny during the trip.

Visiting one stockholder after another, Dwight tirelessly argued on his uncle's behalf: Instead of taking a loss from selling off the company's remains, Clyde Cessna would return it to its former glory, and stockholders would see a far greater gain.[34] While Dwight was traveling in the East, Dwane was making a similar case to every person in Wichita with more than 100 shares of company stock.[35] To hedge their bets, the brothers also purchased 6,000 shares of outstanding stock from the C.M. Key brokerage firm in New York City.[36]

The meeting was held January 17, as planned. A committee tallied the votes of the few attending stockholders, then added up the proxy submissions. Initially, it appeared that Clyde and his nephews failed to bring the company back to life, but then Dwight stood up. He carried an enormous briefcase, which he unzipped, dumping a pile of proxies on the table. When they were counted, it was clear that Clyde had regained control of the company, thanks to his nephews' efforts. "I sure got two smart nephews," he later said.[37]

With Clyde once again as president, Roscoe Vaughn was named vice president, Dwight became secretary/treasurer, Dwane became manager and engineer, and George Harte was appointed the company test pilot.

The C-34

Soon after the factory reopened, Cessna began manufacturing the 4-place craft that Clyde had promised before the vote. The C-34 (Cessna 1934) was truly a family project, conceived by Dwane while still in college and partly engineered by Clyde's son Eldon. It became a reality through the work of engineers Tom Salter and Jerry Gerteis.[38] The C-34 seemed to herald a new era for the company. Its clean, modern design featured Cessna's first use of flaps on the cantilevered wings, and it was powered by a 145-horsepower Warner Super Scarab 7-cylinder radial engine. Although it did not reach the anticipated speed of 185 miles per hour, it came close — 162 miles per hour. The first production C-34 was sold to Ross E. Colley of Tuxpan, Mexico, in November 1935. It was the right product to lift the company's wings

The C-34 boasted a control panel that was sophisticated for the time.

The C-34, given the racing number 75, was used as both a racer and a company demonstrator.

again. Priced at $4,995, nine were built in 1935 and 33 more in 1936.

In 1935, the planes were offered with either 145- or 165-horsepower Warner Super Scarab engines, and were designated either the C-145 or C-165. The fuselage length of the C-165 was increased by four inches.[39]

Test pilot Harte and his protégé Dwane demonstrated the monoplane at air meets and races, winning not only prizes but publicity. From August 30 through September 2, 1935, Harte won the coveted international award in the *Detroit News* Trophy Race by accumulating the most points in the four events.

Cessna seemed to have a lock on the series; Eldon had won the *Detroit News* Trophy flying a Model AW in 1931. The races weren't held between 1932 and 1934.[40]

Dwane won the race again in 1936. He took first place in the Argentine Trophy Race that was also part of the All American Air Races, averaging 156.13 miles per hour on a 25-mile closed course. He received a trophy valued at $2,000 and a cash prize of $350. Since Cessna had won three times in a row, the company was given permanent possession of the cup, and the C-34 was dubbed the "World's Most Efficient Airplane."[41]

The plane got remarkable mileage. Harte and Dwane flew from Wichita to Mexico City, spending only $15.24 on gas and oil. "An average of 16.9 miles per gallon was made on the long hop," noted the newspaper article; it also pointed out that the C-34 easily cleared a 12,500-foot mountain pass on the journey.[42]

Despite the high points, times were tough. During 1934 and 1935, Dwane, Dwight and Clyde worked without salary. Clyde lived off his savings, while Dwight continued to practice law in addition to serving as the company's secretary-treasurer. When Dwane was asked how he made it through those years, he replied, "Hamburgers were only a nickel apiece, and six for two bits," but he gave no indication of how he earned the nickels.

Eldon, with a wife and young child to support, left the company during the summer of 1934 to become an engineer for Northrop Aircraft in California. Clyde hated to see him go but understood why his son had made the painful decision.[43]

Al Zerbe, a Cessna employee from 1927 to 1932, came back to work in 1935. Things were so tough that year that Zerbe finally approached Dwane about the situation. "I told him I just couldn't live on $15 a week," recalled Zerbe. "He took me into his confidence, showed me just what the profit was on a single sale of a [C-34]. He showed me that wages depended

The C-34 Cessna Airmaster became popular with aviation enthusiasts, who founded the Airmaster Club in 1975.

Dwane Wallace (center) accepting the DeSilva trophy from Mr. and Mrs. DeSilva after the Miami All American Air Races in 1934.

on sales. He promised to do better when he could. The company had only a handful of employees, but we had confidence in Mr. Wallace. We liked that guy well enough so that none of us quit our jobs."[44]

Velma Wallace, who joined the company as Dwane's executive secretary in 1937 and married him in 1941, recently reminisced about those early years. Certified to fly both single-engine and twin-engine planes, she worked closely with Dwane during his entire tenure at the company.

> *"The factory had been closed down, and when we started out, Dwane got on the roof and mended it. We were all janitors. We did whatever needed to be done. ... And the employees were there for us. You never saw such dedication and loyalty. Everybody did everything that needed to be done, even if it was after hours or on weekends."*[45]

W.L. "Smitty" Schmidt became part of the staff in 1936, working in final assembly. "I was drawing $65 a month," he said. "I had a wife and baby. When we found that $65 was all we would get, we fitted our household budget to $65 a month and made a go of it." Schmidt later became head of Cessna's experimental department and reaped the benefits of his loyalty during the difficult years.[46]

In 1936, all three local aircraft companies — Stearman, Beech and Cessna — saw an encouraging increase in business. "It was the best year since the boom days of 1928 and 1929," noted the *Wichita Eagle*.

> *"The Cessna Aircraft plant is the one which, more than either of the others, has gone to the front in production during the year. An exact comparison with the previous year cannot be made since the nationally famous Cessna C-34 model was not being made on a production basis the first half of 1935. Since it came out, however, every month has seen more and more of them sold and more and more men employed at the plant. ... Dwane Wallace, general manager at Cessna, said more than 50 planes were built during the past 12 months, which, of course, is several times the number built in 1935."*[47]

During bad times and good, a strong feeling of camaraderie permeated the entire company. In 1937, employees formed the Cessna Employees Club to promote group activities and establish disability benefits. Starting out with 30 members, the club had more than 1,700 by 1941. Friends and family were invited to dances and picnics, and a flower fund was maintained in case of illness in the immediate family of any member.[48] The club, with more than 5,000 members, still exists today.

Clyde Cessna Retires

More than 25 years after Clyde had first taken to the skies, he retired to his farm in Rago, Kansas, at age 57. The move was not surprising, since he had clearly lost his joy for flying. He sold his interest in the company to Dwane and

Dwight, and announced the sale of stock to the board of directors in December 1935. With the proceeds, he purchased 640 acres west of his 40-acre homestead. But even in retirement he could not fully relax. He spent his days farming and inventing farm machinery.[49]

Clyde officially stepped down as president of The Cessna Aircraft Company on October 28, 1936, turning the leadership over to Dwane. Airman Albin K. Longren of Topeka, Kansas, remained vice president, with Dwight as secretary/treasurer. Cecil Lucas, who became sales manager in 1936, often served as test pilot, although Dwane did the majority of experimental and production flight-testing.[50]

"Clyde really gave Dwane his blessings," noted Velma. "He knew what abilities he had, and he respected it. They were very close. They didn't see each other often because Clyde went back to the farm, but as far as being close in thoughts and ideas, there was a very special feeling there."[51]

Dwane, a talented engineer, would prove to be a hands-on leader. "He was an excellent person to work with," recalled Delbert L. Roskam, who joined Cessna in 1942, and would serve as president from 1964 to 1975. Roskam had started out in personnel and served as both production manager and manufacturing manager before becoming president. "He wanted to know what was going on. We both would walk the plants and get to know who the people were. If a department was having trouble, we'd just talk to the foreman and talk to the workers and pretty soon we'd have worked through the problem. ... He was a good people person."[52]

A tribute printed after Wallace's death in 1989 noted that, in the early days, Wallace served as everything from president to waterboy. "City water had not yet reached the factory, so Dwane would regularly haul out five-gallon bottles of drinking water for the crew. In addition, he swept floors, served as chief test pilot, sold airplanes, flew in races and pitched for the lunch hour softball team."[53]

Wallace was also known for his optimism, noted the employee publication *Cessquire* in a 1977 edition celebrating the Cessna's 50th anniversary.

> *"We're constantly reminded of his famous saying of many years back regarding the general aviation business: 'It's early in the morning and the sun is shining.' His optimism has always been and still is infectious. He has*

The control panel of a C-37 Airmaster.

credibility. After all, didn't he almost single-handedly reopen a factory that had been closed three depression years, produce a revolutionary design while living on a hamburger diet, help build it, learn to fly, win air race trophies and money for needed publicity and factory wages? He sure as hell did."[54]

Airmasters

The C-37, an improved version of the C-34 was introduced in 1937, featuring electric wing flaps in place of the manual flaps of the C-34. The width of the cabin was increased by five inches at the top to add comfort, a new cowling was installed, and more efficient landing-gear shock absorbers were added. The plane's unusual stability earned it a prominent place in the aerial photography industry. When equipped with Edo 44-2425 floats, the C-37 was also Cessna's first model to receive seaplane approval.[55]

A total of 47 Model C-37s were built in 1937, with production hitting a high of seven per month in June.[56] On October 11, 1937, Cessna came out with the C-38 prototype. The wing flaps continued to evolve, and in this model they were replaced by a hydraulically operated fuselage flap. The bird sported the same 145-horsepower Warner Super Scarab engine as the earlier planes, but it also had curved landing gear legs, a larger vertical fin, and a Plexiglas windshield in place of the pyrolin used earlier. Sixteen of these were built between 1937 and 1938.[57] Though the C-38 was the first airplane to be called the Airmaster, all Cessnas from C-34 through C-165 became known by the name.[58]

The Airmaster was produced from 1935 to 1942. Fuel-efficient and comfortable, Airmasters served the company well, keeping it in business while the country was struggling to rise out of the murky depths of the Depression.[59]

Top: A C-38 Airmaster, landing with its belly flap down in Spokane, Washington on September 13, 1964.

Above: The C-38 was the first plane officially known as the Airmaster.

Later Airmasters included the C-165 (above) and the C-145 (below).

NEITHER SLEET NOR GRAVITY ...

LIKE EVERY AVIATION enthusiast and entrepreneur, Clyde Cessna was part showman and part pragmatist. In its early days, aviation was considered little more than a novelty, and few foresaw the vast commercial possibilities that air transport offered. Unfortunately, members of Congress fit into the doubters' category and impeded progress that would lead to airmail.

On the other hand, the U.S. Post Office, true to its vow of speedy mail delivery, was one of the first and most passionate proponents of air freight, as related in the book, *Two Hundred Years of Flight in America: A Bicentennial Survey,* first published in 1977:

> *"The Post Office could not obtain Congressional approval for airmail service until 1916, the war then delaying airmail operations for two years. The "Father of Airmail," Assistant Postmaster General Otto Praeger, received permission for trial service between Washington, D.C., and New York via Philadelphia. On May 25, 1918, the first official U.S. operations began, with modified Curtiss JN-4H "Jenny" biplanes flown by Army pilots. One pilot became lost after takeoff from Washington's Polo Grounds (his mail eventually arriving in New York by train), but two others successfully delivered the southbound mail from New York to the Nation's Capital. [On August 12, 1918] Post Office pilot Max Miller inaugurated the world's first permanent mail service, Standard Aero-mail plane."*[1]

But the Postmaster didn't want to run what he felt should be a private-sector business, so in 1925 Congress passed the Kelly Act, which subsidized private companies to haul mail. The legislation encouraged businesses such as The Cessna Aircraft Company to enter the commercial aircraft market.[2] Cessna's Airmaster, designed in 1937, was a popular aircraft used by airmail companies.

The Post Office officially ended its direct involvement in transporting mail in 1927. By then, Post Office pilots had logged more than 10 million miles and carried 7 million pounds of mail.[3]

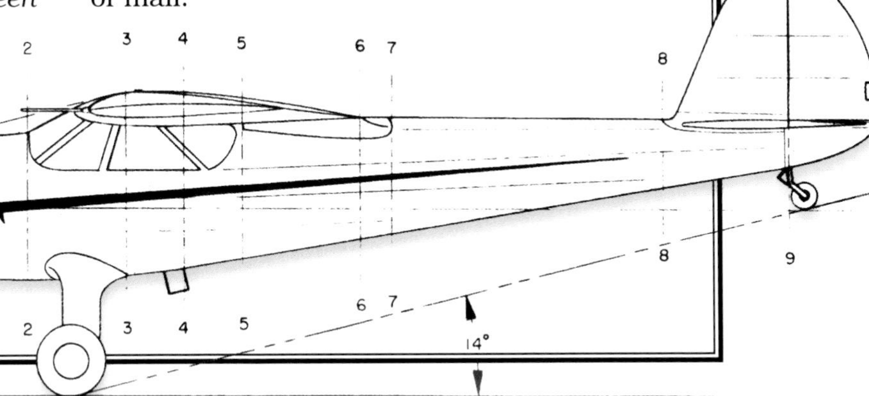

Honoring a Pioneer

Although Clyde Cessna had retired, he remained a local hero, widely recognized as one of aviation's pioneers. When the first airmail was delivered to Kingman County, Kansas, on May 19, 1938, Clyde piloted the Airmaster filled with approximately 1,500 letters.[60]

The festivities were kicked off with a parade in the town of Kingman, near Clyde's farm in Rago, celebrating the modern wonders that aviation had brought to Kansas. Clyde held a position of honor in the parade, riding on a hayrack with a replica of the plane he flew in 1913.[61] Afterward, C.C. Calkin gave a brief talk on "Airmail and Kingman County," praising Clyde for his contributions to aviation. Clyde also gave a brief speech.

As an additional honor for his 25 years of achievements in aviation, a commemorative seal was designed for the envelopes used on air mail from Kingman.[62]

The UC-78, first built in 1942, served as a utility aircraft during World War II. *(Photo courtesy of the Kansas Aviation Museum.)*

The Bobcat Springs to the Nation's Defense

1939–1945

"Yours is a privilege enjoyed by comparatively few in doing a part toward meeting the requirements of this Titanic National Defense Program. To be actually working with your own hands in the creation of training planes gives you the opportunity to serve your country in one of the most important phases connected with this tremendous task."

— Dwane Wallace in the *Cessquire,* 1941[1]

WITHOUT INTENDING it, Cessna had positioned itself for America's entry into World War II by introducing its first twin-engine aircraft in 1939.[2] This new capability would serve two crucial roles during the war: as a training platform for bomber pilots and to haul valuable cargo.

The aircraft, dubbed the Bobcat during the war, was originally intended for the civilian market. Chief engineer Tom Salter and his crew spent three years designing the plane, designated the T-50. The idea had originated with Dwane Wallace, who determined there was a need for a small, five-place twin-engine aircraft with a modest price tag of between $20,000 and $30,000.[3] He planned to market the new model to the airline feeder and charter industries.[4]

Powered by two Jacobs 225-horsepower engines, the aircraft reached top speeds of nearly 200 miles an hour, and yet featured a very tame landing speed of 55 miles per hour.[5] The cabin was a roomy 10 feet in length and five feet in width and height. The baggage compartment, which could accommodate up to 300 pounds, was located behind the rear seat, making it accessible during flight. For loading and unloading, it could be reached through a door on the left side.

With Dwane Wallace at the controls and factory manager Bill Snook riding shotgun, the T-50 prototype made its 20-minute maiden flight on Sunday, March 26, 1939.[6] After some modifications, including changes to the shape of the rear window and tail, the plane was certified in December 1939.[7]

Wallace had never flown a twin-engine plane before, recalled Velma Wallace. "When he finally got all his testing done, he took it to the FAA in Kansas City and went through another test flight with the FAA man. When they landed, the man said he would license the plane. Dwane turned to him and said, 'I don't have my twin-engine license. I wonder if you would sign my ticket for a twin-engine rating.' The man about fell off his chair, but after he recovered, he said, 'Okay. I guess you deserve it.'"[8]

The first production models were offered to the civilian market at $29,675.[9]

Although both the T-50 and Airmaster sold well in 1939, production costs remained high and the

This logo appeared in the 1941 *Air Crafter* magazine to thank Cessna for its efficient production of T-50s for the Royal Canadian Air Force. "Two great democracies are depending upon Cessna to 'Keep 'em flying.'" noted the magazine.

Cessna's legendary T-50, later dubbed the Bobcat, would be used during the war to train bomber pilots and haul cargo.

company was barely breaking even. At one point, Cessna's corporate bank account held the magnificent sum of $5.03.[10] However, things were about to change, both for the company and for the world.[11]

A New Kind of War

On September 1, 1939, Hitler's army overran Poland, officially beginning the war that would claim more than 55 million lives before it would end. Realizing that their policies of appeasement were fruitless, Britain and France declared war on Germany two days later.

Remembering the futility of World War I ("the war to end all wars"), the United States had every intention of remaining clear of this newest European conflict. But following the fall of France in 1940, Great Britain stood alone, and President Franklin D. Roosevelt began preparing the nation for war.

The first peacetime draft in United States history was enacted, and the military budget was dramatically increased. Roosevelt called for 50,000 combat planes per year in his annual budget.[12] Cessna's board of directors, with a keen eye on the activities abroad, anticipated the day when America might enter the conflict and raw materials for production of commercial airplanes would be restricted. If Cessna were to survive, the company would have to produce for the military.

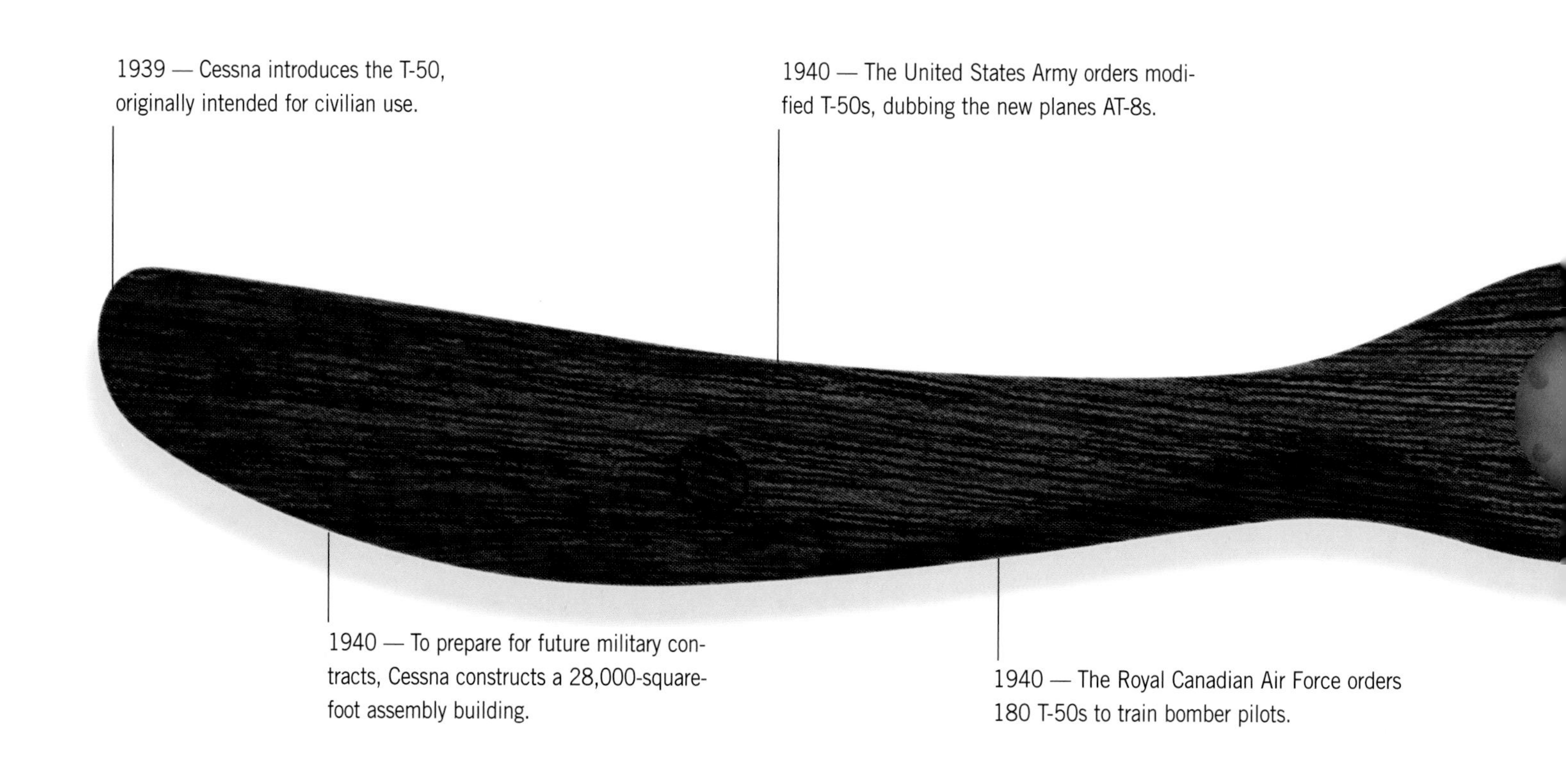

1939 — Cessna introduces the T-50, originally intended for civilian use.

1940 — The United States Army orders modified T-50s, dubbing the new planes AT-8s.

1940 — To prepare for future military contracts, Cessna constructs a 28,000-square-foot assembly building.

1940 — The Royal Canadian Air Force orders 180 T-50s to train bomber pilots.

Air power, which had not played an overwhelming role in World War I, would prove critical during this latest conflict. Reconnaissance remained important, but modern aircraft could now strike deep into the industrial heart of a nation.

Scores of pilots had to be trained to fly multi-engine aircraft heavily laden with bombs. Wallace saw the T-50 as ideal for this training mission, because its twin-engine design was similar to the North American B-25 Mitchell bomber, and was useful to help train pilots to fly the four-engine Consolidated B-24 Liberator and the Boeing B-17 Flying Fortress.[13] Since the T-50 was fuel efficient and constructed from nonstrategic materials, it would not create a drain on scarce resources.

To prepare for potential orders from the military, Wallace launched an expansion program in June 1940. By the end of the month, a 28,000-square-foot assembly building was under construction.[14] Wallace's efforts paid off when the U.S. Army ordered 33 specially equipped T-50s — the largest order in Cessna history at that time.[15]

To meet Army specifications, Cessna switched the 225-horsepower Jacobs radial engines to 290-horsepower Lycoming R-680s, installed hydraulically operated Sperry autopilots and special radio gear, and added windows on the cockpit roof. With these changes, the plane was designated the AT-8 by the Army, becoming one of the first aircraft built for multi-engine training.[16]

Meanwhile, German air raids, designed to weaken Britain for a cross-Channel invasion, were reducing London and the countryside to rubble. Citizens' groups in the United States began sending "bundles for Britain" — food, medicine and other humanitarian supplies — while the United States government sold munitions and "leased" ships and other weapons.

Air Raids

But the famous British Spitfire fighters inflicted heavy losses on the German air force, and Great Britain responded with its own air raids, supported by units comprised of many nationalities, including Poles, Canadians and Americans, all of whom required multi-engine training to fly bombers. To meet this significant challenge, England, Canada and Australia formed the British Commonwealth Air Training Program. Most of the training would take place

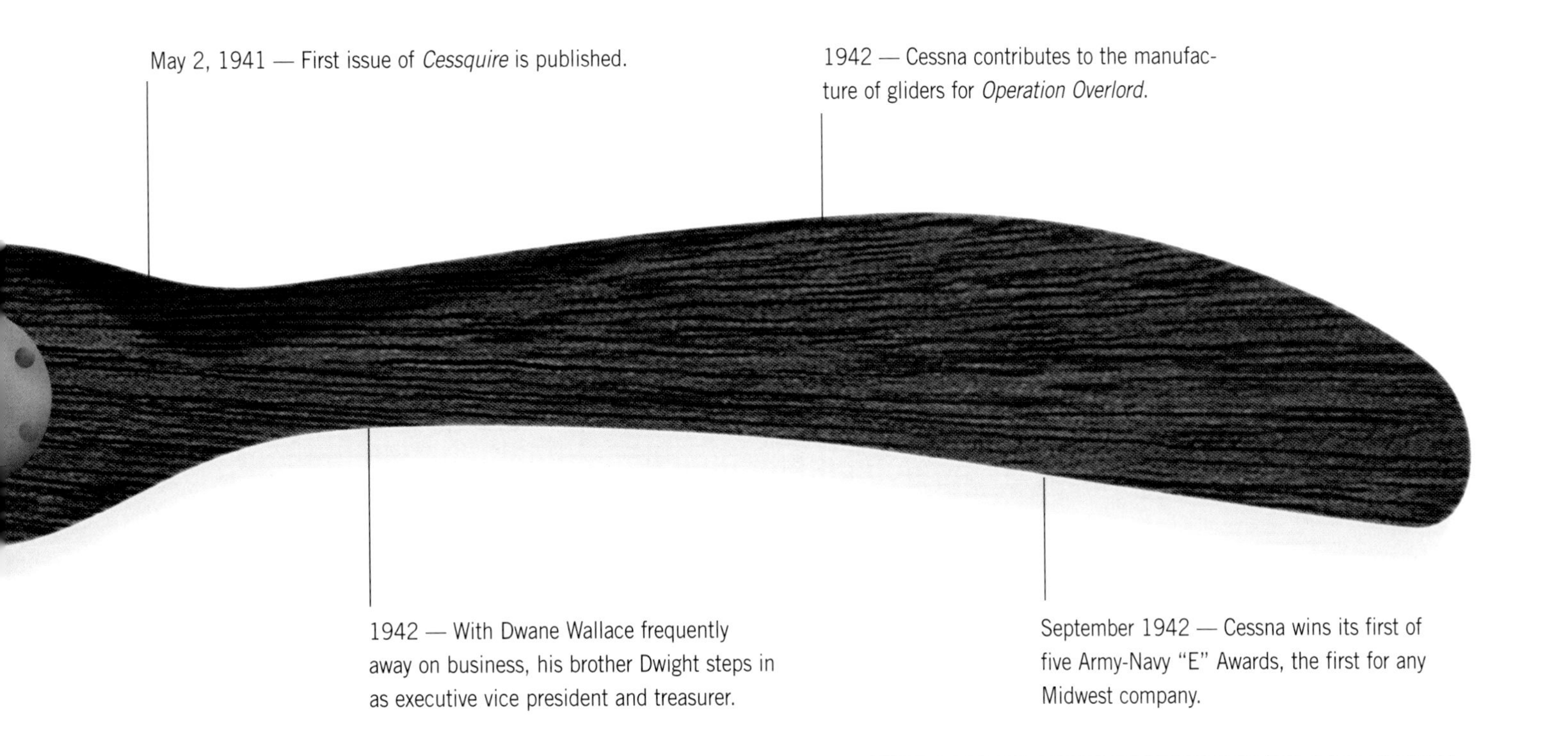

May 2, 1941 — First issue of *Cessquire* is published.

1942 — Cessna contributes to the manufacture of gliders for *Operation Overlord*.

1942 — With Dwane Wallace frequently away on business, his brother Dwight steps in as executive vice president and treasurer.

September 1942 — Cessna wins its first of five Army-Navy "E" Awards, the first for any Midwest company.

in Canada, according to author Edward Phillips. "It represented a continent-sized airbase that stood little chance of being attacked. Would-be aces and bomber pilots flocked to the country, where many of them would learn their deadly trade in twin-engine Cessna airplanes."[17]

In September 1940, the Royal Canadian Air Force ordered 180 T-50s — the largest order to date in all of Wichita.[18] Dwane Wallace had worked hard to win the contract with the British Purchasing Commission, which liked the planes but required proof of Cessna's financial stability before signing an agreement.

Dwane knew that the company was in precarious financial shape, so he contacted his brother Dwight, the attorney, for assistance. In an effort to bolster the corporate account in a hurry, Dwight called upon the president of the Fourth National Bank in Wichita, A.W. Kincade.

A transcript provided by retired Cessna employee Clair McColl gives the following account of what transpired next:

"Nobody in Wichita knew better than Mr. Kincade of the struggle Cessna had made to survive. ... There had been in Wichita 29 airplane manufacturing plants, parts manufacturers and training schools in 1928 and 1929.

"Most of them had failed, but Cessna had survived because of the vision and character of management and labor. Mr. Kincade liked to lend money to people of character. He called his secretary and dictated a telegram to the British Purchasing Commission, saying that his bank would meet all problems by lending Cessna all the financial aid it needed. Mr. Wallace flew back to Wichita with a contract in his pocket."[19]

The Canadians, who named their planes for birds, dubbed the T-50 the Crane, even though Cessnans preferred the more ferocious-sounding Bobcat. Regardless of the name, the plane provided valuable pilot training. Before the contract expired, a second order was placed for an additional $9.5 million worth of Cranes.

As a token of appreciation and a source of inspiration for employees, Cessna published employee yearbooks in 1941 and 1942. The 1941 *Cessna Aircrafter* had this to say about the Cranes:

"Bundles for Britain in the way of skilled pilots are being prepared by Canada. The Cessna T-50's high performance, adaptability to the rigors of student flying, and dependability are blended together to form an instrumental cog in the prepa-

Production of the T-50 went into high gear after the Royal Canadian Air Force ordered 180 in 1940.

ration of just flyers into pilots; ready for any action, any plane, and a match for any foe."[20]

Preparing for War

More manufacturing space was needed in spite of recent additions to the Pawnee Road facility. In early September 1941, Dwane announced a second expansion that would include a new final assembly structure and a two-story administration building.[21] Working around the clock, contractors were able to finish construction in only two months. Even before the entire structure was complete, workers began moving in equipment and assembling aircraft.[22]

In October 1941, the company purchased 320 acres to the east of the main plant to use for aircraft flight testing. Prior to this acquisition, pilots had been forced to taxi across a dirt road to reach the old runway area.[23]

Above: The company's most important wartime aircraft, T-50s, AT-8s and C-165s, are shown here in various stages of production.

Right: The cockpit of a T-50.

Cessna was growing rapidly. Employment spiraled from 200 in July 1940[24] to 2,000 by April 1941.[25] Because of the draft, however, there was a shortage of manpower. "If they looked in one ear and could not see through to the other side, you could pretty much go to work anywhere you wanted at that time," recalled Jack Zook, who joined Cessna's accounting department in 1941 and retired in 1982.[26] Since Zook's wife was about to give birth, the local draft board had told him he

could delay conscription by finding a job in a defense-related industry. He went into the service in 1944, three years after the birth of his child, and returned to Cessna in 1946, where he held a variety of positions in marketing and international sales. Zook eventually became international director of sales in 1961 and director of marketing administration in 1973.

Like most manufacturers during the war, Cessna turned to women to fill out its workforce. The company had always had an abundance of female applicants for secretarial positions. According to one story, 26 such applicants were in the waiting room one day when personnel director Myron Russ called them into his office one at a time and offered each a position as a factory worker. Only six accepted. It was said the others were put off by the somewhat unfashionable dress codes. Women would have to wear overalls in place of skirts that could get caught in whirring machinery, cut their fingernails, and either bob their hair or tuck it under a hat.[27]

Eventually Dwane would tell a reporter in July 1942 that one out of every four Cessna workers was female, and the number was expected to increase to six out of every 10. A *Wichita Beacon* article described Cessna as a pioneer in hiring women and discussed how the company overcame some early difficulties.

> *"Company officials reported that cover-all uniforms, mandatory for girls, has reduced many a 'dangerous curve which formerly distracted masculine eyes and minds from their jobs.'*
>
> *"'When a girl worker used to walk down the assembly line in slacks and sweater, necks craned and the men whistled,' commented the Cessna public relations department. 'But the tables are turned now.'*
>
> *"'Remembering those shrill whistles of the pioneer days, they are giving some of the boys their own medicine. When a handsome new male worker is led out to his job, the girls frequently let*

The T-50s that went to the Royal Canadian Air Force were known as Cranes in keeping with the Canadian tradition of naming aircraft for birds.

To ease the tensions of a frenetic work schedule, the company sponsored two softball teams, the "Bombers" and the "Flyers." In 1941, the "Bombers," shown here, won first place in the Wichita Westside Softball League.

up a chorus of whistling to the embarrassment of the blushing newcomer.'"[28]

By 1941 Cessna employees were laboring in three shifts, 24 hours a day, to build AT-8s and Cranes.[29] In June 1941, a third expansion was announced, and a 3,750-square-foot building was complete by the end of summer. This facility included a cafeteria to feed the growing numbers of workers. But Dwight was worried that long food lines would harm productivity, so he devised a system consisting of 14 electrically heated carts that delivered food to each department, giving employees 20 minutes to eat.[30]

The work was fast-paced and the pressure was high. To reward employees and help them relax after their shifts, the company organized softball teams, picnics, dances and parties. An employee gymnasium provided another opportunity to unwind. To improve communication with employees, Cessna's first official company publication — the *Cessquire* — debuted May 2, 1941, and was published every other Friday. Articles in that first issue highlighted a company and a city experiencing rapid change. One story spoke of the increased traffic hazards in Wichita caused by the thousands of aircraft workers who had flooded the city. Another reminded employees that two five-minute smoking breaks cost Cessna thousands of dollars in time lost over the course of a year. An address by Dwane discussed the importance of Cessna's wartime contributions.

"Yours is a privilege enjoyed by comparatively few in doing a part toward meeting the requirements of this Titanic National Defense Program. To be actually working with your own hands in the creation of training planes gives you the opportunity to serve your country in one of the

most important phases connected with this tremendous task.

"Combat aircraft must be manned for defense; hundreds of trainers are therefore required to train these pilots. A bit of carelessness, a sloppy fit, some little thing not just right may COST A LIFE. Let us exercise all possible care in the construction of CESSNA trainers, and before this is completely effective, it must be extended to the last man.

"Our objective: QUALITY TRAINERS IN QUANTITY."[31]

The United States Declares War

On December 7, 1941, more than 360 Japanese warplanes screamed down from the clouds above Pearl Harbor and shattered the United States Pacific Fleet as it sat peacefully on a Sunday morning. By the end of the attack, five battleships and 14 other ships were sunk or seriously damaged; 2,000 sailors and 400 civilians were killed.

The United States declared war. Despite the military buildup, the nation was still unprepared. The vast manufacturing capability was only partially mobilized, and many soldiers who had been drafted had to drill with wooden rifles. More airplanes were needed — and fast. The original 50,000 planes a year ordered by President Roosevelt was increased to 60,000. By June 1942, Cessna's entire factory was devoted to military contracts; all production for commercial and private aircraft was suspended to meet the needs of war. Recalled Jay Landrum, an electroplater who joined Cessna in March 1941:

"We were sitting on the floor eating lunch when the announcement came over about Pearl Harbor, and our foreman — we called him Shotgun Burke — gave us a pep talk. He said, 'What I want to see from now on is fannies and elbows working hard. We're doing good now, but we have to do better.'"[32]

Engineers had been designing a "Family Car of the Air," a four-seater that would be relatively simple to fly and would have more safety features than any other plane of the time. The company

After the United States declared war, Cessna was forced to suspend plans for a "Family Car of the Air" that would have sold for around the same price as a 1941 Chevrolet.

seas, who often wrote long dispatches to the magazine about their wartime experiences. Each issue served as a vital link between those on the front and Cessna workers keeping the factories running at home. A page of *Service Men's News* kept employees at home informed about their former coworkers. Dramatic wartime adventures, including this story from a 22-year-old woodshop worker, were frequently published.

"Staff Sergeant Ernest V. Swanson, former Cessna employee, was back in Wichita at Cessna last week after having had his share of wartime experience walking 450 miles in Italy to escape from a prison camp. He had spent two months in an Italian prison and although he was not badly mistreated, the food

With thousands of people flocking to Wichita to fill the airplane factories, a housing shortage was inevitable. The federal government built three housing projects with a total of 6,000 barrack-type units. Another 8,300 units were built by individuals, but there was never enough housing.[37]

During the war years, the *Cessquire* was mailed to former employees now fighting overseas, who often wrote long dispatches to the magazine about their wartime experiences. Each issue served as a vital link between those on the front and Cessna workers keeping the factories running at home. A page of *Service Men's News* kept employees at home informed about their former coworkers. Dramatic wartime adventures, including this story from a 22-year-old woodshop worker, were frequently published.

> *"Staff Sergeant Ernest V. Swanson, former Cessna employee, was back in Wichita at Cessna last week after having had his share of wartime experience walking 450 miles in Italy to escape from a prison camp. He had spent two months in an Italian prison and although he was not badly mistreated, the food was scarce and there was little of it given to American prisoners.*
>
> *"Escaping from the prison alone, he walked south toward the boot of Italy; it took him four weeks to cover the 450 miles of mountainous country. Sergeant Swanson said he traveled across country by day and night. There were thousands of Jerries and he had to watch out for them but otherwise he felt comparatively safe as he traveled away from the principally used highways.*
>
> *"After the first few days out a stray dog came along and made the remainder of the trip with him until he met up with the Eighth Air Force from England and they sent him to the American lines. Peasants furnished food to both Sergeant Swanson and the dog during his trip."*[38]

Cessna employees did everything in their power to support the American effort, noted an article in the 50th Anniversary Edition of the *Cessquire*, published in 1977.

> *"Cessnans vigorously supported their country through the purchase of war bonds and stamps. They put their hearts into their work, responding favorably to the need for reduced absenteeism in the hope that their presence and individual contribution to each plane and part might help save a life.*
>
> *"Those waiting anxiously back home occupied their free hours planting victory gardens and running scrap drives, saving metal, rags, rubber and paper to be converted directly or indirectly into weapons. They even saved fats and oils for glycerine to make explosives —'the power to blast the U.S. to victory.'*
>
> *"The Cessna Industrial Guard was formed, becoming the first organization of its type in the country to train its members in actual combat maneuvers in case of emergencies at home.*

To prepare for emergencies, Cessnans participated in the Industrial Guard, a unique organization that trained them in combat maneuvers.

"The challenge of supplying a war-time Air Force was indeed a serious one, as was the task of maintaining a positive and hopeful attitude. Cessna rose to meet those challenges with resolute strength and ardor."[39]

Concern for the community went beyond these efforts. Cessnans had a long history of donating to local charities and serving as volunteers. During the war, several employees took time from their schedules to design a new type of walker for children with cerebral palsy.

"In 1944, Cessna Vice President Dwight Wallace and his wife visited the Institute of Logopedics at the University of Wichita [Wichita State University today.] Dr. Martin Palmer, director of the institution at the time, pointed out the need for a new type of walker to assist the handicapped children in getting around. ...

"Mr. Wallace thought Cessna could devise a better walker to aid these children. The project was taken on by three Cessna employees, and with the assistance of Dr. Palmer, they came up with a radically new idea — the parachute sling. By supporting the child's body in a sling similar to a parachute, the new walker was created.

"The old-style walkers were usually the crutch type, and unless a child had strong arms and shoulders, he could not use these walkers successfully. Any child, regardless of strength, could use the Cessna walker. The parachute sling was designed in the Upholstery Department, and the rest was constructed in the Jig Shop. Twelve walkers were built and given to the institute."[40]

Bobcats

At the request of the United States Army Air Corps, the AT-8 was modified in early 1942 to incorporate an overhead window and some structural changes to the wings that allowed it to carry 5,700 pounds of gross weight instead of 5,100. The Air Corps ordered 450 ships of this new model, designated the AT-17 but known as the Bobcat, a name that eventually caught on for all planes in the T-50 series. However, structural problems in the main spars of some units restricted the weight capacity to 5,300 pounds. These planes were given the designation AT-17E. Bobcat model AT-17B, also built in 1942, sported a silver paint scheme and was powered by two Jacobs R-755-9 engines.

After the United States joined the fighting, Cessna provided more than training planes. The AT series of Bobcats became the C-78 series, used by the Army Air Corps between 1942 and 1944 as a personnel transport and light cargo plane. Similar to the AT-17, the ship carried updated radios and other equipment and radio changes, and was painted olive drab and gray, camouflaging colors that reflected the more direct role these planes would play in the war.

By 1942, the Bobcat series had been in production long enough to have been given such nick-

Airplanes in the T-50 series were powered by Jacobs engines.

In April 1942, Cessna was commissioned to build the outer wing panels of 1,500 Waco CG-4A gliders, large and powerful enough to carry Jeeps into combat.

names as the Bamboo Bomber and the Double Breasted Cub. Three hundred and thirty of these planes were delivered under the C-78 designation, and another 674 identical planes were delivered as UC-78 (the "U" stood for utility).[41]

The UC-78B, capable of hauling greater loads than other designations, became Cessna's most popular wartime aircraft. Its ability to move supplies from the home front to the battlefront was critical, since victory or defeat in battle was usually decided by whoever was able to reinforce and resupply hard-fighting divisions. By the time production ended in 1944, 2,156 of the aluminum-colored ships had been built.

Several experimental ships were also built during the war years. The P-7/T-50A, P-10, C-106 and C-106A were all prototypes aimed at the military market but never put into production (the "P" was used by Cessna to designate experimental projects).[42] In most cases, the military was so pleased with its current Cessnas that there was no reason to switch to something different.

By 1943, Cessna had become heavily involved in maintaining, repairing and rebuilding the military's UC-78, AT-8 and AT-17 airplanes. The company had leased a hangar at the Hutchinson Airport and converted it to an overhaul depot for these machines.[43]

Gliders

As early as 1942, plans were under way for a cross-Channel invasion of Europe, using Great Britain as the launching point. The massive attack, known as *Operation Overlord*, would eventually occur on June 6, 1944. Gliders were needed to airlift elite commandos behind enemy lines, and the United States government ordered CG-4A models from the Waco Aircraft Company of Troy, Ohio. These gliders, with enormous wingspans of more than 83 feet, were strong enough to carry 15 fully equipped commandos, who were assigned among the most daring and dangerous missions of the war. These troops were required to disrupt German communications, hold or destroy decisive targets such as bridges and fields to prevent enemy reinforcements, and accomplish all this without raising the general alarm that the invasion was under way.

The order for gliders was too big for Waco to handle alone, so it was subcontracted to 16 other manufacturers across the United States, including Cessna, Beech and Boeing. Cessna's job was to build the outer wing panels for 1,500 gliders.[44]

Already cramped for space, Cessna purchased 110 acres 50 miles northwest of Wichita near the small town of Hutchinson, Kansas. The property was adjacent to the Hutchinson Airport, facilitating the transportation of parts and personnel. Within a frantic 30-day period, a 108,000-square-foot building was erected and 630 people were employed, working three shifts to construct the glider parts on schedule.[45] Although half of the CG-4A orders were canceled, the first of 750 deliveries was made in September 1942, and the final glider was delivered in January 1943.[46]

The "E" Award

In September 1942, The Cessna Aircraft Company became the first company in the Midwest to win the coveted Army-Navy "E" award, which recognized the company for such wide-ranging accomplishments as quality of production, ability to overcome production difficulties and maintaining fair labor standards.[47] The award ceremony on September 27 recognized all Cessna employees for their good work, noted the 1942 *Cessna Aircrafter.*

> *"Ten thousand Cessna employees and their families thronged the Wichita Forum ... to witness the presentation of the Army-Navy 'E' Award to The Cessna Aircraft Company. The Award, won for excellence in production, entitles all employees to wear the coveted 'E' pin, and the Company to fly the famous 'E' flag.*
>
> *"Dignitaries who participated in the ceremonies were Henry J. Allen, master of ceremonies; Col. Ray G. Harris, Army Air Corps, speaker and representative who presented the Awards; Dwane L. Wallace, president of the Cessna Aircraft Co., who accepted the Award; Honorable Payne G. Ratner, Governor of Kansas and speaker of the evening; and Al Zerbe, oldest employee of Cessna from the standpoint of service, who accepted the award for the employees.*
>
> *"A big picnic barbecue dinner was served to all 10,000 guests, who participated in a full evening of entertainment and fun. Two Cessna orchestras played for the dancing, and members of the Cessna radio show entertained throughout the evening. The weekly radio show* Strictly Personal *climaxed the day's activities."*[48]

Cessna received this prestigious award a total of five times during the war.[49]

The End in Sight

By 1944, the Army had enough trained bomber pilots. What it needed were more bombers. In early 1944, the production of Bobcats was cut back, and Cessna's facilities were converted to support subcontract work for components of the Boeing B-29 Superfortress and Douglas A-26 bomber.[50] For the B-29,

Above: Cessna won the prestigious Army-Navy "E" Award five times during World War II.

Right: In early 1944, Cessna suspended production of the Bobcat series and began manufacturing components for the Douglas A-26 bomber and the Boeing B-29 shown here.

Cessna employees built 1,400 vertical stabilizers, 1,894 rudders, 1,658 heat exchangers, 1,619 pilot and co-pilot instrument panels, 1,536 dorsal fairings, 1,567 elevators, 1,343 wing leading edges and 1,583 rudder pedals. For the A-26, they manufactured 6,500 engine cowlings and 2,046 landing gear sets.

Realizing that the end of the war would mean the end of military contracts, company executives took measures in early 1945 to secure contracts with North American Aviation Incorporated and Fairchild Engine and Airplane Company to build major assemblies for the C-82 Packet Cargo airplane. Another contract was signed for assemblies for the FR-1 Fireball Jet Propelled Navy Deckfighter manufactured by Ryan Aeronautical Corporation.[51]

On August 6, 1945, a single bomb was dropped from a Superfortress over Hiroshima. A moment later, more than four square miles was destroyed, and 60,000 people perished or would die soon after. Two days later, Nagasaki was similarly destroyed, after the Japanese government ignored calls for its surrender.

The Japanese formally surrendered on September 2, 1945. By that time, employment at Cessna had dropped to 1,800, as it became clear that victory was imminent. Eventually, employment dropped to a mere 450, compared to a wartime high of 6,074 workers. Cessna had earned $191.8 million in wartime sales. It was time to return to civilian production. For the next few years, Cessna would concentrate on single-engine airplanes, a line for which it would become famous.[52]

The Wichita Eagle

JAPS QUIT UNCONDITIONALLY: U. S. ORDERS BATTLING ENDED

PRESIDENT ORDERS IMMEDIATE SLASH IN SERVICE DRAFT

Will Accept Japanese Surrender

TRUMAN ANNOUNCES END OF WAR; NAMES MACARTHUR TO ACCEPT FORMAL CAPITULATION OF ENEMY

Hirohito Blames Atomic Bomb for Japs' Defeat

V-J DAY FOR WICHITA

TRUMAN'S STATEMENT ON SURRENDER

Doom Petain to Execution

Surrender Order to Japs

Big Cruiser Indianapolis Sunk; Casualties 1,196

Truman Holds Surrender Message

The *Wichita Eagle* announces the end of the war.

This golfer was able to tee off moments after landing his Model 140 on an airfield adjoining a golf course at Estes Park, Colorado.

CONVERTING TO PEACE

1945–1950

"For Performance, Economy, Safety... you get More for your Money in a Cessna."

— 1946 advertising slogan[1]

THE SECOND WORLD WAR had unleashed terrible carnage throughout the world — the worst ever witnessed — culminating with the splitting of the atom. But the end of the war unleashed two powerful forces of a different nature: two decades of pent-up demand combined with unparalleled prosperity. Americans had weathered privation that began with the Great Depression and lasted through the war. Flush with money from war bonds and wartime earnings, people became aggressive consumers.

The directors at Cessna had already begun converting the company's factories back to the production of civilian airplanes by the time the atomic bombs were dropped.[2] Returning to the commercial sector was expected to be difficult as the market was already saturated with war-surplus planes. Their attractive price tags would make it difficult for new models to penetrate the market.[3]

But the potential appeared enormous. A Department of Commerce official predicted to Congress that light planes "represented the most logical field for postwar expansion of the aeronautical industry,"[4] and expected production to increase to 200,000 aircraft a year.[5] Aeronautical magazines, which had suddenly become popular, published surveys stating that pilots returning from the war "would be unwilling to give up their wings, while other veterans would use GI Bill funds to learn to fly."[6] Prices were expected to fall to the point where buying an airplane would be comparable to buying an expensive automobile.

To gain every possible advantage, Cessna established a nationwide organization of distributors who sold only Cessna aircraft.[7]

Meanwhile, Cessna employees who fought in the war were welcomed back. Most went right back to work in the same positions they had left, but that meant that other people had to be laid off, recalled Lucille Brunton, who joined Cessna's Finance Department in 1942 and retired in 1990 as assistant manager for risk and insurance. Many of the women who had been working in the factory quit when their husbands came home, but there were still too many workers. "Each week, people left the company. We had to make it one way or the other, and we couldn't do it with employees and no work for them," recalled Brunton, who left the company after the war and returned in 1953.[8]

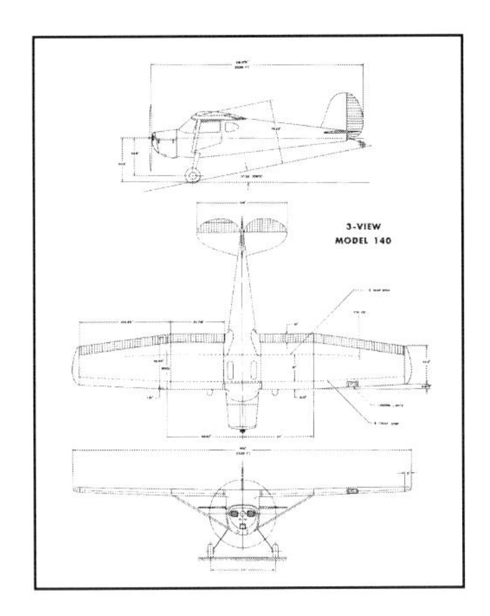

Drawings of the affordable Model 140. Cessna envisioned a day when aircraft ownership would be almost as common as owning a car.

The engine and cowling of a Cessna model 140. The 140 was designed as a trainer and a sport plane.

Models 120 and 140

Just five months after V-J Day, Cessna had fully converted to peacetime production and introduced its first postwar planes, models 120 and 140.[9] Executives had spoken to former military pilots who wanted to continue flying, and designed an aircraft for this ready market. The highly affordable craft reflected the company's belief that flying would someday be nearly as popular as driving.

The 120, designed with the GI Bill for flight training in mind, was a two-seater that sold for $2,695. The 140 was a two-place trainer and sport plane intended for private ownership, with a price tag of $3,245. The 120, able to attain speeds of 120 miles per hour, was basically a stripped-down version of the 140, without the wing flaps, additional side windows and sophisticated electrical system of its more luxurious cousin.[10]

Both were built entirely of metal, except for fabric-covered wings, and were powered by 85-

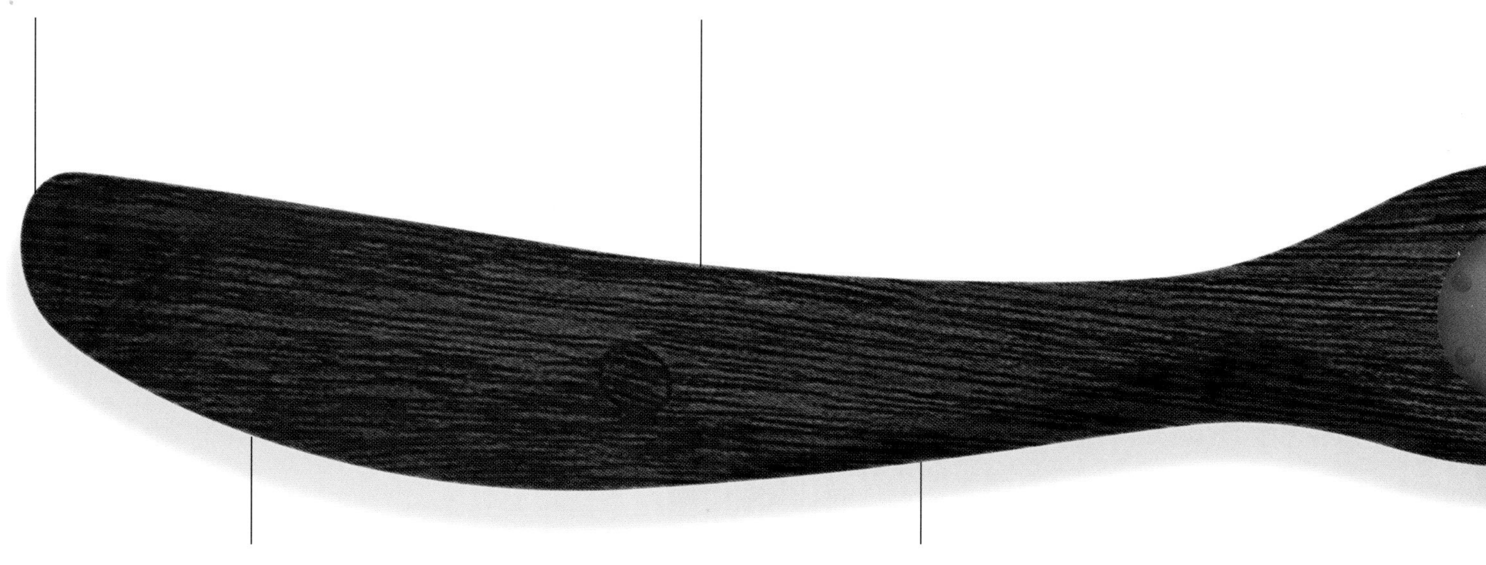

1945 — Nationwide Cessna distribution network is established.

1946 — Cessna begins manufacturing farm machinery components.

1945 — Cessna introduces the two-place models 120 and 140.

1946 — Industrial Hydraulics Division is established.

horsepower Continental engines. The similarities between the two allowed the company to produce them on the same production line.

The 140 was the first to use Cessna's famous "spring steel" landing gear leg — a single piece of metal attached to the fuselage, to which the axle, wheel, tire and brakes were mounted.[11] The spring steel flexed when the plane landed, providing a smoother contact with the runway than conventional landing gear.[12] "It was a good two-place airplane, very economical" said Jack Zook, assistant sales manager at the time. "We really pushed it."[13] The sales department obviously did a good job, with 4,904 built between 1945 and 1949.[14]

By the middle of 1946, Cessna was producing planes as quickly as it could obtain material, noted the *Wichita Eagle*.

> *"Cessna Aircraft Company is one month ahead of its schedule in production of light, two-place, personal plane models, now having production up to*

The Model 140 could carry 80 pounds of baggage in the luggage compartment.

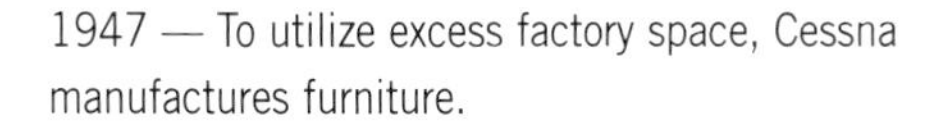

1947 — To utilize excess factory space, Cessna manufactures furniture.

1947 — The 170, a four-seat version of the 140, becomes Cessna's "family car of the air."

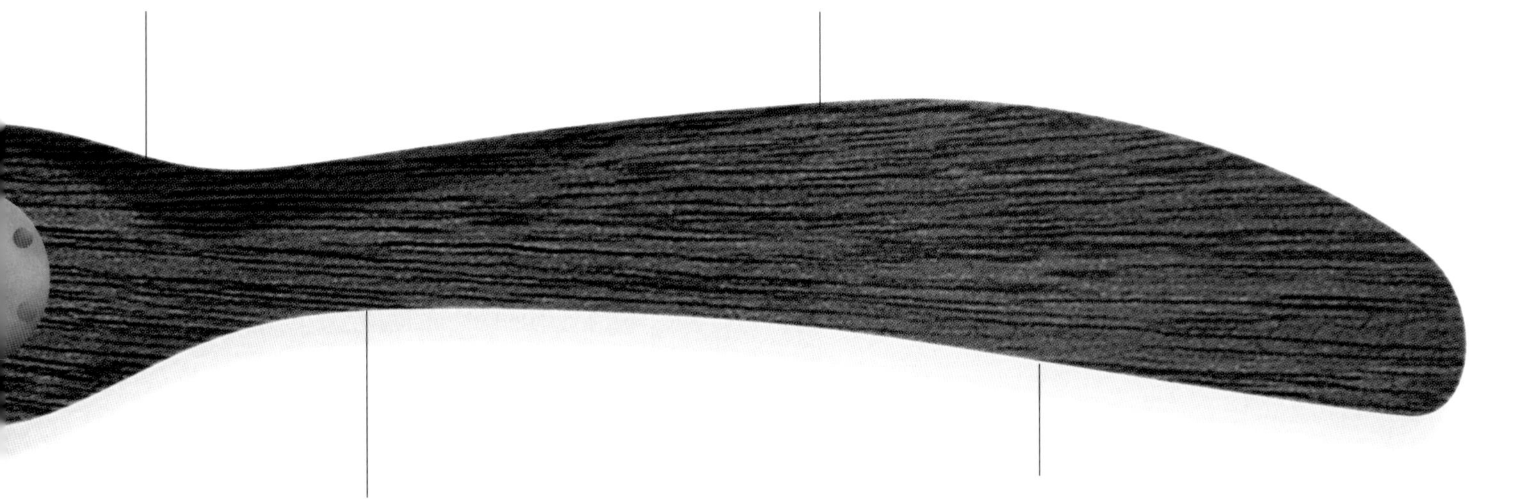

1947 — Models 190 and 195, deluxe five-passenger aircraft, are introduced.

1949 — The United States Air Force orders 15 Model 195s for search and rescue missions in the Arctic. More orders follow.

22 planes a day, company officials announced over the weekend.

"Cessna began its reconversion program immediately after V-J day, retooling the entire factory for volume production of its new light planes, models 120 and 140. Actual production started in March with four planes a day, now increased to 22."[15]

Production peaked at 30 planes a day in September 1946.[16] Both airplanes were advertised in the December 1946 *Air Facts* magazine with the slogan "For Performance, Economy, Safety... you get More for your Money in a Cessna."[17] The 140, for example, could carry 25 gallons of fuel in twin-wing tanks, delivering a range of about 450 miles in more than four and a half hours of flight time. Storage space was increased to handle enough luggage "for two people for two weeks," according to an advertisement.[18]

In 1948, the 140 was honored as "Outstanding Plane of the Year" by the U.S. Flight Instructors Association.[19] It was later used by oil companies as a pipeline patroller to hunt leaks. The following year, it was further refined to incorporate all-metal wings and was dubbed the 140A. The plane could reach a top speed of 125 miles per hour and could cruise at 110 miles per hour.

But the 140A line was temporarily discontinued in February 1951 because military contracts took precedence following the outbreak of the Korean War.[20]

Top: The wing spars and ribs for the Model 140 were constructed of aluminum alloy, which were then covered with fabric.

Inset: Model 140s flying in formation.

Above: The 140 was named "Outstanding Plane of the Year" by the U.S. Flight Instructors Association in 1948.

Models 190 and 195

In December 1946, Cessna's assembly line was closed for five days while existing machinery was rearranged and new tooling installed to accommodate production of two new Cessna models — 190 and 195.[21] Designed primarily as postwar replacements for the Airmaster series, these new airplanes were deluxe-cabin, five-place ships intended for executive use.[22] The 190, described as "big, bullish and beautiful," sold for $12,750, while the more popular 195 was priced at $13,750.[23] Both were powered by 300-horsepower Jacobs engines. With the new executive-class planes, Cessna could compete in a variety of price ranges.

A 1947 newspaper article described them as sleek all-metal machines with all the luxuries a top executive would expect.

"The cabin is as big, as high, and as roomy as the interior of the average modern automobile sedan, seating five persons in complete comfort. Richly upholstered seat cushions are constructed of no-sag springs and foam rubber.

"Another of the outstanding features of the Cessnas 190 and 195 is the patented Cessna safety landing gear, already proven a sensation and successful on the smaller Cessna planes. It requires no maintenance or upkeep and there are no moving parts.

"The gear is constructed of chrome vanadium steel, the finest grade of spring steel, and the shock of landing is absorbed by the flexing of the gear itself. The gear is so aerodynamically clean that there is no appreciable amount of drag, thus eliminating expensive, troublesome and weighty retracting mechanisms."[24]

Above: The prototype 195 in 1945.

Below: A 300-horsepower Jacobs seven-cylinder radial engine powered the Model 195.

In 1949, the United States Air Force began shopping for a fleet of airplanes to be used for search and rescue missions in the Arctic. The five-place ship had to withstand heavy use and frigid weather, and be adaptable to land on unimproved runways, snow or water. In the fall of 1949, Cessna was selected to supply 15 Model 195s for this purpose, designated LC-126As by the Air Force. The planes were delivered in January 1950.

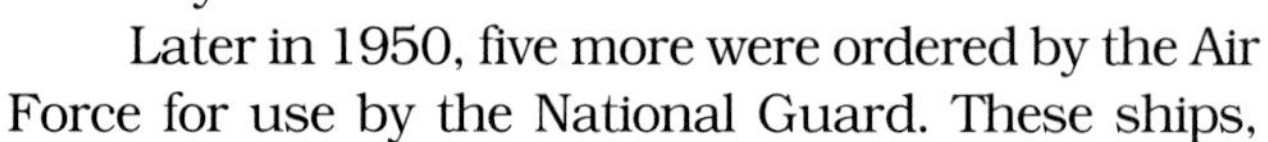

Above: The elegant and logical instrument panel of the 195 contributed to a review stating that the cabin "is as roomy as the interior of the average modern automobile."

Later in 1950, five more were ordered by the Air Force for use by the National Guard. These ships, delivered without skis or floats in January 1951, were designated LC-126Bs. The only other difference between the LC-126A and the LC-126B was the radio equipment installed.

In the spring of 1952, the Army ordered 63 more. A different radio, a larger baggage door and different upholstery warranted yet another military designation. This fleet became the LC-126Cs and was used not only for rescue missions but also for personnel transportation, instrument training and as light cargo transports. First deliveries began in May 1952, and the order was completed by October.[25]

In 1953, Cessna substantially altered the popular Model 195, changing its designation to the A195. The A195 had wing flaps twice as large as those on the 190. A spinner was added to the propeller and the interior styling was updated. When Cessna began building A195s during the summer of 1953, production ceased on models 190 and 195.[26]

Below: The 195 could be adapted as a floatplane, which was used by the National Guard.

Though the 170 was planned for a different market, the plane was superb for traveling executives who wanted to visit customers in spacious comfort. The plane is shown here in front of Cessna's corporate headquarters.

Models 170 and 170A

A four-seat stretched version of the 140, known as the 170, was introduced in 1947. During the war years, Cessna had begun designing a "Family Car of the Air," intended for returning pilots who would want airplanes of their own. The project had been put on hold as wartime production was stepped up. The concept returned in 1947 as the Model 170. Like a family sedan, this safe and comfortable airplane seated four people. Powered by a Continental 145-horsepower engine, it could cruise at 100 miles per hour.[27]

An article in *Air Facts* magazine hailed its comfort and performance and noted that the ship was a natural step up for 140 owners.

"Everything is exactly the same and in the same place. Even the instrument panel is the same, except for two or three inches more of it on each side.

"As you taxi out, however, you find even better over-the-nose visibility, and on rough ground you'll soon find that the gear appears softer than in the 140. Actually it is the 140 gear, but with the additional weight, rides better. It is not overloaded, though, for what happened was that they went overboard slightly on the 140 gear as a hedge against any possible field troubles and realize now that it can be lightened somewhat as it will be at some later date."[28]

Though the airplane was supposed to be a family friendly ship, the agricultural industry used it as a high-speed "farm truck" because of the cabin's spaciousness.

The plane later became something of a classic, according to a 1969 article in *Family Planes*, with models selling between $3,500 and $6,000, depending on condition.

"At least two conditions appear to be essential to lift an airplane from the 'used' or 'old' category into the rarefied heights of the 'classic' airplane. It has to be an unusually good flying machine to start with, and it has to pass through a period where the price is low enough that a large number of low-budget airplane lovers can get their hands on one.

"Note that it is airplane lovers, not the general market of airplane users, who create and sustain the 'classic' category of aircraft. And airplane lovers as a group have lately turned their attention to the ubiquitous Cessna 170, which satisfies both of the conditions to membership in the 'classic' family."[29]

More than just an Aircraft Company: Farm Machinery Components and Furniture

The sudden drop in military contracts left Cessna with excess factory capacity. Having invested heavily on expansion during the war, executives loathed the idea of letting all this space go to waste. The three-year-old Hutchinson, Kansas, facility, touted as the "most complete and modern in the Midwest,"[30] was refurbished in 1946 to produce components for farm machinery — a natural choice for the rural state. Cessna began designing a hydraulic cylinder for a self-propelled combine.[31] The Industrial Hydraulics Division was established, and pumps, valves and a wide array of other components were added to the product line.[32]

Customers included Minneapolis-Moline, John Deere, Allis-Chalmers, Massey-Harris-Ferguson, International Harvester, Ross Gear, J.I. Case and Mid-Western Industries.[33]

Production changed altogether in 1947 when a $6.5 million contract to manufacture furniture was obtained from the Army Quartermaster Corps. Cessna's challenge was to build furniture durable enough to resist corrosive tropical environments without sacrificing the rich beauty of wood. Cessnans covered aluminum-and-steel frames with walnut-veneer plywood.[34]

Cessna's furniture matched the quality of its aircraft, and its line of furniture grew to bureaus with mirrors, dressing tables, stools, desks, dining tables and pivot-top tables. Cessna decided to market its furniture to the general public. In 1950, the furniture was offered through 50 retail outlets.[35]

Cessna furniture won rave reviews when it was displayed at the Chicago Home Show that same

A 1949 Model 170 on floats.

The Model 170, the stretch version of the 140, was originally designed for returning military pilots who wanted to travel comfortably with the family.

year. *House Beautiful* magazine described it as the "first new thing in furniture seen in a long time."[36] At one point, orders were so great that the Pawnee facility was pressed into service to supplement manufacturing in Hutchinson.[37] The line was dropped in 1951. All the military orders had been filled, and the National Production Authority ordered a halt to the use of aluminum in the manufacture of household furniture.[38]

But the furniture was so durable that it can still be found today, noted Floyd Lundy, a Cessnan from 1941 to 1986, who helped weld the all-metal furniture. "The last time I saw the company doctor, he still had some of the chairs in his office," Lundy said.[39]

In 1948, Cessna began building aluminum clothes lockers to fulfill a $1 million contract from the Quartermaster Corporation.[40] By the end of the year the $7 million non-aircraft side of Cessna actually outperformed the aircraft manufacturing component by $46,635.[41]

When the Korean War began in 1950, the Hutchinson facility was once again outfitted to build airplane tails and wings, which were trucked to the Pawnee plant for assembly. Two years later, the Hutchinson plant was cleared of all aircraft assemblies and devoted fully to the production of hydraulic components. Within six months, all hydraulics production was moved from Pawnee Road to Hutchinson, creating Cessna's Industrial Products Division.[42] All aircraft hydraulic components for the company began to be produced solely at the Hutchinson facility.[43]

In the fifties, Cessna would once again become an important wartime manufacturer — starting with the famous L-19 Bird Dog — after North Korea attacked its southern neighbor in a failed attempt to reunify the country under Communist rule.

Thousands of Cessna employees lined the fences and rooftops of the Prospect plant during the summer of 1951 to witness the first flight of the Model 308. Test pilot Bill Thompson flew the airplane.

THE BIRD DOG POINTS THE WAY

1949–1959

"The artillery Bird Dogs often fly deep into enemy territory just to keep an eye on targets that might be moving up into range. If they 'point' some especially juicy 'ducks,' a tank column for instance, they radio back post-haste. Air Force fighter-bombers then arrive to roast the ducks with napalm, stuffing them with rockets and adding cannon shells for seasoning."

— the *Cessquire*, 1952[1]

BY THE END of the 1940s, the United States Army decided it was time to retire its aging fleet of Stinson L-5s and Piper L-4s used during and after World War II for artillery spotting, and requested bids for new aircraft. The bid would result in the manufacture of the famous "Bird Dog," used with great effectiveness in two undeclared wars.

Artillery spotting was risky business. Pilots flew virtually unarmed into enemy airspace to locate targets for forward artillery units. The aircraft were not fighters; if challenged in the air, they had to race to relative safety by hiding in clouds or retreat behind their own lines. They had to fly low enough to pick out targets and determine their coordinates. They often flew low enough to be hit by small-arms fire, as well as anti-aircraft guns.

The aircraft also served in search and rescue roles and transported cargo and personnel. The two-place ship was to be built solely of metal, with high wings and the capacity for both skis and floats. It had to be able to take off from and land on unusually short airstrips.

Like nearly every small aircraft manufacturer in the nation, Cessna was eager to win the contract. The Army requested bids in 1949 and had scheduled a competition for January 1950, so little time was given to design a prototype. At that point, the Cessna engineering department consisted of only 18 individuals, already overloaded with work on the 140, 170, 190 and 195. The only way to meet the deadline would be to use veteran components from other Cessna models.

Construction of the Model 305 began with the wings of a 170. The experimental department constructed a new fuselage, while engineers selected a Continental 0-470-11 engine customized by the manufacturer to deliver 213 horsepower rather than its 190 off-the-shelf rating. The tail from the 195 was added. With little time to spare, the company still had much to do.[2]

The most noteworthy development was the design of 60-degree slotted wing flaps, accomplished with the use of an external hinge bracket that pivoted below the wing. This allowed the plane to fulfill the Army specification of landing over a 50-foot obstacle in a distance of less than 600 feet.[3]

Cessnans worked frantically to meet the deadline, cramming 2,500 man-hours into three short weeks. The prototype was completed December 8, 1949, and made its first flight with chief engineering test pilot H.F. "Hank" Waring at

The L-19B, a variation of the venerable Bird Dog observation and liaison plane.

the controls on December 14.[4] Although the plane was considerably heavier than others in the competition, Cessna executives and engineers were confident. A May 25, 1950 story in the *Wichita Eagle* helped explain why.

"In all particulars, the new two-passenger plane surpasses army requirements.

"The field forces asked for an airplane that will climb 800 feet per minute to a service ceiling of 16,000 feet, take off and land over a 50-foot obstacle in 600 feet, maintain constant altitude and full control at 43 knots, fly for three hours with 20 gallons of fuel, and cruise at 78 knots at 5,000 feet.

"Cessna's 305 answers as follows:

"It climbs at 1,290 feet per minute to 22,900 feet; takes off and lands over a 50-foot obstacle with runs of 560 and 600 feet, respectively; maintains an observation speed of 40 knots with constant altitude and full control; cruises 3.1 hours with 20 gallons of fuel, and cruises at a speed of 90 knots at 5,000 feet with 29 percent of its horsepower.

"The little liaison craft is powered with a Continental E190 engine, which has a normal horsepower of 190 but develops 213 for takeoffs. It can attain cruising speeds up to 145 miles per hour.

"At tests in Dayton, Ohio, several weeks ago, the new Cessna competed with airplanes built for the competition by nearly every U.S. small plane manufacturer. Test pilots of one airplane in the competition took to their parachutes when their ship failed while in the air.[5]

On May 29, 1950, Cessna was verbally notified that it had won the contract. The initial order, worth about $5 million, was for 418 aircraft. "It is a nice piece of business and naturally we are highly pleased since it will ensure steady employment through the next two years of our working force," Dwane Wallace told the *Wichita Eagle*.[6]

The first shipment of 14 L-19s was scheduled for September 1950.[7] However, the date was moved to December to allow for certification by the Civil Aeronautics Administration. The process took longer than usual because of the military's insistence that the ship pass Civil Aeronautics regulations instead of the traditional military standards. Because so many of the main components of the 305 were taken from existing Cessna models, no retooling was necessary to produce the new aircraft.

May 29, 1950 — Cessna wins a contract to manufacture 418 L-19s for the military.

April 11, 1952 — The Seibel Helicopter Company is acquired.

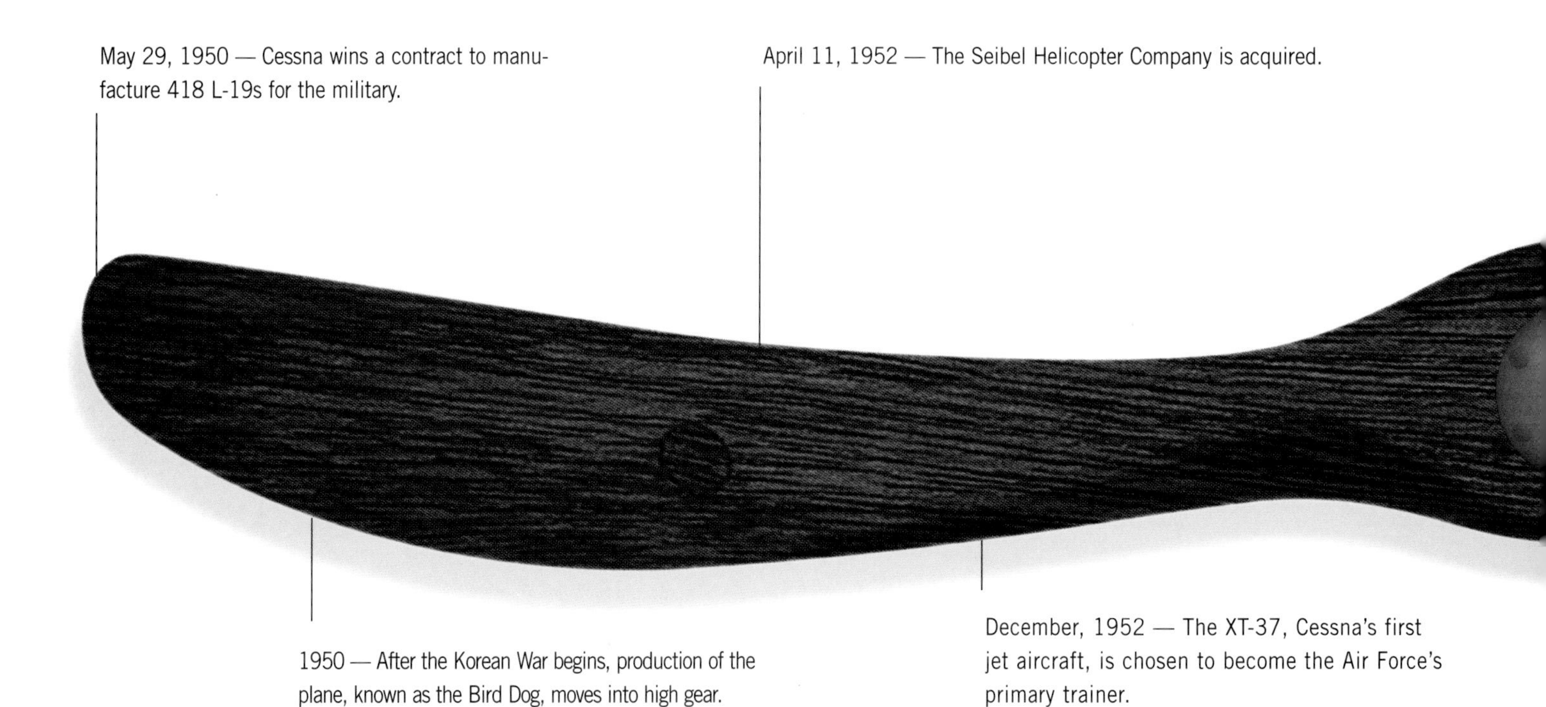

1950 — After the Korean War begins, production of the plane, known as the Bird Dog, moves into high gear.

December, 1952 — The XT-37, Cessna's first jet aircraft, is chosen to become the Air Force's primary trainer.

However, a separate production line was established for it.[8]

The Bird Dog Goes to War

On June 25, 1950, North Korean troops crossed the 38th Parallel, the somewhat arbitrary dividing line between North and South Korea, in an attempt to forcibly reunite the country under Communist rule. Having learned from Europe's failed appeasement policy — which led to World War II — President Harry Truman sent troops to bolster South Korean forces. After months of desperate fighting, victory seemed near after General Douglas MacArthur's army routed the Communist forces and crossed the 38th Parallel into North Korea. But when China entered the conflict, the war bogged down into a bloody contest of wills.

The war in Korea accelerated the production schedule for L-19s into high gear. The Army changed its delivery date from December to October, and in November doubled its order.[9] The plane entered service as an observation plane in Korea on February 16, 1951.[10] Its excellent maneuverability was extremely valuable in the mountains of Korea, as was its ability to lift off within 200 feet, even when carrying 600 pounds of freight. Pilots praised the plane's heating system and said its spring steel landing gear absorbed shocks.

The Army designated the plane the L-19/L-19A, and Cessna employees were encouraged to submit name suggestions for it. "The future name of the L-19 should be one that is appropriate as to either performance, use, durability, maneuverability, or construction, etc. It should be a short name, easily pronounced, and not the slogan type," advised an article in *Cessquire*.[11]

More than 10,000 contest forms were filled out by eager employees. Pre-flight department employee Jack Swayze and Jack O. Lawrence of engineering both chose the winning name of Bird Dog, so a coin toss established Swayze as the winner.[12] In a special ceremony, Gen. Mark W. Clark, then chief of Army Field Forces, presented Swayze with his prize: a week of paid vacation, free transportation within 600 air miles of Wichita for him and his family, plus $200 for expenses.[13] Clark, who served in both world wars and directed the invasion of North Africa in World War II, praised the L-19 as "the best plane the Army has."[14]

July 16, 1953 — The XL-19B sets the world's light aircraft altitude record.

1957 — First shipments of the CH-1 Skyhook helicopter are delivered to the Army.

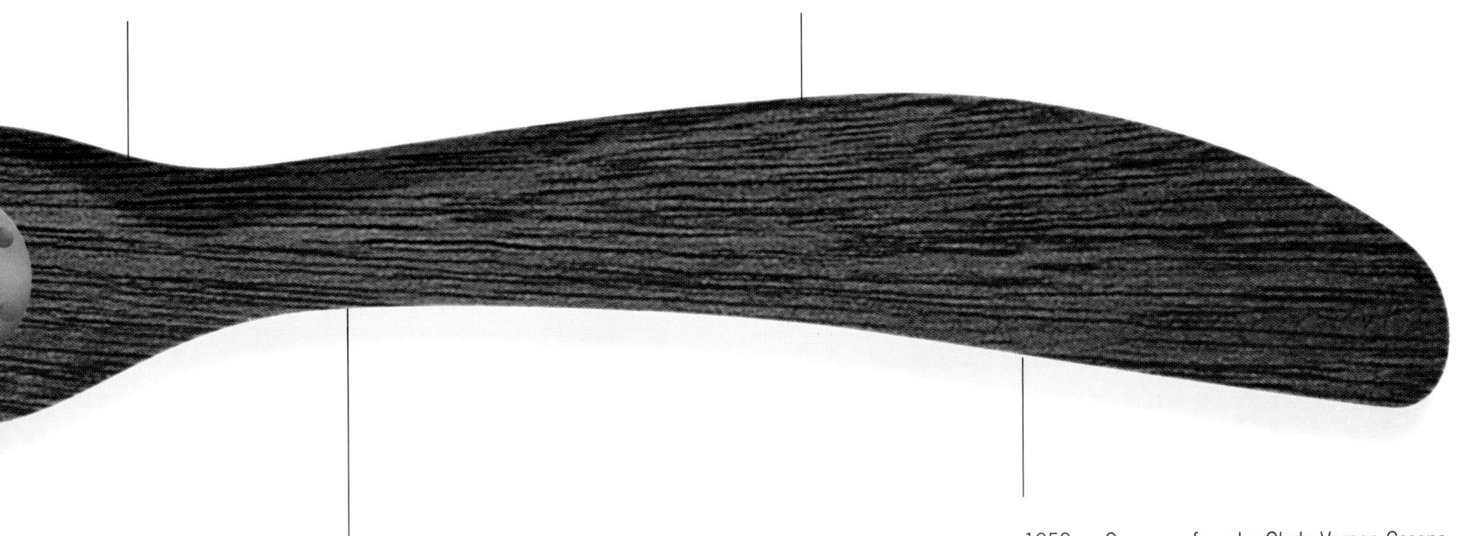

October 12, 1953 — The XT-37 takes its first flight.

1959 — Company founder Clyde Vernon Cessna dies at his Rago, Kansas farm.

"Cessna's distinguished guest advised his attentive audience that he was going to write General Matthew Ridgway, who is intimately familiar with the stellar performance of the L-19 in battle areas, tell him about his visit to Cessna, and ask General Ridgway to write the Cessna people of the L-19 assignments in Korea and of the heroic men who fly them.

"General Clark commended the Cessna Company and its employees for being on time with production schedules for the L-19 and stated frankly that he wished he could say the same for many other organizations engaged in defense production."[15]

Throughout 1951, Cessna produced more than a hundred Bird Dogs a month. Government payment for these remarkable planes took some time, recalled Don Hammer, who retired as manager of credits and collections in 1982. "Our contract was off by less than a dollar," he said. "They accounted for every penny, and in some cases you'd be off by two or three cents, something ridiculous, and then you would have to sit down with the government people and find out where it had disappeared."[16] Eventually, payment was made, he added.

The plane was praised by the pilots who relied on it in life-and-death situations. Capt. Charles Posz wrote a letter to Cessna, saying the plane had saved his life after he was hit by enemy fire at 6,000 feet. One shell tore six feet off the right wing, but Posz was able to jam the controls to the left and fly the plane for a full hour to the nearest Air Force base for a crash landing. "During this period, at speeds never below 110 miles per hour, it's a wonder the severe strain didn't tear off more of the damaged wing," he wrote. "Please accept my heartfelt thanks for building an airplane that could take the beating we gave this one."[17]

The L-19 Bird Dog was not sexy like a fighter or fearsome like a bomber. But it was fast, reliable and crucial to the success of the U.S. Army during the Korean War.

Capt. John J. Walters, commanding officer of IX Corps' 4th Light Aviation Section in Korea, described the Bird Dog as "worth its weight in gold."

"With more than 550 hours of flying time in this light plane, he believes it's got everything that a flier could want for front line flying, including comfort. Speed, maneuverability, and 360-degree visibility have gained recognition for the L-19 as being unbeatable for all-around observation work."[18]

Above and below: The Bird Dog was redesigned with a more powerful engine, a 265-horsepower Continental, and became Cessna Model 321. The military designated it the OE-2.

In July 1951, Lt. D.M. Casselman visited Cessna after 150 hours of front-line action because he wanted to see where the planes were made. "It is certainly the nicest liaison plane I've ever flown," said the 2nd Infantry pilot. "It outperforms anything we had." He noted that the plane required hardly any maintenance, even after it had been riddled with bullet holes. "We'd just file down the hole and rivet a patch on it."[19] The L-19 flown by Casselman played a part in *The Korean Story*, starring Robert Mitchum. The 1952 movie was filmed at Camp Carson, where Casselman was assigned when he returned from Korea.[20]

In 1951, Cessna sent L.A. Vanderlip to Korea to serve as a company representative and advisor. "I never had one minute's trouble with anybody about the L-19," Vanderlip reported. "The product lived up to all expectations so well that it was a pleasure to say that you were with Cessna."[21] The plane was even used by Army engineers.

"The 73rd Engineer Combat Battalion, a typical outfit, is now using the L-19 to make daily reconnaissance flights to see how engineer projects are progressing and to keep a constant check on road maintenance.

"Once a week, the plane is flown over the front lines with an aerial photographer to get a complete picture of the changes made along the front in the 73rd's sector. The photos are used to pinpoint the movements made by the enemy and the United Nation's forces.

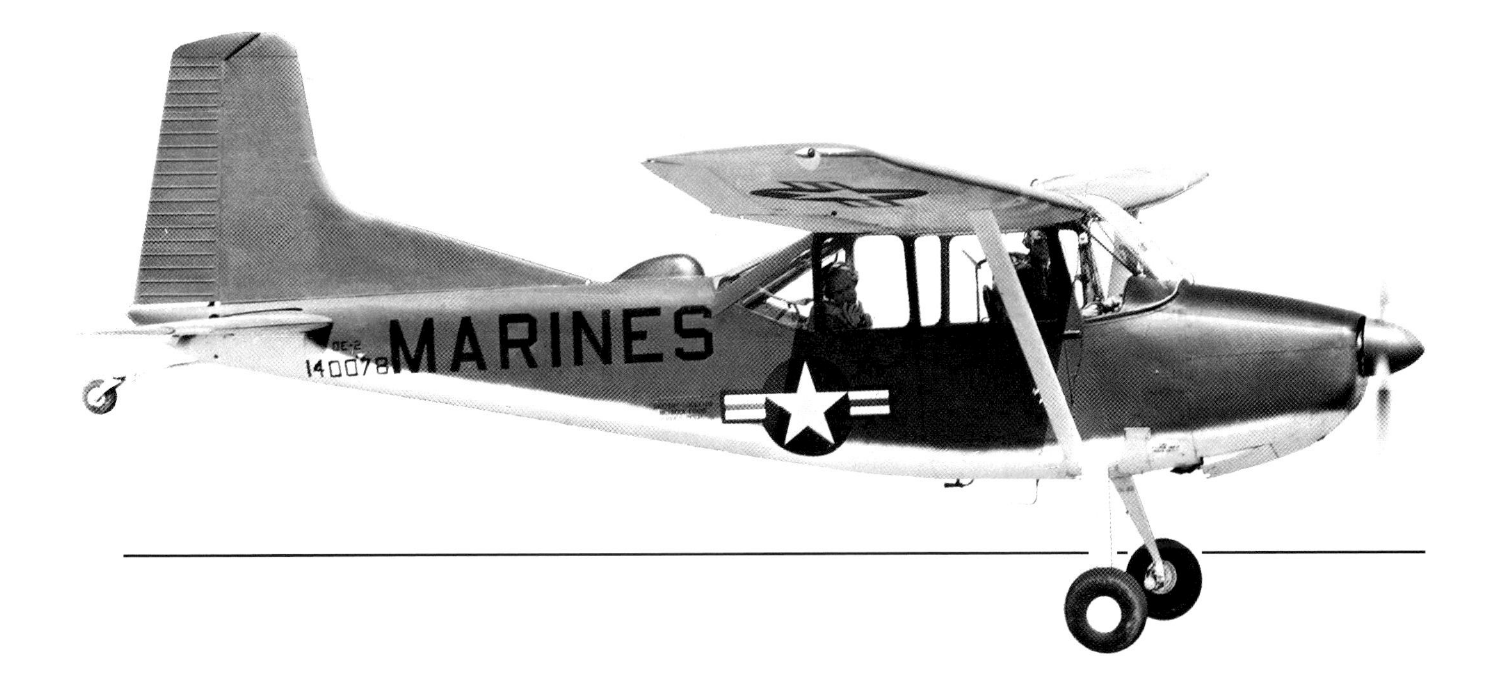

"Especially important, according to Capt. Murray, is the plane's ability to 'change direction and altitude in a helluva hurry,' a handy asset when the enemy opens fire."[22]

News of the L-19's performance reached other branches of the military. The United States Navy placed an initial order for 25, giving the planes its own designation of OE-1 even though they were identical to the L-19s except for their paint scheme. By the end of 1953, Cessna had received orders for 60 OE-1s.[23]

CAA flight certification for a high-performance version of the L-19, the OE-2, was received on May 18, 1955. The Marine Corps ordered 25 in May and additional units in October.[24]

The Bird Dog After the War

Although production of the Bird Dog was officially discontinued in October 1954, Cessna won a contract for 100 L-19s in July 1955. A letter in the *Cessquire* — written from the point of view of the old favorite — explained why it was returning to the production line.

"Dear Cessnans:

"You can't keep a good dog down. Although you bade me a fond farewell last October when the 'last' of my family of 2,480 trotted out of the Pawnee Road factory, I'm coming back!

"You designed me so well and built me so soundly that the army wants a hundred more of me, proving General Mark Clark wasn't exaggerating when he declared I was 'the best plane the army has' back in 1951 when he christened me.

"Believe me, I've seen a lot since then. I've served, and am still serving, wherever the United States Army goes, under all conditions of climate and terrain. You gave me the attributes of success, and I made your name known in far-off places.

"This time I'll be used as an instrument trainer instead of an observation plane. I'll have electrically controlled flaps and two complete sets of instruments, one for the student and one for the instructor.

"You are already ordering materials and making plans for my return. Next summer I'll be coming off the line to take up my new duties. See you then.

Gratefully,
Cessna L-19 Bird Dog"[25]

After it was resurrected, the Bird Dog became a truly international creature. On

A U.S. Army XL-19C, powered by a turboprop engine.

September 24, 1956, Cessna forged an agreement with Fuji Heavy Industries to manufacture L-19s in Japan.[26] The first one rolled off the Fuji Heavy Industries, Ltd., production line in 1957.[27] In 1959, the French government ordered 70 L-19s.

The L-19 was nothing if not versatile. In the early fifties, it received CAA certification for both skis and floats. The prototype with floats was tested in watery New Orleans, Louisiana, while the one fitted with skis was tested in snowy Iowa City, Iowa. Later modifications resulted in the TL-19D, an instrument trainer version, which became available in 1956.[28]

Turbocharging

Another variation of the L-19 was the XL-19B, the world's first turbocharged light airplane. This version was a joint project between the U.S. Army, the U.S. Air Force, Cessna and Boeing, built for evaluation by the Air Force and powered by a 210-horsepower Boeing XT-50-BO-1.[29]

Planes with turbocharged engines offered vast improvements in power over their normally aspirated counterparts, especially in high altitude and high density altitude conditions.

Probably best known for setting the world's light aircraft altitude record of 37,063 feet on July 16, 1953, only one was ever built.[30] The ship was destroyed when the engine failed during an evaluation flight. It flipped over, and the pilot was forced to crash-land into a fence. Though the pilot was injured, he survived.[31]

A 200-horsepower, French-made Continental-Turbomeca Artouste I was installed in a X-19B in August 1953, and the new turboprop version, the XL-19C, made its first flight on September 1, 1953. This new version had twice the fuel capacity of the standard L-19 — a total of 84 gallons in two tanks. Two of these ships were built in 1955, but the turboprop engines were eventually removed and the planes were converted back to standard L-19s, retaining their larger fuel capacity.[32]

In 1962, the United States forces changed its L-19 series designation of the Model 305 to the O-1 designation. The OE-2, also known as model 321, was a higher-performance version of the OE-1 ordered by the Marine Corps. Powered by a 265-horsepower supercharged Continental TSO-470-2, this machine boasted an instrument panel lighted in red, an armor plate for the pilot, and flak curtains. Electrically operated flaps replaced the manual flaps in the OE-1, and the horizontal and vertical tail surfaces were redesigned into a rectangular shape with a large dorsal fin. Larger fuel tanks and a constant-speed propeller completed the upgrade. On the prototype's maiden voyage August 19, 1954, it reached a top speed of 180 miles per hour.

The prototype was first flown by engineering test pilot R.L. "Bob" Crawshaw. It was reported to have reached a top speed of 180 miles per hour with a service ceiling of 26,000 feet. Cessna delivered the first of 25 OE-2s to the Marine Corps in the summer of 1955, but its high price prohibited the military from ordering more.[33]

Fickle Government Regulations

Although Cessna had won valuable contracts from the military, the company sometimes met with frustration when dealing with the government's inevitable red tape. The Model 308 was a good example. The six-place cargo plane had been developed by Cessna in 1951 for deployment by the Army as an aerial ambulance, light cargo and observation aircraft. Army officials had initially expressed interest in a Canadian aircraft, the De Havilland Beaver, but flight restrictions barred them from operating aircraft with gross weights in excess of 5,000 pounds.

With no other aircraft available to meet the Army's specifications, Cessna seized the opportunity to develop a suitable contender. The Model 308 made its first flight during the summer of 1951 and was ready for the Army's evaluation six months later.[34] However, during the evaluation period, the military regulations concerning gross weight were changed and the Army went back to its first choice of the Beaver. Cessna continued to work on the airplane and in the spring of 1953 demonstrated it again to the Army at Fort Bragg. Again, the Army declined to purchase the plane. The Cessna 308 was returned to the plant and disassembled.[35]

Jet Propulsion

In December 1952, Cessna's first jet aircraft, designated the XT-37, was chosen by the United States Air Force as its first jet trainer. The news, as written by the Associated Press, appeared in newspapers across the country on the last day of the year.

"The air force tonight chose a small, light airplane with two French-designed jet engines — the Cessna Model 318 — as its first true jet trainer.

"The plane will be by far the smallest jet aircraft, with the smallest engines in the air force. It will also be that air force rarity, a twin-jet craft, taking its place alongside the only twin-jet fighter, the Northrop F-89 Scorpion interceptor and the not-yet-operational B-57 light bomber, a Martin modification of the British Canberra.

"The air force announced it would award a contract to the Cessna Aircraft Company of Wichita, Kansas, for development of the twin-jet primary training aircraft.

"Heretofore, the air force has been using, for training purposes, combat aircraft or modified combat types. The standard jet trainer is a two-seat-in-tandem version of the single-seat fighter, the F-80 Shooting Star.

"The air force said the Cessna design was chosen for further development from among 15 design proposals submitted by eight aircraft manufacturers. ...

"The plane will be powered by two 900-pound thrust jet engines designed by the Societe Turbomeca, France, and built in the United States by the Continental Motors Corporation, Muskegon, Michigan."[36]

Jet airplanes, with their faster and more efficient engines, were gaining importance after World War II, and Cessna was eager to be part of this emerging new market. The company's proposal for a jet aircraft to train student pilots was chosen over submissions from eight other companies, and on October 12, 1953, a XT-37 made its first flight from the new

The Cessna Model 308 was a six-place cargo plane developed for the Army, which originally wanted to purchase the De Havilland Beaver but could not because of weight restrictions. The restrictions were eventually lifted, to the dismay of Cessna executives.

The T-37 "Tweety Bird" was the military's primary jet trainer for more than 40 years.

Wichita Municipal Airport with Bob Hagan at the controls. Structural tests began in February 1954, and a year later, Cessna received a $1 million contract from the Air Force for production of the T-37.[37] Bruce Peterman, who joined Cessna in 1953 and worked on the T-37, remembered that the Air Force liked the plane for several reasons. "The Air Force had decided it was going to go to an all-jet force, and the twin-engine was unique as well," said Peterman, who became chief engineer in 1972 and retired in 1996 as senior vice president. "Those two things really captured the imagination of the military. ... The T-37 is a remarkable airplane."[38]

In August 1955, one of the prototypes was lost in a crash near Lake Afton west of Wichita during spin evaluation, although test pilot Hagan was fortunately able to parachute to safety, according to the *Cessquire*.

> *"Bob put the plane into a spin deliberately, as a normal part of the testing routine. When the spin became critical he released the spin chute, a device designed to stabilize the plane in recovering from such a maneuver. The spin chute became detached and vanished.*
>
> *"Bob stayed as long as possible in an attempt to save the airplane he had brought home from so many test flights during the last ten months. Finally, at an altitude of 12,000 to 14,000 feet, he was forced to jettison the canopy and eject the seat. His automatic-opening parachute deposited him, uninjured, on a creek bank a mile from the wreckage.*
>
> *"The missing spin chute was found five days later by a Viola farmer and was turned over to an Air Force investigation team in an effort to learn why it failed to operate."*[39]

The spin problem was solved by Cessna engineers Lloyd Long and Harry Clements in November 1956 by lengthening the tail cone and placing five-foot, two-inch-wide metal extrusions, known as strakes, along each side of the jet's nose.

> *"It was a rather unusual problem. According to the National Advisory Committee for Aeronautics (NACA), no other plane with fuel massed in the wings (as the T-37) has ever met similar spin requirements. Although several modifications were involved in the development, the strakes were the final victory.*
>
> *"The British have been using them for years, but as far as I know, this is the only aircraft today with forward strakes. They slow down spins and make recovery easy. From a scientific viewpoint, I think the outstanding achievement is overcoming the weight of the wing fuel when asymmetrically placed.*
>
> *"A number of flight tests determined the strakes' length and width. Final size was fixed after the jet attained normal stall characteristics, which varied with strakes of different sizes.*

U.S. Army Lt. Col. Paul Wagner, center, and Lt. Col. Horace Beaman, right, shown talking to Charles Seibel, Cessna chief helicopter engineer, in front of a Cessna YH-41 Helicopter.

"Upswept dihedral wing tips, ventral fins, and exceptionally large 'up' elevator deflection also aided in ironing out the spin problem."[40]

Shortly after the first shipment of T-37s was delivered, the Air Force signed a follow-up contract for $3.5 million. Though the T-37 was originally used for training, the Army decided in 1957 to use it as a utility reconnaissance airplane.[41] The following year, Cessna received a $12.35 million contract.[42]

The T-37B, which went into production in 1959, featured two major improvements over the T-37A. Its high thrust engines — boosted from 920 pounds to 1,025 pounds — increased reliability and performance while reducing maintenance. State-of-the-art electronic equipment greatly improved navigation and communication capabilities.[43]

To provide appropriate airfield facilities for the jet, construction began in 1956 on a facility across the street from the Prospect Plant and next door to the new Wichita Municipal Airport (now Mid-Continent Airport). The new facility, named the Wallace Plant after Cessna President Dwane Wallace, included a flight hangar built by the city and leased by Cessna. The metal building, located north of the existing municipal hangar that was occupied by Cessna, provided 24,000 square feet of floor space.[44]

By the second half of the fifties, T-37s, used for Air Force training purposes, were affectionately known as "Tweety Bird," or "Tweet," for short.[45] The T-37 was one of the safest, most reliable aircraft in Air Force use — and was its primary trainer for more than 40 years.

Helicopters

The Cessna Aircraft Company entered the helicopter market on April 11, 1952, when it purchased the Seibel Helicopter Company, Inc., its first acquisition. The company, founded in April 1948, had sold several helicopters to the United States government for evaluation purposes, but the company could not afford to stay in business without Cessna's help. As part of the acquisition, Charles Seibel and his engineering staff joined Cessna.[46]

Helicopters were still relatively new, with the first successful flight having taken place in 1936. Because they derive their lift from power-driven rotors instead of fixed wings, the highly maneuverable machines could rise or descend vertically, hover, and move forward, backward or sideways.

After Cessna acquired the Seibel Helicopter Company it began producing the Cessna Skyhook helicopter.

Cessna's first helicopter, the CH-1 Skyhook, began development in 1952 and was ready for test flights in 1953. Intended for the military market, the Skyhook reached a top speed of 120 miles per hour, could climb from sea level to 10,000 feet in under 10 minutes and could hover at an altitude of more than 15,000 feet. The helicopter was powered with a Continental FSO-470-A engine with 260 horsepower. Fuel capacity of 60 gallons allowed a cruise distance of 270 miles with a flight endurance of 3.7 hours.[47]

The CH-1 helicopter received FAA certification in 1955 and underwent demonstration flights for both military and commercial prospects. During one such demonstration, the helicopter hovered over Pikes Peak, in the heart of Colorado's Rocky Mountains.[48] The event was described in the September 30, 1955, issue of the *Cessquire.*

"Climaxing a series of altitude evaluation tests, Cessna's helicopter test pilot, Jack

JET PROPULSION

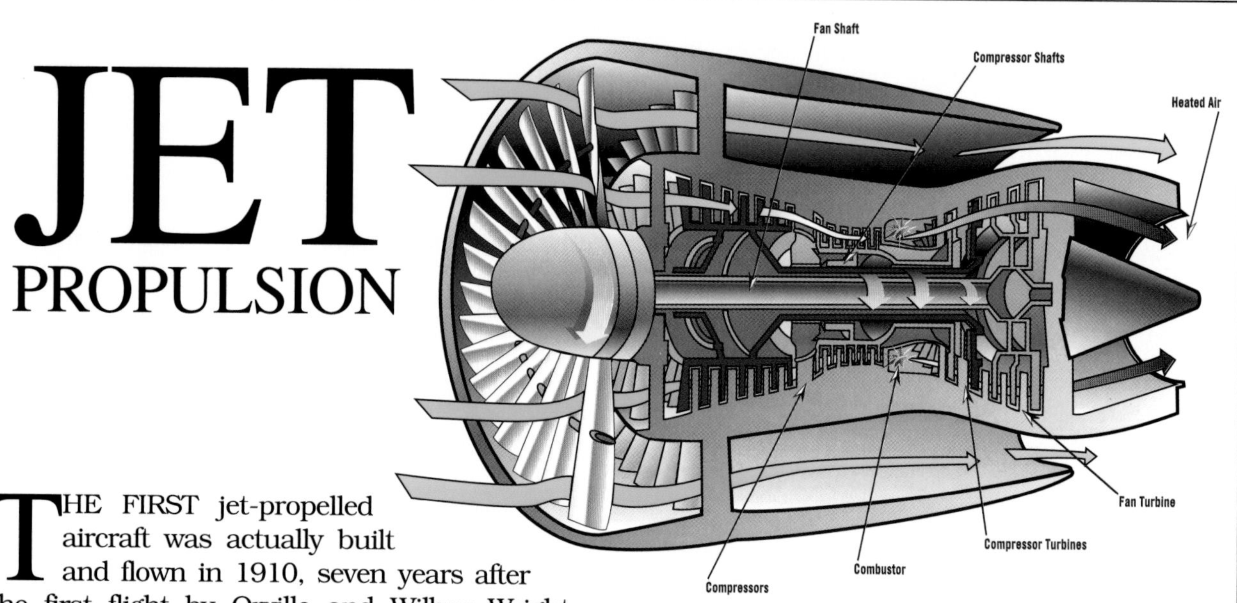

THE FIRST jet-propelled aircraft was actually built and flown in 1910, seven years after the first flight by Orville and Wilbur Wright. French scientist Henri Marie Coanda designed and built a biplane powered by a gas turbine engine, which he called the reaction motor. The idea never caught on, and a discouraged Coanda abandoned the concept.

A jet engine operates by compressing air sucked in through the front of the engine, mixing it with fuel and igniting the mixture, which expands with great force and is exhausted from the rear, pushing the craft forward. This uses the principles of Newton's Third Law of Motion, which states that for every action, there is an equal and opposite reaction.[1]

There are several types of jet engines, but the most popular commercial/general aviation type is the turbofan, a derivative of the turbojet. A large fan in front of the compressor section pulls an enormous amount of air into the engine casing. A small percentage of air is sent through the core to be mixed with fuel for combustion to produce the jet reaction, while the rest flows outside the core case, and inside the engine casing. The fan flow is mixed with hot jet exhaust in the engine's rear, where it cools and quiets the exhaust noise.[2]

The fan itself produces a tremendous amount of thrust, acting as a propeller, while the aircraft is boosted by the jet action at the rear of the engine.

Zimmerman, landed atop Pikes Peak at exactly 7:00 a.m., MST, September 13. After completing the first aircraft landing on the peak its discoverer said would never be climbed, Jack conducted hovering demonstrations over the 14,110-foot summit with Capt. Robert Knowles of Fort Carson as passenger.

"To fully exercise the CH-1's ability, he took aboard a second passenger and hovered over the peak with three aboard. After this, Lt. Gen. John Van Houten, commanding general of Fort Carson, climbed in. The pilot took off, gained approximately 1,000 feet of altitude above the peak, and returned the general to his post at Fort Carson."[49]

Deliveries of the CH-1, designated by the Army as the YH-41 Seneca, began in July 1957. The machine became the Army's highest performance small helicopter.[50]

World headlines were made on December 28, 1958 when an Army Seneca YH-1 piloted by Capt. James Bowman set three world altitude helicopter records above Wichita, soaring to 30,355 feet.[51]

A breakthrough in helicopter design was achieved in 1959 when the new CH-1C was certified by the FAA. It was the first helicopter to achieve inherent stability comparable to that of a fixed-wing aircraft, without dependence on any electronic stabilizing devices.[52]

The Death of a Pioneer

The same year that Cessna entered a new area of aircraft technology, its founder, namesake and first innovator, Clyde Vernon Cessna, died of a heart attack at his Rago, Kansas, farm at age 74. Clyde had retired to the farm with his wife, Europa, in 1936.

After Dwane Wallace helped him reignite the company, Clyde returned to the quiet lifestyle of farming he knew as a boy, supplementing his living by selling farm equipment such as grain augers and chain saws.[53]

After his retirement, Clyde seldom left his home. He did, however, make a public appearance for the opening of Wichita's new Municipal Airport (now the Mid-Continent Airport) earlier in 1954.[54]

During his life, Clyde received many honors and awards for his contributions to aviation. On February 28, 1953, he had received a telegram from President Eisenhower, which read:

"Congratulations for the prominent part you have played in the early development of aviation. Your work has been a splendid contribution to this great industry and Kansas can be proud of your memorable pioneering in this field."[55]

Clyde was buried at the Belmont Cemetery near his parents. A flyover of jet aircraft saluted one of aviation's earliest pioneers.[56]

The Model 180 was equipped with a 225-horsepower Continental engine that yielded top speeds of 165 miles per hour.

THE COMMERCIAL MARKET IN THE FIFTIES

1950–1959

"Personal aviation is no longer to be considered in the light of recreational flying."

— *Wichita Eagle*, 1951[1]

A 1959 advertisement for the Model 150 emphasized the affordability of the two-place trainer.

AFTER THE UNITED STATES entered the Korean conflict, Cessna began turning out the sturdy L-19 Bird Dog in impressive numbers. The war was bloody and miserable, but unlike World War II, it was not an all-encompassing struggle. Although some restrictions were placed on materials, civilians did not have to do without.

Cessna, like so many businesses in America, entered a remarkable period of growth by catering to both military and civilian needs. Aviation had evolved from an adventure to a convenience, particularly for business travelers who needed to cover hundreds of miles on a weekly basis.

"Personal aviation is no longer to be considered in the light of recreational flying," noted the *Wichita Eagle* in 1951. "It is a business proposition and although the same plane that carries an executive about his business during the week may also be used over the weekend on a pleasure jaunt, its principal purpose is to serve industry efficiently, safely and economically."[2]

Cessna filled this new need with planes that were fast, safe and comfortable. The enormous success of the L-19 as a military plane inspired Cessna to offer a similar large-flap wing design to commercial customers. Engineers added the "super-lift flaps" to the popular 170 in 1952, designating it the 170B. The company advertised the improvement by linking the 170 to the Bird Dog.

"Proved in combat on the famous L-19 Bird Dog Army observation plane. ... NOW available to you on the 1952 Cessna 170! These flaps reduce landing speed more than 10 percent. Combined with the Cessna patented landing gear, they give you shorter take-offs, safe landings even on short, rough fields."[3]

The Model 180 was also introduced during this period. Considered a workhorse, the 180 was a four-place monoplane with a high wing design and a 225-horsepower six-cylinder Continental engine that gave it top speeds of 165 miles per hour. The plane, first sold in March 1953, was the first Cessna model to abandon the traditional rounded tail design in favor of a square tail that would be used throughout the remainder of the fifties. A 1954 advertisement claimed that the plane offered the "smoothest power possible ... so smooth

The Model 172 featured a new tail design and Cessna's patented Land-O-Matic tricycle landing gear.

that when the engine is running, you can even rest a glass of water on the cowling without disturbing the water!"[4]

172 and 182

The year 1956 has been described by one aviation author as "momentous" for Cessna: "It was a year that two of their best-selling taildraggers would be modified into two of the most heavily produced tricycle gear airplanes in the world."[5]

The 172, shrewdly marketed toward the growing class of business pilots, was basically a 170B, modified with a patented Land-O-Matic tricycle landing gear and new tail design. The new landing gear replaced the taildragging design, which could cause inexperienced pilots to ground

1952 — The 170B, a Bird Dog modified for the civilian market, is introduced.

1954 — Production of the Model 310 luxury businessliner begins.

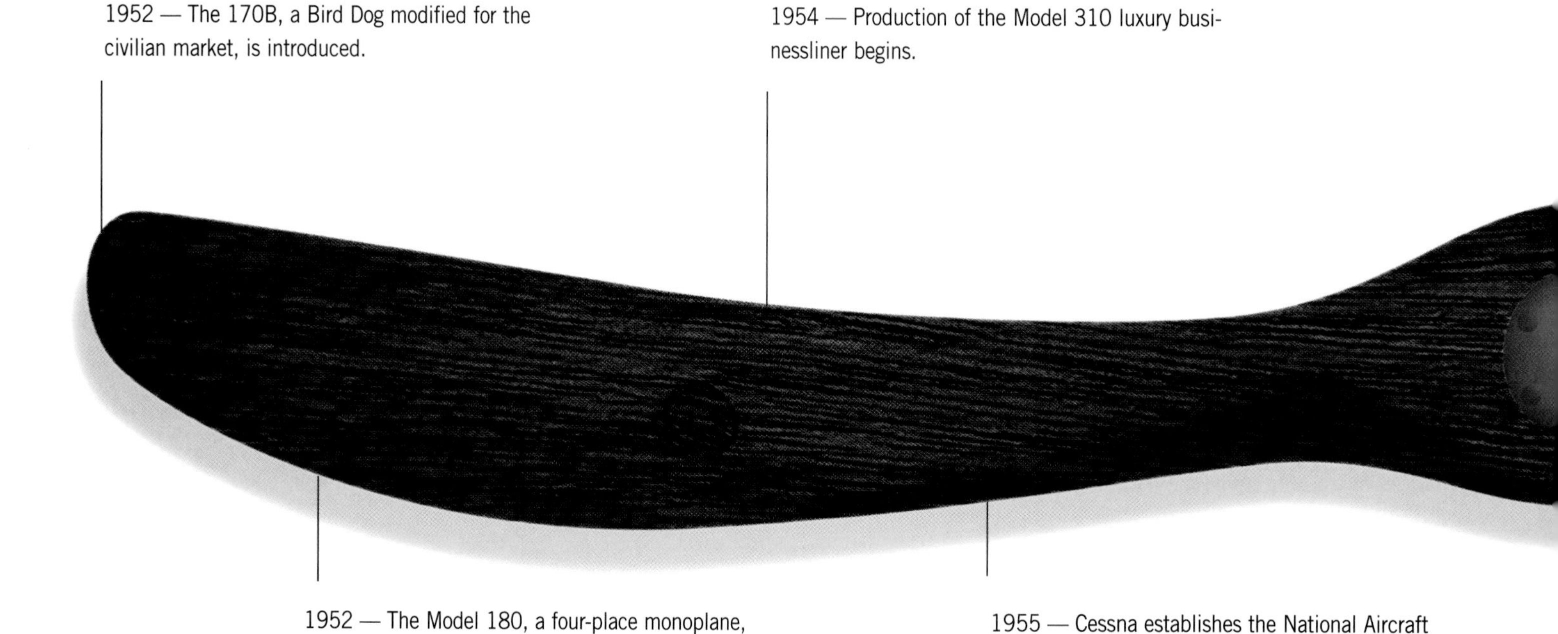

1952 — The Model 180, a four-place monoplane, is introduced.

1955 — Cessna establishes the National Aircraft Finance Company to increase sales of businessliners.

loop on landing. The improved model was introduced with no price increase, selling for $8,295.[6]

The snazzier 182 Skylane was a 180 with the same Land-O-Matic landing gear and redesigned cowling, offered at $13,750. The 182 Skylane was built for the pilot who wanted more of everything, as aviation author James Ellis wrote.

> *"The 182 Skylane is the airplane for the pilot ... who is just a little dissatisfied with the 172, which often seems to be a bit underpowered, a little too light, and a little too little all around. There's nothing too little or too underpowered about the Skylane. This is a big, solid, powerful handful ... an honest airplane."*[7]

Both planes featured Paralift flaps, which made it easier for pilots to reduce landing speed, take off from short runways, and clear obstacles.[8] The new landing gear and lower center of gravity allowed pilots to handle the airplane with much greater ease. A steerable nose wheel improved maneuverability and became one of the model's major selling points, since it allowed the 172 to turn around on a 30-foot taxi strip with room to spare.

Cessna's sales strategy during the fifties was twofold: first sell the concept of using aircraft for business. Then sell the businessman a Cessna by pointing out how popular its planes were. The story of Ward McDowell, who owned a manufacturing business with his brother, was typical.

> *"One day a friend invited Ward to lunch. The friend took him to the airport and then flew him 50 miles. The two had a good meal and were back at work as soon*

A 1958 Model 172.

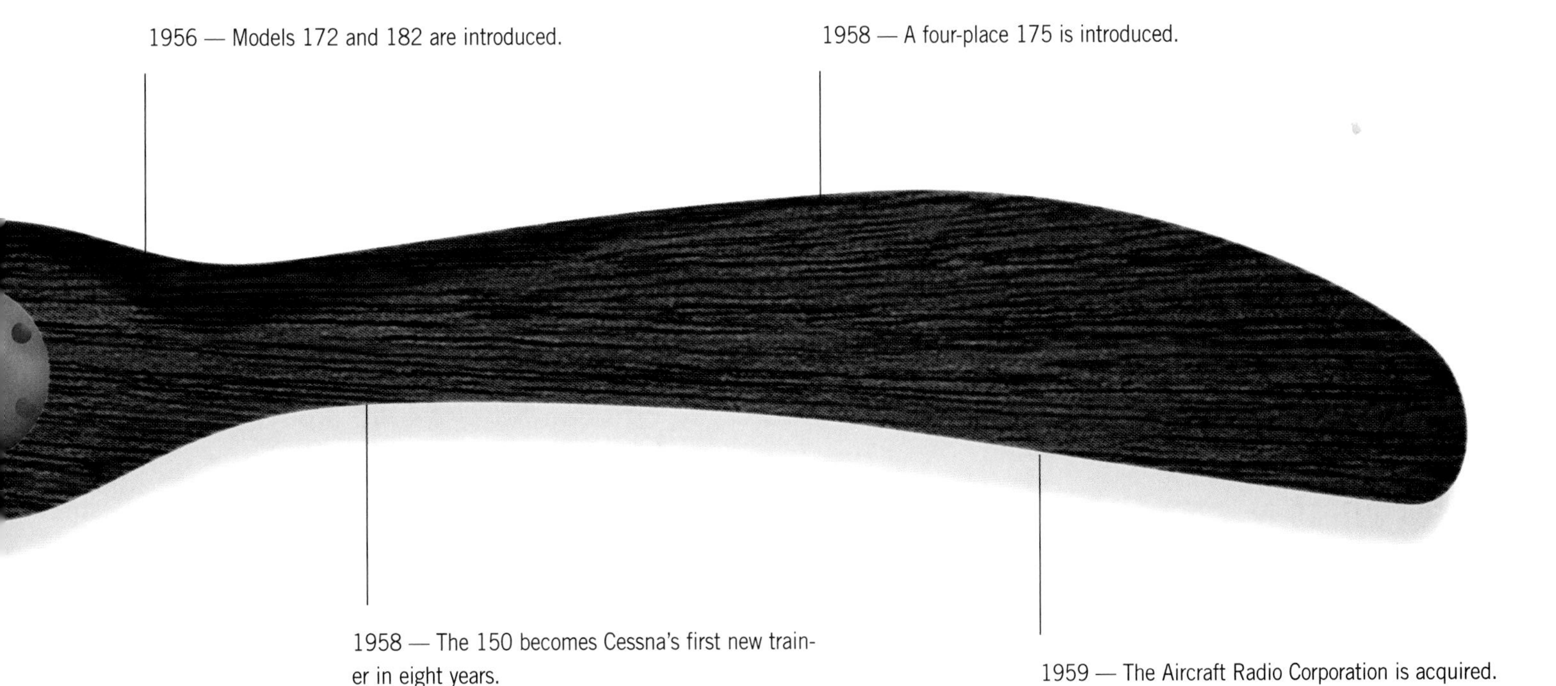

1956 — Models 172 and 182 are introduced.

1958 — A four-place 175 is introduced.

1958 — The 150 becomes Cessna's first new trainer in eight years.

1959 — The Aircraft Radio Corporation is acquired.

Above: A Model 182A showcases its Land-O-Matic gear in 1958.

as if they had dined in the suburbs. The flight made Ward realize how he could save time by flying a plane when calling on the trade.

"The brothers bought a used plane, and in it, after he learned to fly, Ward visited all of his dealers in a fraction of the time he spent while driving a car.

"Then a friend told him of the Cessna Land-O-Matic and Paralift. He went to J.C. Kemper, the Ft. Worth Cessna dealer, who demonstrated the advantages of these two devices. 'That's the plane for me,' exclaimed Mr. Ward McDowell. He traded his used plane for a Cessna 172. It chanced that the sale was the 1,000th 172 since being placed on the market only 10 months before."[9]

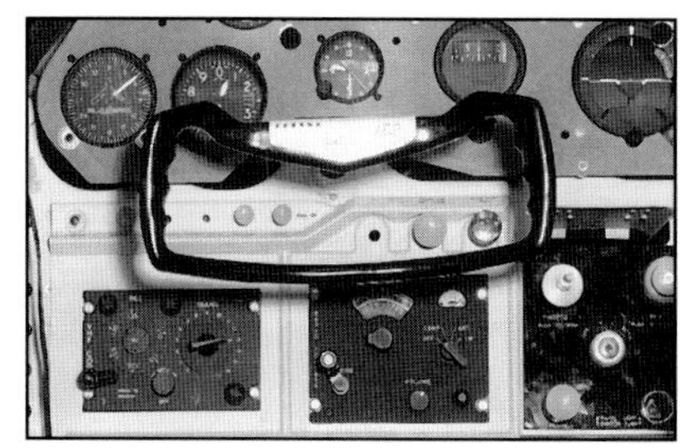

Below: The control panel of a 1957 Model 182A.

The four-place 175 — basically a 172 with a geared engine — was introduced in 1958 to fill the price gap between the 172 and 182. The ship was powered by a six-cylinder 175-horsepower engine, producing a top speed of more than 147 miles per hour, and included adjustable front seats, stainless steel mufflers, and electric fuel and oil gauges as standard features.[10]

In 1960, a deluxe version of the 175, known as the Skylark, was introduced for $13,050.[11] Slightly heavier, with more refined interior appointments, the Skylark also offered an engine-driven vacuum system for gyroscopic flight instruments.[12]

The 310

Production of the Model 310 luxury businessliner began in 1954.[13] "The sleek, all-metal twin-engine ship represented a new beginning for Cessna that had actually started in 1951 when the company realized that many pilots wanted and needed a modern, light, multi-engine airplane," noted author Edward H. Phillips.[14]

Advertised as the newest and fastest executive transportation on the market, the five-place low-winged airplane was powered by two 240-horsepower engines that delivered a cruising speed of more than 205 miles per hour and could climb 380 feet a minute on a single engine.[15] The ship had space for 200 pounds of luggage and sold for $49,950 when it first went on the market.[16]

It was the first twin model to offer wingtip fuel tanks as standard equipment, a design that increased the airplane's lift. The original production line for the Model 310 consisted of about 160 employees who turned out 10 to 12 of the planes a month.[17] Cessna had correctly predicted the emergence of an important market. By 1955, production exceeded 20 planes a month.[18]

The popular 310 helped Cessna lead the entire business aircraft market in 1956.[19] To handle the increased business, a hangar was built in 1956 to house the 310s, a small delivery operations building was erected, and an addition was made to the flight service hangar.[20]

The Model 310B, introduced in 1957, was made even more convenient and luxurious. Updated features included a revamped instrument panel with some updated instruments, minimum windshield glare, and sophisticated interior lighting with four separate zones.[21]

The 310B was featured in the 1950s western *Sky King*, featuring America's only cowboy pilot, Sky (Kirby Grant), and his 310B, *Songbird II*,

Above: Kirby Grant of *Sky King* fame exchanges greetings with a well wisher.

Below: Cessna hoped to capture the growing light twin-engine market with the Model 310, introduced in 1954.

which replaced the show's original *Songbird*, a Cessna T-50.[22]

A military version of the 310 was delivered to the Air Force in 1957. The Army designated the planes L-27A (U-3A) and used them for administrative and light cargo transportation.[23]

Cessna established the National Aircraft Finance Company, Inc., in August 1955, a wholly owned subsidiary to handle financing for commercial aircraft, including leased planes and dealer demonstrators.[24] With this move, Cessna hoped to increase sales of businessliners.[25] Four years later, NAFCO entered the retail aircraft financing business, allowing monthly payments on aircraft with one-quarter of the price down. In addition, the company began offering full insurance coverage, making it possible for customers to purchase, finance and insure their airplanes all in one place.[26]

The entire Cessna fleet is shown in this 1958 advertisement.

A Good Plane at the Wrong Time

Executives of large corporations, hoping to escape the scheduling whims of major airlines, found it cost-effective and more convenient to travel in company planes. But airliners were much safer in bad weather. With this in mind, Cessna introduced the Model 620 in 1956, the world's first four-engine fully-pressurized executive transport, with room for nine passengers and a crew of two.[27] The plane's number was a bit of an inside joke — it was supposed to be twice as much plane as the 310. The preliminary price of $375,000 excluded electronic and wing de-icing equipment.[28] Although the 620 was a good plane, the timing was wrong. Around this time, commercial airlines were purchasing jet planes, which used gas turbine technology to boost speed

and engine efficiency. The planes were also more comfortable. A market glut of traditional aircraft drove down prices to the point where the new 620 could never become profitable.[29]

Unfortunately, a number of employees had been counting on that plane as a tool to recruit new engineers. Don Powell, a recruiter hired in 1952, recalled spending $25,000 on a film and promotional literature. The film, called "Eye to the Sky," generated considerable interest when it was first shown in the auditorium at Wichita State University. The next day, the 620 was canceled.

"Every vestige of the 620 was to be abolished. Immediately. I had little plastic slide rules with '620' on them, all kinds of gimmicks that I handed out in places. When I got back to the office, I asked what the story was. The story I got was that management was under heavy criticism by the stockholders for spending money on a model that had no chance to make money. So they took the plane, took the engines out, and ran a bulldozer over the whole thing."[30]

This Cessna Model 620 was the only one ever built. It was disassembled in 1959.

Diversification

After an eight-year hiatus from the trainer market, Cessna introduced the 150 in 1958. This two-seater was available in three models — Standard, Trainer and Commuter, with prices ranging from $6,995 to $8,545. The day the plane became available, more than 600 orders were placed, creating the single largest day of sales in the company's history.[31]

Despite its low price tag, the 150 offered Cessna's Land-O-Matic and Paralift features, as well as a shock-mounted instrument panel with instant readability. Dubbed the "world's easiest-to-fly airplane," the ship cruised at 121 miles per hour and was available in forest green, damask red and colonial blue.

On June 19, 1959, Cessna opened an East Coast Branch Office at the Municipal Airport in Morristown, New Jersey. The new office complex consisted of a 7,000-square-foot hangar and warehouse area, and 2,400 square feet of office space.[32]

Aircraft Radio Corporation of Boonton, New Jersey was acquired by Cessna on February 2, 1959 by an exchange in stock.[33] The company, which specialized in the development, design and manufacture of electronic communication and navigation equipment, operated as a wholly owned subsidiary, remaining in New Jersey and retaining its management.[34] Cessna would sell ARC to Sperry Corporation in the mid-1980s.

The High Ground of the Cold War

Throughout the 1950s, Cessna took on subcontracting work as it had during World War II, producing various sections to be used in military aircraft: empennages for the B-47 Stratojet; stabilizers for the B-52 Stratofortress, which required the largest tooling program ever undertaken by Cessna;[35] $12 million worth of aft section assemblies for Lockheed Aircraft Corporation's T-33 jet trainer and the F-94B jet fighter; empennage assemblies, vertical fins, rudders and stabilizers for the F-84F jet fighter.

During World War II, Cessna had converted almost totally to war-related production; now it was determined to keep pace with both civilian and military markets. The Pawnee facility was expanded by 105,000 square feet between 1950 and 1954, and another hangar building was constructed at the Pawnee plant to house flight operations and a painting facility.

Right: The Cessna 150, with a top speed of 124 mph, was designed primarily for flight training, business and pleasure flying.

Below: Cessna acquired the Aircraft Radio Corporation of Boonton, New Jersey, in 1959.

Above: The Prospect plant provided Cessna with 150,000 square feet of additional work space.

The company also purchased the former Aero Parts plant, located five miles southwest of Wichita at Prospect, Kansas (now southwest Wichita), providing 150,000 square feet of additional work space to supply sections for the F-94B and the T-33 trainer.[36] A $2 million expansion program for the Hutchinson Plant began in 1959, more than doubling the size of the plant through the addition of 158,000 square feet of space.[37]

The following decade would see more of the same — an economy driven by both military and civilian demand. But Cessna would do more than provide observation or training craft. For the first time, a general aviation company would provide combat aircraft, which would be used over the deadly jungles of a place few Americans knew existed at that time.

The Super Skylane was added to Cessna's line of turbocharged airplanes in 1965.

GUNS AND BUTTER

1960–1970

"The work ethic was such that people stayed on the job, working 12 to 14 hours a day, trying to get 'em ready to leave for Vietnam."

— Arbery Barrett, 1997[1]

CESSNA'S MOMENTUM in the 1950s carried into the next decade, boosted by both commercial and military aircraft production. The economy of the 1960s was spurred by the "guns and butter" approach taken by manufacturers: companies worked to meet the needs of the military without lagging behind in supplying civilian demand. Cessna was able to meet this frenetic schedule by rapid foreign and domestic expansion.

From 1960 to 1970, Cessna introduced 16 new aircraft models, while continuing to improve its existing line of commercial aircraft. By 1970, Cessna customers could choose among 35 different airplanes, including many turbocharged models, helicopters and agricultural planes.[2] The military, meanwhile, continued orders of the vaunted L-19 Bird Dog for the Army and CH-1C helicopters for the Air Force and Navy,[3] along with the A-37B, a close-in support strike aircraft that saw extensive service in Vietnam.

Expanding in a Shrinking World

To meet the needs of military and civilian markets, Cessna grew quickly at both home and abroad. On August 1, 1960, the company acquired McCauley Industrial Corporation of Dayton, Ohio, and entered the propeller manufacturing business. The 22-year-old company offered a comprehensive line of fixed pitch, constant speed and full-feathering propellers for use on both business and private aircraft.

International expansion began in 1960 with Cessna's purchase of 49 percent of Reims Aviation, in Reims, France.[4] Cessna used this facility to manufacture the F-150 and F-172 models, later adding additional models to the production line.[5] The 172 Skyhawk manufactured in France was identical to the American version, except it was powered by Rolls-Royce engines built in England.[6] With scores of improvements and modifications over the years, the Skyhawk is the highest-volume commercial airplane ever produced.[7]

In 1963, construction was completed on a 120,000-square-foot addition to the Wallace Plant to house production of the growing line of twin-engine aircraft. Two years later, another 140,000 square feet were added to the Military and Twin Division in Wichita; 80,000 square feet were added to the Commercial Aircraft Division; and

Most of Cessna's 1960 models included this VOR, localizer and glideslope receiver, a sophisticated navigation instrument to help pilots find the airfield in limited visibility.

construction began on a modern service parts center that would speed the delivery of spare parts to customers around the world.[8]

With hydraulics becoming more widely used, a subsidiary was established in 1961 in Glenrothes, Scotland. Operating under the name Cessna Industrial Products, Ltd., the wholly owned subsidiary supplied industrial hydraulics to the United Kingdom.[9] Continuing its expansion in Europe, Cessna opened a sales and marketing branch office in Geneva, Switzerland, in 1963, which was moved to Brussels, Belgium, the following year when larger facilities became available.[10]

To honor Cessna's overseas expansion, President Lyndon Johnson in 1964 presented Dwane Wallace with the President's "E" for Export Award in a special White House ceremony.[11] A year later, Cessna opened a plant in Mendoza, Argentina, to manufacture the 172 and 182.

Cessna wasn't ready to stop growing. In both 1967 and 1968, facilities in Kansas again

Dwane Wallace receives the "E" for Export Award from President Lyndon Baines Johnson in 1964.

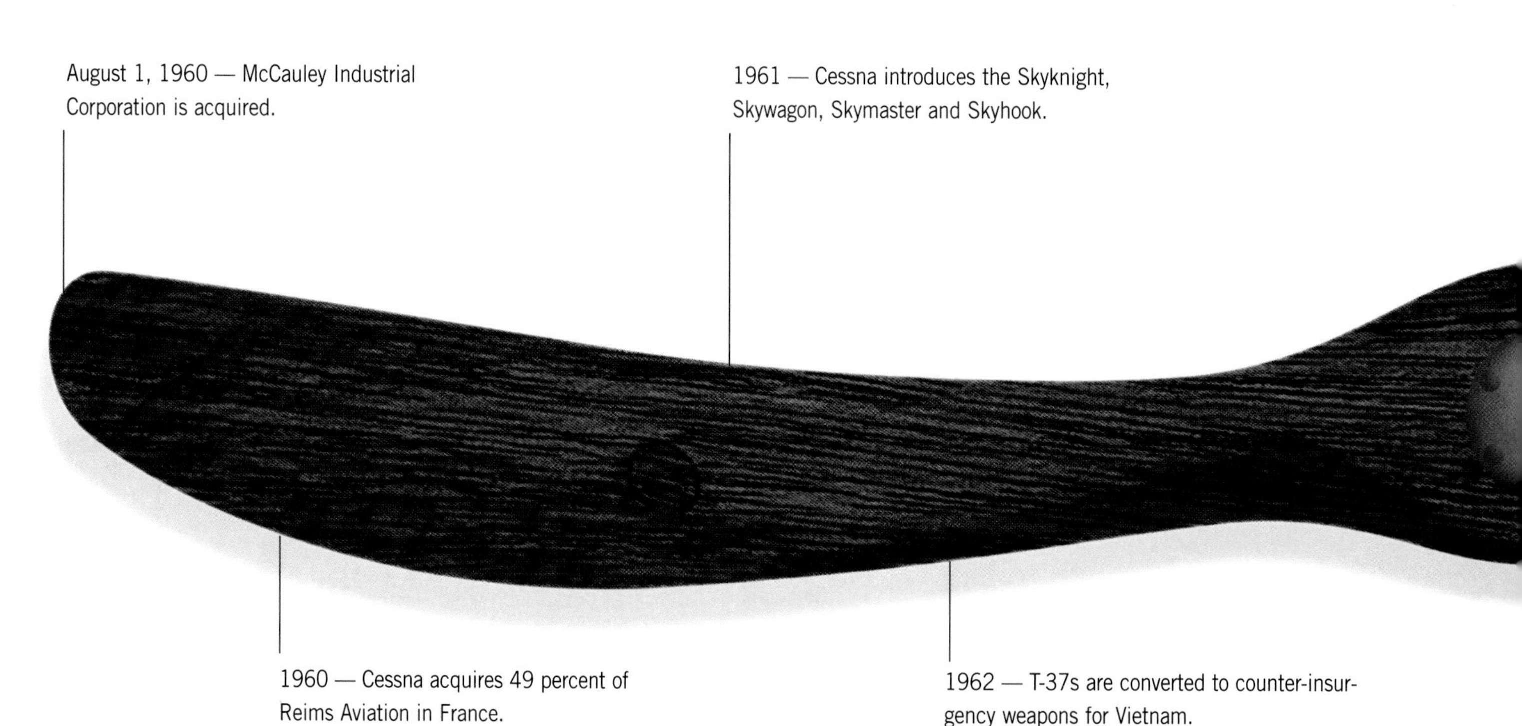

August 1, 1960 — McCauley Industrial Corporation is acquired.

1961 — Cessna introduces the Skyknight, Skywagon, Skymaster and Skyhook.

1960 — Cessna acquires 49 percent of Reims Aviation in France.

1962 — T-37s are converted to counter-insurgency weapons for Vietnam.

had to be expanded. In 1967, an 83,000-square-foot aircraft assembly plant was built at Strother Field, 40 miles southeast of Wichita.[12] In 1968, ground was broken for a 104,000-square-foot Engineering Research and Development Center at the Pawnee facility that would house the engineering and experimental departments for that division.[13]

As Cessna expanded, its corporate operations became more formal. In 1964, Dwane Wallace, the man responsible for Cessna's emergence as a global competitor, would become the company's first chairman, and Del Roskam would succeed him as president.[14] Dwane's new title didn't diminish his rapport with employees. Earl Biggs, a machine shop supervisor who joined Cessna in 1941, said Dwane "would always recognize me and come up to talk to me if he saw me in a store or wherever. ... He seemed ordinary, not like somebody who was running a whole company, but like somebody who was part of the family."[15] Dorothy Naylor, an employee relations representative who joined Cessna in 1955 and retired in 1994, recalled that Wallace didn't embrace the trappings of power. "When he was in charge, we didn't have an executive dining room. When he went to the cafeteria, he went over and sat with the guys from the shop."[16] Cessna today still has no executive cafeteria.

Built in 1969, the engineering building at the Pawnee facility is now known as the Glass House.

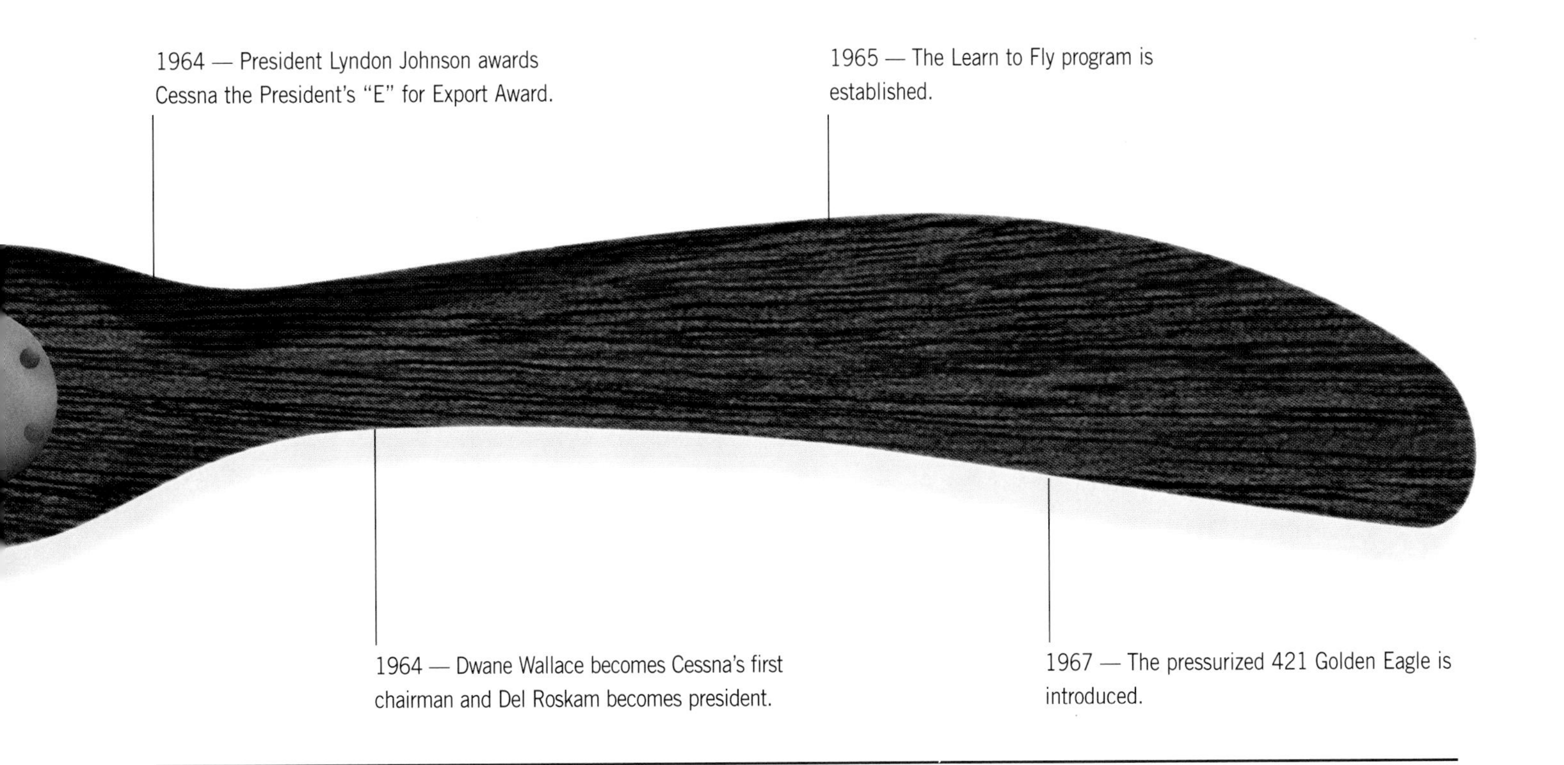

A 1968 turbocharged Centurion, which was introduced alongside the Skylane in 1965.

Wallace and Roskam were so well matched that Roskam has been called "Dwane's interpreter." Dwane would come up with the vision and Del would turn it into a reality. Because Del had to make the difficult decisions, he had a reputation for being tough, but people who knew him well said he had a heart of gold. In a 1997 interview, Del said he and Dwane would argue over an idea until both of them understood each other's position.

"We disagreed sometimes, but we talked until we did agree. He'd want to do one thing, and I'd want to do another. I was more optimistic, while he was often less so. That was good because it kept us from getting in trouble. We would have to come to an agreement. I would say, 'Dwane, I understand what you're saying, but what in hell do you want to do with it? I have to understand it, and when I can understand it, then we agree.'"[17]

Russell W. Meyer, Jr., who would work under Dwane and Del as executive vice president before becoming chief executive officer in 1975, said Dwane was known as Mr. General Aviation. "He always thought about the impact on the industry as well as on the company."

In fact, Wallace was so respected that Del probably didn't get the credit he deserved. "Del's one of these guys that would sit and review his thoughts for a long time," Meyer said.

"He wanted to think through an issue, whether it was a marketing program or an airplane configuration or a personnel issue or whatever. Sometimes he'd talk about it with one person, but more often he would talk about it with five or six people in an effort to reach the correct decision, which he invariably did."[18]

Innovations of the Sixties

In 1960, the Model 210, the first high-wing light airplane in the nation with fully retractable landing gear, was introduced, designed to fit into the sales line between the Skylane and the twin-engine 310D.[19] The 210 featured a new look for Cessna planes. Long and low, the design was accented by a 30-degree sweep in the tail assembly.[20]

Powered by a 260-horsepower fuel-injected engine, the four-seater reached a top speed of 199 miles per hour. Author Gerald Deneau, in *An Eye To The Sky, Cessna,* explained the importance of the hydraulically retractable landing gear.

"With the gear down, the 210 flew and handled like the popular Model 182. But here the comparison ended! For cruising flight, the main gear folded back under the baggage compartment; and the nose gear retracted forward under the engine. This transformed the craft into a speedy, single-engine airplane that filled the customer's performance needs."[21]

The 1960s also marked the beginning of the swept tail for Cessna airplanes. All but two models offered by the company (the 180 and 150) in 1960 had adopted the design, which changed the exterior looks of the ships with a vertical tail that slanted aft.[22] Although this design later benefitted planes by improving aerodynamics, most of the early swept-tail airplanes incorporated the "jet age styling" primarily for cosmetic reasons, the change having been advanced by Richard Ten Eyck Associates, Cessna's styling consultant at the time.[23]

In 1962, a second distinctive appearance improvement was made, this time at the suggestion of chief technical engineer Bruce Peterman. To improve the lateral and directional stability of the twin-engine Model 310, the wingtip fuel tanks were moved up to be flush with the bottom of the wing, canted outboard, and streamlined with a pointed nose and new rear fairings. The style was used on subsequent twins until the mid-1970s, when the tip tanks were removed in favor of internal wing fuel tanks.

In 1961, the company introduced several revolutionary planes, including the Skyknight, the Skywagon, the Skymaster and, of course, the Skyhawk. The single-engine Skyhawk was basically a deluxe version of the 172.[24] An amazing 35,773 of these birds have since been built, and that figure does not include variations such as the Hawk XP, the Cutlass or recent productions.

Aviation author James Ellis stated that the 172 Skyhawk, which first appeared as a prototype in 1955, "quickly outdistanced the 170 in popularity, resulting in the end of 170 production."[25]

"Only Russian World War II fighters beat it out for the honor of the most heavily produced aircraft in the history of aviation. ... It is an airplane that has changed by evolution rather than revolution."[26]

For multi-engine pilots who wanted more performance and speed than the 310, the 320 Skyknight, produced in 1961, was Cessna's first

Above: A 1961 Skyhawk, marketed as a deluxe version of the 172. This plane, and its various enhancements over the years, would prove to be Cessna's most popular aircraft ever.

Right: A 1966 Skyknight Model T320. The Model 320 was Cessna's first turbocharged twin-engine plane.

turbocharged twin-engine airplane. With a price tag of $67,500, the Skyknight was significantly cheaper than competitive turbocharged twins.[27] A May 1961 article in the *Cessquire* described the company's latest offering.

"The Skyknight is a turbocharged twin-engine airplane with speeds up to 265 miles per hour. It is a fast, roomy, five-passenger airplane which will occupy the top position in the Cessna 1962 line. Continental 260-horsepower turbocharged engines with fuel injection will power the Skyknight, providing outstanding high altitude performance.

"With turbocharged engines, the Skyknight will have available the full 260 horsepower of its engines to 16,000 feet, providing greater takeoff and single-engine safety at high altitudes. Single-engine service ceiling is in excess of 17,000 feet.

"The Skyknight has been specifically designed to fly long distances at high altitudes, topping weather conditions over 27,000 feet, and will offer business executives high-speed flight in comfort, with outstanding visibility at altitudes where flying is at its finest. A combination of four seating arrangements, including a lounge, will be available."[28]

The Skywagon Model 185, Cessna's first six-place, single-engine utility airplane, was also introduced in 1961. Powered by a Continental 260-horsepower, fuel-injection engine, it was certified for operation on both skis and floats.[29] One of the plane's most interesting features was a detachable fiberglass Cargo-Pack, which attached to the bottom of the Skywagon fuselage and expanded the ship's cargo capacity by 21.5 cubic feet. "Designed specifically for use on the Skywagon, the Cargo-Pack provides even greater flexibility to the new 'bush country' airplane," noted the *Cessquire*.[30] The rugged Skywagon, "[a] taildragging workhorse, not a racehorse," was also capable of quick takeoffs, as one industry author wrote:

"One New England Yankee aircraft broker routinely used a Skywagon to commute from an

Billed as the station wagon of the air, the six-place Skywagon Model 185 was introduced in 1961, and was available with an optional belly cargo pod.

850-foot island runway to his office at a suburban Boston airport, using aircraft capabilities that also make these planes one of the aircraft of choice by bush pilots in Canada, Alaska, and Maine as well."[31]

The Model 206 Super Skywagon (later Stationair 6) was introduced in 1964, and a new Skywagon, the 207 (later the Stationair 7), was added to Cessna's line of utility aircraft in 1969. This airplane, which could carry seven people with luggage, or nearly 2,000 pounds of cargo, became the industry's largest single-engine model.[32]

The Skymaster

On February 28, 1961, the revolutionary tandem twin-engine Skymaster made its first flight.[33] This Model 336, featuring Centerline Thrust (engines on each end of the fuselage) and twin cantilever tail booms supporting a communal stabilizer, was the culmination of years of research and design to develop a low-cost, safe, comfortable business aircraft.[34] The push-pull action of this novel twin-engine concept gave the Skymaster a ceiling of 27,200 feet. Tailored to the business pilot, this model, priced at $39,950, simplified the transition

Above: The 1965 Skymaster Model 337, a variation of the tandem twin-engine Skymaster introduced in 1964.

Below: The instrument panel of the Skymaster Model 337.

from single-engine to twin-engine aircraft.[35] Lacking the often aggressive yaw which accompanied the loss of an engine aboard most twin-engine aircraft, pilot multi-engine ratings were limited to "centerline thrust." The version of the Skymaster that went into production in 1964 was almost completely re-engineered to include retractable landing gear and provide better flying characteristics, an updated appearance and greater speed.[36] The Turbo Super Skymaster, introduced in April 1967, offered even greater performance.[37]

During the summer of 1968, two Ohio men flew around the world in a Cessna Super Skymaster. In 34 days, A. Clayton Tschantz, general manager of Richland Aviation (a Cessna dealership in Mansfield, Ohio) and Raymond Mion, president of Mansfield Flooring, flew Mion's Super Skymaster a total of 159 hours and 25,000 miles. The trip took more than 18 months to plan. After carefully charting their route, Tschantz and Mion installed long-distance fuel tanks, increasing the Super Skymaster's fuel capacity from 128 gallons to 338.

During their 34 days of travel, the pair was delayed only once — in Brussels, Belgium — because of bad weather. Looking back, Mion said, "I've gained the satisfaction of flying around the world. I wouldn't take a million dollars for the experience, but I wouldn't do it again for a million dollars."[38]

The Skymaster would find its way into the Air Force, which required a fast, tough Forward Air Control ship for use in Vietnam. One version of the Skymaster was armed with rockets, observation windows and a 7.62 millimeter minigun. Another version was armed mostly with speakers and leaflets, used to demoralize the enemy and destroy its willingness to fight.

Above: The first military version of the Skymaster, the O-2A, was delivered to Vietnam in 1967.

Left: Clayton Tschantz and Raymond Mion pose next to the Super Skymaster that carried them around the world.

Learn to Fly

With a wealth of new planes, Cessna's marketing division turned its attention to encouraging the prosperous American population to become pilots. The Learn To Fly program in 1965 and the Air Age Education program in 1967 offered information and incentives to get people interested in flying. The Learn To Fly program offered a $5 introductory flight lesson, and even reduced the price of the two-seater Model 150 trainer by more than 10 percent. With these incentives, the program introduced hundreds of thousands of people to flying, an accomplishment that generated more than $141 million for Cessna dealers.[39]

The Air Age Education program, provided by Cessna dealers, was aimed at elementary schools, high schools, junior colleges and vocational schools throughout the nation.[40]

Cessna was also able to boost sales by helping customers pay for their new planes. In 1967, the National Aircraft Finance Company changed its name to the Cessna Finance Corporation.[41] In 1969, the Cessna International Finance Corporation was formed to strengthen the company's ability to penetrate export markets by providing credit for foreign customers, dealers and wholesalers.[42]

Commercial Aviation

In 1966, Cessna began producing the Model 188 Agwagon, used for low level flight for airborne crop spraying. The Agwagon, fondly known as Pinnochio because of its long nose, was a comfortable, stable ship that met the specialized needs of the agricultural pilot. The ship was built with very light control surfaces because the pilot often spent eight to 10 hours flying over fields, noted Dean Noble, who retired as manager of direct marketing. He noted that the controls on agricultural aircraft required little effort to manipulate, and extra-large wings provided more lift.[43]

The second half of the 1960s also marked the start of a new 400 series of cabin class Cessna twins. In 1965, Cessna's first twin-engine airplane with over 6,000 pounds of gross weight, the 411, was introduced. The all-new design used geared turbocharged engines. In 1967, the models 401 and 402, with simpler straight drive turbocharged engines were introduced — the 401 for passengers and the 402 for cargo. These were later merged into the multipurpose 402, and the 411 was discontinued.[44]

In 1967, the company also introduced the pressurized 421 Golden Eagle, the first general aviation aircraft to combine cabin pressurization with a turbocharged engine.[45] The Golden Eagle, which sold for $187,500, was capable of carrying about 1,100 pounds of payload nearly 1,400 miles at 250 miles per hour.[46] An updated 421 Golden Eagle, introduced in 1975, utilized a bonded wet wing and hydraulically actuated landing gear.[47]

Before the end of the decade, Cessna developed two other notable civilian airplanes, the Model 414 and the 150 Aerobat, a companion model to the 150. The Model 414 was Cessna's third pressurized airplane, a step up for aircraft owners who tired of the ear-popping unpleasantness associated with nonpressurized cabins.[48] The Aerobat, on the other hand, lived up to its name. Level flying was not on the minds of the engineers when designing this highly maneuverable ship, capable of performing barrel and aileron rolls, snap rolls, loops, vertical reverses and chandelles. Used in flight training programs, the economical Aerobat became popular with the world's smaller air forces, in such places as Zaire and Ecuador.[49]

Helicopters

Following eight years of development, a four-place, rotary-wing helicopter dubbed the Skyhook was introduced in 1961. With seating for four, the Skyhook was certified for cruising speeds as high as 122 miles per hour, and featured a maximum cruising range in excess of five hours. With a price tag of $79,960, the Skyhook became the first rotary-wing aircraft in the history of aviation to be supported by a worldwide sales and service organization.[50]

The first production CH-1C, an updated version of the popular Seneca helicopters deployed by the United States Army in the 1950s, made its maiden voyage in July 1960.[51] The Air Force and

However, Cessna elected to leave the helicopter business in December 1962, noted Bruce Learmont, who joined Cessna in 1957 and served as an engineer in the helicopter group. He explained that the helicopters, which were sold through dealers, required more maintenance per flight than Cessna's fixed-wing aircraft of the time. The maintenance training that Cessna provided for dealers proved inadequate. "We did have some accidents due to improper maintenance and we decided this was not working," said Learmont, now a senior project engineer. "We did the right thing by getting out."[54]

Navy used the four-seater to transport military and contractor personnel to and from missile sites.[52] In 1962, Cessna received an Air Force contract to provide four CH-1Cs to a friendly South American country under the Military Assistance Program.

The CH-1C, identical to the commercial version of the Skyhook, was capable of operating over rough mountainous terrain, where roads and highways are nonexistent. The four helicopters introduced a new hoist and litter installation for rescue operations. The hoist was used to deliver personnel and equipment to areas inaccessible by trucks. The interior of the helicopter, with three of the four seats removed, could also be configured for duty as an aerial ambulance.[53]

Above: Both the Army and the Navy relied on the CH-1C during peacetime to transport military and contractor personnel to and from missile sites.

Below: The T-37 was modified in 1962 to become a jet trainer for counterinsurgency in the Vietnam War. *(Photo courtesy of* Air Force Magazine.)

The Vietnam War

Like the Korean War, termed a "police action" by President Eisenhower, the conflict in Vietnam was never officially declared a war. But while the objective in Korea was to push back an invading army over a predetermined line, progress in Vietnam could not be measured by land won or lost. An area that was supposedly cleared of Viet Cong, for example, was often not cleared for very long, and the mission of United States troops was for the most part counter-insurgency.

The Vietnam War differed from conventional wars in two ways: there was no "front" to defend or expand; and the fighting consisted of using overwhelming firepower by United States troops

Above: Two 500-pound bombs are released from an A-37 Dragonfly during one of the final missions flown by the U.S. Air Force in the Republic of Vietnam. *(Photo courtesy of* Air Force Magazine.)

Below: An A-37 and its crew in Vietnam in 1968. *(Photo courtesy of* Air Force Magazine.)

to fight guerrillas who quickly melted into jungles and villages after hit-and-run raids. The Air Force needed a light-strike aircraft that could carry enough weapons of different types to counter the ghostly Viet Cong incursions.

In 1962, the Air Force's Special Air Warfare Center began toying with the idea of converting the T-37 jet trainer into a counter-insurgency weapon. The center's officers wanted to see if these sturdy but light aircraft could be used to assist ground forces in close-support roles. Web Moore and Bert Overfield of Cessna Engineering led the effort to turn these wishes into reality. Two T-37Bs were modified by Cessna to carry increasing amounts of weaponry, eventually doubling the airplane's gross weight to 14,000 pounds and more than doubling the engine thrust — a formidable feat since the size of the airplane did not change. "The ordnance it carries is very sophisticated for that size of airplane," noted Arbery Barrett, currently vice president of aircraft completion and one of the men who helped modify the original T-37s.[55] Barrett, a first level supervisor at the time, recalled that a sense of urgency developed as the value of these aircraft became apparent on the battlefield. "The work ethic was such that people stayed on the job,

working 12 to 14 hours a day, trying to get 'em ready to leave for Vietnam."[56]

The Air Force ordered the conversion of 39 T-37B trainers into light-strike warplanes, equipped with General Electric J85-GE-5 turbojets. By 1967, 25 were operating as a squadron under the A-37A designation, and the apt name of Dragonfly, the first combat designated airplane built by a general aviation manufacturer. The Dragonfly became part of the 604th Air Commando Squadron, based at Bien Hoa, and was used in counter-insurgency roles.[57] By August 1968, the Air Force had ordered 178 of the A-37B attack jets, a contract value of almost $38 million, according to the 1968 Annual Report.

> *"Cessna's A-37 was designed to meet specific requirements of the Air Force for brush and guerrilla-type warfare. The 'A' version, smallest jet in Air Force inventory, has already proved its capability in thousands of combat sorties. It is one of six Cessna models serving in Vietnam.*
>
> *In combat evaluation, the A-37As were highly praised by pilots for their maneuverability, bombing accuracy and maintainability in counter-insurgency and close air support missions.*
>
> *The 'B' model A-37s now in production include higher thrust engines than the 'A' model plus provisions for aerial and single-point ground refueling.*
>
> *Sales efforts for this model are continuing, and Cessna sees excellent market potential for the A-37, both in the U.S. and abroad."*[58]

Other Cessna aircraft saw action in Vietnam. Military versions of the Super Skymaster, designated the O-2A and 0-2B, were first delivered to Vietnam on May 20, 1967.[59] These airplanes joined the O-1E Bird Dogs in the dangerous Forward Air Control mission over the Vietnamese jungles. In November 1967, the *Cessquire* printed an article from the Air Force about the effect of Cessna aircraft on the Viet Cong and on America's pilots.

> *"The Viet Cong have come to fear the small Cessna O-1E Bird Dog flown by forward air controllers in South Vietnam. When they see it circling near them they try to hide, for in minutes after the FAC (Forward Air Control) spots them they most likely will be pounded.*

These O-2Bs were ready for service in dangerous Forward Air Control Missions over the Vietnamese jungles.

"Now the VC are having to become familiar with a new airplane that the FACs of the 20th Tactical Air Support Squadron (TASS) at Da Nang are receiving — the twin-boom, tandem-engine O-2A Super Skymaster.

"The first FAC unit to receive the new bird, the 20th TASS pilots, attended a six-day transition school in Binh Thuy to familiarize themselves with the O-2A. Major James W. Leatherbee, 39, (from Fairborn, Ohio) became the first man in Vietnam to qualify in the O-2A. He is a pilot with the 20th TASS.

"Major Leatherbee made the following remarks about Cessna's modified Super Skymaster after training in it:

"'It's an ideal plane for FACing. The speed and loitering time will give us additional capabilities. We have better visibility in the O-2A because the top of the cabin and the cutouts in the doors are Plexiglas. It will be much easier to keep track of the fighters we're directing.

"'The target marking rocket pods are mounted under the wings. The plane also is equipped with a gun sight so we will be more accurate with the rockets instead of calculating the aim as we have been doing. And with the added speed of the plane, we should perform our mission with no drop in efficiency.'"[60]

An additional order for 12 O-2As was received in 1969. This order, coming from a foreign government, marked the first purchase of the O-2A outside the United States.[61]

As the decade began to wind down, the pace of the war speeded up, and opposition intensified. Americans questioned not only the war but the military as well. Cessna's contribution to aviation was recognized nonetheless, and on April 27, 1968, Dwane Wallace was the first to receive the honor of being named outstanding engineering alumnus by the Wichita State University College of Engineering.

Dwane Wallace, right, accepts the Citation's certification from FAA Central Region Director John Cyrocki on September 10, 1971.

THE CESSNA FANJET 500

"It flew like we anticipated it would, and it flew much better than could be expected for a first flight. In fact, things went so well that we had no apprehension about flying it longer than we'd planned."

— Pilot Milt Sills, after the Citation's first flight[1]

CESSNA'S FIRST business jet, the Fanjet 500, was a breakthrough for the company and the industry. Quieter, simpler, safer and less expensive than other business jets on the market, it was ideal for business travelers. The plane would become the first of the Citation series, which today dominates the corporate jet market.

Perhaps more important were the implications the introduction of this aircraft had for the company itself. The Citation caused Cessna to carefully examine its marketing and sales strategy. The decisions made as a result of this analysis would have a dramatic and lasting impact on the future of the company and how it did business.

By 1967, Cessna's single- and twin-engine planes commanded the lion's share of a worldwide general aviation fleet that had grown to more than 100,000 aircraft. Business aircraft, which usually flew less than 600 miles and carried fewer than three passengers, comprised 34 percent of the general aviation fleet.[2]

The growing popularity of business aircraft was easily explained. Executives had to travel more than ever before, particularly to rural areas where new factories were being constructed. But the major airlines served only 525 of the nation's 9,000 airports, and tended to concentrate on routes between major cities. Sixty-eight percent of all domestic passengers landed and departed in only 22 cities.

In 1966, Cessna executives studied the corporate aircraft market and discovered this niche.[3] The study found a sizable gap between top-of-the-line $580,000 twin-engine turboprops, which flew 300 miles per hour at 25,000 feet, and low-end $800,000 corporate business jets which flew 500 miles per hour at 35,000 feet. Cessna executives also realized that maintaining a jet in the corporate hangar meant additional crew costs, since the FAA required two pilots for jet operation rather than only one pilot for a turboprop.

Cessna leadership conceived of a pressurized aircraft that could fly approximately 400 miles per hour with a maximum altitude of 35,000 feet and carry at least four passengers plus crew in a cabin five feet wide. This new plane would cost about $600,000, be extremely economical to operate and maintain, and represent an easy transition plane for twin-engine pilots. Drawing on experience from manufacturing more than 1,100 T-37 and A-37 jets for the military, Cessna created the Fanjet 500, a six-passenger pressurized business jet that met all these criteria. With short takeoff and landing requirements, it could access airfields previously limited

A 1968 artist's rendering of the Fanjet 500.

to single- and twin-engine aircraft. From the beginning, the plane was designed to be single-pilot certified, a first for business jets.

"Everyone thought we were off our rocker when we came up with that plane because it was a relatively slow jet," said Bruce Peterman, chief engineer in 1972. Peterman had been a Cessnan since 1953, retiring as senior vice president in 1996. "Some of our competitors made comments about bird strikes from the rear. But we just kept producing the airplane and making it better until we wound up with the majority of the market."[4]

Cessna Chairman Dwane Wallace and President Del Roskam unveiled a mock-up of the Fanjet 500 at a press gathering prior to the National Business Aircraft Association convention in Houston on October 7, 1968.[5] "Our primary concern," said Roskam at the introduction, "was the mating of an engine package to a compatible airframe." The Fanjet 500's two Pratt & Whitney JT15D-1 engines were crucial to its success. At the time of the introduction, the engines had completed test runs and begun flight testing for later use with the Fanjet 500 prototype.

To manage Cessna's entry into the commercial jet market, the Commercial Jet Marketing Division (CJMD) was established and placed under the leadership of James B. Taylor, who was appointed its vice president in March 1969.[6] A native of New York who had flown F4U Corsairs in World War II, the 48-year-old Taylor had worked the previous five years as the head of Pan American's Business Jets Division. His leadership grew the division from two employees and one prototype fanjet to sales of 125 aircraft worth more than $155 million.

Taylor's first order of business was to find a more distinctive name for the Fanjet 500.[7] Fanjet engines were universally employed, and the "500" designation was similar to other 500-series aircraft such as the Aero Commander 500, Lockheed L-500, and Howard 500.

In addition, a numerical designation seemed too cold and impersonal for pilots who liked to name their planes, such as the T-37 "Tweety Bird" and the A-37 "Dragonfly." Taylor perused Old West literature, meteorology, astronomy and

Above: James B. Taylor, vice president of the Commercial Jet Marketing Division, used innovative methods to sell the company's first business jet.

Below: After a prolonged search, Cessna chose the Pratt & Whitney JT15D-1 to power the Fanjet 500, which would soon be known as the Citation.

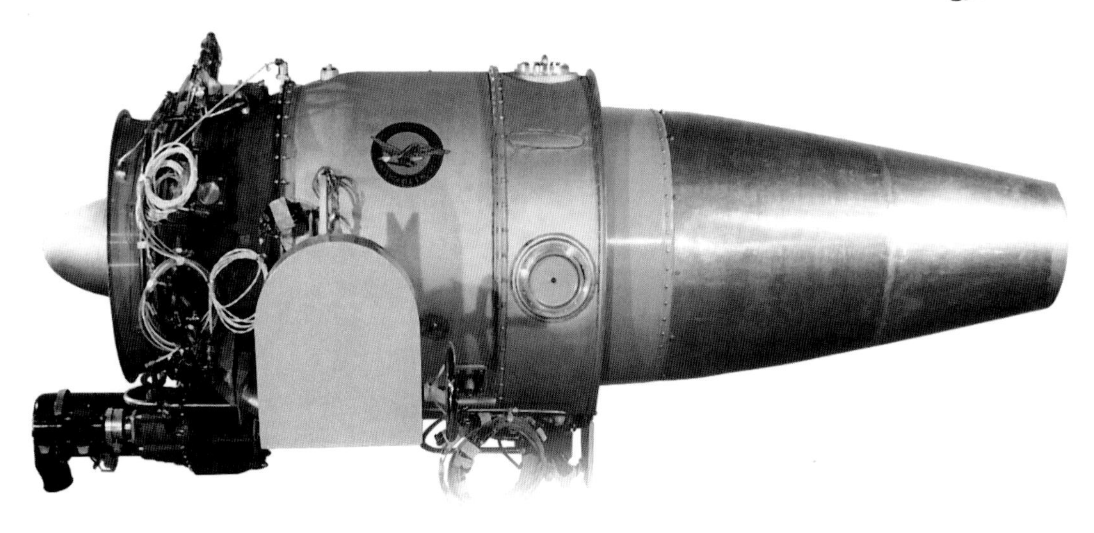

mythology, as well as explorers, heroes, pioneers and innovators to find the right name.

Finally, an executive at the company's advertising agency, Ogilvy & Mather, suggested "Citation," after the horse that won the Triple Crown in 1948. The parallels between the famous racehorse and Cessna's new jet were ideal. Both embodied exceptional performance, flexibility, handling, efficiency and appearance. "We feel we have a real thoroughbred and want the name to reflect it," Taylor said.[8]

The Citation, photographed during its successful first flight. The plane touched down after one hour and 45 minutes in the air.

However, Taylor still had to convince Dwane Wallace and Del Roskam, who were reluctant to abandon the company's tradition of giving planes numerical designations. He purchased pony horseshoes, had them chrome-plated, and placed them on the desks of the two men. The gesture worked, and the plane officially became the Citation.

Meanwhile, preparations were under way for the Citation's first flight. Construction had gone smoothly, but extensive wind tunnel tests called for changes that made the prototype model different from the original mock-up displayed in Houston a year earlier. The vertical tail was lengthened by about a foot. The horizontal stabilizer was lowered to provide more upsweep for better stability. Engine nacelles were placed closer to the fuselage and moved farther back to reduce drag.

Inlet guide vanes in front of the compressor were eliminated to quiet the engine — a crucial move that would later prove beneficial when aircraft noise became a public issue in the early seventies. At 1,000 feet, a Citation flyover registered 81 decibels — the same as popular twin piston-engine aircraft or a busy office. Its relatively quiet engines meant that the Citation could be flown into airports normally reserved for turboprops, thus avoiding congestion with airliners at metropolitan airports. A California-based consulting firm later rated the Citation as the quietest business jet, and CJMD's "Good Neighbor Jet" advertising campaign promoted the Citation's low noise level. The plane's ability to service the same airports served by a growing number of small commuter airlines would be a strong selling point to many early Citation customers.

The Citation's gross weight was increased by 850 pounds to a 10,350-pound takeoff weight, and the fuselage was lengthened by six inches in the cabin area. A new seating configuration was also added, featuring four reclining seats with a lounge on the right side of the cabin instead of a bench-type seat across the rear of the cabin.

By early September 1969, all preliminary testing had been accomplished. On September 15, before a large crowd of Cessna officials, local dignitaries, press, and the many proud engineers, designers and assemblers who had made it possible, the Citation was rolled onto the tarmac for its maiden flight.[9]

Originally scheduled to take off around 9:15 in the morning, low cloud ceilings delayed the Citation's flight until midafternoon. At 3:20, pilot-in-command Milt Sills and co-pilot Jim LeSueur took the Citation into the skies above Wichita's Municipal Airport, adjacent to Cessna's Military and Twin Division where the prototype Citation had been assembled. Observers estimated the Citation's takeoff ground roll to be about 1,500 feet — true to original designs for short runway takeoffs and landings. A Cessna twin-engine 421 flew as a chase plane, carrying two photographers to record the moment. Equipped with a 16-channel telemetry unit in the aft cabin to provide strip recording with simultaneous readouts on the ground, and a camera positioned to record the flight instruments while airborne, the Citation reached a maximum indicated airspeed of 225 knots. Sills and LeSueur tested gear retraction and performed complete system and flight handling checks. Though the flight test regime was originally scheduled to reach 20,000 feet, weather conditions limited the flight to only 10,000 feet.

After one hour and 45 minutes in the air, the Citation landed to applause and cheers. Upon exiting the plane, Sills praised the Citation's performance: "It flew like we anticipated it would, and it flew much better than could be expected for a first flight. In fact, things went so well that we had no apprehension about flying it longer than we'd planned. Originally the flight was to last only 45 minutes."[10]

Years later, Sills, a former Navy pilot who had joined Cessna in 1965 after working as a flight test engineer at McDonnell Douglas, recalled the flight "was a rather comfortable situation. One of the things I appreciated about Cessna was that we were involved in the design of the airplane all the way through before we flew it, so I felt like I had an understanding of how the airplane was going to behave and how it was going to fly."[11] Sills eventually became senior vice president of product engineering.

Dwane Wallace, Del Roskam, James Taylor and Max Bleck, vice president of the Military and Twin Division, draped roses over the nose of the prototype and officially christened it the Citation. With a second prototype scheduled to fly in January 1970, CJMD set its marketing campaign in motion.[12]

Marketing the Citation: An Enduring Legacy

Selling an innovative business jet required an innovative marketing plan. The resulting strategy would have far-reaching consequences and marked a crucial turn in how Cessna viewed its relationship with the customer.

Cessna executives were concerned that existing Cessna dealers and distributors would not be able to adequately support the Citation line. Instead, executives decided that customers of a sophisticated business aircraft like the Citation would be better served by working directly with the manufacturer. This unique marketing concept was based on direct factory-

After the flight, the Citation was christened with a garland of roses. Left to right: Milt Sills, test pilot; Dwane Wallace, Cessna chairman; James Taylor, vice president of the Commercial Jet Marketing Division; Jim LeSueur, test co-pilot; Max Bleck, vice president and general manager of the Military and Twin Division; Bob Lair, senior vice president of aircraft operations; Thor Stevenson, president of United Aircraft Canada Limited; and Del Roskam, president of Cessna.

A marketing and sales meeting in 1971, held in the newly opened Citation Service Center.

to-customer sales. The marketing organization was to include regional sales managers, strategically located domestically and internationally, to personally serve the client base. This strategy placed control of the marketing and sales effort directly with Cessna.[13]

One element of the plan called for the establishment of three company-owned Citation Service Centers, in Poughkeepsie, New York; Wichita; and Sacramento, California, with certified technicians and representatives. The idea was to expand the number of centers as required by fleet population and location. A center was also established in Germany to support Citations in Europe.

This structure, unique in the industry at the time, was more cost-effective than the usual multitiered dealer organization and helped keep Citation prices as low as possible. This strategy would grow in future years, and help create an environment in which Cessna was able to build and enhance personal relationships with its customers, something not typical in the industry. In fact, Cessna's customers would eventually play a key role in helping the company design its aircraft. This concept has proven so successful, others in the industry have followed Cessna's lead.

By April 1970, CJMD had compiled a list of 100,000 names and more than 27,000 businesses as potential customers. Among the prospective customers were companies with annual sales of $10 million to $50 million that operated single-pilot aircraft. Owners of twin-engine piston and turboprop aircraft desiring a step-up plane were among the most promising prospects.

The Citation marketing program was aggressively launched in September 1970 at the National Business Aircraft Association's convention in Denver. The Citation's $695,000 price tag included factory-installed avionics, ground and flight training, and a one-year computerized maintenance program that informed the customer when scheduled inspections and maintenance were due. This standard package, which greatly simplified the

production process, had been carefully selected after an aggressive competition among several avionics companies. The standard package also made pilot training easier because flight simulators could be similarly standardized.

Cessna also negotiated a comprehensive customer support agreement that included a three-year warranty on the airframe and a one-year warranty on factory-installed avionics.

Also impressive and unique in the Citation package were ground and flight training provided at American Airlines' new Flight Training Center at the Greater Southwest International Airport in Fort Worth, Texas. The 80-acre site contained the latest in flight simulators and training methods, and the arrangement made Citation pilots the first outside personnel to use the facilities.[14] "We will sell a complete business aircraft program, not just another airplane," Taylor said.[15]

While marketing plans were being implemented, Cessna began building a 7,500-square-foot CJMD headquarters and Citation Service Center next to the Military and Twin Division in Wichita. The service center could hold as many as six Citations at once in a unique hexagonal design that contained 19,500 square feet of space. It opened in December 1970, three months after CJMD headquarters began operations.

Taylor hand-picked a sales staff to occupy the new facilities. Like every other aspect of the Citation program, qualifications for salesmen were somewhat unusual. Rather than hire seasoned professionals, Taylor wanted people "who haven't bounced around the industry for

Above left: The Citation production line in 1972.

Below: One of Cessna's more unusual promotions was the Citation Convincer, a self-contained demonstration unit that was driven throughout the United States and Canada.

years. They're not bound by a lot of old ways of doing things."[16]

These new salesmen, along with the 80-person Citation marketing team, formed what was to become the world's leading business jet marketing organization. In another innovative move to promote the Citation, CJMD introduced the Citation Convincer in early 1971. The Convincer was a self-contained traveling demonstration unit that featured a full-scale mock-up of the Citation's cabin and cockpit. The mobile unit contained its own conference room with projection and refreshment facilities large enough to accommodate several potential customers at the same time. The Convincer covered more than 10,000 miles throughout the United States and Canada in the months before the first production rollout of the Citation.[17]

By the time the first Citation was delivered, Cessna had spent approximately $35 million on the project — 40 percent of the company's net assets.[18]

Bruce Peterman said the first deliveries were "kind of like the way women talk about giving birth. You forget all the pain after you get to see the little one. It was a lot of pain, but there was a lot of joy, particularly being chief engineer."[19]

A New Way to Build

Even the manufacture of the Citation was unique, reflecting an intensive analysis of the entire assembly process before the line was started. On the production floor, the cabin section was assembled in a vertical jig to allow 360-degree internal and external access and to save space on the factory floor. Both wings were also assembled in vertical jigs for the same reason. In late August 1971, the first production Citation rolled out the factory door. In the next two weeks, it would log 95 hours of demonstration flight time.

On September 10, the Citation was awarded FAR Part 25 certification — the same category received by major airlines. "Granting of this certification marks the climax of nearly four years of design and development work on the new

Above left: Bruce Peterman, who retired as senior vice president in 1996, was chief engineer during the Fanjet 500's development. He is shown here with a new Citation X.

Below: The 250th Citation was delivered to Fed Mart Corporation's Raymond M. Balwierczak in July 1975.

Citation," Dwane Wallace said when he received the certificate from John Cyrocki, director of the FAA's central region. "The success of this development program could not have been accomplished without outstanding cooperation and support of our major Citation suppliers."[20]

FAA regulations require two pilots for aircraft certified to FAR Part 25. But after the aircraft received two-pilot certification, Cessna planned to apply for single-pilot certification. The Citation exhibited excellent low-speed handling characteristics and short takeoff and landing field length capabilities, and the cockpit was ergonomically designed for a single pilot. Cessna initiated a program to convince the FAA that the two-pilot requirement should be re-evaluated. However, early in 1972, it became clear the FAA was not ready to change its position, so Cessna decided to defer the process.

Cessna remained interested in obtaining single-pilot approval, so after working closely with the FAA it was decided to certify both the Citation I and Citation II as small aircraft (aircraft certified to FAR Part 23). These aircraft were known as the Citation I SP (single pilot) and Citation II SP. For single-pilot operation, the aircraft required certain working equipment including an approach-coupled autopilot, push-to-talk switch and boom microphone.

The successful operation of the Citations I and II by single pilots, coupled with the fact that FAR Part 23 certification limited maximum takeoff weight to 12,500 pounds, led Cessna to request an exemption for large aircraft to be operated as single pilot. The request was granted by the FAA in 1984. The exemption applies to the pilot in FAR Part 91 operations only, and established qualifications and training standards to allow Cessna Model 500 series to be operated with one pilot. All subsequent 500 series jets including the CitationJet, Bravo,

Citation V and the Citation Ultra can be flown by a single pilot. Except for FAR Part 23 certified aircraft, including the CitationJet, pilots must meet the requirements for the exemption to operate single pilot. For the CitationJet, a pilot can obtain a single pilot rating to the pilot's type rating.

The Citation is the only jet to have ever been granted single-pilot certification. "It's very meaningful to somebody who's buying it as a two-pilot aircraft because they think, 'If the FAA is going to certify that airplane to be flown by a single pilot, it must be a pretty darn good airplane,'" noted Russ Meyer in a 1997 interview. Meyer would join Cessna in 1974 and rise to become chairman and CEO.[21]

With two Citations completed and 12 in production, the jet was ready for the market.[22] Cessna delivered the first production Citation to American Airlines as a demonstrator in January 1972, and following models were delivered to Citation suppliers such as Bendix (avionics) and United Aircraft Canada Limited (engines) for the same purpose. The first retail customer to own a Citation was Levitz Furniture. With a production rate of six jets per month, the 50th Citation was rolled out in September. Cessna delivered 52 Citations during the year, making it the industry's biggest seller for 1972. Three Citations were sold to customers in Europe where the business jet had received positive reviews at the Paris Air Show a year before, and California Governor Ronald Reagan had a Citation leased for official use after a plague of hijackings forced him to find safer methods of travel.[23]

Aerial view of Cessna's Citation Service Center and marketing facility during the early 1970s.

One of the factors contributing to the Citation's success was the unforeseen energy crisis that wreaked havoc on the general aviation industry during the early seventies. On average, the Citation used 20 to 70 percent less fuel than other jets. The Citation could travel 700 miles on 250 gallons of fuel. Airline flight cancellations and overcrowding also increased the overall appeal of the Citation package, and the energy crisis prompted CJMD to approach oil exploration industries as well as some oil producing nations as potential Citation customers.[24]

By 1975, Cessna set industry and company records by increasing Citation deliveries for three years in a row and delivering more light jets than its competition for each of those years. Annual production had risen from 52 Citations in 1972 to 85 Citations in 1974. A milestone was set in November 1974 when Burlington Industries took delivery of the 200th Citation. By July 1975, the 250th Citation rolled out the factory doors and was delivered to Fed Mart Corporation.

An improved configuration, available in December 1974, had helped to boost sales. The aircraft was designed for longer ranges, and maximum altitude was increased from 35,000 feet to 41,000 feet. This Citation I version proved its long-range capabilities when it made a 2,387-mile nonstop trip from Sacramento, California, to Binghamton, New York, in six hours and 13 minutes, with 30 minutes of reserve fuel still available. With an established production, marketing and sales network, as well as growing customer demand, Cessna engineers and designers began looking at ways to improve and expand general aviation's best-selling business jet.

The Stationair series was marketed as the aerial equivalent of the family station wagon. Shown here is a Stationair II from 1976.

NEW HEIGHTS

1970–1979

"We became more of a marketing company. We began to employ more sophisticated ways of listening to the marketplace, listening to the customer, reading trends and understanding what was important."

— Phil Michel, 1997[1]

THE BOOMING AMERICAN economy of the fifties and sixties had some economists believing that an era of permanent growth had arrived. But the decade of the 1970s was marked by a shattered presidency, the Arab oil embargo, inflation and an economic downturn.

For Cessna, the decade was considerably brighter, with high points that included the hiring of Russ Meyer, Jr., and the development of the Citation series of business jets.

But the immediate challenge to Cessna was a sudden recession after years of record economic growth. By 1970, factors such as the Vietnam War and rising interest rates drained the economy at a time when foreign competition was increasing. Worse still, the United States was becoming more dependent on Mideast oil supplies. These economic difficulties worked to halt Cessna's remarkable sales growth in its tracks. Sales slid from $283 million in 1969 to $227 million in 1970.[2]

Even so, Cessna continued to lead the aircraft industry, commanding 50 percent of the market by the end of 1970. It was the 15th year in a row that Cessna delivered more airplanes — 3,633 commercial and 502 military[3] — than any other aircraft company. It was also the 13th consecutive year in which Cessna held dollar volume leadership in the general aviation industry.[4] And the company still held the edge in both single- and multi-engine aircraft.

The Cardinal RG and the Stationair

Cessna continued to cover the market spectrum with innovations incorporated in the new Cardinal RG and the Stationair, aircraft that served widely divergent purposes. The Cardinal RG demonstrated beauty and performance, while the rugged Stationair served a more utilitarian market as a workhorse.

The original Model 177 Cardinal, which was introduced in 1967, was meant to replace the popular Skyhawk, but its 150-horsepower Lycoming engine was not powerful enough for the new model's heavier frame and larger fuel tanks. In 1969, a 180-horsepower Lycoming was substituted, and in 1970 a constant-speed prop was installed, along with a modified wing that demonstrated better low-speed characteristics. In 1971, the Cardinal was again improved with hydraulically retractable gear and a 200-horsepower fuel-injected Lycoming engine.

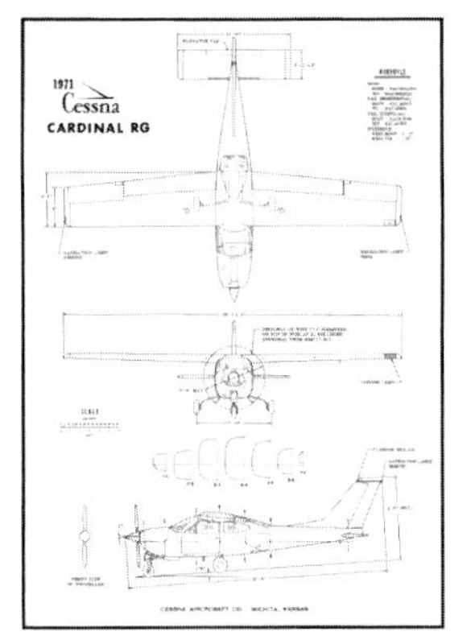

The Cardinal RG, introduced in 1971, brought a retractable landing gear to the midpriced single-engine airplane.

This version was designated the Cardinal RG, described by one aviation author as "sleek, rakish and beautiful" and "one sweet airplane to fly."[5]

The high-winged aircraft offered more spaciousness, comfort and standard features than any other medium-priced plane. More importantly, it brought retractable landing gear to the medium-priced aircraft buyer. The landing gear of this high-performance prop plane went through an interesting evolution. At first, the retractable gear was a mixture of electrical and hydraulically-driven components, but by 1973 hydraulics had replaced the electric solenoids to engage the downlock actuators.

"The new Cardinal RG is an excellent step-up airplane for present owners of lower-priced Cessnas," noted Senior Vice President Bob Lair in 1970. "We think 172/Skyhawk and Cardinal owners will be looking closely at this new airplane. Also, with two retractables in our single-engine line, customers now have a wider choice to fit their price and performance requirements than ever before."[6]

By the time the Cardinal series was discontinued in 1978, more than 4,200 units were built. Improvements in other designs, notably the Hawk XP and Cutlass RG, made the Cardinal obsolete.[7]

The Model 207 Stationair, on the other hand, was the aerial equivalent of the family station wagon. The seven-place plane was noted for its oversized roominess, high cruise speed and rich styling appointments inside and out. Two versions were introduced in 1970 — one with a 300-horsepower fuel-injected engine and the other, the Turbo Stationair, with a turbocharged 310-horsepower engine for operation at higher altitudes and high-elevation airports.

A Cardinal RG II from 1975 — described as "one sweet airplane to fly."

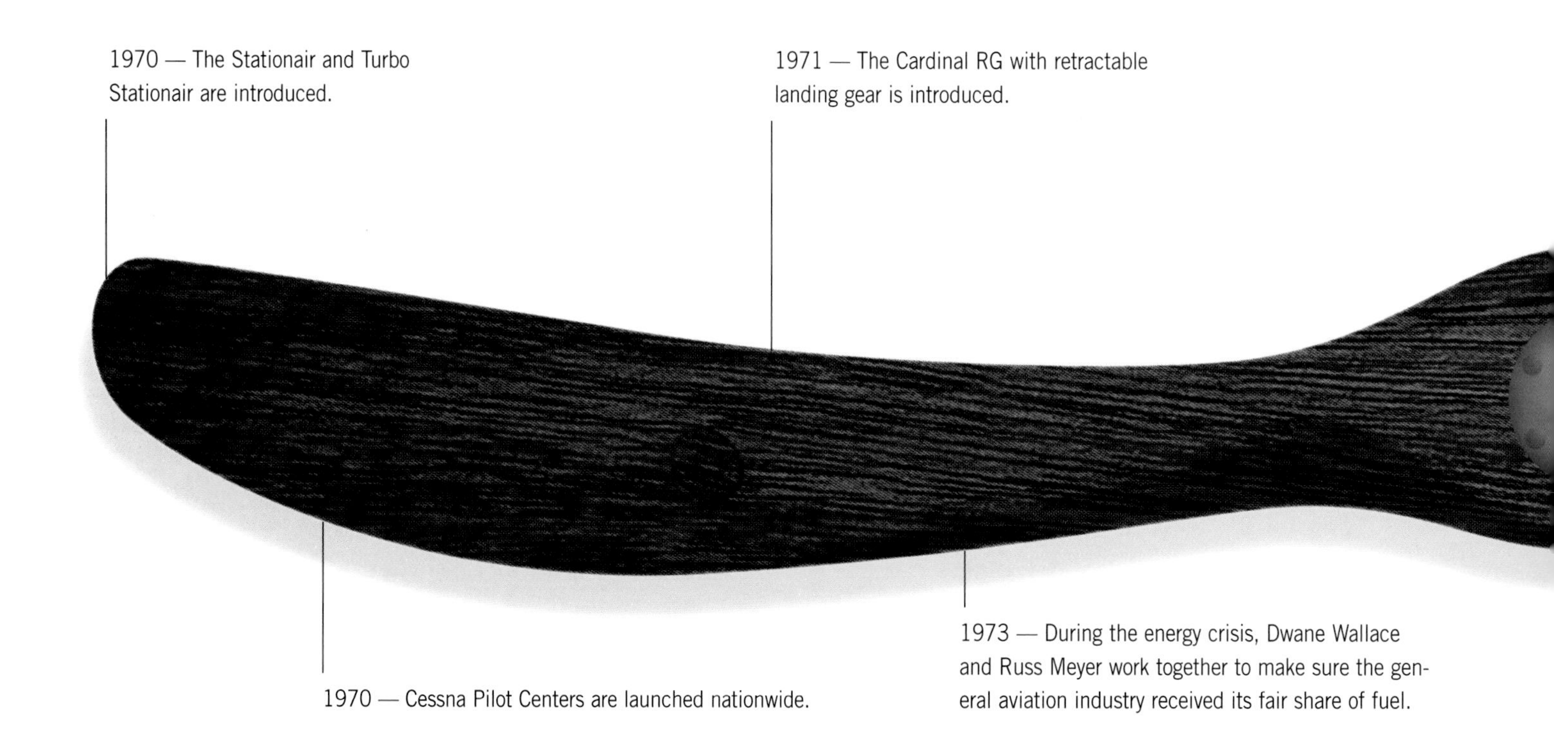

New Marketing Strategies

Cessna responded to the weak economy as it did during other downturns: with creative sales incentives and marketing programs. In 1970, the company launched a nationwide network of Cessna Pilot Centers. The centers featured the company's exclusive Integrated Flight Training System, which used audio-visual education techniques and eliminated the traditional division between ground school and flight training.[8]

Licensed Cessna Pilot Centers were supported by national advertising, standardized management systems and a complete package of instructional materials, making them the first "soft goods" program marketed by Cessna.[9]

The economy remained stagnant in 1971, and Cessna's total sales fell to $168 million, with only 3,847 commercial aircraft and 125 military planes delivered that year.[10] In response, the company changed its marketing focus, again shifting from an emphasis on personal flying to communicate the fact that planes were practical and necessary business tools. Two new slogans were coined: "Cessna Means Business" and "Cessna Thinks Customer." Several customer service programs were initiated, and in 1972, Cessna held its first international meeting devoted to after-sale care for customers.[11]

A company-wide transformation was taking place at Cessna, one that set it apart from competitors. Cessna, like other aircraft manufacturers, had for years been driven by innovation and reliability. But beginning in the late sixties, executives began listening to customers more closely.

The spacious interior of the Stationair II had room for six passengers.

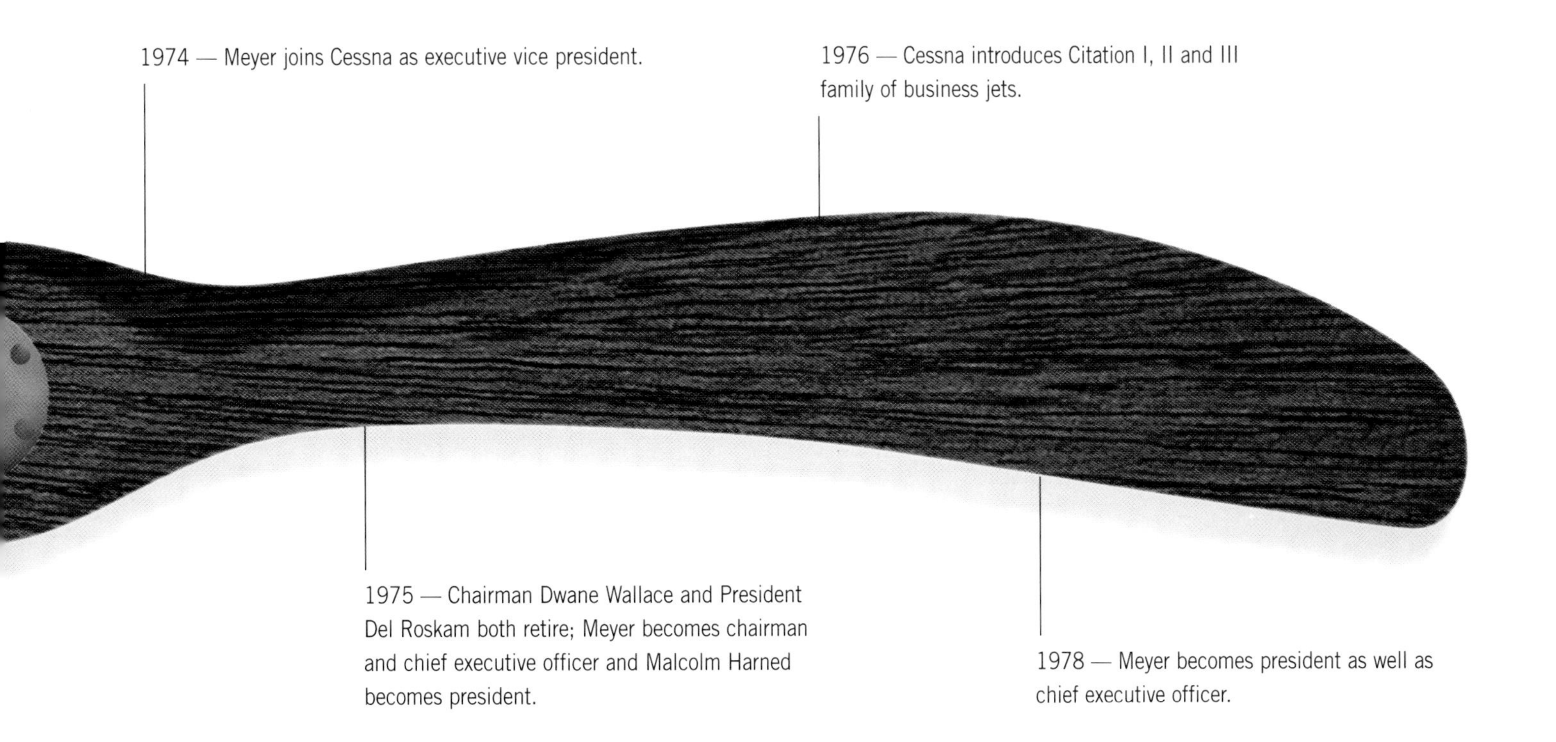

1974 — Meyer joins Cessna as executive vice president.

1975 — Chairman Dwane Wallace and President Del Roskam both retire; Meyer becomes chairman and chief executive officer and Malcolm Harned becomes president.

1976 — Cessna introduces Citation I, II and III family of business jets.

1978 — Meyer becomes president as well as chief executive officer.

Rather than allow complex technology to solely determine how a plane should be designed, Cessna involved the customer in the process, noted Vice President of Marketing Phil Michel, who joined Cessna in 1975.

> *"We became more of a marketing company. We began to employ more sophisticated ways of listening to the marketplace, listening to the customer, reading trends and understanding what was important. I think many airplane companies have a tendency to employ technology for technology's sake, without really trying to understand what value is actually being added for the end user."*[12]

The company's general aviation line in 1972 featured 39 models of business and personal aircraft. Meanwhile, the company continued an almost frantic pace of expansion. In 1972, building projects included a 37,000-square-foot addition to the Wallace Division and a 60,000-square-foot addition at the Hutchinson Plant, which was organized as part of the Cessna Fluid Power Division.[13] The following year, expansion continued at the Fluid Power Division in Hutchinson, Kansas and Glenrothes, Scotland, with an additional 282,416 square feet of floor space.[14]

The company also purchased a 115,000-square-foot manufacturing and office building located on 30 acres at MacArthur Road and the K-15 Highway. The facility, known as Pawnee Plant II, was used to supplement manufacturing at the Pawnee Division Plant on East Pawnee Road. In addition, both Cessna finance subsidiaries, Cessna Finance Corporation and Cessna International Finance Corporation, were housed there.[15] By the end of 1974, the company had expanded its sales organization to include 1,034 dealers worldwide.[16]

The Energy Crisis

In 1973, the American public was abruptly confronted with the fact that it had grown dangerously dependent on oil from the Middle East. When Arab nations refused to sell oil to countries that supported Israel during the 1973 Yom Kippur War, gas prices skyrocketed. Lines at gas pumps stretched

Left: This advertisement for the Cessna Pilot Center included a $5 coupon for an introductory flying lesson in "the world's best trainer," the Cessna 150.

Below: Cessna's Hutchinson facility in 1973, following a substantial expansion.

for blocks as panicked drivers topped off their tanks whenever the needle quivered below full.

Although stocks of oil were relatively full nationwide, the panic created the perception that oil supplies were running out. The almost hysterical reaction of motorists actually created a shortage where one did not previously exist.

In the midst of the panic in November 1973, President Richard Nixon made an ominous announcement, recalled Russ Meyer, who had just been elected chairman of the General Aviation Manufacturers Association (GAMA) and who would join Cessna as executive vice president the following year.

> *"I got a call from Ed Stimpson on Sunday afternoon, who said, 'Nixon is going to make a speech about allocating fuel. We're not going to like it.' So we're sitting there, watching Nixon tell us we have this terrible energy crisis, and they're going to cut general aviation fuel by 50 percent. ... We went to see someone about it, the Secretary of Transportation, but he was not available. Then we accidentally got locked in one of the government buildings. Boy, was this ever symptomatic of what was going on."*[17]

Meyer delivered a speech stating that "this is no longer a question of growth in general aviation. It's a question of survival."[18] Throughout the crisis, Meyer worked closely with Dwane Wallace and other GAMA directors to ensure that "nonessential" (the federal government's designation) industries like general aviation received their fair share of fuel. The incident was one of the first real challenges to GAMA, which had been founded in 1970. By achieving a solution in which general aviation aircraft received equitable fuel allocations, GAMA became an increasingly effective and essential trade organization for the industry.

In February 1974, Wallace offered Meyer a position at Cessna. Meyer turned it down. Not long afterward, however, Wallace told Meyer that he was reorganizing Cessna and wanted to appoint two executive vice presidents. "While there was never any assurance of what was going to happen beyond that, it was fairly clear that one of the vice presidents would succeed Dwane," Meyer recalled. "I thought it was too good an opportunity to pass up. ... I thought Cessna was the best, and I had great respect for Dwane because he was always thinking about the industry as well as the company."[19]

Malcolm S. Harned, an experienced aerospace engineer and manager who had joined Cessna as a vice president in 1970, became the other executive vice president. Harned was in charge of aircraft manufacturing operations, the avionics and accessories divisions, and the fluid power operations while Meyer was responsible for financial and legal activities, marketing of all aircraft products, and personnel.[20]

Russell W. Meyer, Jr.

Growing up in the small Midwestern town of Davenport, Iowa, Russ Meyer enjoyed a childhood that seemed like something out of a Norman Rockwell painting, complete with a paper route, Sunday evenings gathered around the radio and afternoon baseball games.

Meyer was born in 1932, between an older sister and a younger brother. He understood the value of working for a living early in his life. At nine, Meyer got his first job delivering the *Des Moines Register.* The experience was "one of the more meaningful and effective disciplines in my life," he later said.

Left: Dwane Wallace in 1973.

Above: Malcolm S. Harned, who became executive vice president in 1974, would be promoted to president of Cessna in 1975.

"You got up early, seven days a week, at maybe 4:45 a.m. I remember that one of my customers on that route was the principal of the local high school, who absolutely terrified me. I hadn't been on the paper route more than about four days when he came out and told me that if his paper wasn't folded properly and on his porch by 5:45 a.m., I could probably expect to go to prison for the rest of my life. ... I started out with about 50 customers in a one-mile radius. Everybody had porches, and you'd ride your bike and pitch the papers onto the porch. If a little wind got you, and the paper went on somebody's roof, you were in trouble."[21]

Meyer knocked on countless doors to recruit new customers. By the time he hung up his sack about five years later, he had expanded from 50 customers to 128, in a route about one quarter as long as the original. For his efforts, he won such prizes as a Ted Williams baseball glove and a Rawlings football. He faithfully put his earnings, about $4 a week, in the local bank.

Meyer's roots in Davenport and his neighborhood ran deep. His parents were natives, and his paternal grandparents ran a local grocery store just a few blocks away from his house. Active in many sports, he pitched for his varsity baseball team until an appendix operation forced him to quit for four months. He took up golf, winning a city tournament the following year. The sport remained his avocation ever since.

Though his time was divided between games, school and work, he joined his family every Sunday night to listen to Amos 'n Andy, Jack Benny and other popular radio personalities of the day.

Always an excellent student, Meyer attended Yale on a scholarship in 1950. "It was an extraordinary education," he later said, "and very maturing."[22] Meyer started out with an engineering major, but switched to history. It was during the McCarthy era, and as part of a special academic program his senior year, he wrote a 287-page paper about congressional investigations. Although he had an entire academic year to work on the report, he didn't start until January. "I must have worked 18 hours a day for I don't know how long," he said. "My eyeballs were just about crossed."[23] Although he received a good grade for his efforts, he knew he could have done better. The experience taught him the value of long-term planning.

Meyer graduated in 1954 and, after a short stint on Wall Street, signed up for four years with the Air Force, where he served as a fighter pilot. That's where he developed a fierce love of aviation. "The first plane I flew was a T-34, a really nice airplane," he remembered fondly. "In those days, the first thing you did was slide the canopy back. The second thing you did was feel the rush of the wind. ... Then you'd close the canopy and go up and do your thing. Turn it upside down or whatever. ... I just loved that. I remember I sent my parents a telegram when I soloed."[24]

Transferring to the Marine Air Corps Reserves in 1958, he flew FJ-3 Sabre Jets for three years, "which was one of the best experiences of my life."[25]

On August 20, 1960, he married Helen Scott Vaughn of Rochester, New York. Together, the Meyers would have

Above: Russ Meyer, who would lead Cessna into the 21st century, joined the company as executive vice president in 1974 and became chief executive officer the following year.

Left: A Model 421 Golden Eagle from 1970.

Above: The Titan, Cessna's largest business/cargo/commuter twin-engine airplane, was introduced in 1976.

Below: The interior of a Titan configured for freight.

five children — Russell, Elizabeth, Jeffrey, Christopher and Carolyn.

Meyer graduated from Harvard Law School in 1961 and accepted a position with the law firm of Arter & Hadden in Cleveland, where he tried his first case within four weeks of passing the bar. When he won, it reinforced a lesson he had learned in college. "The number one thing I learned is that the guy who is best prepared is going to win 99 times out of 100 as long as he doesn't do something really stupid," he said.[26]

The firm did a lot of work in the aviation industry, and because of his active involvement in this area, Meyer was given an assignment to structure additional financing for American Aviation Corporation, a small company trying to develop and certify a two-place plane. Meyer soon became the company's general counsel, in addition to his work at the law firm.

After practicing for five years and gaining experience in both litigation and general corporate law, Meyer was asked to run American Aviation.

> *"I said, 'You've got to be kidding me. I don't know how to run this little company.' They said they were dead serious, and asked me to take a leave of absence from the law firm. They said, 'We've got to get this airplane certified. When we get it certified, we'll have the choice of selling or going into production.'"*[27]

The law firm was supportive, Meyer recalled, telling him that it offered good experience. The firm suggested a leave of absence, expecting him to return to full-time practice in a year or two.

In June 1966, he became president and chief executive officer. The company was in the process of developing a two-seater called the Yankee. The Traveler and Tiger followed, and in 1972,

The Hawk XP (extra power), with a 195-horsepower engine, was introduced in 1976.

American Aviation acquired the assets of the Gulfstream program from Grumman Corporation in a reverse merger that created Grumman American Aviation Corporation. The new company had a line of products ranging from single-engine and agricultural aircraft to large business jets. It was a big change. "The Traveler weighed 1,800 pounds and the Gulfstream II weighed 60,000 pounds," Meyer said. But the lessons he had learned early in life served him well, both at Grumman American and after he joined Cessna in 1974.

"There is nothing in our business or probably any business that changes if you build a good product, treat the customer fairly and fully support the product over a period of time. ... Size and weight are less important than aircraft quality, good management, employee morale and commitment to aviation."[28]

Moving from Grumman American to Cessna was a big change for Meyer. The two companies were similar in that both produced high-quality light aircraft, the work pace was intense and the senior management was committed to both the company and the industry. But moving to Cessna's size and scope was equivalent to going from the minor leagues to the majors, as Meyer recalled.

"The engineering capability here at Cessna was much broader than what we had at Grumman American, the resources greater and the scale greater. I came from an environment where, if we delivered 50 airplanes a month, plus a couple of Gulfstreams, that was pretty good. When I arrived at Cessna, we were delivering between 400 and 500 airplanes a month, 20 to 30 planes a day. That was impressive."[29]

An Aviation Legend Retires

In 1975, Dwane Wallace, who had led Cessna for four decades, retired. President Del Roskam retired at the same time, although both remained on the board of directors and served as senior consultants.[30] Meyer was elected to replace Wallace as the chairman of the board, while Harned became the company's fourth president.[31]

Interviewed in 1997, Roskam said he knew Dwane was ready to retire while remaining a director. "We decided to retire at the same time."[32]

Added Meyer: "I think they felt that they had the right management structure in place. They said, 'We'd like you to be chairman and chief executive officer and we want to elect Mal [Harned] as president and chief operating officer.'"[33]

Until Meyer made the announcement at a senior management meeting, few people knew he

had been chosen as successor. Handing over control of the company must have been a difficult decision for Wallace. He had helped resurrect a defunct company started by his famous uncle, and had devoted his life to building it into a global organization. "Dwane didn't play golf. He didn't play tennis. He had absolutely no avocation. Cessna was his avocation," Meyer said.[34]

In 1978, Meyer became president as well as chairman and chief executive officer. He is widely credited with continuing an atmosphere at Cessna that was begun by Clyde Cessna and fostered by Dwane Wallace. Gifford Booth, who joined Cessna in 1962 and retired as director of marketing communications in 1980, praised Meyer's leadership ability. "According to Russ Meyer, the most important thing we have are people. ... Just like at home, you can kick your kids in the butt and they'll turn into a bunch of bums, or you can train them and make wonderful citizens out of them."[35]

"I remember Russ saying that, no matter how busy we get, it will be OK if we keep our sense of humor," said Marilyn Richwine, director of corporate affairs.[36]

Marketing out of a Slump

Meyer took control of Cessna at the right time, as the company's marketing efforts were clearly paying off. To improve fuel efficiency, the company

CESSNA was blessed with a talented and dedicated management. Booth and Richwine were just two invaluable components of Cessna. Others included Bill Adams, who retired in 1996 as vice president of manufacturing and support services. Adams made the necessary changes in production and manufacturing to handle additional product lines and production of the Citation series. Bernie Bogard, who retired in 1983 as vice president of commercial aircraft sales, was vital in the development of worldwide sales for propeller-driven single- and multi-engine aircraft.

While Bogard developed the sales, L.C. Gartin, who retired in 1982 as vice president of product support, developed the propeller support organization. Gartin helped lead the support group during the tremendous growth years of the seventies. Jack Zook, who retired in 1981 as director of marketing administration, was a key figure in devising administrative policy, marketing strategy and dealer support services for the worldwide sales and marketing organization. The late Ed Chase, who was head of the Cessna Finance Corporation for many years, developed the original financing organization in the fifties. The wholly owned subsidiary gradually grew to become the largest finance company in aviation. Peter Redman succeeded Chase in 1986 as president of CFC, which remains vital to Cessna's future.

Above: Del Roskam was often considered "Dwane's interpreter" because he put Wallace's ideas into action. He retired in 1975 after 13 years as president of Cessna.

Right: The P-210 Centurion was the world's only pressurized single-engine piston airplane when it was introduced in 1977.

The Ag Husky, introduced to the agricultural market in 1976, was the only turbocharged agricultural airplane in the world.

had substantially refined the aerodynamics of its planes in 1975, while keeping all airplane prices at the same level as the previous year.[37] Perhaps for those reasons, sales of all product lines increased in 1975, reaping total revenues of almost $492 million, and the company increased its market share of the general aviation industry to nearly 54 percent.[38] The market share was driven by two milestones: in 1975, Cessna delivered its 1,000th Golden Eagle and produced its 100,000th single-engine airplane.

Sales for 1976 were up slightly from the year before, at $493 million, in spite of a five-week strike in July and August 1976. The strike was unusual for the company; the previous one, which had lasted only four days, had been in 1959. Aircraft deliveries increased from 7,673 to 7,705[39] units, and employment surpassed the 15,000 mark.[40] New designs also went into production, such as the Ag Husky, the only turbocharged agricultural airplane in the world.[41]

Deliveries of the Model 404 Titan, the company's largest business/cargo/commuter twin-engine airplane, began in 1976.[42] The turbocharged aircraft was offered in three versions: the Ambassador, featuring a business interior; the Courier, which could be quickly adapted from a passenger aircraft to a cargo plane; and the Freighter, which had extra-wide doors and was considered a heavy-duty cargo plane.[43]

Also in 1976, the Hawk XP (Extra Power) was introduced. Described as the powerful big brother to the Skyhawk, it sported a 195-horsepower fuel-injection engine and a constant-speed propeller.[44]

When Cessna celebrated its 50th anniversary in 1977, employment had reached 16,000 and sales totaled $620 million.[45] Aircraft deliveries increased 9 percent over the previous year, to 8,430.[46] The P-210 Pressurized Centurion, the world's only pressurized single-engine piston airplane was among the 47 commercial models manufactured in 1977.[47]

In 1978, the McCauley Accessory Division moved to a new facility at Dayton International Airport in Vandalia, Ohio. That same year, Cessna became the first in the industry to offer weather radar aboard a single-engine aircraft.[48]

The Conquest Series

Cessna's first propjet, the Model 441 Conquest, made its maiden flight in 1975, and was certified and ready for delivery in 1977.[49] The 441 (which would be designated the Conquest II in 1983) was watched with great interest by the aviation industry because it promised such superior performance in speed, climb and fuel efficiency.

The 441 was powered by Garrett TPE-331 engines, and was by far the fastest, most fuel-efficient aircraft in its class. Shortly after its certification in 1977, Russ Meyer flew the Conquest II to the Paris Air Show, stopping once in Newfoundland, then nonstop from there to Paris.

Deliveries began in the summer of 1977. But the aircraft's success was dimmed by a tragic accident in November 1977 which killed seven people.[50]

The accident shocked Cessnans because the Conquest II had undergone a rigorous development and FAA certification program. Cessna took immediate action by grounding the fleet of Conquests until the problem could be solved. Cessna provided its customers with alternate transportation during this time.[51]

It was determined that the accident had been caused by a lack of adhesive bonding in the leading edge of the horizontal stabilizer. Cessna redesigned the stabilizer and replaced it on every aircraft in the fleet.

Cessna had taken immediate action, fixed the problem and returned the aircraft to flight status before the end of 1977. Since that time, the Conquest II has maintained an excellent safety record, and the fleet has accumulated more than a million hours of flight time.

Cessna President Mal Harned noted that the 441 "exceeded almost every performance standard set for it before the certification process began." The Conquest could reach speeds of 332 miles per hour, and boasted "fuel efficiency unmatched by any other jet or prop-jet aircraft."[52]

Shortly after the Conquest debuted, Cessna introduced a second turboprop called the Model 425 Corsair. This model was renamed Conquest I in 1983. The Conquest I was powered by the reliable Pratt & Whitney PT6 series engines, flat rated to 400 pounds of thrust. Introduced in 1980, the Conquest I was extremely well received by the operators. Like its big brother, the Conquest I continues to provide exceedingly good service, and almost all are still in operation.

Cessna built 234 of the Conquest I and 359 of the Conquest II. These aircraft were an important part of the Cessna product line and continue to hold exceptional value in the marketplace. Cessna stopped building the line because of the severe economic recession in the aviation industry in the mid-eighties, one which was detrimental to all manufacturers.

Improving an Old Standard

In 1978, the 150, still favored for beginning pilots, was refined and given a new 110-horsepower engine and a new designation — the Model 152.[53] The updated plane featured a dual impulse coupling that increased voltage to the magnetos, and a four-cylinder direct primer. The new system injected fuel evenly into all four cylinders, providing prompt ignition and uniform combustion. "This new starting system will appeal to students and operators alike. When a trainer starts easily, the students love it and the operator has substantially reduced downtime and maintenance costs," noted Cessna Senior Vice President Bob Lair.[54]

Other improvements included a new glare shield that enhanced forward visibility, a redesigned throttle control fitting, a "stepped" green arc on the tachometer that provided easy reference to power settings at different altitudes, a new avionics control panel and vertically adjustable pilot seats.[55]

The end of the seventies was marked with several other accomplishments: the certification of the Turbo and Pressurized Centurions for flight into known icing, the only production singles approved for this capability, and the introduction of the Cutlass RG, which would become the world's most popular retractable gear airplane in its first year of production.[56]

But during the next decade, these accomplishments would be overwhelmed by the greatest challenges faced by Cessna since it reopened its factory doors. Another recession, deeper and longer than anything encountered since the Depression, would cut into the company's ranks. Rising insurance premiums would force the company to halt production of all piston-engine aircraft plus the two Conquest turboprops, and Russ Meyer would take on the federal government in an attempt to revive an industry that was falling on hard times.

The Conquest was Cessna's first propjet.

The Citation VII, a more advanced version of the Citation III, helped fill the market niche for a high-performance midsize jet.

A GROWING FAMILY OF CITATIONS

"The Citation has a wonderful image. It has a great safety record, it is an affordable business jet, and it is just so popular. It's a natural choice to show the actual workings of business aviation."

— Dorothy Cochran, curator, National Air and Space Museum, 1997[1]

IN 1976, CESSNA released what was probably the most significant announcement ever made by a general aviation company when it unveiled an expanded Citation family at the 29th National Business Aircraft Association convention in Denver, Colorado. The Citations I through III represented Cessna's largest commitment to new products.

The Citation I was a carefully designed upgrade of the popular two-pilot Citation. Boasting increased wing span and thrust, the upgrade resulted in improved performance, range, climbing abilities, cruise speed and passenger accommodations.[2] The Citation I's most noteworthy aspect, however, was its certification by the FAA for single pilot operation. This was the first business jet to achieve single-pilot certification.[3]

The Citation II was a new business jet that used many of the same proven components and systems as the Citation I.[4] The fuselage was stretched by four feet, providing an eight-seat configuration, and the wings from the Citation I were attached to a new carry-through structure.[5] Able to reach an altitude of 43,000 feet, the Citation II had the shortest takeoff requirements — at 2,990 feet — of any jet in its class. The Citation II was certified in 1978. It quickly became the best selling business jet of all time, and stayed in production for 16 years.[6]

This version was quieter in both take-off and cabin sound levels, and more fuel efficient as well. "The Citation II had considerably better range," said test pilot Ellis Brady. "It retained all the other characteristics of [the original Citation] but gave us significant improvement in cabin volume and then got the range up to where it could perform a lot more missions."[7] The Citation II could also be flown by a single pilot, either in the II/SP version or with a Part 91 exemption to the pilot's certificate. The II/SP included instrument modifications and a boom mike which made it easier for a single pilot to operate the aircraft.

The Citation III was a totally new swept-wing high-performance business jet in the midsize category. It was also Cessna's largest financial commitment to a single product in Cessna's history.

"Citation III was an airplane that came about after a lot of advanced design study, which included a three-engine plane," recalled Milt Sills, vice president of engineering. "We investigated a three-engine airplane for a while and finally concluded there was not really a suitable market for it. We weren't sure it was a suitable market for anybody."[8]

The sweptback wings of the Citation III are highlighted in this photo.

The Citation II offered more cabin volume than the original Citation.

Inset: The cockpit and panel of a Citation II.

The Citation III's advanced technology wings, developed in cooperation with Dr. Dick Whitcomb at NASA, were important to its performance. The unique airfoil design significantly reduced the wave drag associated with standard airfoil designs on jets flying at similar speeds.

The plane was Cessna's first to be certified to 51,000 feet, recalled Sills, an altitude so high that pilots cannot remain conscious more than a few seconds without pressurized cabins. Engineers introduced several technologies that went beyond the requirements of the already stringent FAA rules. The plane was designed so that in the event of rapid cabin decompression, the autopilot would fly the aircraft from 51,000 feet to 14,000 feet in three minutes and 30 seconds and then level off automatically.

But the Citation III's most impressive features related to its performance.[9] At high altitudes, the Citation III remained the fastest aircraft in its class, with exceptionally stable handling characteristics, low operating costs (due to its fuel efficiency) and ability to climb quickly.[10]

The first Citation III customer was legendary professional golfer Arnold Palmer, a longtime pilot and Citation owner, who praised the new "III iron's" performance in company advertisements. "I couldn't run my businesses nearly as effectively without the unique capabilities of the Citation III. It is without question the finest business jet I've ever flown. And I've flown them all."[11]

Executive Jet Aviation

The Citation S/II, which debuted in 1984, featured a modified supercritical wing, which was much more efficient at higher speeds. This particular wing was one of the main reasons for the later success of the Citation V. The S/II also featured improved sound reduction, increased baggage space, and greater useful load. As in the case of the Citation II, it could be operated by a single pilot as long as the pilot had a Part 91 exemption.[12]

In 1986, a company called Executive Jet Aviation purchased six S/IIs to launch its unique fractional share program. The company, founded in 1965 as a charter organization, had been purchased in 1984 by Richard Santulli, who had developed a concept called "NetJets" to sell fractional shares of ownership while still guaranteeing that the planes would be available when needed. Customers, for example, purchase one-eighth of an airplane, entitling them to 100 hours of flight time per year. The customer is charged only for the time he occupies the aircraft.

The program was widely disliked by many aircraft salesmen who thought it would attract customers who might otherwise purchase a jet of their own. But Cessna realized that EJA not only would purchase a large number of airplanes, but would introduce many potential customers to the Citation family of business jets.

EJA has since purchased approximately $2 billion worth of Citations. Santulli, the company's chairman, said he likes working with Cessna because the company provides excellent planes and first-rate customer service. "With the kind of operation we run, which is 24 hours a day and seven days a week, with quick response time a requirement, it's very important that we have uninterrupted service, that our inspections are as quick as possible and our unscheduled maintenance events don't happen often. Cessna's service centers are second to none."[13]

More than Just a Business Jet

With its exceptional performance and value, criteria that quickly became associated with Citations, the aircraft has also been pressed into service for missions such as flight inspections, air ambulance and surveillance. Citations were used for special United States government needs. The U.S. Customs Service, for example, has relied on Citations for patrol service since the seventies. The planes are equipped with sophisticated military radar and infrared systems that can read the identifying numbers of planes flying at low altitudes at night.

Another Citation modified for government use was the T-47A, used for radar intercept training maneuvers at the Pensacola Naval Air Station in Florida. Cessna provided these training systems between 1984 and 1991.[14]

Two adaptations of the Citation III were introduced in the early 1990s. The Citation VI was a more affordable midsize jet that provided the outstanding performance of the Citation III with updated, standardized features to keep efficiency high and operating costs low. From 1983 to 1994, Cessna delivered 240 Citations III and VI.

The Citation VII offered more significant improvements to make it climb more quickly and fly even faster at high altitudes; better ice and rain removal for the cockpit windows; and more powerful Garrett TFE731-4 engines. Cruising speed was increased to 550 miles per hour. Several modifications reduced drag, such as a smaller dorsal-fin air inlet. The outboard thrust reverser stangs were redesigned.[15]

Above: Assembling the Citation III required skilled craftsmen and state-of-the-art techniques.

Right: The Citation S/II was selected by Executive Jet Aviation to launch its fractional share program.

The Citation S/II offered improved flight performance over the Citation II.

In addition to the exterior modifications, the cabin offered an expanded selection of custom-type options for interior fabrics, finishes and woods. Certified in March 1992, the Citation VII began customer deliveries a month later.

Building a Better Business Jet

Like the original Citations, the new models were manufactured with meticulous care.[16] A Production Inspection Record was maintained at each stage of assembly to assure quality control. This PIR book contained signatures of the assembly worker and FAA-approved inspector responsible for each stage of the process. Contributing to the Citation's quality control program was the testing of almost every part and assembly used on the aircraft before it ever arrived on the manufacturing floor, including parts from outside vendors.[17] The efficiency of the Citation's production team made it possible to produce a record 140 Citations during 1979.[18]

By 1981, that number increased to 196 Citations, and on January 27, 1982, Cessna deliv-

Above: The sweptback wings of the Citation III were assembled in vertical jigs during production.

Below: The Wichita Citation Service Center is the largest facility of its kind.

ered its 1,000th Citation, making it the only general aviation company in the world to have delivered that many business jets in such a brief time span. The 1,000th delivery, a Citation II, was received by Indium Corporation of America, based in Utica, New York, the world's largest producer and refiner of pure indium metals used in the microelectronics industry. By that time, the Citation had captured 55 percent of the business jet market.[19]

The Citation's reputation was also recognized in the Far East. In 1981, the People's Republic of China purchased its first business jet ever — the Citation II.[20] Ursula Jarvis, vice president of administration, was in charge of working out the agreement. Cultural differences made the job more challenging than usual, she said, since the Chinese continue negotiating even after a contract has been signed.[21]

Though many people contributed to the Citation's success, two Cessnans stood out. Joe Solomon and J. Derek Vaughan fulfilled crucial management roles during the development years of the Citation program. Solomon, who retired in 1989 as vice president of product support and aircraft completion, guided the development of the Citation product support effort during the program's growth years. He was a key figure in expanding the number of company-owned Citation Service Centers. Vaughan, who left Cessna in 1983 as senior vice president and general manager of the Citation Marketing Division, played an important role in developing worldwide sales of the Citation during the seventies and early eighties.

The Robert J. Collier Trophy

Cessna, Russ Meyer and the entire Citation series received a special honor in 1986 when they were chosen as winners of the 1985 Robert J. Collier Trophy. Perhaps the most coveted aeronautical honor in America, the Collier is "awarded annually for the greatest achievement in aeronautics or astronautics in America, with respect to improving the performance, efficiency, and safety of air or space vehicles, the value of which has been thoroughly demonstrated by actual use during the preceding year."

Prior recipients included Orville Wright in 1913 and the astronauts aboard the historic Apollo 11 moon landing in 1969.[22]

Above: A Citation III prototype on the tarmac.

Below: In 1986, Russ Meyer (right) received the Robert J. Collier Trophy in recognition of the excellent safety record of the Citation series.

The award was named for Robert J. Collier, a prominent publisher and aviator, who was also the first person to purchase a plane from the Wright brothers for personal use. Collier commissioned and donated the 525-pound bronze trophy to the Aero Club of America in 1911, the year the first award was given to Glenn H. Curtiss for development of the hydro-aeroplane. The trophy is now on permanent display at the National Air and Space Museum in Washington, D.C.

The award citation read: "Russell W. Meyer, the Cessna Aircraft Company and its line of Citation business jet aircraft for the safety record in 1985 of almost 1,400 Citation aircraft."[23]

Meyer accepted the honor May 16, 1986 at a presentation and banquet in Washington, D.C. Addressing an audience that included Kansas Senator Nancy Kassebaum, Transportation Secretary Elizabeth H. Dole and Arnold Palmer, Meyer praised Cessna employees for the company's outstanding safety record.

"That safety record was not achieved by good luck. It was achieved because we have the best air traffic control system, because we are building better aircraft and equipment, providing more useful and necessary information to our operators through standardized manuals and handbooks, and because we have developed much more effective training programs and simulators for both new students and professional pilots."[24]

Riding on the crest of these achievements, Cessna rapidly expanded its Citation family during the late 1980s and early 1990s.

In September 1987, two months after the successful Special Olympics Airlift (see sidebar), the Citation V was introduced at the annual National Business Aircraft Association convention. Designed as an evolutionary model of the S/II, the V featured a cabin 18 feet long, 20 inches longer than the S/II. Its two Pratt & Whitney JT15D-5 turbofan engines provided 2,900 pounds of takeoff thrust. These 800 additional pounds of thrust translated into a top cruising speed of 427 knots and a ceiling of 45,000 feet. Standard equipment included such features as an eight-passenger configuration, radar, Honeywell autopilot, thrust reversers, a flight guidance system and two external baggage compartments.[25] Contributing most to the popularity of the Citation V was the supercritical wing, adapted from

The Citation V, introduced in 1987, was a much improved version of the S/II, featuring a more spacious cabin and more powerful engines.

the S/II but modified along the leading edge to make room for a new de-icing system.[26]

Citation V Project Engineer Roy Phillips described the alterations: "We kept the same airfoil used in the Citation S/II. It's a supercritical wing that's uniquely different from the Citation II wing, and it was totally developed by Cessna."[27] So successful was the design team in creating a marketable improvement to the S/II that 70 orders had been placed for the new V before a model was available for flight and customer demonstrations.[28]

In September 1994, another evolutionary step was taken with the first delivery of the Citation Ultra. Its overall design was created to expand on the strengths of the V. The Ultra could cruise further and faster, and outclimb the V. The airframe of the Ultra is identical to the V,[29] but significant changes were made in cabin design, flight control system, pilot displays and operating performance.[30] Twin Pratt & Whitney JT15D-5D engines provide 3,045 pounds of thrust — the key to the Ultra's performance improvements.[31]

At maximum weight takeoff, the Ultra can climb to 41,000 feet in only 20 minutes, and its short takeoff requirement of 3,180 feet contin-

Above: The cockpit and control panel of the Citation V (left) and Citation Ultra (right).

Below: A Citation III in flight.

ues this traditional key Citation attribute. Its ability to carry eight passengers, as well as its large cockpit, exceptional standard flight operating equipment, and ability to fly at a faster speed than the V with the same amount of fuel,[32] earned the Ultra the "Best Business Jet" award by *Flying* magazine in 1994. The Ultra was chosen for "offering more performance, more comfort and more speed but costing no more money to operate."[33]

CitationJet

With the improvements and evolution of the numerous Citation models, Cessna went back to the drawing board in the late 1980s to design an entry-level business jet similar in marketing principle to the original Citation and Citation I of the 1970s. The result was the CitationJet.

The challenge to Cessna's engineering team was to design an entry-level jet with a cabin as large as the Citation I, but with higher speed and longer range while using much less powerful engines. The Citation I's JTI5D-1A engines delivered 2,200 pounds of thrust; the CitationJet's Williams FJ44-1 engines, on the other hand, would deliver just 1,900 pounds.

The solution was to design a lighter and more efficient airframe, which included a laminar flow wing airfoil and an innovative design of the carry through structure. The structure followed the exterior contour of the fuselage, and

This page: The interior and exterior of the Citation VII.

greatly simplified the attachment of the wings to the fuselage.

As a result, the CitationJet had a cabin with more usable space, but the gross weight was reduced from 11,850 to 10,300 pounds. Although fuel capacity was reduced from 3,780 to 3,220 pounds, the aircraft was faster than the Citation I, and had considerably more range.[34]

Some of the concepts that made the CitationJet an impressive breakthrough were subsequently used in the development of both the Citation X and Excel. The CitationJet was designed to recapture the entry-level market its two predecessors had created. The CitationJet first flew on April 29, 1991.[35]

The twin Williams/Rolls-Royce FJ44 turbofan engines were simpler than the Pratt & Whitney models, containing only 700 parts. The aircraft was carefully tailored for reduced drag so that even with less thrust, the CitationJet performance exceeded that of its predecessors,

THE SPECIAL OLYMPICS AIRLIFT

CITATION SPECIAL OLYMPICS AIRLIFT

THE IDEA FOR THE CITATION Special Olympics Airlift began in 1985, when the Kansas Special Olympics Committee asked Cessna Chairman Russ Meyer if he could provide transportation for the state's team to the Winter Games in Salt Lake City. Meyer readily supplied two Citations with crews. The operation went so well that Meyer decided to take it further.

When he accepted the Collier Award in 1986, Meyer announced his plan for flying hundreds of Special Olympians and their coaches to the Summer Games in South Bend, Indiana. "Before he made the announcement, he came into my office and said, 'I have the greatest idea,'" recalled Director of Corporate Affairs Marilyn Richwine, who would eventually spearhead the project. "He wanted to know what I thought of it. Well, what do you say to the boss? You can't tell him his idea is crazy. So I said, 'That sounds like it would be really nice.'"[1]

Described as "the largest peacetime airlift in aviation history,"[2] the event took 14 months to coordinate. The first step was to send three letters to the CEOs of companies that used Citations. The first letter was from Special Olympics founder Sargent Shriver, the second was from Meyer, and the third was from Senators Ted Kennedy and Bob Dole, who put aside their political differences for the cause.[3]

Held every four years, the Special Olympics was originated to provide the experiences of personal growth, camaraderie and physical fitness for mentally handicapped children and young adults.

Corporations responded with enthusiasm, and by the time of the event, 132 Citations had been organized to transport the entire delegation east of the Rocky Mountains — nearly 1,000 athletes and coaches — to the games, which attracted 4,600 athletes from all 50 states and 72 foreign countries. Using volunteer pilots, the airlift saved Special Olympics community programs close to $2 million in travel expenses.[4]

For six and a half hours on July 31, 1987, a Citation took off from an airport staging point in 16 cities every three minutes, each carrying four to eight Special Olympians.[5] The planes also arrived in two- to three-minute intervals, in order to keep state delegations together. Since the six different models of Citations traveled at different speeds, organizing the event was a logistical challenge. And, 10 days later, the Citations and their passengers were sent winging homeward.

and its unusually low operating costs made it as affordable as a twin turboprop.[36]

By 1993, approximately 100 orders had been placed for the CitationJet. Thirty percent of those were from current Citation owners, with another 30 percent coming from turboprop owners.[37] Roger Whyte, senior vice president of marketing and sales, said the plane had been on back order since before it was ready for the market. "Within three days of its announcement, we had 53 orders on the books for an airplane that had no metal on it yet," he said.[38]

As the Citation family evolved during the eighties and nineties, Cessna maximized its opportunities within the marketplace. The company's share of the light business jet market grew from 51 percent in 1981 to more than 75 percent by 1991.[39]

The Bravo and Excel

In 1996, Cessna announced a replacement for the Citation II with the introduction of the Citation Bravo.[40] The new model used Pratt &

"There wasn't a person among us who didn't have a little bit of doubt that we could pull it off," said Dean Humphrey, then director of public relations for Cessna. "Nothing like this has ever been done before on this scale in civil aviation."[6]

The event, which Cessna repeated for the 1991 and 1995 games, was memorable for all involved.

"A 16-year-old swimmer found her Citation III flight was addictive. 'I don't EVER want to go anywhere any other way,' she says. 'I didn't get sick. I always get sick in the car.'

"It wasn't just the youngsters and the coaches who enjoyed the flights. The Citation flight crews had their own memorable experiences.

"One of the pilots, having landed at South Bend and taxied to the disembarkation point, helped unload the athletes and their baggage. Then, prepared to reboard the Citation, he was halted by one of his young passengers, who gave him a mighty hug. One by one, the other athletes stepped up to embrace him — the Special Olympians' universal expression of appreciation and affection. The pilot was still beaming as he taxied the aircraft away.

"'Those kids made us feel like heroes,' another veteran pilot with white hair observed. 'They were so open and genuine. I don't know when I've enjoyed anything this much.'"[7]

Whitney PW530A engines that increased speed by approximately 8 percent and consumed 10 percent less fuel.[41]

The Bravo also had a new trailing link landing gear, a new digital flight control system with larger displays and a sophisticated flight management system. The company marketed the new aircraft as a direct challenge to turboprops, emphasizing that it could travel 135 miles per hour faster and climb at least two miles higher than popular business turboprops on the market. The luxurious interior seated as many as 10, including two pilots, and the aircraft was exceptionally easy to operate. "Things have changed since the days when one could rationalize the turboprops' lower speeds, lower altitudes, higher noise and vibration levels on the basis of 'saving the company money.' Now the savings go to those who use the more advanced technology," noted a marketing brochure.[42]

In 1993, Milt Sills and his advanced design team conceived a simple, large-cabin Citation that would combine the wings, tail and systems of the Citation V. Though the engineering team argued that the resulting plane would be a relatively straightforward way to gain market advantage, management and marketing were concerned that the cruise speed would not be acceptable. Nonetheless, they assembled customer focus groups which gave the concept a favorable endorsement.

Being an "extra large" version of the Model 560, the new aircraft became the Model 560XL, Citation Excel. With some further design and manufacturing refinements, Cessna introduced the Citation Excel in 1994 as "the first business aircraft ever to combine the spaciousness of a stand-up cabin with the simplicity, versatility and short-field capability of a light jet."[43] Market acceptance was immediate and enthusiastic.

The Excel's enormous success is not surprising, because engineers carefully designed the aircraft to fit the requirements developed by a Citation Advisory Council. The council comprised people involved in a broad range of corporate flight operations, with varying fleet sizes

The CitationJet, introduced in 1989, marked Cessna's return to the entry-level business jet market.

The Citation Excel, introduced in 1994, combined the spaciousness of the Citation VII with the versatility, ease of operation and fuel economy of the Citation V.

and specific missions. The most important requirements included cabin size, short-field performance, reliability, baggage space, acquisition price and low operating costs.

The council said that Cessna would have a world-beating aircraft if the company could provide a spacious stand-up cabin; ample baggage for eight passengers; balanced field length of 3,500 feet, and a purchase price within $1 million of the price of an Ultra, with similar operating costs and the same speed and range.

Cessna delivered on the council's requirements, and as a result the company had built an order backlog in excess of 200 aircraft, including 50 for Executive Jet Aviation, prior to the first customer delivery. Market response has been extraordinary, and FAA and production schedules remained on track. Russ Meyer said he expects Cessna to sell more than 1,000 Excels.

The Excel's roomy cabin is three to four inches shorter between passenger bulkheads than the Citation VII, but is longer than the VII between pressure bulkheads. In addition, the Excel's lavatory is considerably larger. Powered by new Pratt & Whitney PW545 engines, the aircraft boasts a cruising speed of more than 500 miles per hour, can take off and land from runways as short as 3,500 feet, and climb to 41,000 feet in 20 minutes.

The family of Citations is sure to continue winning awards and recognitions. In 1998 and 1999, the Citation will highlight an exhibit on business aviation at the Smithsonian Institution in Washington, D.C. "The Citation has a wonderful image," said Dorothy Cochran, curator of the Aeronautics Department at the Smithsonian's National Air and Space Museum. "It has a great safety record, it is an affordable business jet, and it is just so popular. It's a natural choice to show the actual workings of business aviation."[44]

Rollout of the first high-performance Citation III in 1983 was one of the highlights of a decade marked by stark reductions in payroll and production.

LOSING ALTITUDE

1980–1989

"We thought we had seen the bottom of the piston market on two or three different occasions. ... Then we'd find out we had to take hundreds more people out of the workforce."

— John Moore, 1997[1]

DURING THE EARLY 1980s, good economic news was hard to come by for Cessna, and many American corporations. Skyrocketing interest rates meant people couldn't afford to borrow the money to buy airplanes. A declining export market and increased liability insurance premiums aggravated an already strained situation.

Cessna struggled through the early years of the eighties, drastically cutting payroll and consolidating operations. When faced with earlier downturns, Cessna always managed to market itself out of the slump, offering incentives and implementing special programs. It did so again, but this recession threatened to tear the heart out of the company.

By 1986, the company's workforce would plunge from 18,000 to 3,000, and Cessna would be acquired by General Dynamics, the $8 billion defense company. Though Cessna saw a turnaround by 1989, that year was marred by the death of Dwane Wallace, one of only three chief executives in the company's history, and the man who helped resurrect Cessna in 1934.

Painful Cutbacks

The company's financial challenges began in 1980, when high interest rates scared many potential customers away from the aviation market. To remain viable during this difficult period, Cessna responded with a series of cost reduction and cash conservation programs.[2] Excess aircraft inventory was discounted and short-term borrowing was decreased by $57 million.[3] Worse still, from a human point of view, were the severe layoffs.

On March 14, 1980, 750 employees of the Pawnee Division were laid off. "We planned a gradual decrease in the rate of production to coincide with normal employee attrition and hoped to avoid major changes in employment levels," said CEO Russ Meyer in a press release. "However, the rapid escalation of interest rates in just the last two weeks has already resulted in reduced credit for aircraft purchasers, and many of our customers are unable to obtain financing, or unwilling to borrow at such high rates."[4]

By the end of the month, Cessna had shut down both its propeller aircraft and Citation assembly lines for four weeks, forcing layoffs of

Cessna's growing line of business jets, including the entry-level CitationJet, helped it survive a difficult time.

800 employees and furloughs of an additional 1,500 at the Wallace Division.[5]

This pattern would repeat itself for several years.[6] John Moore, head of human resources since joining Cessna in 1982, said many executives kept believing they had seen the worst in the piston-engine aircraft market.[7]

> *"Between 1982 and 1984, we thought we had seen the bottom of the piston market on two or three different occasions, and the problem was we never saw the bottom of it. We would think we had plateaued, and we would go out and communicate accordingly and conduct ourselves accordingly. Then we'd find out we had to take hundreds more people out of the workforce."*[8]

"The wheels were coming off in the whole industry," recalled Gary Hay. "We were discontinuing models, closing offices and of course laying off a lot of people. Those were rough times."[9] Hay, who became vice chairman in 1996, began his career at Cessna in 1966. He served in both the piston-engine and the Citation sides of Cessna marketing, witnessing the pain and joy that came from each.

> *"Thank goodness there were areas of the company like Citation that were pretty buoyant financially, but we went from something like 18,000 employees down to 3,000 in a matter of three years, and nobody knew from day to day — certainly on the piston engine side of the business — whether they were going to have a job."*[10]

More bad news was on the way. Malcolm S. Harned, former senior vice president of technology at Cessna, died October 21, 1980. During Harned's 10-year tenure at Cessna, he had served as a vice president, senior vice president, executive vice president, and president and chief operating officer. He had also served six years on the board of directors.[11]

The year-end results were mixed. Despite the cost-cutting, sales of $1 billion yielded pre-tax earnings of $55 million, down from $90 million in 1979. The company sold 6,927 planes, down 16 percent but still representing a record share of the general aviation market.[12]

By this time, the most popular planes sold by Cessna were the business jets in its Citation series, which Hay noted "was carrying the company in terms of its financial contribution."[13] Other new

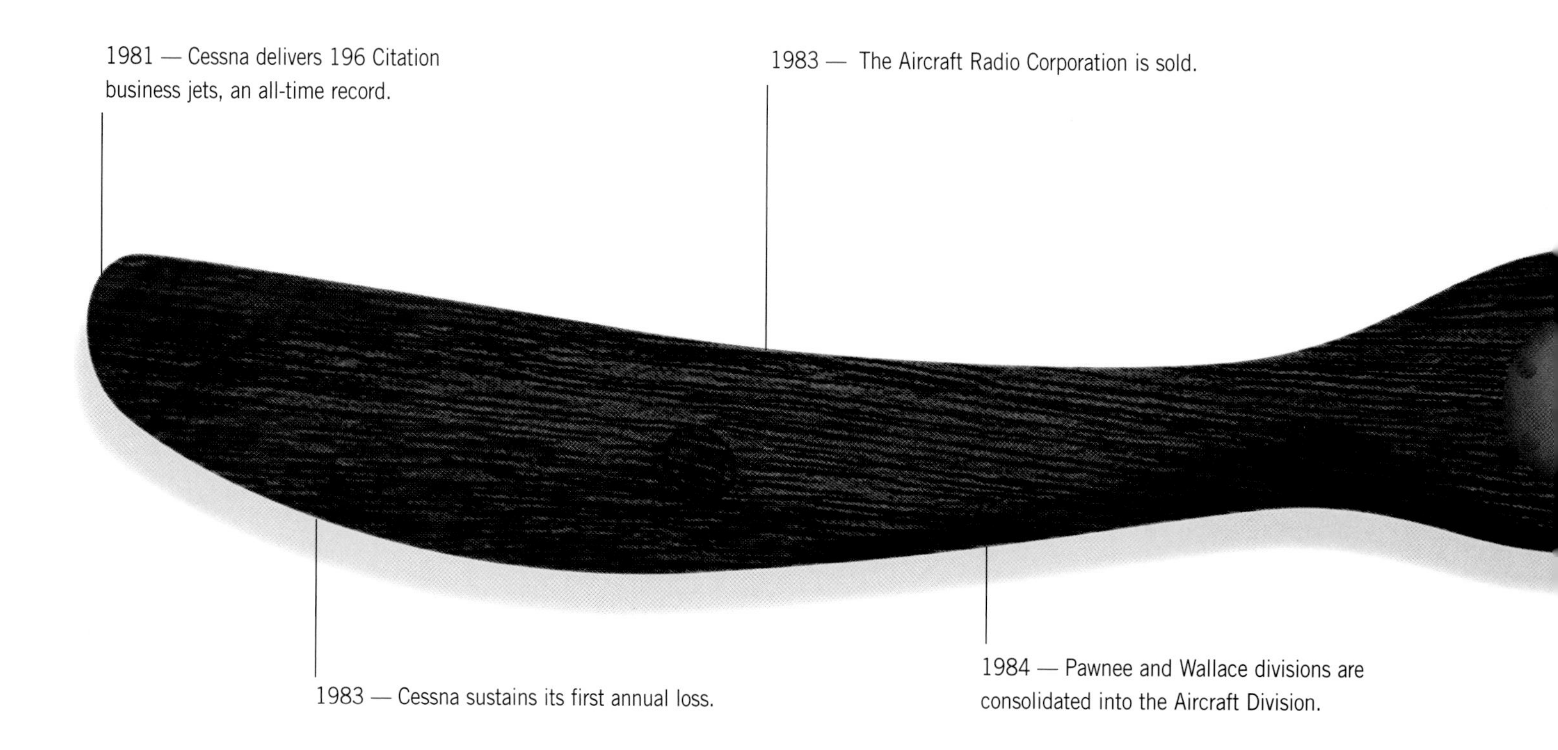

The Model 425 Corsair debuted in 1980.

planes offered in the early eighties were generally modifications of existing models, with improved interiors, aerodynamics and instrumentation. One new plane was the Corsair, an 8-place propjet that began deliveries in 1980.[14]

Marketing Innovations

In addition to the consolidations and cutbacks caused by the economic downturn, the company unveiled aggressive marketing strategies to entice new enthusiasts to flying. In November 1981, the company introduced the nation's largest flight-training program, called "Cessna Flight Plan," by offering a fixed price of $2,990 to obtain a private pilot's license. Promoted through Cessna's nationwide network of Cessna Pilot Centers, it allowed for payments to be made and financed with bank credit cards.[15]

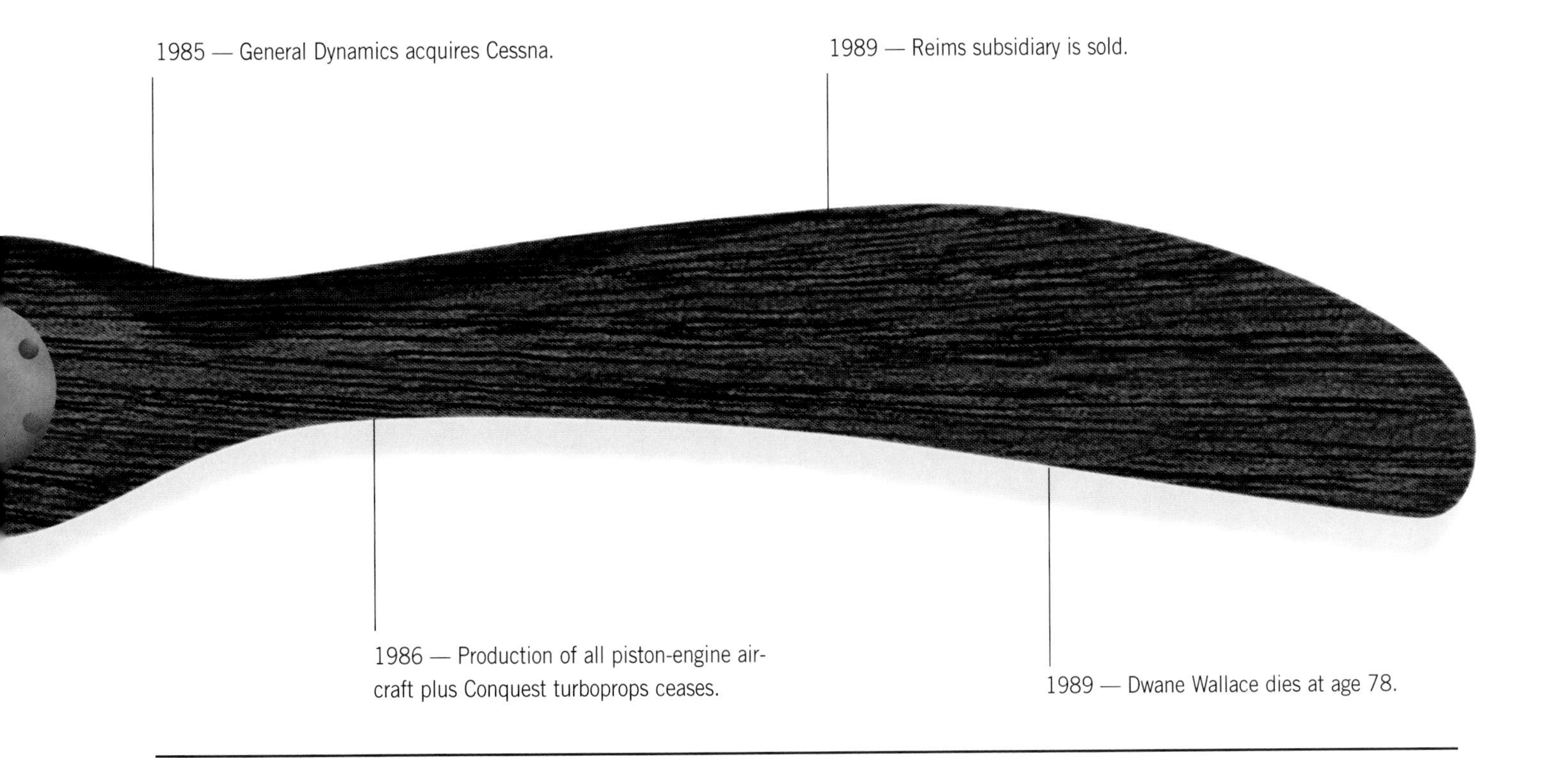

Economic conditions improved in 1981, when Cessna introduced the Crusader, a six-place twin-engine aircraft with counter-rotating propellers.

By the end of the year it appeared the hard work and belt-tightening were beginning to pay off. Sales reached $1.06 billion, and earnings were $61 million with 5,331 aircraft sold in 1981.[16]

One new plane introduced that year was the Crusader, which went into production in 1981 and saw its first delivery in September. The six-place piston-engine twin featured a wide oval cabin with more volume and baggage capacity than competitive craft.[17] Its distinctive cruciform tail provided advanced aerodynamics with superb longitudinal stability. Equipped with two 250-horsepower Teledyne Continental engines, the Crusader could reach a cruising speed of about 240 miles per hour.[18]

The year 1981 was a period of expanding capital-expenditure programs, due in part to accommodate the popular Citation series. "We have invested $98 million in research and development since 1979, significantly broadening our lines of general aviation and fluid power products," noted Meyer in his annual letter to shareholders.[19] The company also spent more than $19 million to expand and update the Wallace Division's Mid-Continent Airport site; $8.5 million for machine tooling and equipment for new product development at the Fluid Power Division; and $2 million in capital equipment at the Pawnee Division facility for production of the new Crusader light twin.[20]

In a further effort to reduce costs, Cessna streamlined its marketing and support organizations in 1982, and created a new Propeller Aircraft Marketing Division led by Robert L. Lair, senior vice president of marketing. Other elements of the reorganization were intended to improve effectiveness of Cessna's dealer organization.[21] Just five months later, Cessna consolidated the aircraft sales and marketing and product support divisions to achieve further economies of scale.[22]

Peter Redman, who joined Cessna in 1978 and became general manager of the Cessna Finance Corporation in 1982, recalled that the company had to change its strategy to deal with the slow economy. "In the early eighties, dealers had all the inventory and the retail customers weren't buying. The dealers would run through the interest-free period and the terms of the note, and they were unable to sell their airplanes, so we ended up with a tremendous number of repossessions," he said.[23]

To solve this problem, Cessna introduced a flurry of financing programs in an attempt to get inflation-shocked customers back into the aviation market. One program, the "Prime Leader," set interest rates as low as 7 percent for the purchaser of a Conquest I or II for the first two years of a five-year contract.[24] The "Fiscal Fitness" program, which featured zero interest terms for the first year and allowed customers to finance as much as 85 percent of the purchase price, led to the sale of more than 700 planes during the year.[25]

Another program, "Company Airline," provided the owners of Conquests and Citations with all maintenance, hangar, insurance and miscellaneous expenses for a five-year contract period. On request, Cessna would even train and manage the flight crews. Customers only needed to pay a modest refundable deposit and small fixed monthly payments.[26]

However, high interest rates, inflation and persistent recession made 1982 the most challenging year in two decades for general aviation. Aggravating the situation were liability lawsuits that sent insurance premiums through the roof. From 1979 to 1982, sales of single-engine aircraft declined 80 percent.[27] Cessna's sales were only $831 million, and pre-tax earnings dropped precipitously to $35 million.[28] "We didn't recognize until 1982 that we were in for a very serious long-term recession," said Bob Conover, a sales manager in the early eighties who is now director of Caravan sales. "Before, every time our sales went down we'd come up with a sales incentive program that would stimulate the market."[29]

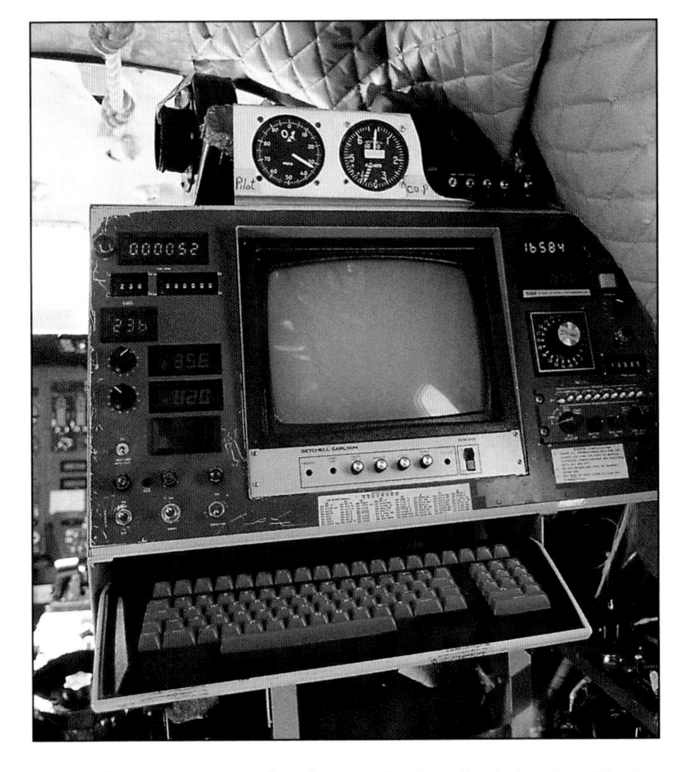

Above right: An experimental aircraft flight test station used to measure and record data aboard a test aircraft.

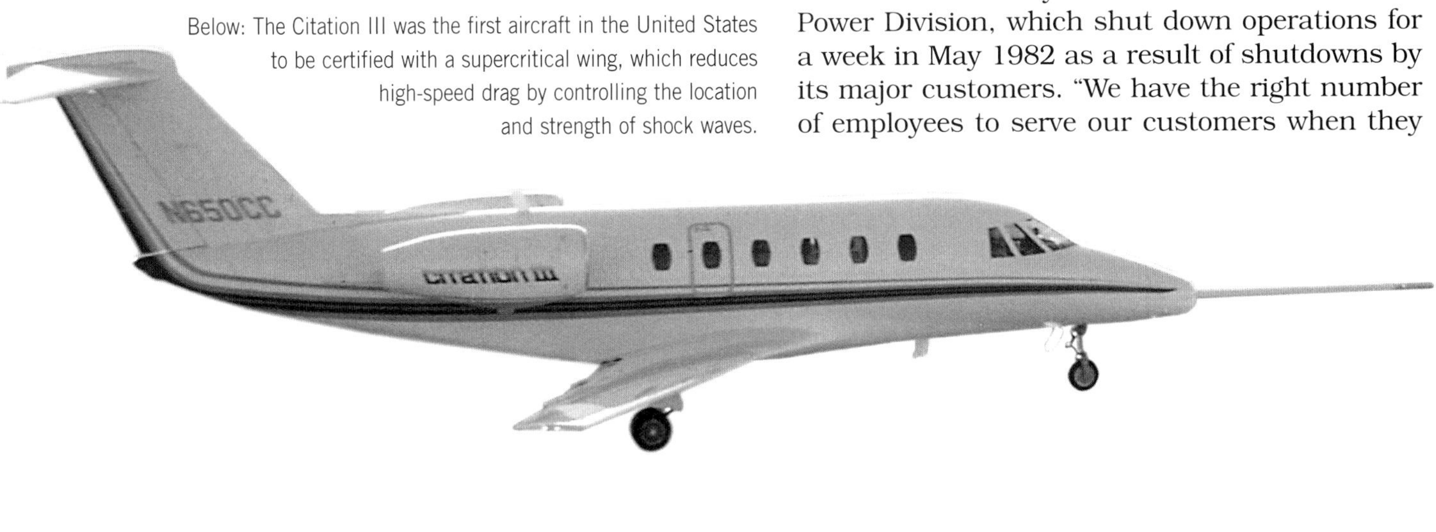

Below: The Citation III was the first aircraft in the United States to be certified with a supercritical wing, which reduces high-speed drag by controlling the location and strength of shock waves.

The company had no choice but to institute another round of layoffs. On March 30, nearly 650 employees in the Wallace Division were furloughed while the propjet production line was put on hold.[30] Another 300 Wallace Division employees were laid off May 28.

The economic cloud of doom hovering over the aircraft industry also affected Cessna's Fluid Power Division, which shut down operations for a week in May 1982 as a result of shutdowns by its major customers. "We have the right number of employees to serve our customers when they are operating, so a temporary shutdown of our own production is necessary," commented Thaine Woolsey, vice president and general manager of the Fluid Power Division.[31]

Despite these drastic measures, conditions did not improve, and the company recorded its first annual loss in 1983. With sales of only $524 million, the company recorded a net loss of $19 million.[32]

The End of an Era

On January 5, 1983, Dwane Wallace resigned from the company's board of directors. In June 1983 he was hospitalized with heart difficulties, and following surgery, he suffered complications from which he never fully recovered.[33] He died on December 21, 1989, at the age of 78.[34]

Russ Meyer credited Dwane Wallace for providing outstanding leadership for both Cessna and the industry. Wallace was fondly described by his peers as "Mr. General Aviation," a nickname that was well earned. He had been elected chairman of GAMA when it was organized in 1970, and was always a source of counsel after his retirement. He remained a director of Cessna until 1983. Wallace lived a very quiet life, especially after he encountered a series of health problems in the eighties. Nevertheless, he always remained fiercely loyal to Cessna and left a heritage of commitment to aviation. "If it weren't for Dwane Wallace, the company wouldn't exist today," noted his wife, Velma.[35]

In 1985, Wallace received the first Kansas Aviation Honor Award at the Wright Brothers Celebration Dinner, recognizing his leadership in the aviation industry. Lt. Governor Tom Docking presented the award on behalf of Governor John Carlin.[36] "Dwane was a very strong and guiding force in the aviation industry, and he deserved that trophy," said Russ Meyer.[37]

Wallace was so engrossed in the company that he didn't seem to need hobbies. "He was a relatively quiet guy," said historian Craig Miner. "But when he did something, there was a lot of thought behind it and often a lot of wit."[38] Bruce Peterman, a Cessnan since 1953, remembered Wallace as "one of the best engineers and one of the best businessmen in the general aviation industry."[39]

The *Wichita Eagle* also described him as "a legend in the world of aviation, for his skill both as a businessman and an aircraft designer."[40]

"Although Wallace's name wasn't on the company or its products, aviation historians say he belongs in the pantheon of Wichita's leading aviation pioneers, including Clyde

With Cessna's innovative financing programs, customers could purchase a Conquest I or II and pay interest as low as 7 percent.

The Citation III was Cessna's first plane to be certified to 51,000 feet.

Cessna, Walter Beech and Lloyd Stearman. 'Dwane Wallace played an integral role in aviation history,' said Edward Stimpson, president of the General Aviation Manufacturers Association. 'Under his leadership, Cessna Aircraft made the planes that taught the world to fly.'"[41]

Reorganization

Economic conditions resulted in the sale of Cessna's Aircraft Radio Corporation Division, which had been acquired in 1959 and had operated as a wholly owned subsidiary in New Jersey. The division was sold to the Sperry Corporation, which provided avionics for most of the company's Citations and Conquests.

In August 1983, Bill Van Sant was elected president, chief operating officer and a member of Cessna's board of directors. Van Sant was a 26-year veteran of Deere & Company in Moline, Illinois, the world's largest manufacturer of farm equipment, where he had most recently served as vice president of engineering and manufacturing services. He would leave Cessna in 1986.[42] In November 1983, Del Roskam retired from the Cessna board of directors, replaced by General Dynamics Corporation Chairman David S. Lewis.[43] At the same time, General Dynamics purchased a small percentage of Cessna stock, said Meyer.

"The stock was to be dedicated to joint technology projects. Both Dave and I felt that we were the leading company in general aviation, and General Dynamics was one of the leaders in high-performance military aircraft. We felt that there could be value to both companies by jointly evaluating various projects and advanced tech-

nologies. From the start, it was a very friendly and meaningful relationship."[44]

In June 1984, Cessna announced a consolidation of the Wallace and Pawnee divisions into the Aircraft Division, strengthening the company by reducing duplication of effort.[45]

In large part because of these consolidations, revenues for 1984 increased 32 percent, reaching more than $693 million, and the company barely returned to profitability, with earnings of just under $1 million. Aircraft deliveries dropped from 1,371 to 919, but dollar volume increased.[46] Nonetheless, production at the Pawnee Division was shut down for three months, affecting nearly half of its employees.

"I've seen people go out of here with 25 and 30 years of service," recalled Regene Prilliman, a benefits supervisor who started out at Cessna in 1961. Prilliman was in human resources during the tough years. It wasn't a time she remembers with fondness. "That has to be one of the most frightening things that can happen to a person."[47]

To streamline operations, the propeller aircraft sales and marketing operations were consolidated into one Aircraft Marketing Division in February 1985.[48] Cessna's management structure was also streamlined, and top executives were given additional responsibilities.[49]

Still, the company underwent more layoffs during 1985. Production of many models was suspended, and plans were made to consolidate assembly for those that remained during the balance of 1985 and 1986.[50] In 1985, only 885 aircraft were sold. It was obvious that something had to change.[51]

"I concluded that it would be in the best interest of shareholders to explore the possibility of a merger," Meyer said. General Dynamics, which already enjoyed a strong relationship with Cessna, was a logical candidate. "We ended up negotiating a deal with General Dynamics without really discussing it with any other companies," he said.

"Whether or not we should merge with another company was a difficult and complex decision. Cessna had been an independent company for almost 60 years, and as the leader in general aviation there was considerable interest in retaining that status.

Production of the single-engine Stationair 8 came to a halt in the eighties.

Production of the 152 also stopped when Cessna halted production of all single-engine aircraft.

"On the other hand, the entire industry was suffering from both the economy and the decimating impact of the cost of product liability. Despite our personal preference to remain independent, we recognized that our number one priority was to Cessna shareholders. With a fair price for the stock and with the financial stability and growth opportunities provided by a partner like General Dynamics, it was clear that a merger was the best decision and the vote was unanimous.

"This decision and the subsequent negotiations required an enormous amount of time by both management and our directors. Cessna was fortunate to have four outside directors, Don Slawson, Ken Wagnon, John Stewart and Larry Jones, who were totally committed to the success of the company and who devoted a substantial amount of time to the merger.

"In retrospect, this merger was beneficial to everyone: our shareholders, our employees, the industry and the community. Our continued investment in new products and expanded facilities during those very difficult years created the foundation which has enabled us to expand our worldwide leadership in the industries we serve. Since the date of the merger, we have enjoyed 12 consecutive years of growth, increased employment from 3,000 to almost 11,000, and set the stage for even greater growth in the next century."[52]

General Dynamics

Cessna announced its acquisition by General Dynamics on September 13, 1985. General Dynamics Chairman Dave Lewis, who was also a member of Cessna's board of directors, made it clear that the defense company understood "that their expertise was in defense and our expertise was in general aviation," Meyer said.[53]

The merger was completed in March 1986, and made Cessna a wholly owned subsidiary of General Dynamics. Cessna continued to operate independently, and Meyer remained chairman of Cessna, while also becoming an executive vice president and board member of General Dynamics.

General Dynamics, with headquarters located at that time in St. Louis, is among the

A Citation III assembly line. Sales of Citations remained strong while the company was forced to halt piston-engine production.

oldest and largest defense manufacturers in the nation, with more than 100,000 employees. The company began in 1899 when John Holland founded Electric Boat Company, a ship and submarine builder. During both world wars, Electric Boat manufactured submarines for the U.S. Navy, as well as PT boats and ships. In the fifties, the company launched the *Nautilus*, the world's first atomic-powered submarine.

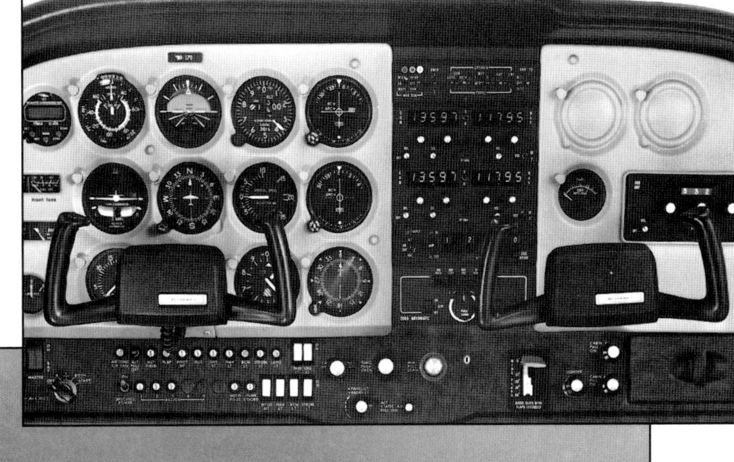

The Skyhawk was among the last of the piston models whose production was halted in 1986.

After World War II, Electric Boat CEO John Jay Hopkins purchased Canadian aircraft builder Canadair, and formed General Dynamics in 1952 by merging Canadair and Electric Boat. In 1954, the company purchased Consolidated Vultee Aircraft, which manufactured both civilian and military aircraft.

A March 4, 1986 article in the *Wichita Eagle-Beacon* summarized the benefits of the acquisition during a time when the entire aviation industry was suffering.

A Citation III in line for takeoff. The versatile plane could be flown from large airports as well as more remote locations.

"Analysts said the merger gives Cessna the backing of a giant corporate parent as it competes against manufacturers such as Beech Aircraft Corporation, which is owned by Raytheon Co., Piper Aircraft Corporation, which is owned by Lear Siegler, Inc., and Gulfstream Aerospace Corporation, which is owned by Chrysler Corporation.

"For General Dynamics, analysts say the deal provides a way to diversify beyond its military business in fighters and submarines and obtain added manufacturing capacity. However, a few analysts question whether General Dynamics, with $8.2 billion in sales, could obtain much diversification from a relatively small, $700 million company like Cessna."[54]

In his annual letter to shareholders, General Dynamics CEO Stanley Pace, who had recently succeeded Lewis, was upbeat in describing the merger. "We believe Cessna is exceptionally well-positioned to take advantage of a future upturn in the general aviation market."[55]

The acquisition did not immediately improve Cessna's situation. In 1986, delivery of aircraft for the general aviation industry reached its lowest level since World War II — only 540 for the year, generating sales of $539 million.[56] By this time, employment had dropped to barely 3,000, a decline from Cessna's peak employment a few years earlier.

Piston-Engine Aircraft Production Stops

A major cause of the drop was the company's decision in 1986 to halt production of its final line of single-engine airplanes, in large part because liability lawsuits had sent insurance rates soaring. Production would not resume until 1996, after Meyer helped establish legislation that limited such lawsuits. (See Chapter 16.)

Meyer described the decision as one of the toughest of his career, but said the company had no other option. "Product liability was becoming a real cancer," he recalled.[57]

Bruce Peterman recalled that piston production had been dropping since 1978. "Everyone was aware of the strong decline. And the thing that went through my mind was that we've got to make Cessna survive. If the litigation and all the problems associated with the piston airplanes meant that we had to stop production on the pistons in order to concentrate on the jets, that's what we ought to do. The company simply had to survive."[58]

The inevitability of the decision didn't make it any easier. Dean Humphrey described it as "very traumatic. ... Even though there had been production suspensions and interruptions over the years, I don't think anything of this magnitude had ever been announced."[59]

Return to Prosperity

Bruce Peterman became senior vice president of operations.[60] Peterman, a 43-year veteran who retired in 1996, had been involved with almost every Cessna aircraft for 20 years, noted Russ Meyer.

> *"I have never worked with a finer gentleman than Bruce Peterman. He probably had a broader range of engineering expertise than anyone in the industry. He was the perfect role model: unselfish, competent, professional in every respect and totally devoted to Cessna."*[61]

The company's improving bottom line owed a great deal to its relationship with General Dynamics. "The significance of the arrangement was that it enabled us to ride out a couple of very difficult years," noted Meyer.

> *"Without General Dynamics, it would have been difficult for us to sustain the engineering development on such critical programs as the Citation V. That enabled us to put a fair amount of distance between us and the competition when other companies were having similar problems in terms of the economy."*[62]

Dean Humphrey said he was pleasantly surprised at the degree of autonomy maintained by Cessna. "I think Russ Meyer was a big part of that," he said. "He held his ground, and to give credit to the General Dynamics board, they said, 'We're military and we don't know anything about the general aviation business.' By then, we were coming back strong with the Citation line."[63]

Cessna also had a profitable year in 1988, with orders for Citation jets continuing to strengthen the company.[64]

In March 1989, Cessna sold its French-based Reims subsidiary to a French company. Reims Aviation S.A. had been owned by Cessna since 1960, and assembled models such as the 150, 152, 172, the Skylane 182, the twin-engine Skymaster and the 406. When it was sold, Reims purchased the type certificate to continue to assemble the F-406.

"We purchased Reims for the right reason, but the right reason never materialized," Meyer said. "The right reason was the European nations in the mid-fifties were discussing a very, very high import tax on a number of products, including airplanes. So we acquired an operation in France."[65]

Reims had been ably operated by Pierre Closterman from the time Cessna purchased the company. Closterman's business acumen was just one facet of a fascinating profile. A World War II ace, Closterman had been a member of the Free French Movement. He flew with the Royal Air Force, shooting down more than 30 enemy aircraft. As head of Reims, Closterman helped devise a special finance program that increased Cessna's market share in Europe.

The decade closed on a positive note. Cessna held 50 percent of the worldwide market in light and mid-size business jets. Backlogged orders in 1989 doubled to more than $850 million, requiring the addition of 1,500 employees during 1990. The widespread acceptance of the Citation contributed to a prosperous outlook for the years to come.[66]

President Bill Clinton signs the General Aviation Revitalization Act August 17, 1994, as key legislators and industry leaders look on. From left to right: Monte Mitchell; Pat Lehman; Congressman Dan Glickman; Vice President Al Gore; Cessna Chairman Russ Meyer; Gerald Baliles, chairman of the Airline Commission; Senator Nancy Kassebaum; Congressman James Hansen; and Ed Stimpson, president of GAMA.

THE GENERAL AVIATION REVITALIZATION ACT

1986–1994

"I've often wondered if the people who unjustly sued us knew, or even cared, how many families their greed put out of work."

— Russ Meyer, 1996[1]

THE PISTON-ENGINE aircraft industry, wildly successful in the sixties and seventies, witnessed a precipitous decline in the eighties, in large part because of liability lawsuits that raised insurance premiums beyond acceptable levels. With the entire industry in a downward spiral and foreign competition picking up the slack, Cessna was forced to halt production of all piston-engine aircraft in 1986. Cessna Chairman and CEO Russ Meyer took a leadership role in the industry when he helped enact landmark legislation to restrict liability lawsuits and restore viability to an important American industry.

The General Aviation Revitalization Act, approved in 1994 after years of struggle, owes its success to the hard work of Senators Bob Dole and Nancy Kassebaum of Kansas, Congressman Dan Glickman of Kansas (later to become secretary of agriculture), the General Aviation Manufacturers Association, the Aircraft Owners and Pilots Association and Meyer himself.

"Nancy [Kassebaum] took the lead on that, but I helped as majority leader," said Dole. "It was a big issue, and I certainly give Nancy and Dan Glickman a lot of credit for carrying the heavy water. I might have turned on the hose a few times. ... But when you boil it down, it was Russ Meyer's sheer persistence. He kept hammering away at it."[2]

Liability Problems

During the sixties and seventies, tens of thousands of single- and twin-engine piston aircraft were manufactured and sold. These light aircraft were extremely popular with a wide variety of aviation enthusiasts, from businessmen using them to travel to rural destinations where new factories were located, to individuals using them for private transportation. Special-purpose aircraft were used for agriculture, wildlife study, law enforcement, medical evacuation, and to battle forest fires.

But as the seventies drew to a close, general aviation manufacturers (particularly Cessna, because it had produced so many aircraft), fell prey to a threat many in the industry had seen coming for years — rising insurance rates.

While insurance rates had remained relatively constant over the years, product liability premiums for aircraft manufacturers had skyrocketed. The main culprit was a sharp increase in lawsuits filed by families of pilots and passengers killed or injured in accidents — even accidents caused by pilot negligence. Higher insurance premiums put piston-engine

A 1980 Skyhawk II, one of many Cessna single-engine airplanes forced out of production by high liability costs.

airplanes out of the financial reach of a growing number of potential customers.

Trial lawyers found they could play on the emotions of juries, and aircraft manufacturers were forced to defend a substantially increased number of claims. As early as 1974, liability rates began to rise above all other coverage elements,[3] even though general aviation accident and fatality rates had declined to their lowest point in 29 years.[4] "All of a sudden, by 1978 or 1979, instead of carrying 50 cases, we had 250 cases, and the insurance carriers said we were going to have to increase the self-insured portion," recalled Meyer. "So we went from $1 million to $2 million to $3 million and ultimately to $30 million of self-insurance."[5]

The increase grew partly out of the concept of "crashworthiness," which began in the automotive industry, explained Tom Wakefield, vice president and general counsel at Cessna. "This was a spin-off from strict liability. The basic theory was that even if someone is 100 percent at fault in an accident, he or she can still try to recover damages if they can show that the design of the restraint system, the seat, the rails, the panel or anything else enhanced their injuries," Wakefield said.[6]

Cessna's prominence in the light airplane industry made the Kansas manufacturer particularly vulnerable to lawsuits. Noted Meyer: "Cessna was spending more to defend itself in court than on research."[7]

In one remarkable lawsuit, Cessna and several component manufacturers were sued by a plaintiff who attempted to fly his Model 152

This graph shows the dramatic decline in airplane shipments between 1978 and 1993.

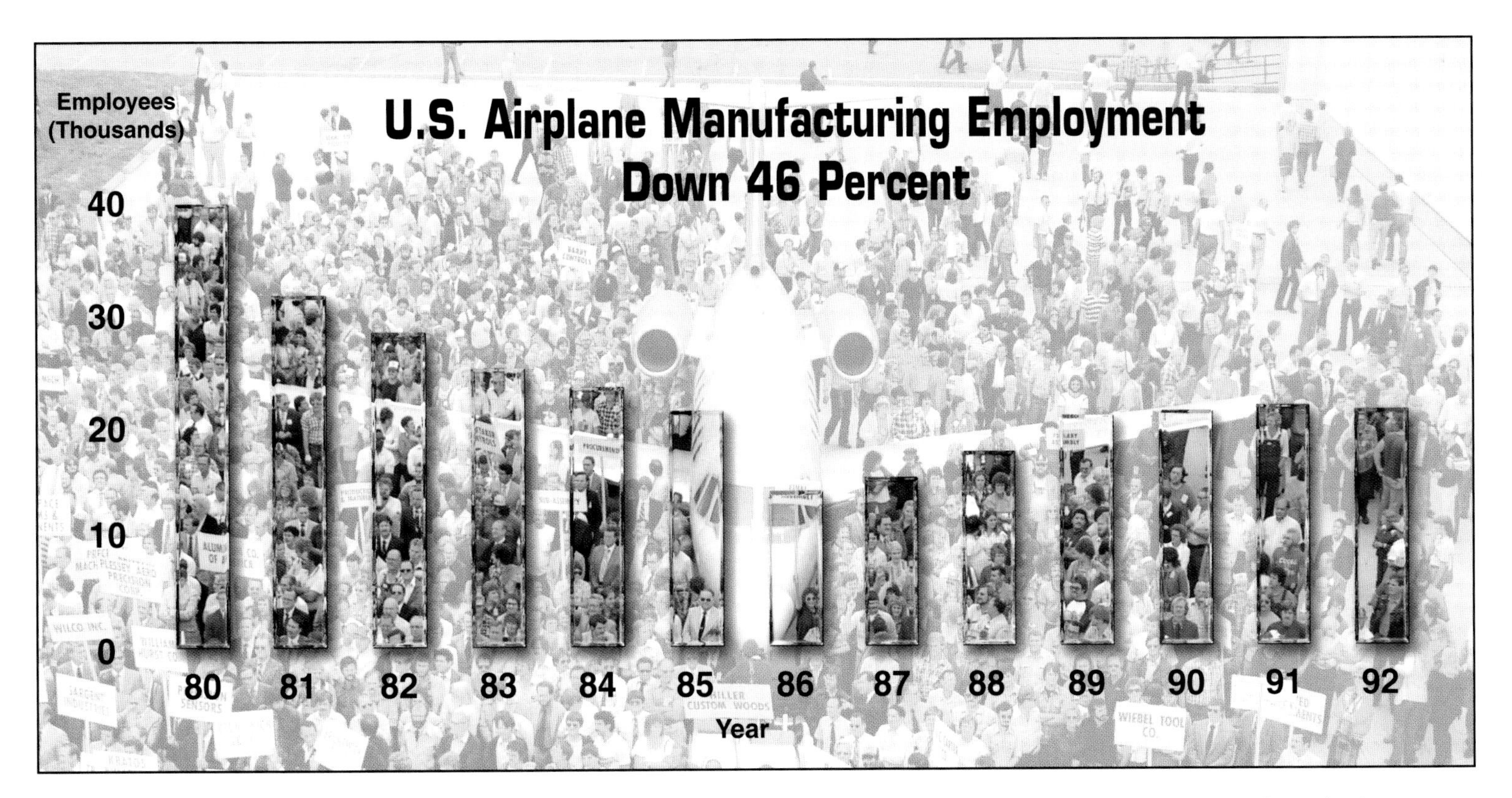

Between 1980 and 1992, the number of employees working in aircraft manufacturing dropped 46 percent.

from Tennessee to Louisiana while severely intoxicated.[8] Three hours after the crash, the pilot's blood alcohol level was measured at 0.2 percent, far above the current FAA maximum of 0.04 percent. The primary problem faced by Cessna and other general aviation companies was the cost of defending against such groundless lawsuits. In 1994, Cessna was even sued in an accident involving a 1946 Model 140 that had run out of fuel.[9]

As John W. Olcott, president of the National Business Aircraft Association, stated: "As interpreted by the courts, product liability applied to general aviation is simply a lottery funded by the general aviation community and promoted by lawyers."[10]

Besides the cost of litigation, economic conditions continued to worsen as interest rates climbed. To combat this negative trend, Cessna instituted a series of programs in the early 1980s to attract new customers. Double warranties, rebates, avionics packages, free flight training classes, and even a safe pilot sweepstakes that offered a 1982 Skyhawk II as the grand prize failed to improve the drastic situation facing piston-engine production.[11]

After six consecutive years of depressed sales, Cessna announced on May 28, 1986 that it was suspending production of all single- and twin-piston engine aircraft. New models of such favorite aircraft as the Skylane, Skyhawk, Centurion and Stationair 6 were put on hold, and 900 salaried and nonsalaried employees were laid off.[12] "That was the blackest time of my business career," Meyer later recalled. "Imagine going to work every day knowing you were going to lay off more people. ... I've often wondered if the people who unjustly sued us knew, or even cared, how many families their greed put out of work."[13]

Cessna's unfortunate situation was shared throughout the general aviation community, as shown by dramatic statistics from the General Aviation Manufacturers Association (GAMA), which represents 39 United States companies that manufacture more than 95 percent of all general aviation aircraft and equipment. In 1980, 40,000 employees were involved in general aviation production, but by 1986 only 12,000 remained. Between 1978 and 1986, annual United States airplane shipments dropped from 17,811 to 4,000. These conditions led to an alarming increase in foreign piston-engine aircraft production. In 1980, the United States had 29 piston-engine airplane manufacturers while only 15 were located in foreign countries. By 1993, the United States had only 9, while manufacturers in foreign countries had risen to 29.[14]

"The industry really came to a halt for small planes," said GAMA President Ed Stimpson. "The economy was also a factor, but the key factor for small airplanes in this country was product liability."[15]

Leaders of the general aviation community knew that it was time to address the situation.

In 1986, GAMA and its members petitioned federal legislators about the burdensome inequality of product liability laws.[16] Every year between 1986 and 1993, these leaders worked to have favorable legislation passed. Each year, however, the efforts failed. "We'd get it reported by a committee, and it would get stalled in the Judiciary Committee," Stimpson said.[17]

The main opponent was the powerful American Trial Lawyers Association. "They are very involved politically and very powerful," noted former Kansas Congressman Dan Glickman. "Because of that, they are able to provide a lot of contributions and work the system. And they had a particular power on the House and Senate Judiciary Committees."[18]

Meanwhile, conditions in the aviation industry continued to deteriorate. Piper, Cessna's chief competitor in the piston-engine market, was forced to declare bankruptcy in 1991.[19] In 1993, piston-engine employment had dropped to around 1,800 workers manufacturing only 34 models, down from 110 models in 1978.[20] In the face of these dismal statistics, progress finally began to take place.

Above: GAMA President Ed Stimpson worked with Russ Meyer to pass meaningful product liability reform, which benefited both the aviation industry and consumers.

Piston Airplane Production Has Moved Out of the U.S.

Below: When piston airplane production dropped in the United States, foreign competitors picked up the slack.

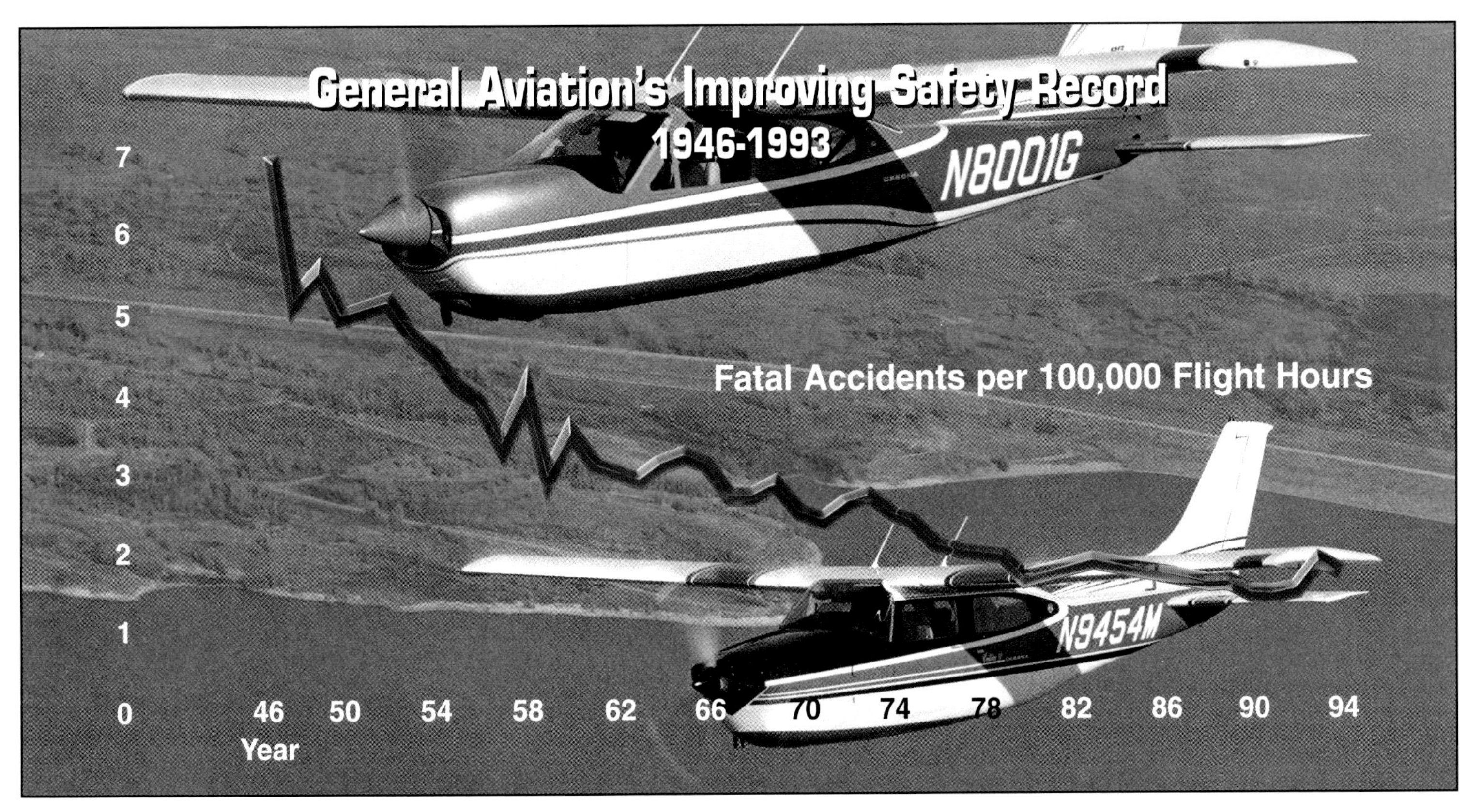

Liability claims seemed unrelated to the safety of the aircraft — while fatalities dropped, claims increased.

The General Aviation Revitalization Act

Senator Nancy Kassebaum introduced the General Aviation Standards Act of 1993, a comprehensive liability bill similar to earlier versions. In February 1994, members of GAMA's Product Liability Committee met with Utah Congressman James Hansen, who suggested the bill was too complex. GAMA officials agreed. After discarding another version written by a Washington, D.C.-based law firm, officials from GAMA and senior attorneys with several general aviation manufacturers agreed on a new bill known as the General Aviation Revitalization Act (GARA) of 1994. This version contained a 15-year statute of repose starting with the delivery date of the aircraft, making it impossible to sue for deficiencies in aircraft older than the limitation.

Hansen and Glickman secured more than 300 co-sponsors in the House and Kassebaum more than 60 in the Senate.[21] "We were blessed that we had Kassebaum and Glickman on this bill," Stimpson said. "They are both highly respected and highly regarded."[22]

Russ Meyer contributed to the bill's momentum by assisting Kassebaum and Glickman in drafting the language. Meyer cast the legislation as a jobs bill rather than a product liability reform bill in order to gain the support of organized labor.[23] And he insisted that the legislation focus specifically on the single issue of a statute of repose, a move that won additional support from consumer organizations.[24]

"Russ Meyer deserves specific praise for being the initiator of this idea," Glickman said. "Russ suggested that we limit this to the issue of the statute of repose. He said if we take out the other parts of the bill, this is the one that makes the biggest difference to manufacturers."[25]

In 1993, President Bill Clinton appointed Meyer to the National Commission to Ensure a Strong Competitive Airline Industry. From that post, Meyer convinced the commission to recommend approval of GARA legislation to the president.[26] The commission noted that "production of

After signing GARA into law, President Clinton congratulates Russ Meyer.

light piston-engine aircraft has been reduced to a trickle by the enormous ongoing cost of open-ended product liability," and added that the GARA would rectify the situation, creating jobs and improving the trade balance in the process.[27]

On March 8, 1994, Kassebaum placed the bill as a rider to the Fiscal 1994 FAA Reauthorization Bill sponsored by Senator Ernest F. Hollings of South Carolina. A longtime opponent to liability reform of any kind, Hollings had to decide whether to filibuster against his own bill, worth $2.05 billion, or let it pass as amended, leaving it to be rejected in the House Judiciary Committee by its chairman, Jack Brooks of Texas. Brooks had stopped many earlier attempts at liability reform. Kassebaum, her patience exhausted after listening to GARA opponents all day, was approached by Hollings with a compromise — if she would drop the GARA amendment, he would send it to the Senate floor as its own bill, with the statute of repose increased from 15 to 18 years. Kassebaum agreed, and within the week, the Senate passed the GARA in a lopsided vote of 91 to eight.[28] At long last, the industry had achieved a meaningful milestone in its efforts to gain relief. However, the House presented its own unique challenge.

Despite the bill's 300 supporters in the House, the Senate's version sat for two months, as expected, under the thumb of Jack Brooks. Unwilling to see their efforts foiled once again by Brooks, Congressmen Glickman and Hansen began gathering signatures for a discharge petition, which would allow the legislation to bypass committee and go immediately to the floor for a vote. The process was made easier by a year-old provision that made signatures on discharge petitions public, holding legislators accountable to their constituents. "In the old days, it was all done in secret, so you never knew who had signed it and who hadn't signed it," Stimpson explained.[29]

Recognizing that the bill might bypass his committee, Chairman Brooks immediately scheduled hearings on it. In June, the House Judiciary Committee approved minor modifications passed by House Public Works and Transportation Subcommittee Chairman Norm Mineta of California, creating a statute of repose of 15 years for piston-powered aircraft, 18 years for turboprops and 22 years for business jets. The modified bill passed a vote on the House floor in July and was sent to the Senate for approval in its new version.[30]

As supporters and opponents of general aviation product liability reform faced off for the final showdown, Russ Meyer announced Cessna would resurrect piston-engine aircraft production as soon as the president signed the bill. His courageous statement offered tangible visions of new jobs, expansive growth, research into new technologies, reduction of foreign competition, and a strengthened of the United States general aviation industry. With that, the bill — with its original 18-year statute of repose — passed the Senate on August 2 and the House on August 3.[31]

GARA had triumphed. "I've done a lot of things in my congressional career, but I think this was my highest individual achievement," said Glickman.[32]

In an Oval Office signing ceremony on August 17, President Clinton praised the new legislation. "This is a job-creating and job-restoring measure that will bring good jobs and restore economic growth back to this industry," he said. "It will also help United States companies restore our nation to the status of the premier supplier of general aviation aircraft to the world, favorably affecting our balance of trade."[33]

With the long-awaited passage of GARA, the devastated general aviation industry was given the confidence to move forward. Phil Boyer, president of the Aircraft Owners and Pilots Association (AOPA), traces a surge in confidence among members directly to the approval of GARA.

"In 1992, we asked members if they were optimistic or pessimistic about the future of general aviation, and about two-thirds were pessimistic and one-third were optimistic. When we asked the same question late last year, the answers were reversed, with two-thirds optimistic and one-third pessimistic. We've asked that question twice every year for the past five years, and we could see where the lines crossed. And they crossed right when that bill was signed."[34]

And Cessna? Within 24 hours, Cessna announced that it was considering 16 sites to locate a new, state-of-the-art, piston-engine aircraft manufacturing plant.[35]

Phil Boyer, president of the Aircraft Owners and Pilots Association, said GARA brought new confidence and energy to the aircraft industry.

Unlike other Cessna aircraft, the Caravan was not a design of aesthetic beauty, but its rugged hauling power made it very attractive.

THE CESSNA CARAVAN

"With a design not to coddle the pinstripe set, but to make money for their somewhat more utilitarian counterparts ... you start to understand why the airplane appears headed for success."

— Caravan customer, 1985[1]

THE CARAVAN, introduced by Cessna in 1985, is renowned for its size, simplicity, lifting power and versatility. Though not as fast or as beautiful as the company's more glamorous business jets, the prop-driven Caravan could "haul heavier loads to more places at lower cost than virtually anything else on the planet," as one magazine writer put it.[2]

Company officials began to scout out the utility aircraft market in the late seventies. They found that these planes, used primarily in remote areas where extreme weather changes, mountainous terrain, and rough landing conditions took their toll, were rapidly becoming old and outdated.

The popular twin-engine Douglas DC-3, for example, had been sold as surplus after World War II. The DHC-2 Beaver and DHC-3 Otter, manufactured by de Havilland of Canada since the 1950s, and called Stoneboats because of their cold, rough rides, were "waiting to be replaced."[3] The Beech King Air series, Piper's Cheyenne, and Cessna's own Conquest turboprop also saw use as utility transport aircraft.[4]

Cessna market analysts were confident that a reliable single-engine turboprop utility aircraft with low operating and maintenance costs could sell around 40 units a year in rugged Canada and Alaska, and succeed in the international market, where most utility aircraft were used.[5] In addition, a powerful single-engine utility turboprop could be used by government agencies in law enforcement, air ambulance services, police, military, agencies ferrying aid to Third World nations and missionary organizations worldwide.[6] Notably absent from the initial list was overnight cargo, which would become one of the most important uses for the new airplane.

On November 20, 1981, the go-ahead was given to create an airplane that Cessna hoped would become "the best value in the general aviation utility category."[7] Engineers at Cessna's Pawnee engineering facility set out to create the utility plane described in the research.[8] John Berwick, chief engineer at Pawnee, supplied the leadership that resulted in a superior airplane designed for the operator. Working with Cessna on the Caravan development project were two former executives from de Havilland who had long urged the Canadian company to develop the same type of plane. Russ Bannock, who offered marketing and operational advice, had recently retired from de Havilland after a successful career that began in the 1950s as a sales manager. Dick Hiscocks, who

The Caravan was the first Cessna single-engine airplane with a turbine engine to go into production.

Above: A 600-horsepower Pratt & Whitney PT6A-114 engine was chosen to power the Caravan because the engine was famous for its low-maintenance requirements and dependability.

Below: The Caravan's wings are over 52 feet wide and contain almost 280 square feet of surface area — needed for short field operations.

provided technical assistance, had retired as vice president of engineering for de Havilland in 1979. Both men attended monthly review meetings in Wichita.[9]

"We had a design philosophy to make it rugged," recalled Project Engineer Larry VanDyke. "Make it go to the field and operate for days on end, with little or no maintenance. It had to be as simple to use as possible. A number of operators would fly the airplane all over the world. The airplanes come into the maintenance base on Friday night or Saturday night. They spend Sunday doing routine maintenance, and it goes back to work, often to remote villages, and stays out all week."[10]

Engineers started with the fuselage of the six-place Model 207 Stationair — a particularly roomy plane — and split it open to insert additional space. The modified fuselage was fitted with a Canadian Pratt & Whitney PT6A-112 turboprop engine. This strategy was soon abandoned because there was not enough room for fuel storage, Meyer said. "The more we looked at it, the more we realized that if we were going to build a truly new and expanded utili-

ty airplane, it had to be designed from scratch," he added.[11] Although the first prototype incorporated some 207 parts, its design was entirely new.

Engineers turned to Pratt & Whitney's PT6A-114 turboprop engine, known for its ability to withstand rugged use with minimal maintenance.[12] The 600-horsepower engine weighed less than 350 pounds and took up minimal space, giving engineers room to place additional features for reliability, such as two ignition exciter boxes.[13] It was the first time that a major aircraft manufacturer had put a turbine engine in a production single-engine airplane. The large size of the Caravan made it possible.

The engine also provided important advantages to pilots flying in remote regions. It operated on fuels that were common worldwide and could even fly short distances on diesel or avgas.[14] Its overhaul service period of 3,500 hours meant that the planes could fly for several years before the engines had to be removed for service.[15]

Dwane Wallace, who remained a consultant as well as a member of the board, insisted on large fuel tanks for remote operators and a strong landing gear to deal with rough terrain.[16] Accordingly, the plane's large wings, designed for quick liftoffs on short, rough runways, contained fuel tanks capable of carrying 335 gallons of fuel.[17] As for the landing gear, an oil-only strut in the nose gear absorbed the hard impact during landings while a spring stabilized the plane during taxis.[18]

The landing gear was designed to be easily replaced by floats, increasing the plane's versatility in remote regions.[19] "The plane had to be able to change from a land plane to a float plane very quickly," said engineer Larry VanDyke. "Our goal was to accomplish the change in eight hours. Most of the other planes took two or three days to change. For an operator, that's a lot of down time. ... We achieved our goal, and I have heard that some operators in the field have cut that down to four hours."[20]

On December 9, 1982, the Caravan prototype made its first flight.[21] The servo tabs fitted on the ailerons to lighten the control forces limited the plane's ability to produce a satisfactory roll rate — a flight characteristic necessary for pilots operating in short, mountainous airstrips. Roll spoilers were added to rectify the problem.[22] The surface area of the wing had to be increased to create more lift — especially for the 25-second maximum water run required for amphibious and straight float models.[23]

Federal Express

Around this time, Federal Express was gaining prominence as an extremely fast and reliable overnight delivery service. However, the company was still using trucks to transport packages from small towns to "feeder" cities where larger and faster aircraft would pick them up. Packages delivered from these smaller communities natu-

An oil-only strut in the nose gear absorbs the impact during landings. The tricycle gear itself was designed to be easily and quickly replaced with floats.

rally took longer to reach their destinations, and company executives had decided to replace the trucks with airplanes.

Although the Caravan had not been designed with this application in mind, Russ Meyer realized that the utility aircraft still in development would be perfect. He called his friend Fred Smith, the founder and CEO of Federal Express. Smith had started the overnight delivery business in 1971, using an idea that had earned him a C on a term paper at Yale. The company turned a profit within three years, becoming the first service company in history to reach $1 billion in sales in 10 years.[24]

Smith initially was opposed to the single-engine Caravan because the company had been considering twin-engine aircraft. But he agreed to a demonstration. "It was a hands-down winner compared to any other airplane because of the operating costs and reliability," noted Meyer.[25]

"It was a very extensive effort on our part to find a small airplane that would allow us to provide express services into smaller communities that had never been able to get fast service, much less overnight service, from many places around the country," commented Fred Smith.

"We looked all over the world. We had to have an airplane that was very economical and very reliable. But the traditional designs did not meet either of those two essential criteria. Other planes were more expensive, and they weren't reliable, at least to our standards. We became aware of Cessna's innovative approach to the utility airplane business: taking a rugged design and marrying it to the very proven PT6 in a single engine versus a traditional twin-engine configuration. And the rest is history."[26]

In 1985, Federal Express announced it would use the new planes as feeders for its worldwide delivery fleet. To accommodate the delivery giant, Caravan engineers designed a cargo pod

Cessna's design of the Caravan cargo pod met FedEx's needs.

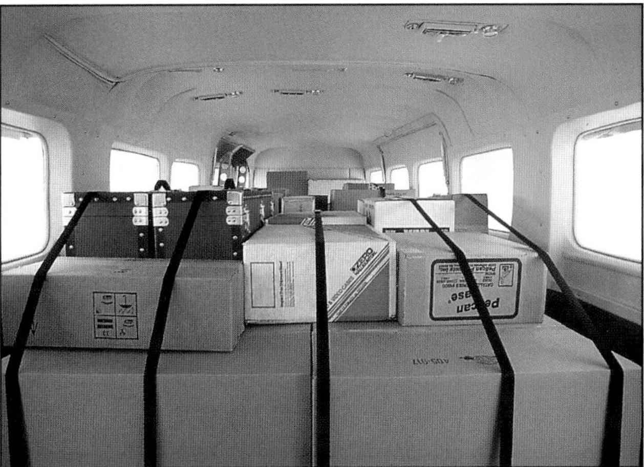

that could carry an additional 820 pounds of cargo.[27] "It's used by everybody else now, but the cargo pod was developed specifically for Federal Express," VanDyke said.[28]

Federal Express ordered 30 of these planes, which would log more than 2,000 hours of flight time and obtain a 99 percent reliability rating in their first six months of operation.[29]

Also at the request of Federal Express, Cessna designed a longer version of the Caravan, the 208B, which lacked windows but included an additional four feet of fuselage for more cargo space.[30] "It was just a big pickup truck," said John Daniel, product manager for the CitationJet and Caravan model lines, who began his Cessna career as an entry-level mechanic in 1979.[31] The 208B evolved into the Grand Caravan and Super Cargomaster, which are still in production.

Cessna also designed a support program specifically for Federal Express, noted Mark Blair, vice president of feeder operations for Federal Express. Blair had been with Cessna for 15 years and had been responsible for the Federal Express account before moving to the delivery company in 1990.

"Cessna wasn't traditionally in the business of supporting a scheduled airline like ours. From the outset, we told them we needed unique product support, and we sat down together and designed the concept and the package. It has evolved through the years and is very, very effective."[32]

In 1996, Federal Express celebrated 1 million hours of Caravan flight, noted Blair. "People are impressed that we have accumulated more than a million flight hours and get better than 99.7 percent dispatch reliability," he said. Federal Express had taken delivery of 300 Caravans by 1997.

"It's because we've got a tried and true engine. We have a fundamentally sound design concept and production concept in the airframe, and everything in the airplane is simple. I think it says a lot about Cessna that they're very innovative, but they tend not to throw away fundamentals."[33]

Above right and left: The Caravan 208B's 450 cubic feet of space enabled pilots to increase their payload. The space could easily be converted to transport passengers as well.

Left: The Caravan can carry as many as 10 standard 55-gallon oil drums.

Noted Meyer: "It's been a great relationship. It's brought overnight service to literally hundreds of communities."[34]

Initial Reaction

The first Caravan was delivered to Federal Express in February 1985. Later that day, the second one was delivered to Hermens Air Service in Alaska.[35]

The Caravan 208 was extremely easy to operate, and though designed with doors on either side for two pilots, it could be flown by a single pilot. The Caravan's 24-item pre-takeoff checklist, outside visibility, landing ease, and handling qualities made it a simple transition for pilots familiar with Cessna's popular single piston-engine models.[36] Pilots could make small adjustments in heading or banking simply by using the foot-operated rudder pedals — a benefit to a pilot whose hands were occupied with maps and microphones.[37] The Caravan's 970-foot takeoff distance appealed to customers who often had to land on short, unprepared fields. Early operators proudly nicknamed the Caravan "tur-ban" and "aerial truck."[38]

By the time Federal Express received its first Model 208B "stretched" version in October 1986, Caravans were operating in South America, Africa, North America, Europe, Australia and New Zealand.[39]

In Venezuela, Caravans gave tourists the scenic view of 9,000-foot Angel Falls — the highest waterfall in the world.[40] Relief agencies flew Caravans in Mozambique, Zaire and Ethiopia, where a Caravan carried 2,800 pounds of grain to villages isolated by the country's plateaus and gorges.[41] A trip that would take days by truck could be flown in only 12 minutes.[42]

Project Engineer Walt Thompson, a 26-year veteran at Cessna, recalled a letter from a customer in Africa with a rather unique problem: "The customer was having problems with hyenas and lions eating his tires and brake lines. He wanted to know if we could do something about it. His solution was to rub garlic on the tires and brake lines. We thought about it, and without putting a lot of money into some sophisticated way to keep the lions and hyenas away, we told him to keep using garlic as he was having success with it."[43]

New Versions

With the success of the Caravan, new features followed close behind. An amphibious Caravan was certified in March 1986, with deliveries two months later.[44] The plane carried two large floats, each capable of carrying 200 pounds of gear within watertight bulkhead compartments. Retractable water rudders at the stern of each float provided water taxi authority. Although the combination of floats and struts weighed more than 955 pounds, the amphibious Caravan still had a takeoff weight of 8,000 pounds.[45] Engineers added vertical fins to the horizontal stabilizer to provide more control, due to the large float surface.[46]

Canada's myriad natural waterways and lakes created an ideal market for the amphibi-

Above: Caravan's amphibious model had little structural difference from other Caravan models except for fins added to the horizontal stabilizers to compensate for its huge floats.

The Caravan Super Cargomaster is a basic 208B Caravan outfitted exclusively for freight hauling.

Inset: The Grand Caravan was simply a Model 208B outfitted for luxury passenger service. These versions were specially painted for Cessna's "Count On It!" advertising campaign celebrating the Caravan's reliability and 10-year anniversary.

ous Caravan, and one early customer was the Royal Canadian Mounted Police (RCMP), which needed a replacement for its aging de Havilland Beaver. Based in Montreal, the plane would serve the 600,000-square-mile province of Quebec and fly almost 1,100 hours during its first 12 months in service.[47]

"A lot of areas where we fly have no airstrips but do have lakes, so the amphibious floats allow investigators to carry out wildlife enforcement in remote fishing camps," said Neal Melsness, director of air services for the RCMP. Not long after delivery to the RCMP, Canada's British Columbia Telephone purchased an amphibious Caravan for use in its remote service regions.

Around half of amphibious Caravan sales were to individuals who used them for recreation or business. One Caravan owner with waterfront property in New York used his floating airplane as a home office.[48]

The Caravan's popularity among freight operators led Cessna to introduce the Cargomaster 208 and Super Cargomaster 208B in October 1986. These planes, with their large cargo doors and lack of passenger windows, were ideal for such bulky cargo as snow machines, construction equipment and lumber. The Super Cargomaster could carry 750 pounds more than the Cargomaster 208.[49] Pilots found the Cargomasters even more load friendly, and the Super Cargomaster's extra four feet of fuselage made it easier to trim in flight.[50]

In 1990, Cessna delivered its first Grand Caravan, a multimission model that could be changed from a cargo to a passenger configuration in only 20 minutes. An airstair on the right side of the plane allowed entry for passengers, while a large, two-piece door on the left served cargo operators. Depending on flight regulations for the country of operation, the Grand Caravan could carry as many as 14 passengers.[51] Its Pratt & Whitney PT6A-114 was replaced by the PT6A-114A to produce 675

Cessna's 500th delivery of the Caravan, which was made to FedEx.

horsepower — 75 more horsepower than other Caravan models.[52] Although it was the largest single-engine turboprop aircraft in production, pilots found the Grand Caravan "responded quite swiftly to control inputs and generally handled like a large Cessna 182."[53] Brazil Central Airlines, operating out of Sao Paulo, relied on the Grand Caravan for its feeder and commuter routes. By 1996, the South American airline would operate a fleet of more than 30 Caravans, serving more than 30 cities with a 99.5 percent dispatch reliability rate.[54]

Modified versions of the Caravan also operated in what were known as special mission roles. As early as 1987, Caravans equipped for maritime surveillance and medical evacuation made an appearance at the Paris Air Show.[55] The Brazilian Air Force used Caravans to patrol its 600-mile Colombian border.[56] The Caravan's cabin versatility and customized roll-up cargo door were beneficial to parachutists operating in a variety of conditions.[57] Houston-based LCT, Inc., performed its aerial mineral and petroleum searches in a Caravan. The detachable cargo pod provided a perfect location for such equipment as computers, manuals, and even a 30-foot antenna.[58]

Bob Conover, who joined Cessna in 1960 as a parts clerk and is now director of Caravan sales, described how the Caravan became an international aircraft in the early nineties.

"Through the 1985-1989 time frame, the majority of the Caravan activity was focused around the freight industry, and with the exposure we were getting from the Federal Express group, we concentrated quite heavily on the domestic overnight package business. Then in 1990, we really went back after the international market talking about the reliability and how the airplane can be used for many missions. We still carry that theme today."[59]

Service Programs

When the Caravan celebrated its 10th birthday in 1995, Cessna introduced the "Count On It!" marketing campaign to promote the plane's exceptional service record. A Caravan 208 and Grand Caravan — painted burgundy and white, with the phrase "Count On It!" painted in gold on the fuselage — embarked on a tour of Europe and the United States.[60] By early 1996, more than 750 Caravans were in use in more than 50 countries.[61] Supporting an aircraft operating in every corner of the globe was a challenge, but Caravan service and support met operators' needs through a variety of programs.

Early in the Caravan's history, Cessna had established authorized service stations with certified mechanics and personnel. By 1995, there were 57 such facilities in 26 countries. New Caravan owners were given flight training in a Caravan simulator, maintenance training, operating publications, information regarding engine serviceability, and at least four follow-up phone calls during the first six weeks of operation with the aircraft.[62]

With 20 years of experience in customer service, Steve Charles, director of propeller product support, has his share of interesting Caravan stories. On one occasion, a Caravan operated by Mission Aviation Fellowship in Indonesia was damaged in a forced landing. The Caravan was disassembled, placed in a crate and shipped from Jakarta, via Singapore and Los Angeles, to Wichita, where it was slipped into the production line, repaired, and returned to the owner.[63]

Charles noted that most Caravan customers are experienced pilots who know their planes well. "They're self-sufficient in most respects, but when something is beyond them technically, or they need spare parts, then the phone rings and we need to do our part," he said.

> *"The key is to get all the elements in place to really take care of the airplane. The person who works on it has to be trained, he has to have the right tools, he has to have spares if he needs them. He also needs technical support to back him up if he doesn't know how to fix it."*[64]

A dedicated Caravan Customer Center, with presentation facilities, demonstration tours, flight instruction and conference rooms, was completed at Cessna's Mid-Continent facility in 1992.[65]

With innovative manufacturing methods, Cessna managed to deliver every Caravan on time for seven years.[66] Building the versatile Caravan was a well-trained, experienced Caravan manufacturing team operating in the company's Mid-Continent facilities. John Daniel, who took over the Caravan production line in 1996, helped deliver a record 107 Caravan models during the year.[67] He credited the people on the assembly line for the success:

> *"A lot of the people who have worked on the airplane have been with it since the very beginning, so we've got a lot of high experience on this line — and it clicks! The people are proud of it, they like what they're doing, and they have the knowledge to make it work."*[68]

In January 1997, Cessna delivered its 850th Caravan. Telford Aviation received the delivery for use with its seven other Caravans. Telford President Telford Allen III commented that the Caravans "are tremendous aircraft. They can carry a ton of cargo, and they are the most dependable aircraft we've ever operated."[69] The Cessna Caravan had achieved record deliveries, performance and reliability. "The huge, single-engine turboprop, with its boxy fuselage and enormous wings ... may be the best-flying single Cessna has ever produced."[70]

The future of the Caravan is extremely bright. Record unit sales were recorded in 1997, bolstered by the announcement in the fall that the performance of the standard Caravan would be enhanced by the installation of the Pratt & Whitney PT6A-114A engine. The new Caravan 675 was an instant sales success.

During 1998, Cessna will deliver the 1,000th Caravan model, and with increasing acceptance of turbine single-engine commercial operations worldwide, many more are destined to follow.

The world's fastest business jet, the Citation X is also the world's fastest non-military jet, after the Concorde.

CITATION X: FAST TRACK TO THE FUTURE

"While the beauty and performance of the Citation X speak for themselves, it is important to remember and honor the fantastic dedication of the men and women of Cessna whose talent and pride are best evidenced in the quality of this crowd. We would like to take this opportunity to thank you for making the Citation X a reality."

— Russ Meyer at the 1993 rollout[1]

FROM THE TIME the first Citation X was delivered in 1996, this remarkably capable business jet amazed pilots and passengers alike. Traveling at Mach .92 — nearly the speed of sound — it could fly from Los Angeles to New York in four hours and New York to London in less than six hours.

The aviation world first heard about the Citation X in October 1990, during the National Business Aircraft Association Convention in New Orleans. Typical of Cessna's Citation family, a new Citation X, priced at just under $12 million, would offer superior performance to jets priced between $20 million and $25 million.[2]

Designing the Citation X

Creating this high-performance jet required the right combination of power plant and wing design. Extensive negotiations were held with engine manufacturers to make sure that the chosen engine met Cessna's demanding criteria. These included temperature margins at high altitudes, high performance with low fuel-burning characteristics, reliability, maintainability, low noise and emissions, and a wide thrust margin. Most importantly, however, the engine had to come with a 2,500-hour or five-year guarantee for the end user.[3]

Cessna looked at several engines, including the Garrett CFE 738 and the Pratt & Whitney PW300 series, but decided they lacked sufficient power.[4] Finally, Cessna selected the Allison 3007C turbofan engine, the only engine to promise the desired thrust and specific fuel consumption. The engine offered a bypass ratio of five to one, which meant five times as much air passed through the bypass duct as was compressed and burned within the engine core. It was a large engine, almost twice as long as the Citation III's Garrett TFE 731, while providing 64 percent more thrust. The Allison 3007C, like the Citation X, was developed with new technology to allow room for both airframe and engine to mature together.

While the engine was being selected, engineers also worked on wing designs, cooperating with Boeing specialists who had just completed the Boeing 777 wing computations. The completed Citation X wing featured a 37-degree sweptback design — the most sweep of any business jet or airliner except the 747, which also had a 37-degree sweep.[5] This aerodynamic design provided efficient cruising at high speeds and higher altitudes.[6] The supercritical airfoil design controlled pressure on

The Citation X is Cessna's flagship business jet.

Above: Each Citation X's spacious interior is designed to specific customer requirements (inset).

Below: The jet's state-of-the-art cockpit features Honeywell's Primus 2000 avionics system, with five electronic flight information system (EFIS) display screens including dual multifunction displays (MFD), dual primary flight displays (PFD) and an engine indicating and crew alerting system (EICAS).

top of the wing so that supersonic shock waves were generated farther aft, reducing drag.[7]

Also unique to the wing design was the lack of winglets, boundary-layer energizers, fences, vortillons, and vortex generators.[8] The nearly 500 technicians and engineers involved during the peak of the Citation X's development had designed the wing so well it was unnecessary to add additional stabilizing attachments.[9] The entire effort was under the skillful leadership of Milt Sills, who was promoted to senior vice president of product engineering in December 1997.[10]

Development of the fuselage concentrated on reducing drag and was highly sculptured behind the wing for Mach .92 speeds. In fact, the finished plane was actually flown at Mach .99 during some dives by test pilot Rick Trissell, since FAA regulations required .07 Mach margin from the speed that could be consistently demonstrated in tests. This was judged to be Mach .99, so the limit was set at Mach .92.[11] Ellis Brady, director of advanced design and engineering test flight, led the aerodynamic development from the first wind tunnel tests to the final certification. He said he had never felt so much a part of any airplane.

The forward fuselage and cockpit were derived from the Citation III but built longer.[12] Efforts by

Cessna's Citation X Integrated Design Team and Citation Customer Advisory Council helped create maximum cabin interior space. The floor and seats were lowered nearly two inches for greater headroom. The center aisle was just under 24 feet long, and the cabin was five feet, 10 inches high.[13]

A large belly fairing under the wings, extending from the end of the nose gear to the rear tailcone section, minimized drag effects along the fuselage. This new fairing also enabled control cables, hydraulic lines and ducts to be positioned under the composite fairing, allowing more room in the cabin.[14]

Honeywell's Primus 2000 avionics system was installed, featuring five, eight-inch-by-seven-inch electronic flight information system (EFIS) display screens that contained dual multifunction displays (MFD) and dual primary flight displays (PFD), and an engine indicating and crew alerting system (EICAS). Like other Citations, the Citation X did not locate switch panels above the pilot's head, and several controls were moved forward to reduce the pilot's need to look down.[15] The avionics, along with the airframe, engines and other components, came with full five-year warranties.[16]

On September 15, 1993, exactly 24 years after the maiden flight of the Fanjet 500, the first Citation X prototype was rolled out of the Experimental Engineering Hangar in Wichita. Before a crowd of Cessna employees, aviation dignitaries and local media, Meyer described the event as a major turning point in aviation history. "While the beauty and performance of the Citation X speak for themselves, it is important to remember and honor the fantastic dedication of the men and women of Cessna whose talent and pride are best evidenced in the quality of this crowd. We would like to take this opportunity to thank you for making the Citation X a reality."[17]

On December 21, the Citation X took its 45-minute initial flight with Doug Hazelwood, director of engineering flight test, at the controls. In addition to checking handling, he and co-pilot Ken Kimball tested the landing gear, flaps, slats and aircraft systems.[18] Two production class aircraft, assembled in the Experimental Department, were added to the flight test program. Two years, five months and 3,000 flight test hours after the first flight, the Citation X received certification from the FAA.[19]

The Citation X's rollout on September 15, 1993 attracted a large crowd of Cessna employees, aviation enthusiasts and media.

Above: During flight tests of the Citation X, the superfast jet sometimes broke the sound barrier.

Below: Arnold Palmer shakes hands with Cessna Chairman Russ Meyer upon receipt of the first Citation X.

Production

Production went smoothly, in large part because the manufacturing and inspection personnel knew what to expect, having worked closely with the mechanics and engineers as they designed the Citation X. "They saw the planes being built from the ground up and identified problems," said Donald Van Burkleo, vice president of quality and reliability. "When we started the production line, those people brought that knowledge back with them."[20]

Hazelwood said Cessna's emphasis on cooperation was important to him when he joined the company in 1966, and it remains important today. "That was one thing that impressed me more than anything. ... At Cessna, you work with the airplane. You work with the people that work on the floor. The engineers work with them, too. You have a much more hands-on experience."[21]

In all, Cessna spent more than 18 months preparing for the first delivery of the Citation X, noted Ronald Chapman, vice president of customer service. As part of the preparation, the company put together a first-class support system.

"We have a complete organization over here that is a subset of product support called Team X, dedicated to doing nothing but taking care of

those airplanes as they begin to hit the marketplace. We are prepared to launch trained people at a moment's notice, with tools and parts, to help a customer do whatever he needs to get his aircraft back in the air."[22]

Vice Chairman Gary Hay said maintaining a direct relationship with the customer through company-owned service centers "has been a cornerstone of our strategy from day one as it relates to supporting Citation."[23] The engine's warranty covered 100 percent of all parts and labor, including removal, transportation to a service facility for necessary repairs, and reinstallation for a period of 2,500 hours or five years. Allison also had a well-established, worldwide support network that would match the Citation tradition of accessible high-quality service.[24]

Cessna expanded its customer support and availability of parts for the Citation X around the globe. A new company-owned Citation Service Center, for example, was announced for Paris. In addition to the 10 Cessna owned and operated Service Centers, other authorized parts and support facilities are located in Singapore, Sao Paulo, Brazil and Zurich, Switzerland.

On August 29, 1996, the first Citation X was delivered to Arnold Palmer, who had been friends with Meyer since the sixties and had owned virtually every Citation model since the Citation I. Palmer, an accomplished pilot, recalled that he had taken an active interest in the jet from the beginning.

"I was on the edge of my seat the whole time waiting for the X to happen. I was in the factory a lot when they were doing the planning. I was very excited about it. I got to the point where I knew most of the people working on the airplane and would talk to them about the various functions. ... By the time it was delivered, I had heard and read and been told so much about it that the only direction I could have gone would have been disappointment rather than surprise, and I wasn't disappointed at all. It did all the things they said it would do, which was amazing."[25]

By that time, 14 Citation Xs were in production to meet the 30 orders already placed.[26] With the Mach .92 dream announced at the NBAA Conference in 1990 finally a reality, it was time for the world's fastest business jet to show what it could do.

This promotional shot conveys the speed and power of the Citation X.

On one flight westbound over the Rocky Mountains, the pilot of a Citation X passed three airliners flying below. The pilot recalled: "when they (airliners) keyed the mike, they all wanted to know what kind of airplane was blowing past them at 43,000 feet. When the controller said it was a Citation, there was silence."[27]

The chairman of General Motors, flying to the West Coast, couldn't believe how quickly he arrived at his destination. About a week after General Motors took delivery of its first Citation X, President and COO Charles Johnson, then vice president of operations, received a call.

> *"I came in at 7 on a Friday morning and my phone was ringing. It was the director of transportation for General Motors. I normally don't get nice phone calls that early on a Friday morning, so my blood went cold and my adrenaline went up. Then he said, 'Charlie, I've got to tell you that our chairman and vice chairman just looked at the X,' and you could tell by the voice he was very enthusiastic, and he said, 'It's the best airplane we've ever received at General Motors. Best impression an airplane's ever made, the quality level, the detail level, all that stuff.' The Citation X went into service faster than any airplane General Motors has ever put into service. They're just absolutely thrilled."*[28]

Another time, a Citation X was speeding past an airliner on a trip from Chicago to New York at 37,000 feet, recalled Johnson. The Citation was told to "slow it down," he said. Instead, the Citation was permitted to fly 4,000 feet higher and pass the airliner in excess of Mach .9. "The Citation pilots said it was just so much fun to do that."[29]

Palmer said he enjoys the comments from air traffic controllers as he flies the world's fastest business jet. "The other day, on a trip down to Florida, the air traffic controller said, 'Hold up a minute, Arnie. I'm going to see if that pilot ahead of you will let you play through.' I get a kick out of that."[30]

Johnson, formerly chief pilot for Palmer, said the guiding philosophy behind the Citation X was pure Cessna: "Since day one, the philosophy has been to build an extremely safe, very reliable and very economical airplane."[31]

And Cessna's strength has been the ability to attract highly dedicated people who adhere to this as a common goal, noted Gary Hay, vice chairman of Cessna.[32] Hay became involved in the Citation line in 1986, and was promoted to director of worldwide sales for Citation about three years later. He said the development of the Citation X began with a new approach.

Drawing on the experience gained with the Citation III, Meyer, Hay, and other executives met with "opinion leaders" — aviation department managers, chiefs of maintenance, etc. — around the country where there was a hotbed of business aviation activity and sat down with them to discuss their likes and dislikes, and what sort of support they wanted when buying a business jet.

> *"I give a lot of credit to Russ for really capturing the value of this. We went around the industry and found what we thought were the top 25 aviation department managers and chiefs of maintenance and invited them to sit on an Advisory Council."*[33]

Richard Santulli, chairman of Executive Jet Aviation, said his jet sharing organization has ordered 33 Citation Xs. "You can buy one-eighth of a Citation X for $2 million," he said. "That's a lot of money, but if you fly 100 hours a year,

Left: Charles Johnson was named president and COO of Cessna in 1997.

Right: Vice Chairman Gary Hay joined the company in 1966, while still in college.

Milt Sills (inset) was instrumental in the development of the Citation X, which was built to combine first-class business comfort with sustained speed. It has repeatedly demonstrated that, with the sole exception of the supersonic Concorde, it is the world's fastest non-military aircraft.

you've got the best airplane available. It's just a spectacular airplane."[34]

The Robert J. Collier Trophy

Cessna's dedication to performance and customer satisfaction was acknowledged on May 7, 1997, when the company and the Citation X Design Team received the 1996 Robert J. Collier Trophy in Washington, D.C., "for designing, testing, certifying and placing into service the Citation X, the first commercial aircraft in United States aviation history to achieve a cruising speed of Mach .92."[35] It was the second time in 11 years that Cessna had won the prestigious award for its Citation airplanes. During the award ceremony, Russ Meyer called Milt Sills, vice president of engineering, to the podium, singling him out for his brilliant leadership in developing the Citation X.

Paul Kalberer, director of engineering projects for Cessna, said the award validated the company's hard work on the plane.

"One of the reasons it makes me feel good is because there was a lot of doubt in the industry as to whether or not we could pull this off. It was a push for us, aerodynamically, to have a .92 Mach airplane, and it was a little scary. You start designing it on a piece of paper, and all the formulas and all the equations and all the computer codes say it's possible, but you never really know until you fly the airplane how it's going to work."[36]

To demonstrate why the Citation X earned the honor, the plane was flown 2,321 miles from Seattle, Washington, to Washington, D.C., in only three hours and 34 minutes — a speed of 642 miles per hour.[37]

Meyer stressed how important it was to have demonstrated performance throughout the organization. And he wants customers to know the individuals in Cessna responsible for the top performance. If a customer is concerned with a particular feature, these individuals seek to improve it.

"Every morning we receive a summary of customer support issues and dissatisfiers for every Citation, including the Citation X. I see this summary, Gary Hay sees it, Charlie Johnson sees it, Milt Sills, sees it. We've got a team of people over in the Customer Support building, on duty 24 hours a day."[38]

The Citation fleet. Clockwise from back row center: Citation X, Citation Excel, Citation Bravo, CitationJet, Citation Ultra and Citation VII.

STRENGTH AND DIVERSITY

THE NINETIES

"This is a proud, proud day for Cessna and a huge milestone in the history of aviation in this country. ... By working together and meeting our commitments, we will make it possible for literally thousands of young men and women in practically every country in the world to learn to fly in Cessna aircraft."

— Russ Meyer, 1996[1]

IN JANUARY 1991, viewers around the world sat glued to their television sets, watching the real-life drama unfolding in the Persian Gulf. Cessna Chairman and CEO Russ Meyer was among the many Cessnans who watched and prayed for loved ones serving in Operation Desert Storm. His oldest son, Russ, an F-16 fighter pilot with the South Carolina Air National Guard, flew 50 combat missions during the conflict, winning several air medals for his service.[2] After the war, Russ Meyer III patrolled Iraqi air space from bases in Turkey, helping to halt Saddam Hussein's assault on the Kurds during Operation Provide Comfort.

As it had during every major American conflict, Cessna turned out to support the troops. Yellow ribbons competed with the red, white and blue banners and posters that festooned Cessna's plants. Donations were collected to buy amenities to make life in the desert more bearable, and hundreds of letters were written, sometimes to soldiers who were "adopted" by a particular department. A retrospective was published in the *Cessnan* after the brilliant 100-hour ground war demolished the Iraqi Army.

"When the long-expected Desert Storm blew across the long, bleak horizon between Saudi Arabia and Iraq, Cessnans — like their fellow citizens all over the nation — were ready.

"Here at Cessna, it unleashed a great outpouring of support and feeling for our military forces committed to the war. ... In Department 130 there is an artistic presentation of a listing of troops in the Gulf adopted by Department employees. (One of the names, Cory Williams, is a fellow employee serving in the Desert Storm forces.) ... It's a very intimate, very effective tribute to the fact that our troops are real people, with real names, who deserve our support."[3]

Although Desert Shield and Desert Storm dominated international news, Cessna achieved recognition in its own right for several aviation milestones in 1990. The Citation X, which would become the fastest business jet ever produced, was announced, and the Citation VI and VII were introduced, along with the Grand Caravan, a passenger version of the 208B Caravan turboprop.

In February 1990, plans were unveiled to build the world's largest business jet aircraft service facility at Wichita's Mid-Continent Airport. Operational by 1992, the company-owned service center was built on 44 acres of airport property, next to the existing Citation Service Center, which was then

The statue, Wings, by Gary Price, symbolizes the natural love and fascination with flight. The statue is a favorite of Chairman and CEO Russ Meyer.

James E. Morgan, vice president of service facilities, inside the Citation Service Center in Wichita.

converted to an aircraft completion facility. With 111,800 square feet devoted to hangar space, the center was designed to inspect and service as many as 40 aircraft at one time.

Up for Sale

Cessna did well in 1990, achieving $106 million in income on sales of $716 million and commanding 60 percent of the worldwide light- and medium-sized business jet market.[4] But its parent company, General Dynamics, was struggling with both the recession and deep defense contract cutbacks. The fall of the Berlin Wall in 1989 and the break-up of

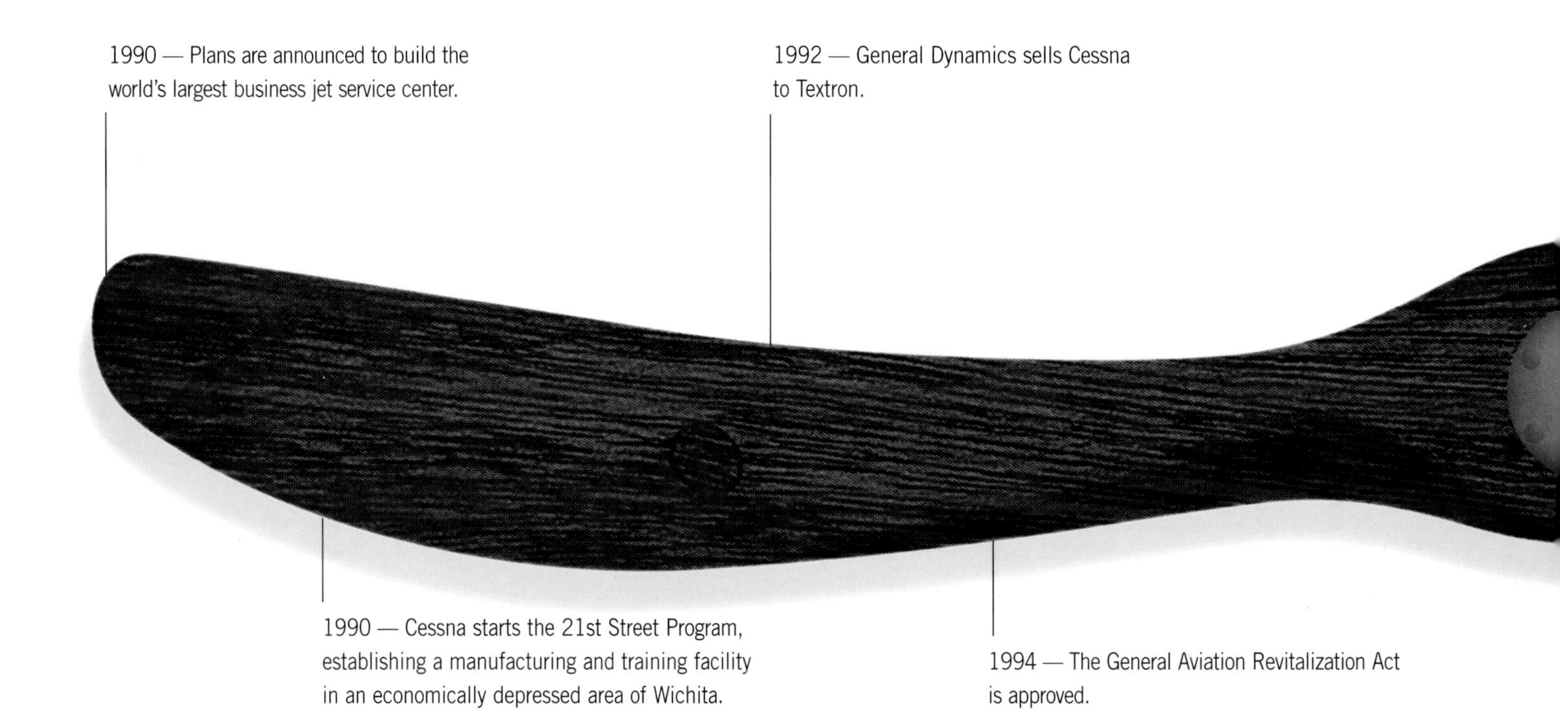

the Soviet Union in 1991 meant that the decades-old Cold War was truly at an end. William Anders, then chairman and CEO of General Dynamics, explained the challenges facing the defense company in a 1990 letter to shareholders.

"The easing of Cold War tensions, welcomed from a humanitarian point of view, is removing a major market stimulus for U.S. defense spending, which was already under stress due to the increasing federal deficits. ... From a business perspective, then, it is not enough simply to produce weapons that work and work well. A revision of our business strategies is called for."[5]

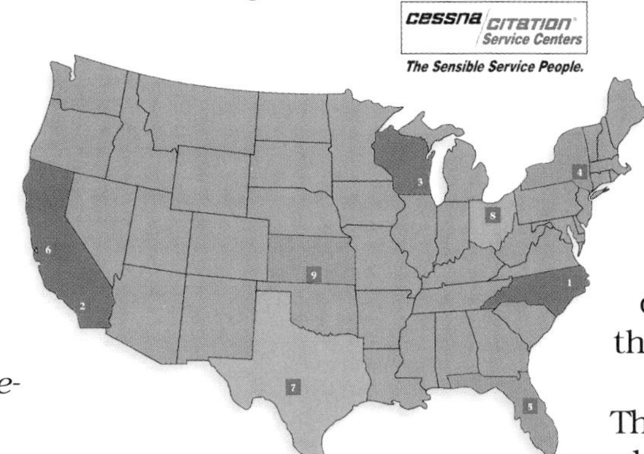

By 1997, Cessna operated nine domestic and one international company-owned Citation Service Centers. Customer support has remained a vital part of Cessna's mission.

As part of this revision, General Dynamics announced in 1991 that it intended to sell Cessna in order to "focus on our core defense businesses and to build the increased financial strength and flexibility necessary to adapt to the new realities of the defense industry."[6]

Russ Meyer assured employees that the move "should have no effect whatsoever on our day-to-day operations. I encourage all employees to continue to concentrate on the tasks which must be accomplished to maintain our excellent performance during the rest of 1991 and the future."[7]

Employees continued to do so. That year, the 500th Caravan was delivered to Federal Express, the CitationJet pre-production prototype made its inaugural flight, and Greensboro, North Carolina, was selected as the site for the eighth company-owned Citation Service Center. Other milestones included delivery of the 100th Citation V, and FAA certification and delivery of the Citation VI.

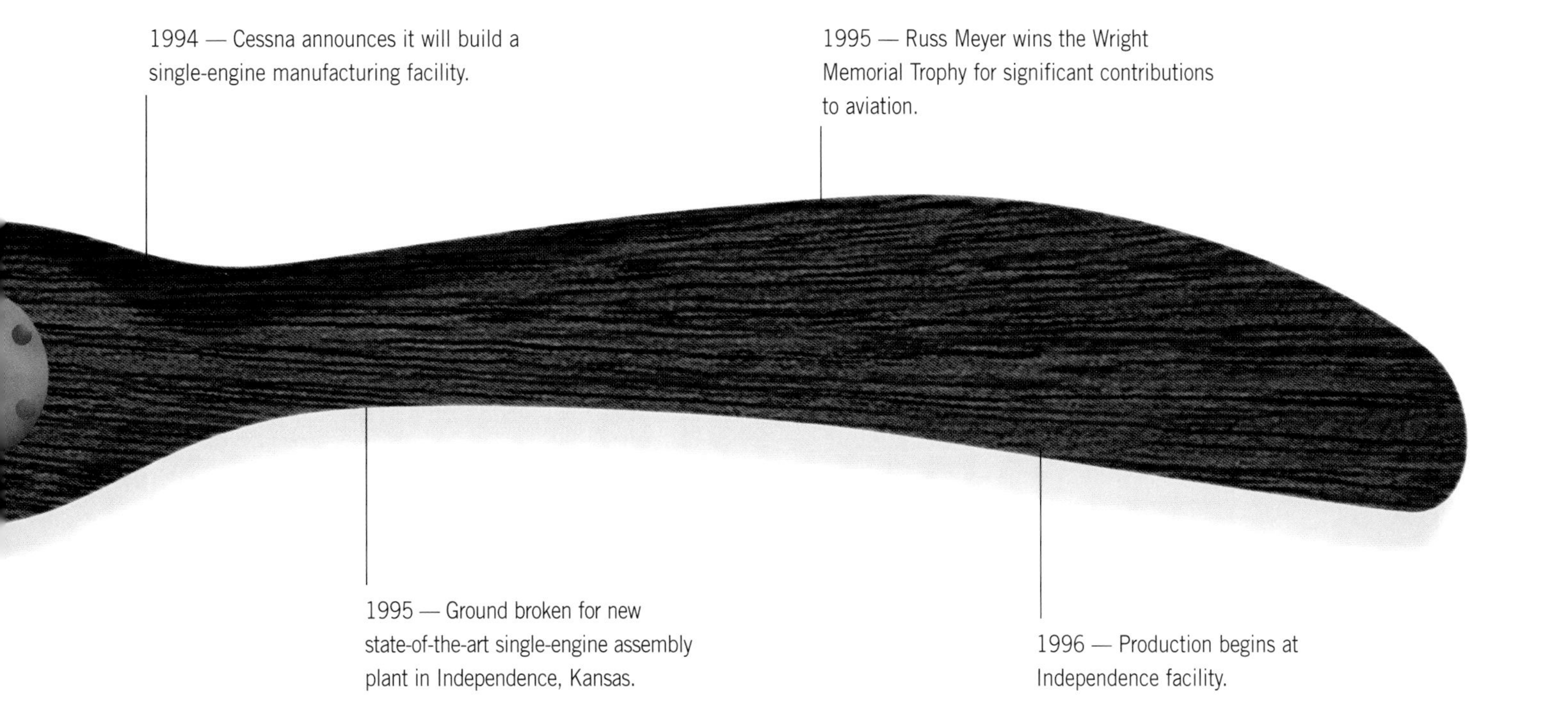

1994 — Cessna announces it will build a single-engine manufacturing facility.

1995 — Russ Meyer wins the Wright Memorial Trophy for significant contributions to aviation.

1995 — Ground broken for new state-of-the-art single-engine assembly plant in Independence, Kansas.

1996 — Production begins at Independence facility.

Cessna ended 1991 with 5,400 employees, sales of more than $820 million, and continuing status as the world's leading designer and manufacturer of business jets and utility turboprop aircraft. The impending introduction of the Citation X further increased the company's luster, and corporate suitors wooed General Dynamics for the chance to buy the company. Textron, Inc. won, and on January 20, 1992, the globally diversified company purchased Cessna for $600 million in cash.[8]

Later that same year, Gary Hay, who joined the company in 1966 while still in college, was promoted to senior vice president, overseeing worldwide marketing and sales for all product lines. By 1997, as vice chairman of the company, his responsibilities had been expanded to include customer service, Cessna's single-engine business, strategic planning and corporate communications.

21ST STREET: THE ROAD TO SELF-RELIANCE

IN 1989, LIQUOR STORES and abandoned buildings made up the landscape on 21st Street in Wichita, with loiterers dominating the street corners. "You could buy liquor, dope, guns, run numbers, prostitution, anything you wanted," noted John Moore, Cessna's senior vice president for human resources."[1]

Not one to sit back and watch his adopted city sink into despair, Cessna Chairman and CEO Russ Meyer took action. With the cooperation of the city of Wichita, the state of Kansas and the Department of Housing and Urban Development, Cessna renovated a 12,000-square-foot former grocery store at 21st and Piatt streets and turned it into a job-training site and subassembly facility for the aircraft industry.

Meyer said the 21st Street Project would address one of the community's most serious problems. "This issue is the widening and sharply defined gap between those of us fortunate enough to have an education, to have a job and to be able to provide for our families, and those of us who have none of these advantages," he said.[2]

On November 29, 1990, the center opened for business with a staff of five headed by Johnnie Cartledge, a manufacturing engineer at Cessna since 1986. The first class of trainees consisted of 16 single mothers who had been relying on welfare support. Paid while in training and given medical benefits, these women learned how to manufacture aircraft components and develop good work habits.

Cessna takes lead role on northeast site

By Jim Cross 1/23/90 FRONT PAGE
The Wichita Eagle

Cessna Aircraft Co. officials say they have found a building in the depressed neighborhoods of northeast Wichita that could be renovated to house a subassembly operation.

Company Chairman Russ Meyer is to meet tonight with black business leaders to report on the status of the project.

It is too early to predict whether the project will succeed, Cessna officials said Monday. But they are progressing in the early planning stages, they said.

"We've found a facility we like," said John Moore, senior vice president of human resources for Cessna. "We've identified some work we could do there. Now is the time to turn this thing into reality or to find out what the obstacles are to keep us from doing it."

Meyer is to meet at 6 p.m. with members of the National Business League, a group of minority-owned businesses. The meeting will be at Rollin' & Smokin' Bar-B-Que, owned by state Sen. Eugene Anderson, D-Wichita.

Sedgwick County Commissioner Billy McCray said he was optimistic that Cessna would open the plant near 21st in the city's predominantly black neighborhoods.

"I think there is a better than 50-50 chance," McCray said. "I think the company is interested in doing something down there. I think it will go."

Moore declined to identify the building the company has in mind because the owner doesn't know the company is interested.

The building will have to be renovated, he said.

Cessna does not want to own the building, he said, and is looking into ways to finance the project.

The company wants to do "productive work" — not just training — in the new facility, Moore said. But profit is not Cessna's only motivation, he said.

"It's never been our intention to make a big money-maker out of this," he said. "If we wanted to do that, we could leave things the way they are."

McCray and Anderson both said they were willing to help the company apply for public assistance for the project.

"Maybe we could assist with transportation of the trainees, or pick up the cost of child care," Anderson said. "I want to meet with Russ and talk about incentives."

Cessna Chairman Meyer first publicly mentioned his subassembly plant proposal at a Nov. 14 banquet to recognize area philanthropists.

The plant, he said, would employ unskilled people recruited from the 21st Street neighborhood for training in assembly-line tasks.

The operation would offer literacy training, high school degrees and counseling on such fundamental subjects as how to manage a personal budget, he said.

Billy McCray
"I think there is a better than 50-50 chance. I think the company is interested in doing something down there. I think it will go."

Depending on their existing skills, some would take longer than others to complete the program. But all were assured that jobs at Cessna awaited them upon graduation. An editorial in the *Wichita Eagle* noted that the program helps both the trainees and the area's aircraft industry, including Cessna. "The goal is to move 30 to 50 successful trainees every year from the 21st Street plant to the main factory," the *Eagle* stated. "For every graduate, a new trainee will quickly be brought in."[3]

Cessna executives had several reasons to establish the center. They wanted their city to thrive, and they wanted to employ people who had been trained at the center. "At that point, we were a 63-year-old company, and we had always been headquartered here. This is where the majority of our employees live and work, and we wanted to do something in the city that was unique," said Moore.[4]

Robert Neubecker

Textron

Founded in 1923, Textron is among the largest and best-performing multinational, multi-industrial conglomerates in the world. It owns a diverse array of businesses involved in industrial, automotive, aircraft, and finance industries, with subsidiaries that include Bell Helicopter, Avco Financial Services, Textron Fastening Systems, and the Textron Automotive Company.

The corporation which would evolve into an international conglomerate started in 1923 as a struggling synthetic yarn factory called Special Yarns, founded by Royal Little and two partners, Harry Mork and Eliot Farley.[9] The company struggled for years, alternating between prosperity and desperation, and changing its products from synthetic yarn to sewn products such as parachutes during World War II.

The Harvard George S. Dively Award for Corporate Public Initiative

Cessna Aircraft Company

Keynote Address

November 13, 1991

Russell W. Meyer, Jr.
Chairman and Chief Executive Officer

Center for Business and Government
John F. Kennedy School of Government
HARVARD UNIVERSITY

The center's success has been spotlighted in *The New York Times* and on *Dateline*. In 1991, Cessna won Harvard's George S. Dively Award for Corporate Public Initiative for the program. "This program is working for a number of reasons," Meyer said when he accepted the award.

"It's working because we try to provide support to each trainee in other aspects of his or her life. We deal routinely with domestic issues, transportation and housing problems, stress, eviction, utility shutoffs, child care, severe indebtedness, birth control, personal hygiene, drug usage, pregnancies, court appearances and lack of self-confidence.

"We generate great excitement among these trainees when we give them their Cessna employee badges the day they arrive at 21st Street. The badge has their picture. It gives them an identity, a sense of belonging. And by the way, it gives them the ability to cash a check at a bank.

"They gain confidence in themselves from little victories, and we provide them as often as possible."[5]

Today, the learning center helps students earn their GED certificates and offers classes in manufacturing-related mathematical skills, personal finance management, clerical operations, and more. "We have over 200 success stories," Moore said. "They are either employed with us, still in training or employed somewhere else."[6] The center sparked a revitalization of the entire street, which now has a bank, a library, and a police and fire substation.

Meyer hopes other companies will follow Cessna's lead. "If we could somehow convince 10,000 companies to participate in this kind of caring crusade, we would create a whole new world for 2 million people in just two years. And that would make a difference."[7]

11/30/90

The Wichita Eagle

BUSINESS & FARM

Cessna Chairman Russ Meyer vows that participants in the training program will succeed.

Renaissance on 21st

Rhetoric becomes reality at Cessna center

By Bob Cox

The training center's dedication draws applause from County Commissioner Billy McCray, left, City Council member Rip Gooch, Cessna Chairman Russ Meyer and Mayor Bob Knight.

Cessna's 21st Street Program enabled the company to give something back to the community by training previously unemployable people. Cessna helped itself by hiring many of these loyal workers to help build its aircraft.

It didn't become "Textron" until 1945. According to an internally published history, the new name was initially going to be Senorita Creations. "Within a few days, however, wiser heads prevailed and 'Textron' was substituted."[10]

Textron began its strategy of diversification in 1952. The purpose, according to the book *Textron ... from the beginning,* was to:

> *"... eliminate the effect of business cycles by having many divisions in unrelated fields. Lessen Justice Department and Federal Trade Commission monopoly problems by avoiding acquisitions in related businesses. Eliminate single industry temptation to overexpand at the wrong time."*[11]

By 1960, the company had 50 subsidiaries producing such diverse goods as plywood, fasteners, pistols, chain saws and clotheslines.

That year, Textron purchased Bell Aerospace, which owned Bell Helicopter, manufacturer of the famous "Huey," used extensively in Vietnam. Bell Helicopter Textron is today the leading worldwide supplier of helicopters around the world, and has pioneered the commercial helicopter market. Bell also pioneered the tilt-rotor technology being introduced to military and commercial markets.

By 1997, Textron had become a global leader with $17 billion in assets and a workforce of 59,000 in more than 100 countries. However, like General Dynamics, Textron felt the bite of the post-Cold War defense market. The purchase of Cessna would "help offset the lower level of activity we foresee in Textron's defense business," the company predicted in 1991.[12]

Like the other major business segments of Textron, Cessna operates as a separate entity. Together with Bell Helicopter, the aircraft segment exceeded $3 billion in revenues in 1997.[13]

Above: By the time Textron purchased Cessna in 1992, it was no stranger to the flight industry. In 1960, Textron had purchased Bell Helicopter, which recently developed the 609, the first civilian tilt-rotor.

Below: The introduction of the CitationJet, pictured here on its first flight in 1991, brought jet speed to smaller businesses for less cost than a turboprop.

State-of-the-Art Customer Service

In 1992, Cessna opened a state-of-the-art customer center that featured marketing offices, a large area for full-scale mock-ups of all Citation models, and a computerized pictorial display that enabled customers to view an image of the cabin interior designed to their specifications. Cessna had this technology well in advance of the competition.[14] Unique in the industry, the center showcased Cessna's dedication to customer needs.

"We have made a much greater investment in our customer, as evidenced by our facilities, by our product line expansion and by our product support organization," noted Bob Knebel, who joined Cessna as a regional sales manager in 1990 and is today vice president of domestic sales. "It absolutely overshadows anything that our competitors do."[15]

Donald Van Burkleo, vice president in charge of quality and reliability, said the company's emphasis on service and support has been a key component of its success. "Cessna has an excellent reputation for servicing and maintaining the product," he said.

> *"We have Service Centers all around the United States, and service agreements around the world. Almost anybody who owns a Citation can get to an authorized service station."*[16]

By 1997, the company had 10 Cessna-owned Citation Service Centers and 25 authorized centers, with 20 of these outside the United States. James Martin, vice president of materiel, explained that, in addition to the Citation, the company still supports every airplane it ever built. "We deal with in excess of 600,000 part numbers in our data system," he said. "Even though we're not selling many of those actively today, they're in the database and we have the ability to either manufacture or buy those parts."[17]

By the end of 1997, about one-third of the company's business was outside the United States, so it was important to create an infrastructure to support aircraft flying throughout the world, noted James Morgan, vice president for service facilities. "A Citation takes off or lands someplace in the world about every 20 seconds," he said.

> *"They're operating in South Africa. They're in China. They're in all the countries of Latin America. All of Western Europe. Some are even in Eastern Europe, the Middle East, Indonesia, Singapore and other places. We've created an infrastructure to support those airplanes, both with independent organizations and with field service people spread around the globe. We have parts we can distribute through contacts with freight forwarders around the world, and we've been very successful in supporting our products in this fashion."*[18]

Expanding into such emerging markets as China is a challenge for Cessna, noted Mark Paolucci, vice president of international sales.

To keep its customers flying, Cessna's Parts Distribution centers operate 24 hours a day. Stocking for different models means 73,000 different parts are always ready to ship worldwide.

The CitationJet has rapidly become one of the world's most popular light jets.

"There are dreams of China being a big market for us someday. It won't happen this year or next year, or the year after that. Whether it will happen in five years or 10 years is difficult to determine because they have a lot of problems to overcome. They need air traffic control upgrades, they need places to service airplanes, they need places to train pilots, they need ramp space to park airplanes, somebody to put fuel in the aircraft. And all of that needs to happen before that market is really going to grow to the size that its population and its gross domestic product say that it should be."[19]

When these markets begin to take off, Cessna will be ready with a wide variety of aircraft, said Phil Michel, vice president of marketing. "We have always had the vision of serving a wide span of general aviation because we see general aviation as an entity. Flight training, personal use of airplanes, charter operations, business or utility airplanes, we have a deep-seated passion for it all."[20]

The company also has about 350 Cessna Pilot Centers throughout the United States and Canada, and in early 1997 Cessna announced that King Schools would develop a new computer-based training system for the centers. "King understands how important the enthusiasm is for people in the early stages of learning to fly," said Michel.[21]

Cessna's healthy growth in the early nineties did not mirror the nation's general business climate. President George Bush, who enjoyed incredible approval ratings immediately after the Gulf War, struggled to persuade the nation that the economic downturn was merely an "interruption in the longest peacetime economic expansion in history." Unemployment, crime and drug use rose, and a sense of pessimism caused many writers to question whether the American Dream was dead.

Many corporations would not accept that view, however, and Cessna was one of them. In 1990, the company started the 21st Street Project. A deserted building in an economically depressed area of Wichita was transformed into a unique training and manufacturing facility, where people who were previously considered unemployable were trained and hired by the company. (See sidebar beginning on page 226.)

JPATS

In 1992, Cessna announced it was entering a variant of the CitationJet, which had been FAA-certified that year, into the $7 billion Joint Primary Aircraft Training System program.[22] The winner would supply 764 trainer aircraft for U.S. Air Force and Navy pilots beginning in 1998. Of the 10 competitors, only Cessna offered to supply an "all-American" training system, completely designed and built in the United States.[23]

The aircraft was powered by twin Williams engines — the military version of the same type used on the commercial CitationJet — and shared the same landing gear and hydraulic, fuel and electrical systems. This helped keep costs down and reliability high.[24] Despite these advantages, in 1995 the contract went to Raytheon, which built the single-engine turboprop MkII.[25]

Movement Toward Excellence

Cessna continued to find ways to learn what its customers needed and expected from their aircraft. The Movement Toward Excellence program was an outcome of this ongoing concept. The program was so successful that executives applied it to every product line, noted Ron Alberti, vice president of manufacturing, who joined Cessna in 1986 as superintendent of components manufacturing.

Russ Meyer at the Independence plant's groundbreaking on May 19, 1995. Meyer quickly and enthusiastically led Cessna back into production of piston-engine aircraft.

FLIGHTSAFETY AND CESSNA: PARTNERS IN SAFETY

TO HELP ITS CUSTOMERS become accomplished pilots, Cessna relies on the services of FlightSafety International, a unique organization that trains more than 50,000 pilots and aircraft maintenance technicians each year using sophisticated aircraft simulators.

Through MarineSafety International, the company also trains ships' officers. But the company's roots are firmly planted in aviation, and FlightSafety has gained a worldwide reputation for training pilots for private, commercial and military flight.

"We try to come up with a training system so that people will be able to operate airplanes safely," explained Al Ueltschi, who founded the company in 1951 and is still its president. In the early years, he said, it was difficult to convince people that training was important. Unable to turn a profit with FlightSafety, he kept his job at Pan Am while he tried to get the organization off the ground. In 1968, at age 50, Ueltschi retired from Pan Am and devoted his energy to FlightSafety. He is a passionate believer in the importance of flight training.

"If you're going to fly, you ought to be trained properly. I try to tell people that they don't have a right to fly an airplane; it's a privilege. You don't have a right to kill people. That's against the law. So if you're going to fly, you better do it right."[1]

FlightSafety is on the leading edge of simulator technology. In 1997, the organization had 174 simulators, which allow pilots to experience every imaginable maneuver and situation they might encounter in a particular aircraft. The simulators allow pilots to earn certification for most aircraft before they sit behind the controls of the real thing. Ueltschi recommends that pilots who get certified this way fly for several hours with a check airman. "It's kind of silly to get a type rating and put a load of passengers in and take them on their first rides," he said.[2]

Ueltschi and FlightSafety have had a long successful relationship with Cessna and its chairman, Russ Meyer. Ueltschi praised Meyer as a great man who has made Cessna the company it is today. "Our only problem with him is that he continually changes models. He comes out with two or three new airplanes every year, and every time he builds a new airplane, we have to build a new simulator. So it gets to be very expensive. That's a smart thing for him to do, but from our standpoint, it's very expensive."[3]

FlightSafety was recently acquired by Berkshire Hathaway, the famous investment firm run by billionaire Warren Buffett. "He and I sat down for an hour and a half and we made a deal for $1.5 billion," Ueltschi said. "He had a hamburger and I had a hamburger and he had a cherry Coke and I had a cherry Coke, and we put the deal together. He had a philosophy that I admire, and we got along great because I think his values are pretty much the same as mine."[4]

"Warren Buffett and I have a deal," Ueltschi said. "He never splits stock. But when I get to be 100, he said he'll split my age. I'll get to be 50."[5]

"The idea is to be responsive to customers' needs and be proactive in terms of ongoing improvement of the product. The idea is to identify the issues and gather the right people around those issues to find the solution and work to incorporate them as early as possible."[26]

The program called for forming teams of people from manufacturing, engineering and customer support, said Meyer. "Customers were not as happy as they should have been, and we put together what has become the standard at Cessna, the MTE teams."[27]

Since then, the CitationJet has proven itself as the favored step-up aircraft for previously non-Citation owners, noted John Hall, director of CitationJet sales. "Over 80 percent of our CitationJet business has been to non-Citation owners. What we're doing is bringing new people into the Citation family, who in turn become prospects for our future business as well."[28]

Reincarnation of Single-Engine Cessnas

Within 24 hours of the General Aviation Revitalization Act being signed into law by President Bill Clinton, Cessna announced it would build a new, state-of-the-art, single-engine aircraft manufacturing plant in one of

Cessna Single Engine General Manager Pat Boyarski addresses the crowd attending the dedication of the Independence facilities.

Above: Russ Meyer was awarded the Wright Memorial Trophy in 1995 for "significant public service of enduring value to aviation in the United States."

Below: The Stationair 206. Like the Skyhawk and Skylane, the new Stationair is equipped with a fuel-injected engine and state-of-the-art avionics.

16 Kansas communities under evaluation.[29] The original list was pared down to five — Emporia, Hays, Manhattan, Pittsburgh and Independence. Although offers came from other states, Meyer was adamant about keeping Cessna in its native state, as he told the *Independence Daily Reporter.*

> *"Despite requests by many other states to enter this competition, we were committed to remaining in Kansas from the very start of this process. Cessna was founded in Kansas in 1927; we owe our worldwide leadership to the efforts of our employees here; we had invaluable assistance from Senators Kassebaum and Dole and Representative Glickman; this is where we have our roots and Kansas is where we will once again produce single-engine aircraft."*[30]

The five communities lobbied heavily for high stakes: 1,000 new jobs, with an annual payroll estimated at $40 million. In Independence, a button campaign urged residents to "Smile for Cessna," and the city offered generous tax incentives.[31]

On December 21, 1994, the *Independence Daily Reporter* announced in a screaming 120-point headline that the city, population 13,000, had been selected for the 500,000-square-foot facility. City leaders described the choice as "one of the best things that has ever happened to Independence in our entire history."[32]

Above: The 172 Skyhawk was the first aircraft returned to production at Cessna's new Independence plant.

Ground was broken May 19. Construction began slowly because the site was very wet, practically a bog, from heavy rains, and the initial earth-moving phase took longer than anticipated. But when the plant was completed in July 1996, it immediately began producing a new generation of the Model 172 Skyhawk and the Model 182 Skylane. The Model 206 Stationair and Turbo Stationair soon followed. The rebirth of Cessna's single-engine line prompted Russ Meyer to designate Independence as the "light aircraft capital of the world" at the plant's dedication ceremony, held in 1996.

> *"This is a proud, proud day for Cessna and a huge milestone in the history of aviation in this country. ... By working together and meeting our commitments, we will make it possible for literally thousands of young men and women in practically every country in the world to learn to fly in Cessna aircraft."*[33]

Pat Boyarski, general manager of the plant, was part of a task force charged with finding ways to quickly produce aircraft while maintaining high quality. "We recommended that we go to a self-directed work-team concept where people have broader job responsibilities, so they

Below: On January 18, 1997, AOPA President Phil Boyer (center) hands a check to Russ Meyer, while receiving his keys to the first Independence-built Skyhawk from Vice Chairman Gary Hay (right).

are responsible for a lot more than just a small repetitive job done a million times a day. The teaming environment was part of the plan from the very beginning."[34]

Consequently, prospects were rigorously interviewed. "The hiring process takes six steps because it is geared toward teamwork," noted Michael Wright. "For example, I am Team Leader of the 172 Back Shop. The words 'foreman' and 'supervisor' are not used here." The team concept has resulted in a highly motivated workforce that writes the names of the customers on individual planes, to remind them who they are building these aircraft for, Wright added. "Everybody enjoys knowing where it's going."[35]

The Wright Memorial Trophy

The aviation community honored Russ Meyer in 1995 by awarding him the prestigious Wright Memorial Trophy for "significant public service of enduring value to aviation in the United States."[36] The program listed more than just his and Cessna's accomplishments in aviation. Also noted were the company's involvement in the Special Olympics and the 21st Street Project. Dean Humphrey, who directed public relations from 1976 to 1993, said Meyer had instilled a wonderful ethic at Cessna.

"Even though it's a large company and a leader in the industry, it's still a very small company in the way it conducts business, the way it treats employees, and the way it stands behind its products."[37]

Frank Harris, director of product safety and engineering services, said the company's family atmosphere has been the key to its success,

The 1997 Model 182 Skylane, another revitalized single-engine aircraft in flight over Independence.

The Cessna headquarters and facilities at the Mid-Continent Airport in Wichita, Kansas. Cessnans are ready to meet the challenges of the new millennium.

even after it was acquired by one giant and sold to another.

> *"I would not have survived in the Boeing or McDonnell Douglas culture. Here, everybody helps. If you had a problem or a question, there has always been someone to turn to, from the time Dwane Wallace was here to now. The management was picked not only for ability to do the assignment, whatever the assignment was, but because they were family-oriented people. We are the best company in the world to work for."*[38]

Meyer's work on GARA received particular attention. The program noted that "with typical enthusiasm, [Meyer] organized rallies on Capitol Hill, personally met with many members of Congress, contacted thousands of constituents and testified before several Congressional committees."[39]

> *"Russ promised that Cessna would begin producing light aircraft again as soon as product liability reform legislation was enacted. This commitment to provide a substantial number of jobs proved to be compelling testimony. ... It was a great day for aviation, and Cessna responded as promised, breaking ground for a new facility in Independence, Kansas, where at least 2,000 new aircraft per year will be produced. ... Russ has shown tremendous consistency in his industry leadership."*[40]

In a recent interview, Wichita Mayor Bob Knight described Cessna as "an amazing company. ... It's not just my local pride saying that. From Meyer on down to the line people, every one of them has a world-class skill. That is something very special, and they deserve respect and appreciation and status."[41]

Building a Platform for the Future

Cessna has achieved remarkable milestones and overcome adversity through the years, but 1997 will go down as one of the most phenomenal years in its history. Backlog orders reached $3 billion for future deliveries, the highest ever for the company. By year's end, Cessna had 40 Citation Xs in service, and orders had been taken for more than 325 Citations, another industry record.

The company also had successfully re-started its venerable single-engine production lines, and reclaimed its position as the world's leader in single-engine piston production.

The Caravan continued to hold its position as the most popular single-engine utility turboprop ever built, with a record 120 orders received in 1997.

Nearing FAA certification in late 1997 was the Citation Excel. This newest Citation had racked up almost 200 orders by the end of the year — before the aircraft even went into production. "The Excel is the most significant airplane I think anybody has introduced," Meyer said. "It is a pre-emptive product."[42] The business jet embodies the most crucial points developed by a customer focus group: cabin size, short-field performance, reliability, range, ample baggage, operating cost, maintenance cost and price. Cessna will build between 60 and 70 Excels a year, and Meyer expects Cessna to sell more than 1,000 over the life of the aircraft.

For the first time in many years, the company employed more than 10,000 people. Its ongoing commitment to research and development into safer, more reliable aircraft earned Cessna ISO-9001 certification. The ISO-9001 certification is earned by meeting the requirements of a very strict, internationally recognized standard of quality and continuous improvement.

Two graduates of the 21st Street Project, Jodee Bradley (left) and Tonya Oden (right), present a model Citation to President Bill Clinton. Standing behind the graduates is Secretary of Agriculture Dan Glickman.

A Fair Shot at a Good Job

Some of Cessna's most meaningful accomplishments in 1997 directly benefited the community and the nation. Cessnans' contributions to such worthy causes as The United Way, The Kansas Food Bank and particularly the Special Olympics are well known. In fact, Cessna announced the largest airlift ever for the 1999 Special Olympics. More than 2,000 athletes and coaches will travel by Citation business jets to the World Summer Games, being held in North Carolina's Raleigh Durham and Chapel Hill "Triangle." This is the fourth Citation Special Olympics since Cessna began the airlift in 1987.

But Cessna's 21st Street Project is perhaps the company's most important contribution because it provides enduring value to individuals, the community and Cessna itself. In 1990, Cessna recognized that most of the country had begun to enjoy a robust economic recovery. Employment levels were up, corporate profits were climbing and income levels were rising.

Russ Meyer realized, however, that not everyone was participating in the prosperity and economic recovery enjoyed by Cessna, the community and the country. Many less fortunate individuals, previously considered "unemployable," had been left on the sidelines. The 21st Street Project tackled the welfare issue before welfare-to-work topped political and legislative agendas. In 1997 federal and state governments rolled back welfare programs by placing time limits on financial assistance. Without training, many people could fall through the widening gaps in the safety net.

Cessna's program demonstrated how corporations could fill the gap by providing quality training, a fair chance and a good job. At the same time, Cessna helped itself by finding and training good workers. In November, the company moved the job training program to a new campus comprising a learning center, a fully functioning subassembly plant, and an on-site day care facility. About half of the 50 workers in the 24,000-square-foot plant come from 21st Street and surrounding neighborhoods.

President Bill Clinton, in Wichita to help dedicate the new facility, called the program a "victory for American dignity."

> *"Every company in America ought to take note of what Cessna is doing. It's a model for the nation. It proves once again that the best social program ever devised is a job — a good job with dignity that allows people to support their children. ... The real idea behind all of this is that ... it's up to those of us who have made it, as Russ said, to create a system where everybody who wants to has a shot."*[43]

In his own speech, Meyer emphasized that taking people off welfare without preparing them for jobs is not a solution. "The only effective long-term solution — in my view — is for those of us in the private sector to accept this issue as our responsibility."[44]

> *"And I mean really accept it. To give it the same high priority as our other business goals, and in partnership with government, provide adequate training and the guarantee of full-time employment to a specific number of people year after year."*[45]

Into the Next Century

As Cessna's production lines and employment rolls continue to grow, its challenge going into the 21st century will be to maintain the company's famous Midwestern work ethic and family atmosphere while keeping quality high. The task will not be easy because Cessna is going through a changing of the guard as veterans retire. By the end of the decade, possibly more than 70 percent of the workforce will have been hired sometime in the 1990s.

In an interview, Meyer said Cessna will continue to stress teamwork as one of the keys to maintaining quality.

> *"You can't have 60 percent of the world's light and mid-size business jet market if you don't have a combination of products and performance and reliability and demonstrated support and relationships with hundreds and hundreds of people."*[46]

Treva West, a preflight inspector who retired in February 1997 after 44 years with Cessna, said the new hires will have big shoes to fill, and she offered some advice: "You have to build quality into the aircraft. You can't put it in there afterward. After the airplane is built, you can rework it and rework it, but it still has to have quality at the time it's first completed."[47]

Gary Hay, vice chairman of Cessna, said this commitment extends throughout the organization, on every level.

> *"Everyone wants to accomplish the same things. It doesn't matter whether it's the guys out in operations, whether it's the people in human resources,*

Cessna's winning team. Seated left to right: Gary Hay, vice chairman; Russ Meyer, chairman and CEO. Standing (left to right): Mike Schonka, senior vice president, CFO; Charlie Johnson, president and COO; and John Moore, senior vice president, human resources.

marketing, product support, or wherever. We all want to satisfy the customer. We used to be an engineering-driven company, but we began to put ourselves in the role of the individual shopping for an aircraft. There is a spirit of support, cooperation and confidence in your teammates here."[48]

The pioneering spirit that has characterized the company for so many years will go on, as new technology is developed and evaluated to meet the changing needs of customers. Cessna is committed to maintaining its leadership role in producing safe, reliable, high quality aircraft that represent the best value in general aviation.

Overall, executives are confident in the abilities and dedication demonstrated by new and future Cessnans. "The folks that we have coming in are dynamite," commented Charlie Johnson. "They're enthusiastic. They want to solve problems and contribute to the product. They don't want to just drive rivets."[49]

Johnson's own enthusiasm and skills led to his promotion in December 1997 to president and COO of Cessna. In making the announcement, Meyer commented he has "had the privilege of knowing and working with Charlie Johnson for almost 30 years, and he has a uniquely broad combination of skills and experience. ... He is dedicated to aviation and will provide excellent leadership at Cessna well into the next century."[50]

Johnson, who joined Cessna in 1979, served as a fighter pilot in Southeast Asia, and has accumulated more than 10,000 hours of commercial flight time, including three years of service as chief pilot for longtime Cessna customer Arnold Palmer.

Likewise, Milt Sills, a 32-year Cessna veteran, was promoted to senior vice president of product engineering. In making the announcement, Meyer said, "Milt was the test pilot on the first flight of the very first Citation, which earned him a very special place in our company history."[51]

Meyer reflected how Cessna's work ethic grew the company from the dark days of the eighties to a company poised to meet the challenges of the new millennium.[52] Whatever form the company takes, safety and quality will remain at the heart of the plan.

"If I were starting the day after tomorrow, I'd say, 'Guys, everything we're doing is great. Now what's next?' You can't beat a formula where you bring in the customer and you do the job for him, and you never let him go."[53]

The management team at Cessna is well prepared for the challenges of the future, and that future looks bright well into the next century. A number of major milestones are due for accomplishment during 1998 alone. The company will deliver 200 Citations during the year, and the 1,000th Caravan will enter service. The resurging single-engine piston business will see 1,000 deliveries during 1998, and Cessna will strongly support the revival of flight training by introducing its totally new computer-based instructional system, developed in cooperation with King Schools. Finally, a number of significant new Citation model development programs will be made public late in the year. Said Meyer:

"Everyone who has worked for Cessna in the past and all of our current employees should be exceptionally proud of the long list of accomplishments during our first 70 years. By working together we have built more aircraft than any other company in the world, and we're the industry leader in every market segment we serve. The name Cessna has become synonymous with general aviation and it would be accurate to say that we have taught the world to fly.

"While it is gratifying to look back over a history filled with significant achievements, the real excitement is to look forward to the enormous opportunities of the 21st century. Every year in the 1990s has been better than the last, and we are confident that this momentum will extend into the year 2000 and beyond.

"We have outstanding facilities, the finest product line in the industry and a huge base of loyal, enthusiastic customers throughout the world. Most importantly, we have thousands of employees who take pride in our heritage, who are excited about making their careers here, and who are totally dedicated to maintaining Cessna's leadership in aviation.

"Here's to 70 more great years!"[54]

NOTES TO SOURCES

Chapter One

1. *Our Times*, based on the 1926 study by Mark Sullivan, abridged, copyright 1996 Dan Rather, Scribner, New York, New York, p. 110.
2. John W.R. Taylor and Kenneth Munson, *History of Aviation: The Full Story of Flight*, Crown Publishers, Inc., New York, New York, 1977, p. 10.
3. *Ibid*, p. 10.
4. "Aviation," Microsoft (R) *Encarta* (R) 96 Encyclopedia, 1993-1995, Microsoft Corporation.
5. Courtlandt Canby, *A History of Flight*, Vol.3, Hawthorn Books, Inc., New York, New York, 1963, pp. 5-10.
6. *Our Times*, p. 110.
7. Sherwood Harris, *The First to Fly: Aviation's Pioneer Days*, TAB/AERO Books, 1970, 1991, p. 15.
8. *Our Times*, p. 113.
9. "The Wright Brothers," taken from a brochure of the same title, © 1990 Henry Ford Museum & Greenfied Village, *http://hfm.umd.umich.edu/histories/wright.html.b oys*, February 10, 1997.
10. "Wright," Microsoft (R) *Encarta* (R) 97 Encyclopedia, 1993-1996, Microsoft Corporation.
11. *Our Times*, p. 114.
12. Henry Ford Museum and Greenfield Village.
13. *Our Times*, p. 120.
14. *Ibid.*, p. 122.
15. John Blake, *Aviation, the First Seventy Years*, Ruine Books, London, England, 1973, p. 10.
16. Larry Forrester, *Skymen: Heroes of Fifty Years of Flying*, St. Martin's Press, Inc., 1961, p. 31.

Chapter Two

1. Jack Abbott, "A Witchita Pilot Who Taught Himself How to Fly: Clyde Cessna Looks Back Fifteen Years When He Built and Flew His First Airplane Without Instructions," *The Witchita Eagle Sunday Magazine*, June 20, 1926, p. 6.
2. Anne Pellegreno, *Iowa Takes To The Air*, Vol. 1, Aerodome Press, Story City, Iowa, 1980, p. 246.
3. Edward H. Phillips, *Cessna: A Master's Expression*, Flying Books Publishers and Wholesalers, Eagan, Minnesota, 1985, p. 5.
4. *Kingman County History, Kingman County Kansas and Its People*, Kingman County Historical Society, Taylor Publishing Co., Dallas, Texas, 1984, p. 67.
5. *Ibid*, p. 125.
6. Gerald Deneau, *An Eye to the Sky: Cessna*, Unpublished manuscript, date unknown, p. 1.
7. *Cessna: A Master's Expression*, p. 7.
8. *Ibid.*
9. *An Eye to the Sky: Cessna*, p. 1.
10. *Cessna: A Master's Expression*, p. 7.
11. *An Eye to the Sky: Cessna*, p. 2.
12. *Cessna: A Master's Expression*, pp. 8-9.
13. *Kingman County History, Kingman County Kansas and Its People*, p.125.
14. *Cessna: A Master's Expression*, p. 8.
15. *Ibid.*
16. *Wichita Eagle Sunday Magazine*, June 20, 1926, p. 6.
17. *Wichita Beacon*, December 5, 1954, p. 3.
18. *Cessna: A Master's Expression*, p. 10.
19. *Aviation History* "Clyde Cessna And The Birth Of A Legend," January 1996, p. 28.
20. *Ibid.*
21. *Cessna: A Master's Expression*, p. 10.
22. *Aviation History*, p. 30.
23. *Cessna: A Master's Expression*, p. 12.
24. *Ibid.*, p. 11.
25. *Ibid.*, p. 13.
26. *Ibid.*, p. 12.
27. *Oklahoma Events*, "Monoplane Exhibited Free," March 9, 1911.
28. *Cessna: A Master's Expression*, p. 13.
29. *Ibid.*
30. *Ibid.*
31. *Jet Pilot*, undated article by Clyde Vernon Cessna.
32. "Clyde Cessna Looks Back," p. 6.
33. *Cessna: A Master's Expression*, p. 13.
34. *An Eye To The Sky: Cessna*, p.3.
35. *Cessna: A Master's Expression*, p. 13.
36. *Ibid.*, p. 14.
37. O.C. Emery, "He Expects his Plane to Set New Records," *Wichita Eagle*, no date available.
38. *Cessna: A Master's Expression*, p. 14.
39. *Ibid.*
40. "He Expects His Airplanes to Set New Records."
41. *An Eye To The Sky: Cessna*, p. 3.
42. "Clyde Cessna Looks Back," p. 6.
43. *Ibid.*
44. Hugh Amick, "How $65 Kept Clyde Cessna of Wichita in the Air: Lack of a New propeller in 1911 Made Things Look Drab Until Friends Came Through," *Wichita Eagle*, October 1, 1930.
45. *Ibid.*
46. *Cessna: A Master's Expression*, p. 14.

Chapter Three

1. "Kingman Youth Flies To Market And For Fairs," *Topeka Capital*, September 19, 1915.
2. Gerald Deneau, *An Eye to the Sky: Cessna*, Unpublished manuscript, date unknown, p. 4.
3. Edward H. Phillips, *Cessna: A Master's Expression*, Flying Books Publishers and Wholesalers, Eagan, Minnesota, 1985, p. 14.
4. "Cessna Will Fly At Lakewood, All Arrangements Made for Local Birdman to Aviate July 4," *Oklahoma Events*, June 22, 1911.
5. *Cessna: A Master's Expression*, p. 16.
6. *Ibid.*
7. *Ibid.*
8. "Airship Flight A Failure," *Jet*, August 24, 1911.
9. *An Eye to the Sky: Cessna*, p. 4.
10. *Cessna: A Master's Expression*, p. 18.
11. *Ibid.*, p. 18.
12. *Ibid.*, p. 19.
13. *An Eye to the Sky: Cessna*, p. 5.
14. *Cessna: A Master's Expression*, p. 18.
15. *Ibid.*
16. *Ibid.*
17. *Ibid.*, p. 19.
18. *Ibid.*, p. 20.
19. *Ibid.*
20. *Ibid.*
21. *Ibid.*
22. *An Eye to the Sky: Cessna*, p. 5.
23. *Cessna: A Master's Expression*, p. 20.
24. *Ibid.*, p. 24.
25. *Ibid.*, p. 22.
26. Ed Phillips, "Clyde Cessna — Wichita's Aviator," Wichita Aeronautical Historical Association, Vol. 5, No. 1, Fall 1986, p. 3.
27. *Ibid.*
28. *Cessna: A Master's Expression*, p. 23.
29. *An Eye to the Sky: Cessna*, p. 6.
30. *Cessna: A Master's Expression*, p. 23.
31. *Ibid.*, p. 23.
32. "Kansas Farmer Flies To Town," *Kansas City Times*, June 10, 1914.
33. *Topeka Capital*, "Kingman Youth Flies To Market And For Fairs," September 19, 1915.
34. "Clyde Cessna - Wichita's Aviator," p. 3.
35. *Cessna: A Master's Expression*, p. 24.
36. "Cessna History, Chapter 2,"*Cessquire Magazine*, Vol. 17, No. 3, March 1977, p. 9.
37. *Cessna: A Master's Expression*, p. 24.
38. Mitch Mayborn and Bob Pickett, *Cessna Guidebook*, Volume I, Flying Enterprise Publications, Dallas, Texas, 1973, p. 3.
39. *An Eye To The Sky: Cessna*, p. 6.
40. Jean Hays, "Headstrong Clyde Cessna Toiled On Plane Day, Night," *Wichita Eagle-Beacon*, October 29, 1984.
41. Edward H. Phillips, "Clyde Cessna and The Birth of A Legend," *Aviation History*, January 1996, p. 73.
42. *An Eye to the Sky: Cessna*, p. 7.
43. "Birth of a Legend," p. 73.
44. *Ibid.*
45. *Ibid*, p. 74.
46. *Cessna: A Master's Expression*, p. 27.

Chapter Four

1. "Records Smashed By Clyde Cessna, Travels at 124.62 Miles From Blackwell — His New Plane Very Speedy," *Wichita Eagle*, July 6, 1917.
2. Edward H. Phillips, *Cessna: A Master's Expression*, Flying Books Publishers and Wholesalers, Eagan, Minnesota, 1985, p. 27.
3. Edward H. Phillips, "Clyde Cessna and The Birth of A Legend," *Aviation History*, January 1996, p. 74.
4. Edward H. Phillips, "Clyde Cessna - Wichita's Aviator," Wichita Aeronautical Historical Association, Vol. 5, No. 1, Fall 1986, p. 3.
5. *Aviation History*, p. 76.
6. *Ibid.*
7. "His New Plane Very Speedy."
8. *Cessna: A Master's Expression*, p.33.
9. *Ibid.*
10. *Ibid.*
11. *Ibid.* p. 28.
12. *Ibid.* p. 29.
13. Mitch Mayborn and Bob Pickett, *Cessna Guidebook*, Volume I, Flying Enterprise Publications, Dallas, Texas, 1973, p. 2.
14. Frank Joseph Rowe and Craig Miner, *A Century of Aviation in Kansas: Borne on the South Wind*, The Witchita Eagle and Beacon Publishing Co., Witchita, Kansas, 1994, p. 59.
15. *Ibid.*, pp. 62-65.
16. *Ibid.*, p. 67.
17. "Fifty Years of Flying Progress, Wichita: The Air Capital," OX5 Club of America publication, August 24, 1961, No page numbers.
18. Lew Townsend, "Aviation Pioneers Link Boeing, Beech, Cessna," *Wichita Eagle And Beacon*, Sunday, February 8, 1976, p. 6C.
19. Ken Weyand, "Wichita: How America's Air Capital Got That Way," *Pilot News*, July 1985, p. 26.
20. Jean Hays, "Headstrong Clyde Cessna Toiled on Plane Day, Night," *Wichita Eagle-Beacon*, October 29, 1984.
21. "Aviation Pioneers," p. 6C.

22. *Cessna: A Master's Expression*, p. 36.
23. "Aviation Pioneers," p. 6C.
24. "How America's Air Capital Got That Way," p. 27.
25. "Aviation Pioneers," p. 6C.
26. *A Century of Aviation in Kansas*, p. 79.
27. "Cessna History, Chapter 3," *Cessquire*, Vol. 17, No. 4, April 1977, p. 8.
28. *Cessna: A Master's Expression*, p. 38.
29. *Ibid*, p. 39.
30. "Cessna History, Chapter 3," p. 8.
31. *A Century of Aviation in Kansas*, p. 79.
32. "Cessna History, Chapter 3," p. 8.
33. *Ibid.*
34. *Cessna: A Master's Expression*, p. 39.
35. *Wichita Magazine*, no article title or author available, October 15, 1953, p. 9.
36. *Aviation History*, p. 77.
37. *Cessna: A Master's Expression*, pp. 40-41.
38. *Ibid.*, p. 40.
39. Gerald Deneau, *An Eye to the Sky: Cessna*, Unpublished manuscript, date unknown, p. 11.
40. *Cessna: A Master's Expression* , p. 40.
41. "Cessna History, Chapter 4," *Cessquire*, Vol. 17, No. 5, May 1977, p. 9.
42. *Wichita Magazine*, October 15, 1953.
43. *Cessna: A Master's Expression* , p. 41.
44. *Wichita Magazine*, October 15, 1953.
45. *Cessna: A Master's Expression*, p. 43.
46. "Cessna History, Chapter 3," p. 10.
47. *A Century of Aviation in Kansas*, p. 81.
48. *Cessna: A Master's Expression*, p. 45.
49. "Cessna History, Chapter 3," p. 10.

Chapter Four Sidebar

1. "Air Warfare," Microsoft (R) *Encarta* (R) 97 Encyclopedia, 1993-1996, Microsoft Corporation.
2. *Jane's Encyclopedia Of Aviation*, compiled and edited by Michael J.H. Taylor, Crescent Books, Studio Editions Ltd., 1980, 1989, p. 242.

Chapter Five

1. Unpublished manuscript received from retired Cessna Division Commercial Controller, Clair McColl, p. 10.
2. "Lindbergh, Charles Augustus," Microsoft *Encarta* 96 Encyclopedia, (c) 1993 — 1995, Microsoft Corporation, (c) Funk & Wagnalls Corporation.
3. Frank Joseph Rowe and Craig Miner, *A Century of Aviation in Kansas, Borne On The South Wind*, Wichita Eagle and Beacon Publishing Co., Wichita, Kansas, 1994, p. 83.
4. *Ibid.*, p. 84.
5. *Ibid.*, p. 81.
6. *Ibid.*, pp. 81, 83.
7. Mitch Mayborn and Bob Pickett, *Cessna Guidebook*, Vol. 1., Flying Enterprise Publications, Dallas, Texas, 1973, p. 2.
8. Edward H. Phillips, *Cessna: A Master's Expression*, Flying Books, Publisher & Wholesalers, Eagan, Minnesota, 1985, p. 45.
9. Gerald Deneau, *An Eye To The Sky: Cessna*, Unpublished manuscript, date unknown, pp. 15, 16.
10. *An Eye to the Sky: Cessna*, p. 14.
11. "50 Years Of Cessna Growth," *Flight Magazine*, Air Review Publishing Corporation, Dallas, Texas, October 23, 1961, p. 13.
12. *An Eye To The Sky: Cessna*, p. 16.
13. *Ibid.*
14. *Ibid.*
15. *Ibid.*
16. *Cessna: A Master's Expression*, p. 46.
17. *Ibid.*, p. 47.
18. *Ibid.*, p. 53.
19. *Ibid.*
20. *Ibid.*
21. *Ibid.*
22. *Ibid.*
23. *Ibid.*, p. 54.
24. *Ibid.*, p. 56.
25. *Ibid.*
26. *Ibid.*, p. 57.
27. *Ibid.*
28. *Ibid.*, p. 58.
29. *Ibid.*
30. *Ibid.*
31. *Cessna Guidebook*, p. 14.
32. *Cessna: A Master's Expression*, p. 62.
33. *Ibid.*, p. 66.
34. *An Eye To The Sky: Cessna*, p. 19.
35. "The Cessna Story 1927–1977," *Cessna 50th Anniversary: 50 Years of Leadership*, program for November 12, 1977 opening of the Wallace and Commercial Jet Marketing Divisions, no page numbers.
36. "50 Years Of Cessna Growth," p. 13.
37. "Cessna History, Chapter 5," *Cessquire*, Vol. 17, No. 6, June 1977, p. 9.
38. *Ibid.*
39. *Cessna: A Master's Expression*, p. 66.
40. "Cessna History," Manuscript included in a 1972 promotional kit titled "Cessna's First 100,000 Airplanes," p. 2.
41. *Cessna Guidebook*, pp. 14-15.
42. "The Cessna Story 1927–1977," no page numbers.
43. David Shi, George Tindall, *America*, W.W. Norton & Company, New York, New York, 1989, p. 698.
44. "Cessna History, Chapter 5," p. 10.
45. Copy of an undated booklet titled *Cessna*, the beginning of which is titled "Cessna History," p. 2.
46. *Cessna: A Master's Expression*, p. 75.
47. *Ibid.*
48. *An Eye To The Sky: Cessna*, p. 22.
49. "The Cessna Story 1927–1977," no page numbers.
50. *Cessna: A Master's Expression*, p. 79.
51. *Jane's Encyclopedia Of Aviation*, compiled and edited by Michael J.H. Taylor, Crescent Books, Studio Editions Ltd., 1980, 1989, p. 242.
52. "The Cessna Story 1927–1977," no page numbers.
53. *Cessna: A Master's Expression*, p. 79.
54. *Ibid.*, p. 80.
55. "The Cessna Story 1927–1977," no pages.
56. "Thad C. Carver is Elected President of Cessna Company," *Wichita Eagle*, January 23, 1931, p. 2.
57. *Ibid.*
58. Clair McColl manuscript, p. 10.
59. *Ibid.*
60. "Cessna History, Chapter 5," p. 10.
61. Karl Boyd, interviewed by Nola Norfleet, April 22, 1997. Transcript, p. 8.
62. Clair McColl manuscript, p. 10.

Chapter Six

1. Edward H. Phillips, *Cessna: A Master's Expression*, Flying Books, Publisher & Wholesalers, Eagan, Minnesota, 1985, p. 100.
2. *Ibid.*, p. 85.
3. *Ibid.*, p. 86.
4. *Ibid.*, p. 87.
5. *Ibid.*
6. Mitch Mayborn and Bob Pickett, *Cessna Guidebook*, Volume I, Flying Enterprise Publications, Dallas, Texas, 1973, p. 3.
7. "Cessna History, Chapter 6," *Cessquire*, Vol. 17, No. 7, July 1977, p. 8.
8. *Standard Catalog Of Cessna Single Engine Aircraft*, compiled by Jim Cavanagh, Revised, 2nd Edition by Kim Shields, Jones Publishing, Inc., Iola, Wisconsin, 1995, p. 10.
9. Gerald Deneau, *An Eye To The Sky: Cessna*, Unpublished manuscript, date unknown, p. 27.
10. *Cessna Guidebook*, p. 21.
11. Unpublished manuscript received from retired Cessna Division Commercial Controller, Clair McColl, p. 13.
12. *Wichita Morning Eagle*, Section A, Jan. 5, 1932, p. 2.
13. *Cessna: A Master's Expression*, p. 89.
14. *Ibid.*, pp. 89, 90.
15. "Cessna History, Chapter 6," p. 8.
16. "Wichita Airport Smashed," *Wichita Eagle*, June 19, 1932, p. 1.
17. "Cessna History, Chapter 6," p. 10.
18. "Wichita-Built Planes Steal Show in American Air Races 35-Mile Feature at Chicago," *Wichita Eagle*, July 4, 1933, p. 1.
19. *Cessna Guidebook*, p. 22.
20. *An Eye To The Sky: Cessna*, p. 29.
21. *Cessna: A Master's Expression*, p. 98.
22. "Cessna History, Chapter 6," p. 11.
23. *An Eye To The Sky: Cessna*, p. 29.
24. "Cessna History, Chapter 6," p. 11.
25. *Cessna Guidebook*, p. 23.
26. *An Eye To The Sky: Cessna*, p. 30.
27. Walt Shiel, *Cessna Warbirds: A Detailed & Personal History of Cessna's Involvement in the Army*, Jones Publishing, Inc., Iola, Wisconsin, 1995, p. 15.
28. *Cessna Guidebook*, p. 23.
29. *Cessna: A Master's Expression*, pp. 99, 100.
30. *An Eye To The Sky: Cessna*, p. 31.
31. "Cessna History, Chapter 7," *Cessquire*, Vol. 17, No. 8, August 1977, p. 8.
32. Clair McColl manuscript, p. 12.
33. *Cessna: A Master's Expression*, p. 100.
34. Clair McColl manuscript, p. 13.
35. *Cessna: A Master's Expression*, p. 100.
36. *Ibid.*, p. 100.
37. Clair McColl manuscript, p. 13.
38. *Cessna: A Master's Expression*, p. 111.
39. *Ibid.*, pp. 169-170.
40. *Cessna Guidebook*, pp. 3, 23-25.
41. "Cessna History, Chapter 7," p. 10.
42. "Cessna Ship Makes Cheap Hop," article in the Cessna archives, date and publication unknown.
43. "Cessna History, Chapter 7," p. 10.
44. Clair McColl manuscript, p. 15.
45. Velma Wallace, interviewed by the author, June 6, 1997. Transcript, p. 5.
46. Clair McColl manuscript, p. 15.
47. "Report $2,500,000 Airplane Business Here During 1936," *Wichita Eagle*, December 27, 1936, p. 5.
48. *1941 Cessna Aircrafter*, an employee yearbook.
49. *An Eye To The Sky: Cessna*, p. 34.
50. *Cessna: A Master's Expression*, p. 104.
51. Del Roskam, interviewed by the author, February 21, 1997. Transcript, p. 25.
52. Tribute to Dwane Wallace, printed after his death December 21, 1989. Date and author unknown.
53. *Cessquire Magazine: Special 50th Anniversary Edition*, "General Aviation's Tall Man: Dwane L. Wallace," 1977.
54. *Cessna: A Master's Expression*, p. 105.
55. "The Cessna Story 1927–1977," *Cessna 50th Anniversary: 50 Years of Leadership*, program for November 12, 1977 opening of the Wallace and Commercial Jet Marketing Divisions, no page numbers.
56. *Cessna Guidebook*, p. 27.
57. *Ibid.*
58. *Cessna: A Master's Expression*, pp. 169, 170.

59. "Crowd In Kingman For Air Mail Celebration, Clyde Cessna Is Pilot on First Air Mail Plane, Parade, Program Draw Crowd to Kingman Thursday," *The Leader–Courier*, Kingman Kansas, May 20, 1938, p. 1.
60. "Air Mail Celebration To Be Held In Kingman Next Thursday Afternoon, Parade at Two, Program At Field, Start At Three, Hundreds Expected To Mail Letters On Special Flight," *The Leader–Courier*, Kingman, Kansas, May 13, 1938, page not known.
61. "Clyde Cessna Was Pilot on First Air Mail Plane From Kingman," *Cessquire Magazine: Special 50th Anniversary Edition*, 1977, pages unknown.

Chapter Six Sidebar

1. *Two Hundred Years of Flight in America: A Bicentennial Survey*, American Astronautical Society, San Diego, California, Volume 1, 1981, p. 156.
2. *Ibid.*
3. *Ibid.*

Chapter Seven

1. *Cessquire*, Vol. I, No. I, May 2, 1941, pp. 1, 2.
2. "Five Decades Of The Pioneer Spirit," *Cessquire Magazine: Special 50th Anniversary Edition*, 1977, pages not numbered.
3. Gerald Deneau, *An Eye to the Sky: Cessna*, Unpublished manuscript, date unknown, p. 37.
4. Edward H. Phillips, *Cessna: A Master's Expression*, Flying Books, Publishers & Wholesalers, Eagan, Minnesota, 1985, p. 110.
5. *Wichita Eagle*, March 27, 1939, p. 5.
6. *An Eye to the Sky: Cessna*, p. 37.
7. *Ibid.* p. 38.
8. Velma Wallace, interviewed by the author, June 6, 1997. Transcript, pp. 13-14.
9. Mitch Mayborn and Bob Pickett, *Cessna Guidebook*, Volume I, Flying Enterprise Publications, Dallas, Texas, 1973, pg. 30.
10. Walt Shield, *Cessna Warbirds: A Detailed & Personal History of Cessna's Involvement in the Army*, Jones Publishing, Inc., Iola, Wisconsin, 1995, p. 16.
11. *Cessna Guidebook*, p. 3.
12. David Shi and George Tindall, *America*, W.W. Norton & Company, New York, New York, 1989, p. 748.
13. *Cessna: A Master's Expression*, p.112
14. *Ibid.*
15. "World War II." Microsoft (R) *Encarta* (R) 97 Encyclopedia, 1993-1996, Microsoft Corporation.
16. *Cessna: A Master's Expression*, p. 113.
17. *Ibid.*
18. *Ibid.*
19. Unpublished manuscript received from retired Cessna Division Commercial Controller, Clair McColl, p. 20.
20. *1941 Cessna Aircrafter*, an employee yearbook.
21. *Cessna: A Master's Expression*, p. 113.
22. "Cessna: The Cessna Aircraft Company, Wichita," Internal publication of The Cessna Aircraft Company published circa 1968, p. 4.
23. "Sisterhood Sells Land Near Airport To Cessna Company: All–cash Deal Involving Approximately $88,000 Is Revealed Thursday, 320 Acres In Tract," *Wichita Eagle*, March 27, 1939, p. 5.
24. *Cessna: A Master's Expression*, p. 112.
25. "Rapid Growth Features Cessna Defense Contracts, Twin–Motor Plane Used By U.S. Army, Canada as Trainer, Output is Rising Rapidly in Plant Increased in Size by 600 percent, 2,000 are employed," *Wichita Eagle*, April 20, 1941, p. 20.
26. Jack Zook, interviewed by Nola Norfleet, February 20, 1997. Transcript, p. 3.
27. Clair McColl manuscript, p. 23.
28. "60 Percent Women Now Being Employed: Cessna Now Has One Female Worker Out of Every Four Laborers With Figure Mounting Steadily," *Wichita Beacon*, July 12, 1942,
29. "High Production & Morale Mark Cessna During The War," *Cessquire: Special 50th Anniversary Edition*, 1977, no page numbers.
30. *Cessna: A Master's Expression*, p. 115.
31. *Cessquire*, Vol. I, No. I, May 2, 1941, pp. 1, 2.
32. Jay Landrum, interviewed by the author, February 19, 1997. Transcript, p. 4.
33. *Cessna Guidebook*, p. 3.
34. Clair McColl manuscript, p. 25.
35. *Ibid.*
36. Wallace interview, p. 6.
37. Clair McColl manuscript, p. 27.
38. *Cessquire*, Vol. III, No. 19, January 7, 1944, p. 14.
39. "High Production & Morale Mark Cessna During The War," *Cessquire Magazine: Special 50th Anniversary Edition*,1977, no page numbers.
40. "Cessna: A History of Community Service," *Cessquire Magazine: Special 50th Anniversary Edition*, 1977, no page numbers.
41. *Cessna Guidebook*, pp. 30–34.
42. *Cessna Warbirds: A Detailed & Personal History of Cessna's Involvement in the Army*, p. 16.
43. *Cessna: A Master's Expression*, p. 120.
44. *Cessna Guidebook*, pp. 3, 36–38.
45. *An Eye to the Sky: Cessna*, p. 41.
46. *Cessna Guidebook*, p. 3.
47. "Cessna History, Chapter 8," *Cessquire*, p. 13.
48. *1942 Cessna Aircrafter*, an employee yearbook.
49. "Cessna History, Chapter 8," p. 13.
50. *An Eye to the Sky: Cessna*, p. 43.
51. Cessna Annual Report, 1945.
52. *Cessna Warbirds: A Detailed & Personal History of Cessna's Involvement in the Army*, p. 17.

Chapter Eight

1. *Air Facts Magazine*, advertisement, December 1946.
2. Cessna Annual Report, 1945.
3. "Cessna History, Chapter 9," *Cessquire*, Vol. 17, No. 10, October 1977, p. 11.
4. *Two Hundred Years of Flight in America: A Bicentennial Survey*, American Astronautical Society, 1979, San Diego, California, 1977, p. 124.
5. *Ibid.*
6. *Ibid.*, 125.
7. Cessna Annual Report, 1946.
8. Lucille Brunton, interviewed by Kenneth Hartsoe, March 25, 1997. Transcript, p. 4.
9. *Air Progress*, "The Cessna Story," Winter 1960, p. 51.
10. Mitch Mayborn and Bob Pickett, *Cessna Guidebook*, Volume I, Flying Enterprise Publications, Dallas, Texas, 1973, pp. 38-39.
11. Black three-ring binder filled with specifications of various Cessna aircraft, from the Cessna legal department. No page numbers.
12. Paul Kalberer, interviewed by the author, April 28, 1997.
13. Jack Zook, interviewed by Nola Norfleet, February 20, 1997. Transcript, p. 10.
14. *Cessna Guidebook*, pp. 38 & 39.
15. "Cessna Production Now 22 Ships Daily, Officials Disclose, Company One Month Ahead of Schedule on Models 120 and 140, Dollar Volume High," *Wichita Eagle*, March 17, 1946, p. 5.
16. *Standard Catalog Of Cessna Single Engine Aircraft*, Compiled by Jim Cavanagh, Revised, 2nd Edition by Kim Shields, Jones Publishing, Inc., Iola, Wisconsin, 1995, p. 11.
17. *Air Facts Magazine*, advertisement, December 1946.
18. "Cessna Production Now 22 Ships Daily," p. 5.
19. "Cessna History Began In 1911," *Cessna Is Growing, And Growing, And Growing*, supplement published by *Cessquire*, undated, p. 3.
20. "Cessna to Drop Two–place Plane, Halt in Production Slated in February," *Wichita Eagle*, December 20, 1950, p. 5.
21. "Cessna's Assembly Line To Be Closed Down During Week, New Machinery Is Being Installed to Take Care of Model Changes, 1,800 Employed Now," *Wichita Eagle*, December 9, 1946, p. 5
22. Cessna Annual Report, 1947.
23. Edward H. Phillips, Wings of *Cessna: Models 120 to the Citation X*, second edition, Flying Books International, Eagan, Minnesota, 1994, p. 43.
24. "New, Bigger Models Unveiled by Cessna, Roomy Cabin Seating Five Persons Handily One of Features of 190 and 195; Pay Load Is High." *Wichita Eagle*, May 10, 1947, pp. 1, 4.
25. Gerald Deneau, *An Eye To The Sky: Cessna*, Unpublished manuscript, date unknown, pp. 51, 52.
26. *An Eye To The Sky: Cessna*, p. 57.
27. "The Cessna Story 1927–1977," *Cessna 50th Anniversary: 50 Years of Leadership*, program for November 12, 1977 opening of the Wallace and Commercial Jet Marketing Divisions, no page numbers.
28. Leighton Collins, "The Cessna 170," *Air Facts*, Vol. 11, No. 5, May 1948, p. 22.
29. "Cessna 170. There Are Lots of Them Around and the Price is Getting Right," *Family Planes*, undated article, circa 1969.
30. "Growing, Growing, Growing, Hydraulics," *Growing, Growing, Growing, Cessna*, published by the editors of *Cessquire*, p. 11, undated.
31. *An Eye To The Sky: Cessna*, p. 49.
32. Clair McColl manuscript, p. 38.
33. "Growing, Growing, Growing, Hydraulics," p. 10.
34. Cessna Annual Report, 1947.
35. "Growing, Growing, Growing, Hydraulics," p. 10.
36. Unpublished manuscript received from retired Cessna Division Commercial Controller, Clair McColl, p. 42.
37. Cessna Annual Report, 1947.
38. *The Cessna Aircraft Company: A Study*, Kidder, Peabody & Co. (booklet), circa 1953–54, p. 3.
39. Floyd Lundy, interviewed by the author, April 2, 1997. Transcript, p. 4.
40. Cessna Annual Report, 1948.
41. Clair McColl manuscript, p. 39.
42. "Growing, Growing, Growing, Hydraulics," p. 10.
43. *An Eye to the Sky: Cessna*, p. 49.

Chapter Nine

1. "Up Front with the L-19: Pointing the Ducks," *Cessquire*, February 15, 1952.
2. William D. Thompson, *Cessna: Wings for the World, The Single–Engine Development Story*, Maverick Publications, Inc., Bend, Oregon, 1991, pp. 174, 175.
3. Walt Shiel, *Cessna Warbirds: A Detailed & Personal History of Cessna's Involvement in the Armed Forces*, Jones Publishing, Inc., Iola, Wisconsin, 1995, p. 77.
4. *Wings for the World*,pp. 174-175.
5. "Liaison Plane Details Given, Cessna More Than Fills Requirements," *Wichita Eagle*, May 25, 1950, p. 4.
6. "$5,000,000 Job Goes to Cessna, Employment at Plant Due to Hold Steady," *Wichita Eagle*, May 30, 1950, p. 5.
7. "Cessna Produces Final L–19," Cessna press release, undated.
8. "$5,000,000 Job Goes to Cessna," p. 8.
9. "Cessna Produces Final L–19."
10. *Cessna Warbirds*, p. 79.
11. "Contest Brews to Pick Name for Army L-19: Cessnans at Three Plants Invited to Participate," *Cessquire*, July, 1951.
12. *Cessna Warbirds*, p. 80.
13. *Ibid.*
14. "Growing, Growing, Growing, Cessna," by the editors of *Cessquire*, December 9, 1955, p. 8.
15. "Jack A. Swayze Submits Winning Name Chosen by General Mark W. Clark," *Cessquire*, August 28, 1951.
16. Don Hammer, interviewed by Alex Lieber, February 25, 1997. Transcript, p. 4.
17. "Korean Liaison Pilot Owes Life to Sturdiness of Cessna L-19," *Cessquire*, March 14, 1952.
18. "Up Front with the L-19: With IX Corps in Korea," *Cessquire*, February 15, 1952.
19. "Veteran Liaison Pilot Visits Cessna," *Cessquire*, July 13, 1951.
20. "L-19 Has A Part In Mitchum Movie," *Cessquire*, January 25, 1952.
21. "Vanderlip Tells of Praise for Liaison Plane in Korea," *Cessquire*, July 27, 1951.
22. "Up Front with the L-19, Birddogging with the Engineers," *Cessquire*, February 15, 1952.
23. Gerald Deneau, *An Eye to the Sky: Cessna*, Unpublished manuscript, date unknown, pp. 52, 53.
24. "Model OE-2 in Production For Marine Corps," *Cessquire*, Vol. 15, No. 6, May 27, 1955, p. 3.
25. "L-19 Announces Return," *Cessquire*, Vol. 15, No. 8, July 29, 1955, p. 2.
26. Cessna Annual Report, 1956.
27. Cessna Annual Report, 1957.
28. *Cessna: Wings for the World, The Single–Engine Development Story*, Maverick Publications, Inc., Bend, Oregon, 1991, pp. 175, 176.
29. *An Eye to the Sky: Cessna*, p. 53.
30. "Cessna History." Unpublished manuscript from the Cessna legal department, p. 4.
31. *An Eye to the Sky: Cessna*, pp. 52-53.
32. "Cessna History Chapter 10," *Cessquire*, Vol. 17, No. 11, December 1977, pp. 11-12.
33. *Cessna: Wings for the World, The Single–Engine Development Story*, Maverick Publications, Inc., Bend, Oregon, 1991, p. 180.
34. "Cessna History Chapter 10," p. 12.
35. *An Eye to the Sky: Cessna*, p. 54.
36. "Cessna to Build Nation's First True Jet Trainer, Air Force Selects Company's Small, Light Plane Model 318; To Use French- designed Engines, Rare Twin–jet Craft to Be Developed here For Pilot Primary Training; Chosen from 15 Designs Submitted by 8 planemakers," *Wichita Eagle*, January 1, 1953, pp. 1, 20.
37. "T-37 First Plant Tenant," *Cessquire*, Vol. 16, No. 10, August 24, 1956, p. 7.
38. Bruce Peterman, interviewed by the author, April 1, 1997. Transcript, pp. 5-6.
39. "T-37 Program Not Affected By Plane Loss," *Cessquire*, Vol. 15, No. 8, July 29, 1955, p. 3.
40. "Cessna Spin Win Cited," *Cessquire*, Vol. 16, No. 16, November 16, 1956, p. 6.
41. "Twin Jet to Try Out for Army Reconnaissance Role," *Cessquire*, Vol. 17, No. 5, May 17, 1957, p. 11.
42. Cessna Annual Report, 1958.
43. Cessna Annual Report, 1959.
44. "New Hangar For T-37 And 620 Flight Groups," *Cessquire*, Vol. 15, No. 2, February 21, 1955, p. 7.
45. *Skyword*, Vol. XI, No. 3, March 1970, p. 5.
46. Cessna Annual Report, 1952.
47. "CH–1 Opens New Vistas," *Cessquire*, Vol. 15, No. 5, April 29, 1955, pp. 3, 4.
48. "The Cessna Story 1927–1977," *Cessna 50th Anniversary: 50 Years of Leadership*, program for November 12, 1977 opening of the Wallace and Commercial Jet Marketing Divisions, no page numbers.
49. "Proves Prowess On Pike's Peak,"*Cessquire*, Vol. 15, No. 11, September 30, 1955, p. 3.
50. "Seneca Bound for Army Testing," *Cessquire*, Vol. 17, No. 8, August 16, 1957, p. 2.
51. "Army Reaches New Helicopter Heights in YH-41," *Cessquire*, Vol. 18, No. 1, January 24, 1958, p. 2.
52. "The Cessna Story 1927–1977."
53. Dirk Broersma, "The Plane Truth: Cessna's Son Claims Role in Aircraft's Success," *News–Pilot*, February 3, 1992, p. A6.
54. Ted Thackrey, "He Left the Farm and Soared Into the Air," *Wichita Beacon*, December 5, 1954, p. 3.
55. News clipping found in Cessna's archives, newspaper and date unknown.
56. "He Left the Farm and Soared Into the Air."

Chapter Nine Sidebar

1. "Airplane," Microsoft (R) *Encarta* (R) 97 Encyclopedia, 1993-1996 Microsoft Corporation.
2. *Ibid.*

Chapter Ten

1. "Big Increase in Personal Plane Sales Last Year," *Wichita Eagle*, Cessna Special Edition, January 15, 1951, p. 1.
2. *Ibid.*
3. Advertisement from February 1954 *Flying*, reprinted in Edward H. Phillips, Wings of *Cessna: Models 120 to the Citation X*, second edition, Flying Books International, Eagan, Minnesota, 1994, p. 31.
4. *Flying*, April 1952.
5. James E. Ellis, *Buying and Owning Your Own Airplane*, Iowa State University Press, Ames, Iowa, 1991, p. 212.
6. "Better Than Ever 170 Costs No More,"*Cessquire*, Vol. 15, No. 12, October 28, 1955, p. 3.
7. *Buying and Owning Your Own Airplane*, p. 212.
8. Unpublished manuscript received from retired Cessna Division Commercial Controller, Clair McColl, p. 48.
9. *Ibid.*, pp. 48-49.
10. "Something New in the Blue," *Cessquire*, Vol. 18, No. 3, March 28, 1958, p. 3.
11. "The Cessna Story 1927–1977," *Cessna 50th Anniversary: 50 Years of Leadership*, program for November 12, 1977 opening of the Wallace and Commercial Jet Marketing Divisions, no page numbers.
12. *Wings of Cessna: Models 120 to the Citation X*, p. 23.
13. Cessna Annual Report, 1952.
14. *Wings of Cessna: Models 120 to the Citation X*, p. 58.
15. Gerald Deneau, *An Eye to the Sky: Cessna*, Unpublished manuscript, date unknown, p. 59.
16. Reprint of ad slick that ran in 1955 issues of *Flying, Flight, Air Facts and Skyways* magazines.
17. Cessna Inter–Office Communication from Paul Zeh to Bob Pickett, subject: end of 210 line, May 6, 1981.
18. *An Eye to the Sky: Cessna*, p. 59.
19. Cessna Annual Report, 1958.
20. "310B Goes to Hollywood," *Cessquire*, Vol. 18, No. 2, February 28, 1958, p. 2.
21. "Something New In the Blue," *Cessquire*, Vol. 17, No. 7, July 19, 1957, p. 3.
22. "310B Goes to Hollywood," p. 2.
23. Cessna Annual Report, 1957.
24. "The Cessna Story 1927–1977," *Cessna 50th Anniversary: 50 Years of Leadership*, program for November 12, 1977 opening of the Wallace and Commercial Jet Marketing Divisions, no page numbers.
26. Cessna Annual Report, 1959.
27. "Craft Makes Maiden Flight, Cessna 620 Planned For Executive Use," *Wichita Eagle*, August 12, 1956, p. 4A.
28. Cessna Annual Report, 1956.
29. Cessna Annual Report, 1957.
30. Don Powell, interviewed by the author, February 19, 1997. Transcript, p. 6.
31. Cessna Annual Report, 1958.
32. "Cessna Opens New East Coast Branch Facilities," *Cessquire*, Vol 19, No. 6, July 1959, p. 2.
33. "The Cessna Story 1927–1977,"
34. Cessna Annual Report, 1958.
35. *Cessquire*, December 23, 1954, p. 20.
36. "Cessna to Open New Unit Jan. 1, President Outlines Expansion Plans," *Wichita Eagle*, September 20, 1950, p. 5.
37. "The Cessna Story 1927–1977,"

Chapter Eleven

1. Arbery Barrett, interviewed by the author, April 1, 1997. Transcript, p. 3.
2. Cessna Annual Report, 1969, p. 13.
3. Cessna Annual Report, 1960, p. 10.
4. "Cessna: The Cessna Aircraft Company, Wichita," Internal publication of The Cessna Aircraft Company, published circa 1968, p. 5.
5. "Cessna History," Unpublished manuscript, from the Cessna legal department, p. 6.
6. Cessna Annual Report, 1964.
7. James E. Ellis, *Buying and Owning Your Own Airplane*, Iowa State University Press, Ames, Iowa, 1991, p. 150.
8. "Cessna: The Cessna Aircraft Company, Wichita," p. 6.
9. Cessna Annual Report, 1961, p. 3.
10. "Cessna: The Cessna Aircraft Company, Wichita," p. 6.
11. *Ibid.*
12. Cessna Annual Report, 1967, p. 2.
13. "Engineering Center Started, "Cessna Shareholder Report, Vol. 1, No. 1, August 1968, p. 3.
14. "Engineering College Honors Dwane L. Wallace," *Cessquire*, Vol. 9, No. 5, May 1968, p. 5.
15. Earl Biggs, interviewed by the author, February 19, 1997. Transcript, p. 10.
16. Dorothy Naylor, interviewed by Karen Nitkin, February 19, 1997. Transcript, p. 6.

17. Del Roskam, interviewed by the author, February 21, 1997. Transcript, p. 33.
18. Russ Meyer, interviewed by the author, May 18, 1997. Transcript, p. 31.
19. "The Cessna Story 1927–1977,"
20. "Cessna To Unveil 210 In Fall," *Cessquire*, Vol. 19, No. 3, April 1959, p. 16.
21. Gerald Deneau, *An Eye to the Sky: Cessna*, Unpublished manuscript, date unknown, p. 68.
22. "Cessna: The Cessna Aircraft Company, Wichita," p. 5.
23. Paul Kalberer, interviewed by the author, May 15, 1997.
24. Cessna Annual Report, p. 8.
25. James E. Ellis, *Buying and Owning Your Own Airplane*, Iowa University Press, Ames, Iowa, 1991, p. 150.
26. *Ibid.*
27. "Cessna: The Cessna Aircraft Company, Wichita,"
28. "The Skynight, World's First Business Turbocharged Twin Announced," *Cessquire*, Commercial Aircraft Division, Vol. 2, No. 5, May 1961, p. 4.
29. Cessna Annual Report, 1960, pp. 7-8.
30. "Cessna Six-Passenger Skywagon Increases Cargo Capacity With External Cargo-Pack Attachment," *Cessquire*, Commercial Aircraft Division, Vol. 2, No. 5, May 1961, p. 2.
31. *Buying and Owning Your Own Airplane*, p. 210.
32. Cessna Annual Report, 1969, p. 17.
33. Cessna Annual Report, 1962, p. 8.
34. *Jane's Encyclopedia Of Aviation*, compiled and edited by Michael J.H. Taylor, Crescent Books, Studio Editions Ltd., 1980, 1989, p. 249.
35. Cessna Annual Report, 1961, p. 4.
36. Cessna Annual Report, 1964.
37. Cessna Annual Report, 1967, p. 15.
38. "Super Skymaster Flies Around The World," *Cessquire*, Vol. 9, No. 9, September 1968, p. 10.
39. "Cessna History."
40. *Ibid.*
41. *Ibid.*
42. Cessna Annual Report, 1969, p. 19.
43. Dean Noble, interviewed by Karen Nitkin, February 20, 1997. Transcript, p. 9.
44. Comments from Bruce Peterman, June 20, 1997.
45. "Cessna History."
46. *Skyword*, Vol. XI, No. 1, January 1970, p. 7.
47. "The Cessna Story 1927–1977," *Cessna 50th Anniversary: 50 Years of Leadership*, program for November 12, 1977 opening of the Wallace and Commercial Jet Marketing Divisions, no page numbers.
48. "Cessna History," p. 9.
49. Cessna Annual Report, 1969, p. 14.
50. Cessna Annual Report, 1960, p. 7.
51. "1911 to 1960: The Cessna Aircraft Company, Part I," magazine article from unknown source reprinted with permission of *Air Pictorial* magazine, 19 Park Lane, London, England, pp. 83-84.
52. Cessna Annual Report, 1960, p. 11.
53. "Cessna Receives Military Helicopter Contract," *Cessquire*, Vol. 3, No. 3., March 1, 1962, p. 9.
54. Bruce Learmont interviewed by Karen Nitkin, June 25, 1997.
55. Barrett interview, p. 3.
56. *Ibid.*
57. Maurice Allward, et al., *The Encyclopedia of World Air Power*, Crescent Books, New York, New York, 1980, pp. 139-140.
58. "A-37B Deliveries Begin," Cessna Shareholder Report, Vol. 1, No. 1, August 1968, p. 2.
59. "Cessna History," p. 3.
60. "V/C Fear Cessna's O-2A," *Cessquire*, Vol. 8, No. 11, November 1967, p. 4.
61. Cessna Annual Report, 1969, p. 21.

Chapter Twelve

1. Milt Sills, interviewed by the author, February 21, 1997. Transcript, p. 6.
2. Robert B. Park, "B/CA Salutes 25 Years of Business Aviation," *Business and Commercial Aviation*, January 1983, p. 61.
3. James B. Taylor, "Cessna Citation Design Factors and Philosophy," Speech to the Society of Automotive Engineers, National Business Aircraft Meeting, Wichita, Kansas, March 18-20, 1970, p. 5.
4. Bruce Peterman, interviewed by the author, April 1, 1997. Transcript, p. 16.
5. Ralph Piper, "Cessna Citations — First of the Mini-Fans," *Business and Commercial Aviation*, March 1971.
6. "Fanjet 500 Mock-Up Shown," *Cessna Shareholder Report*, November, 1968, p. 3.
7. Cessna press release, February 10, 1969.
8. "What's In A Name Anyway?" *Business and Commercial Aviation*, 1969, p. 14.
9. "Cessna Fanjet 500 Renamed Citation; Makes Maiden Voyage," *Business Aviation*, September 19, 1969, p. 81.
10. "Citation's Flight Meets Expectations," *Skyword*, October 1969, p. 1.
11. Sills interview, p. 6.
12. "Citation Takes Wing," *General Aviation News*, September 22, 1969, p. 1.
13. Notes from Russ Meyer, July 22, 1997.
14. "Cessna Model 500 Makes Initial Flight," *Aviation Week and Space Technology*, September 22, 1969, p. 28.
15. "A New Kind Of Challenge For Salesmen," *Fortune*, April 1974, p. 164.
16. Charles E. Schneider, "Cessna Citation Marketing Emphasizes Aircraft Utility," *Aviation Week and Space Technology*, February 22, 1971, p. 60.
17. "Cessna Unveils Marketing Tool," *Fort Pierce News Tribune*, March 14, 1971; "Unique Marketing Tool," *General Aviation News*, March 8, 1971, p. 9.
18. "Cessna Makes Room For The Citation," *Midwest Industry*, May 1970; Marvin Barnes, "FAA Certifies Cessna Business Jet," *Wichita Beacon*, September 10, 1971.
19. Peterman interview, p. 28.
20. "Cessna Citation Jet Production Started," *Aviation Week and Space Technology*, June 7, 1971, pp. 52-53.
21. Russ Meyer, interviewed by the author, November 22, 1997. Transcript, p. 8.
22. "Citation Aircraft To Increase Citation Jet Output Again," *The Wall Street Journal*, September 13, 1972, p. 3.
23. "Fuel Efficiency," *Army Journal International*, January 1974, p. 11.
24. *Ibid.*

Chapter Thirteen

1. Phil Michel, interviewed by the author, April 3, 1997. Transcript, p. 14.
2. Cessna Annual Report, 1970, p. 3.
3. "The Cessna Story 1927–1977," *Cessna 50th Anniversary: 50 Years of Leadership*, program for November 12, 1977 opening of the Wallace and Commercial Jet Marketing Divisions, no page numbers.
4. Cessna Annual Report, 1970, p. 3.
5. James E. Ellis, *Buying and Owning Your Own Airplane*, Iowa State University Press, Ames, Iowa, 1991, p. 157, 218-219.
6. Cessna press release, 1970.
7. "Cessna Cardinal Classic, RG Close Out Production With End of '78 Model Year," Cessna press release, August 14, 1978.
8. "Cessna History," Unpublished manuscript from the Cessna legal department.
9. Cessna Annual Report, 1970, p. 8.
10. "The Cessna Story 1927–1977."
11. *Ibid.*
12. Phil Michel, interviewed by the author, April 3, 1997. Transcript, p. 14.
13. "Hutchinson Plant Gets New Name," *Skyword*, Vol. XII, No. 10, October 1971, p. 3.
14. "The Cessna Story 1927–1977."
15. "New Cessna Facility Adds 115,000 Square Feet To Pawnee," *Cessquire*, Vol. 14, No. 10, October 1973.
16. "The Cessna Story 1927–1977."
17. Russ Meyer, interviewed by the author, May 18, 1997. Transcript, volume II, p. 26.
18. *Ibid.*
19. *Ibid.*
20. "The Cessna Story 1927–1977."
21. Russ Meyer, interviewed by the author, May 18, 1997. Transcript, p. 9.
22. *Ibid.*, p. 22.
23. *Ibid.*, p. 26.
24. *Ibid.*, p. 31.
25. Ibid., p. 33.
26. *Ibid.*, p. 44.
27. *Ibid.*, p. 44.
28. *Ibid.*, p. 23.
29. Meyer interview, pp. 33-34.
30. "The Cessna Story 1927–1977."
31. *Ibid.*
32. Del Roskam, interviewed by the author, February 21, 1997. Transcript, p. 35.
33. Meyer interview, p. 43.
34. *Ibid.*, p. 50.
35. Gifford Booth, interviewed by the author, April 2, 1997. Transcript, p. 16.
36. Marilyn Richwine, interviewed by the author, February 20, 1997. Transcript, p. 8.
37. "The Cessna Story 1927–1977."
38. Cessna Annual Report, 1975, pp. 3-4.
39. Cessna Annual Report, 1976, p. 2.
40. "The Cessna Story 1927–1977."
41. "Cessna Milestones, 1911-1982," published by Cessna.
42. "The Cessna Story 1927–1977."
43. Edward Phillips, *Wings of Cessna: Model 120 to the Citation X*, Flying Books International, Eagan, Minnesota, 1994, p. 75.
44. "Cessna '79 Skyhawk/Hawk XP, The World's Most Popular Airplane ... and Its High Flying, Swift Cruising, Powerful Big Brother," Cessna sales brochure.
45. Cessna Annual Report, 1977, p. 1.
46. Cessna Annual Report, 1977, p. 2.
47. "Cessna Milestones, 1911-1982."
48. *Ibid.*
49. *Ibid.*
50. David M. North, "Conquest Certification Review Planned," *Aviation Week & Space Technology*, November 28, 1977, p. 19.
51. *Ibid.*
52. "Cessna Conquest Propject Receives FAA Certification," Cessna press release, September 27, 1977.
53. "Cessna Milestones, 1911-1982."
54. Cessna press release, 1978.
55. "1979 Cessna Model 152: The World's Standard In Training Aircraft," Cessna press release, August 14, 1978.
56. "Cessna Milestones, 1911-1982."

Chapter Fourteen

1. Dorothy Cochran, interviewed by the author, May 6, 1997. Transcript, p. 7.

2. "The New Citation I," Cessna Marketing Brochure, The Cessna Aircraft Company, May 1977, p. 2.
3. "Comparison Profile: The Citation I/SP," *Business and Commercial Aviation*, February , 1977.
4. "Cessna Citations — The Best Selling Business Jets," *Business and Commercial Aviation*, April, 1983.
5. Hugh Field, "Citation II in the Air," *Flight International*, April 7, 1979, pp. 1059, 1060.
6. "Cessna Citations — The Best Selling Business Jets."
7. Milton Sills, interviewed by the author, February 21, 1997. Transcript, p. 12.
8. *Ibid.*
9. *Ibid.* p. 16.
10. John W. Olcott and J. Mac McClellan, "Status Report: Cessna Citation III," *Business and Commercial Aviation*, January 1980, pp. 39-41.
11. "Arnold Palmer's New III Iron," Cessna advertisement, November 1985.
12. "Exciting New Citation S/II Offers More Performance And Comfort," *Directions*, October, 1983, pp. 1-2.
13. Richard Santulli, interviewed by the author, July 16, 1997. Transcript, pp. 5-17.
14. Jim Lyle, interviewed by Karen Nitkin, June 25, 1997.
15. "Cessna Jets — Celebrating Forty Years of Achievement," Cessna brochure, 1995.
16. Chris Sorensen, "Hand-Building The Citation," *Professional Pilot*, October 1979.
17. *Ibid.*
18. Cessna press release, January 30, 1979.
19. Cessna press release, January 27, 1982.
20. Letter to Shareholders and Employees, Cessna Annual Report, 1981.
21. Ursula Jarvis, interviewed by the author, February 18, 1997. Transcript, p. 10.
22. "The 1985 Collier Trophy Presentation and Banquet Program," Hosted by the National Aviation Club and Sponsored by the National Aeronautic Association, The Shoreham Hotel, Washington, D.C., May 16, 1986, pp. 1, 7.
23. *Ibid.*
24. Speech given by Russ Meyer at the Collier Trophy Award Banquet, Washington, D.C., May 16, 1986, pp. 1, 4, 7.
25. Gordon A. Gilbert, "Cessna Announces Citation V," *Business and Commercial Aviation's NBAA Show Daily*, September 29, 1987, p. 1.
26. Richard N. Aarons, "Cessna's New Citation V," *Business and Commercial Aviation*, May, 1988, p. 55.
27. "Enhancing Proven Technology," *Directions*, Summer 1989, p. 2.
28. J. MacClellan, "High Five," *Flying*, August 1989, p. 57.
29. Fred George, "Citation V Ultra," *Business and Commercial Aviation*, December 1993.
30. "Cessna Jets — Celebrating Forty Years of Achievement," Cessna brochure, 1995.
31. Fred George, "Citation V Ultra," *Business and Commercial Aviation*, December 1993.
32. J. MacClellan, "The Citation V Ultra Exceeds Expectations," *Flying*, November 1994, pp. 77, 78, 80.
33. "Flying's Best of the Past Year," *Flying*, February 1995, p. 70.
34. "CitationJet Makes Its First Public Flight," *General Aviation News and Flyer*, May 1991, p. 1.
35. Graham Warwick, "Affordable Jet," *Flight International*, May 29-June 4, 1991, p. 67.
36. Richard L. Collins, "Personal Turbines," *AOPA Pilot*, May 1991, p. T-14.
37. David M. North, "Single-Pilot CitationJet Primed For Competition," *Aviation Week and Space Technology*, May 3, 1993, p. 42.
38. Roger Whyte, interviewed by the author, April 3, 1997. Transcript, p. 7.
39. Graham Warwick, "Affordable Jet," *Flight International*, May 29-June 4, 1991, p. 67.
40. Citation Bravo, Cessna marketing brochure, October 1996.
41. "Cessna Jets — Celebrating Forty Years of Achievement," Cessna brochure, 1995.
42. Citation Bravo, Cessna brochure, October 1996.
43. Citation Excel. marketing brochure, October 1994.
44. Cochran interview, p. 7.

Chapter Fourteen Sidebar

1. Marilyn Richwine, interviewed by the author, February 20, 1997. Transcript, p. 9.
2. Program for The 48th Annual Wright Memorial Dinner, honoring Russ Meyer, December 15, 1995, p. 10.
3. "Cessna's Uplifting Experience," *Business & Commercial Aviation*, March 1996.
4. "Citation Special Olympics Airlift To Fly Special Athletes To International Games," Special Olympics press relesae, undated.
5. "Airlift Excited All Involved," *Directions Extra*, 1987.
6. "Cessna's Uplifting Experience," p. 83.
7. "Airlift Excited All Involved," pp. 1,3, 5.

Chapter Fifteen

1. John Moore, interviewed by the author, February 18, 1997. Transcript, p. 6.
2. Cessna Annual Report, 1980, p. 2.
3. *Ibid.*, p. 4.
4. "Cessna Announces Employee Reductions At Its Pawnee Division Facilities," undated Cessna press release.
5. "Cessna Announces Layoff And Assembly line Shutdown At Wallace Division," Cessna press release, March 25, 1980.
6. "Cessna Announces Additional Employment Reductions At Pawnee Division," Cessna press release, April 3, 1980.
7. "Cessna Announces Additional Employment Reductions At Its Pawnee Division Plant In Wichita," Cessna press release, May 22, 1980.
8. John Moore, interviewed by the author, February 18, 1997. Transcript, p. 6.
9. Gary Hay, interviewed by the author, February 18, 1997. Transcript, p. 16.
10. *Ibid.*, p. 40.
11. "Malcom S. Harned Dies," Cessna press release, October 24, 1980.
12. 1980 Annual Report, p. 2.
13. Hay interview, p. 16.
14. Cessna Annual Report, 1980, p. 4.
15. Cessna Annual Report, 1982, p. 3.
16. Cessna Annual Report, 1981, p. 2.
17. "Cessna Purchases United Hydraulic Corporation," Cessna press release, October 27, 1981.
18. "Cessna's New Crusader Is Certified; Enters Marketplace," Cessna press release, August 28, 1981.
19. Letter to Shareholders and Employees, Cessna Annual Report, 1981.
20. "Cessna Announces $36 Million Capital Expenditure Program At Its Wichita And Hutchinson Facilities," Cessna press release, November 6, 1980.
21. "Cessna Restructures Marketing Organizations," Cessna press release, February 23, 1982.
22. "Cessna Reorganizes Marketing and Product Support Divisions," Cessna press release, July 6, 1982.
23. Peter Redman, interviewed by the author, April 1, 1997. Transcript, p. 5.
24. "Cessna Announces Prime Leader Finance Plan For Propjets," Cessna press release, September 21, 1982.
25. Cessna Annual Report, 1982, p. 3.
26. *Ibid.*
27. "We're Back!" *Directions*, Spring 1996, p. 40.
28. Cessna Annual Report, 1982, p. 9.
29. Bob Conover, interviewed by Kenneth Hartsoe, April 15, 1997. Transcript, pp. 7, 8.
30. "Cessna Adjusts Production And Employment At Its Wallace Aircraft Division," Cessna press release, March 30, 1982.
31. "Cessna's Fluid Power Division Will Close For One Week In May," Cessna press release, April 21, 1982.
32. Cessna Annual Report, 1983.
33. "Death Closes an Aviation Era: Dwane Wallace Took Cessna to The Top," *Wichita Eagle*, December 22, 1989.
34. Cessna press release, undated.
35. Velma Wallace, interviewed by the author, June 6, 1997. Transcript, p. 7.
36. Wichita Aeronautical Historical Association, Vol. 5, No. 1, Fall 1986.
37. Russ Meyer, interviewed by the author, May 18, 1997. Transcript, p. 60.
38. Bob Cox, "Death Closes an Aviation Era," *Wichita Eagle*, December 21, 1989.
39. Bruce Peterman, interviewed by the author, April 1, 1997. Transcript, p. 29.
40. "Death Closes an Aviation Era."
41. *Ibid.*
42. Cessna press release, January 5, 1987.
43. "Cessna Nominates General Dynamics Chairman As Board Member; Announces Joint Technology Development Program," Cessna press release, November 7, 1983.
44. Russ Meyer, interviewed by the author, July 14, 1997. Transcript, p. 4.
45. "Cessna Announces Consolidation Of Two Aircraft Manufacturing Divisions," Cessna press release, June 11, 1984.
46. "Cessna Reports Improved Fourth Quarter and 1984 Fiscal Year," Cessna press release, October 17, 1984.
47. "Cessna Restructures Sales And Marketing organization For Piston And Propjet Aircraft," Cessna press release, February 21, 1985.
48. Regene Prilliman, interviewed by the author, February 18, 1997. Transcript, p. 6.
49. "Cessna Announces Reorganization At Its Wallace Aircraft Division," Cessna press release, January 18, 1984.
50. Memorandum to all Cessna Employees from Chairman Russ Meyer and President Bill Van Sant, July 11, 1985.
51. General Dynamics Annual Report, 1985, p. 32.
52. Russ Meyer, interviewed by the author, July 14, 1997. Transcript, p. 5.
53. "Cessna And General Dynamics Announce Merger Agreement," Cessna press release, September 13, 1985.
54. Nunzio Lupo, "General Dynamics Takes Cessna into Its Corporate Nest," *Wichita Eagle-Beacon*, March 4, 1986.
55. General Dynamics Annual Report, 1985, p. 3.
56. General Dynamics Annual Report, 1986, p. 20.
57. Meyer interview, p. 67.
58. Bruce Peterman, interviewed by the author, April 1, 1997. Transcript, p. 22.

59. Humphrey interview, transcript, p. 7.
60. Cessna Memorandum to all employees from Russ Meyer, January 16, 1987; Meyer interview, p. 42.
61. Notes supplied by Russ Meyer, August 29, 1997.
62. Meyer interview, July 14, 1997, p. 7.
63. Humphrey interview, p. 10.
64. General Dynamics Annual Report, 1988, pp. 25, 31.
65. Russ Meyer interview, November 22, 1997. Transcript, p. 14.
66. General Dynamics Annual Report, 1989, p. 23.

Chapter Sixteen

1. "We're Back," *Directions*, Spring 1996, p. 40.
2. Bob Dole, interviewed by the author, May 7, 1997. Transcript, pp. 3-4.
3. "Aircraft Insurance Rates Are Trending Upward," *Business and Commercial Aviation*, July, 1974, p. 15.
4. "The 1974 General Aviation Accident Rate Was The Lowest In 29 Years," *Business and Commercial Aviation*, March 1975, p. 23.
5. Russ Meyer, interviewed by the author, May 18, 1997. Transcript, p. 66.
6. Tom Wakefield, interviewed by the author, February 20, 1997. Transcript, p. 3.
7. "We're Back!" *Directions*, Spring 1996, p. 40.
8. Statement of John W. Olcott, President, National Business Aircraft Association, Inc., before the Committee On Public Works and Transportation, United States House of Representatives' Hearing On H.R. 3087, The General Aviation Revitalization Act of 1993, October 27, 1993.
9. *Ibid.*
10. *Ibid.*; Richard Collins, "Cessna Boss Talks About The Future," *Flying*, August 1994, p. 82.
11. Cessna press releases, February 5, 1982, May 5, 1982, December 15, 1982.
12. Cessna press release, May 28, 1986.
13. "We're Back!" *Directions*, Spring 1996, p. 40.
14. General Aviation Manufacturers Association Confidential Presentation To United States Senate and Congressional Leaders, General Aviation Manufacturers Association, Washington D. C., May 2, 1994, Appendix pp. A4-A6.
15. Ed Stimpson, interviewed by the author, May 6, 1997. Transcript, p. 4.
16. Mark A. Gottschalk, "General Aviation Experiences A Rebirth," *Design News*, September 11, 1995, p. 27.
17. Stimpson interview, p. 5.
18. Dan Glickman, interviewed by the author, May 7, 1997. Transcript, p. 4.
19. "General Aviation Experiences A Rebirth."
20. General Aviation Manufacturers Association Confidential Presentation To United States Senate and Congressional Leaders, General Aviation Manufacturers Association, Washington D. C., May 2, 1994, Appendix pp. A1, A5.
21. "What Effect Is GARA Likely To Have On General Aviation Claims?" Speech delivered by Tom Wakefield to the Aviation Space Law, Tort, and Insurance Practice Section at the Aviation Liability Into The 20th Century Conference, Washington D.C., October 9-10, 1996. Transcript, p. 2.
22. Stimpson interview, p. 23.
23. "What Effect Is GARA Likely To Have On General Aviation Claims?" Transcript, p. 2.
24. Stimpson interview, p. 5; "We're Back!" *Directions*, Spring 1996, p. 40.
25. Glickman interview, pp. 2-3.
26. "What Effect Is GARA Likely To Have On General Aviation Claims?" Transcript, p. 2.
27. Robert M. Jenney, "General Aviation Needs More Than Tort Reform," *Aviation Week and Space Technology*, October 3, 1994, p. 58.
28. "Victory In The Senate," *Aviation Week and Space Technology*, March 21, 1994, p. 23.
29. Stimpson interview, p. 7.
30. "Victory In The Senate," *Aviation Week and Space Technology*, March 21, 1994, p. 23.
31. "What Effect Is GARA Likely To Have On General Aviation Claims?" Transcript, p. 4.
32. Glickman interview, p. 15.
33. "Clinton Signs GA Liability Bill," *Airport Report Express*, Vol. 4 No. 67, August 22, 1994.
34. Phil Boyer, interviewed by the author, June 9, 1997. Transcript, p. 5.
35. Stacy Shapiro, "Product Liability Reform Revitalizes General Aviation," *Business Insurance*, May 15, 1995, p. 15.

Chapter Seventeen

1. Peter Lert, "Cessna Caravan," *Air Progress*, July 1985, p. 36.
2. Bob Cox, "Panel Truck for the Airways," *Cessna Owner*, September 1996, p. 23.
3. "Engineering Project Activation Memo Model 298," Prepared by Phil Hedrick — Project Engineer, Report Number M-208-11, Revision K-4-14-83, The Cessna Aircraft Company Archives, Wichita, Kansas, January 29, 1982, p. 3.
4. J. Mac McClellan, "Caravan I," *Flying*, June 1985, p. 49.
5. William C. Hogan, interviewed by Kenneth D. Hartsoe, April 15, 1997. Transcript, p. 14.
6. "Engineering Project Activation Memo Model 298," Prepared by Phil Hedrick, project engineer, January 29, 1982, p. 3.
7. *Ibid.*, p. 61, 2.
8. John W. Olcott and Richard N. Aarons, "Inflight Report: Cessna's Caravan I," *Business and Commercial Aviation*, June 1985, p. 49; Notes provided by Larry Van Dyke, project engineer, April 1997, p. 5.
9. "Cessna's B-I-G Utility Single," *Canadian Aviation*, August 1984, p. 16.
10. Larry VanDyke interviewed by the author, April 15, 1997, p. 9.
11. Russ Meyer, interviewed by the author, July 14, 1997. Transcript, p. 14.
12. J. MacClellan, "Caravan I," *Flying*, June 1985, p. 49.
13. Peter Lert, "Cessna Caravan," *Air Progress*, July 1985, p. 37; John W. Olcott and Richard N. Aarons, "Inflight Report: Cessna's Caravan I," *Business and Commercial Aviation*, June 1985, p. 49.
14. "Traffic Pattern," *Business and Commercial Aviation*, March 1984, p. 94.
15. *Ibid.*, p. 95.
16. "Inflight Report: Cessna's Caravan I," p. 50.
17. "Cessna Caravan," Cessna internal marketing document, 1996.
18. *Ibid.*
19. Notes provided by Larry Van Dyke, Project Engineer, The Cessna Aircraft Company, Wichita, Kansas, April 1997, p. 5.
20. VanDyke interview, p. 7.
21. "Inflight Report: Cessna's Caravan I," p. 50.
22. *Ibid.*
23. "Cessna's B-I-G Utility Single," *Canadian Aviation*, August 1984, p. 16.
24. Milton Moskowitz, Robert Levering and Michael Katz, *Everybody's Business: A Field Guide to the 400 Leading Companies in America*, Doubleday: New York, New York, 1994, p. 616.
25. Russ Meyer interview, July 14, 1997. Transcript, p. 18.
26. Fred Smith, interviewed by the author, August 4, 1997. Transcript, p. 2.
27. "FedEx Takes Delivery of First 'Stretched' Caravan," *Caravan News*, November 1986, p. 1.
28. VanDyke interview, p. 14.
29. Cessna press release, August 22, 1984.
30. Robert S. Grant, "Chiquita Banana," *Air Progress*, April 1989, p. 53.
31. John S. Daniel, interviewed by Kenneth D. Hartsoe, April 15, 1997, Transcript, p. 2.
32. Mark Blair, interviewed by the author, July 18, 1997. Transcript, p. 10.
33. *Ibid.*, p. 7.
34. Russ Meyer interview, July 14, 1997. Transcript, p. 19.
35. "Inflight Report: Cessna's Caravan I," p. 50.
36. Robert S. Grant, "Tur-Ban," *Canadian Aviation*, June 1985, p. 36.
37. "Inflight Report: Cessna's Caravan I," Business and Commercial Aviation, June 1985, p. 50.
38. "Tur-Ban," *Canadian Aviation*, June 1985, p. 36; "Traffic Pattern," *Business and Commercial* Aviation, March 1984, p. 94.
39. Cessna press releases, March 5, 1986 and October 31, 1986.
40. "Chiquita Banana," p. 53.
41. "Caravans In Venezuela," *Caravan News*, Volume 4 Number 2, 1990, p. 1.
42. "Flying In Relief: Revisiting The Caravan In Africa," *Caravan News*, Volume 3 Number 2, p. 1.
43. Walt Thompson, interviewed by Kenneth D. Hartsoe, April 16, 1997, Transcript, p. 13, 14.
44. "Cessna Caravan," Cessna internal marketing document, p. 5.
45. Nigel Moll, "Floats Like A Butterfly," *Flying*, September 1992, p. 95, 98.
46. Daniel interview, p. 7.
47. "Chiquita Banana," *Air Progress*, April 1989, p. 56.
48. Daniel interview, pp. 5-6.
49. "Chiquita Banana," p. 53.
50. *Ibid.*
51. Cessna press release, October 3, 1990.
52. Mark R. Twombly, "Room With A View," *AOPA Pilot*, June 1991, p. 49.
53. Edward H. Phillips, "Grand Caravan Features Rugged Airframe, Simple Systems Befitting Its Utility Role," *Aviation Week and Space Technology*, December 2, 1991, p. 68.
54. Cessna press releases, June 29, 1993 and June 9, 1995.
55. "Caravans Complete Tour De Force of Paris Air Show," *Caravan News*, Vol. 2, No. 2, 1987, p. 2.
56. "Brazilian Air Force Blazes New Trails With Caravan I," *Caravan News*, Vol. 5, No. 1, 1990, p. 1.
57. "Cessna's Special Mission Propjets," Cessna brochure, Commercial Propjet Marketing Division, p. 2.
58. "LCT, Inc. — Leaders In Gravity and Magnetics," *Caravan News*, Vol. 10, No. 4, 1996, p. 4.
59. Bob Conover, interviewed by Kenneth D. Hartsoe, April 16, 1997. Transcript, pp. 13-14.
60. Cessna press release, June 9, 1995.
61. Cessna press release, March 7, 1996.
62. Matt Amsden, "When Profitability Counts, Service And Support Is a Matter of Dollars and Cents," *Caravan News*, 1995, p. 7.
63. Steve Charles, interviewed by Kenneth D. Hartsoe, April 15, 1997, Transcript, pp. 6-7.
64. Charles interview, pp. 5-7.

65. "Customer Needs Came First In Redesign of Caravan Customer Center," *Caravan News*, Vol. 9, No. 1, Winter 1994, pp. 12-13.
66. Daniel interview, p. 9.
67. "The Caravan Trail," *Aviation Week and Space Technology*, December 9, 1996, p. 17.
68. Tour of Caravan Manufacturing Facilities, April 15, 1997. Transcript, pp. 4-5. p. 1.
70. J. MacClellan, "Caravan I," *Flying*, June 1985, p. 35-36.

Chapter Eighteen

1. "Citation X Prototype Rolls Out Of The Cessna Factory," *Directions*, Fall 1993.
2. Rick Gralert, "Cessna Bares 'Fastest Bizjet In History' Here," *NBAA Convention News*, October 4, 1990, pp. 1, 19.
3. Richard N. Aarons, "Cessna's Citation X," *Business and Commercial Aviation*, February 1991, pp. 54, 51.
4. Nigel Moll, "Citation X Is A Ten," *Flying*, June 1991.
5. J. Mac Mc Clellan, "Cessna Citation X," *Flying*, May 1996, p. 67.
6. Joanne R. Julius, "Citation 10," *Professional Pilot*, February 1991, p. 58.
7. "Citation X Is A Ten."
8. Fred George, "Cessna Citation X," *Business and Commercial Aviation*, December 1995, p. 49.
9. "Raising The Bar," *Aviation Spotlight*, May 1997, p. 8.
10. "Citation X Is A Ten."
11. Paul Kalberer, interviewed by the author, April 2, 1997. Transcript, p. 12.
12. "Cessna's Citation X," *Business and Commercial Aviation*, February 1991, p. 51; "Citation X Is A Ten," *Flying*, June 1991.
13. Terry Brisco, "Citation X and Falcon 2000," *Business Aviation and Regional Travel*, May 1993, p. 25.
14. "Cessna Citation X," *Flying*, May 1996, p. 68.
15. Fred George, "Cessna Citation X," *Business and Commercial Aviation*, December 1995, p. 50.
16. Terry Brisco, "Citation X and Falcon 2000," *Business Aviation and Regional Travel*, May 1993, p. 20.
17. "Citation X Prototype Rolls Out Of The Cessna Factory," *Directions*, Fall 1993.
18. "Citation X and JPATS Make First Flights," *Flying*, March 1994, p. 31.
19. "Citation X Receives FAA Certification," *Cessnan*, May-June 1996, p. 8.
20. Donald Van Burkleo, interviewed by the author, April 3, 1997. Transcript, p. 12.
21. Doug Hazelwood, interviewed by the author, April 1, 1997. Transcript, p. 21.
22. Ronald Chapman, interviewed by the author, February 20, 1997. Transcript, p. 5.
23. Gary Hay, interviewed by the author, February 18, 1997. Transcript, p. 28.
24. "Cessna's Citation X," *Business and Commercial Aviation*, February 1991, pp. 54, 51; "Citation X and Falcon 2000," *Business Aviation and Regional Travel*, May 1993, pp. 24, 25; "Cessna Citation X," *Flying*, May 1996, p. 68; "Citation X Is A Ten," *Flying*, June 1991.
25. Arnold Palmer, interviewed by the author, July 11, 1997. Transcript, pp. 5-7.
26. David M. North, "Cessna Citation 10 Offers Speed, Mission Flexibility," *Aviation Week and Space Technology*, September 23, 1996, p. 54.
27. J. MacClellan, "Cessna Citation X," *Flying*, May 1996, p. 66.
28. Charles Johnson, interviewed by the author, February 20, 1997. Transcript, p. 17.
29. *Ibid.*, p. 18.
30. Palmer interview, p. 11.
31. Johnson interview, p. 9.
32. Hay interview, p. 54.
33. *Ibid.*, p. 47.
34. Richard Santulli, interviewed by the author, July 16, 1997. Transcript, p. 16.
35. Tom Webb, "Cessna Proudly Lays Claim To Aviation's Robert Collier Trophy," *Wichita Eagle*, May 8, 1997, p. 17A.
36. Kalberer interview, p. 7.
37. Transcript, Speeches From The Collier Trophy Awards Ceremony, Washington D. C., May 7, 1997, p. 5.
38. Meyer interview, p. 94.

Chapter Nineteen

1. Cessna press release, July 12, 1996.
2. Cessna press release, July 22, 1996.
3. *The Cessnan*, Vol. 4, No.1, January-February 1991, pp. 3, 6.
4. General Dynamics Annual Report, 1990, p. 23.
5. *Ibid.*, p. 6.
6. General Dynamics press release, October 17, 1991.
7. Memo from Chairman and CEO Russ Meyer to all employees, October 17, 1991.
8. Textron Annual Report, 1991, p. 3.
9. *Ibid.*, p. 8.
10. *Ibid.*, p. 8.
11. *Ibid.*, p. 71.
12. Textron Annual Report, 1991, p. 3.
13. Notes supplied by Russ Meyer; Bell Helicopter Website: http//www.textron.com/businesses/air-craft/profile.html.
14. *Directions*, Cessna Citation magazine, New Facilities Edition, 1992.
15. Bob Knebel, interviewed by the author, February 20, 1997. Transcript, pp. 3-6.
16. Donald Van Burkleo, interviewed by the author, April 3, 1997. Transcript, p. 10.
17. James Martin, interviewed by the author, April 2, 1997. Transcript, p. 4.
18. James Morgan, interviewed by the author, April 3, 1997. Transcript, p. 17.
19. Mark Paolucci, interviewed by the author, April 3, 1997. Transcript, p. 14.
20. Phil Michel, interviewed by the author, April 3, 1997. Transcript, pp. 7-8.
21. Michel interview, p. 23.
22. Cessna press release, November 24, 1992.
23. The JPATS Citation Jet, Cessna brochure.
24. *Ibid.*
25. Cessna press release, July 7, 1995.
26. Ron Alberti, interviewed by the author, February 23, 1997. Transcript, p. 14.
27. Russ Meyer, interviewed by the author, May 18, 1997. Transcript, p. 93.
28. John Hall, interviewed by the author, February 20, 1997. Transcript, p. 7.
29. Stacy Shapiro, "Product Liability Reform Revitalizes General Aviation," *Business Insurance*, May 15, 1995, p. 15.
30. "Cessna's Statement," *Independence Daily Reporter*, December 21, 1994, p. 1.
31. "Site Selection Culminates Months of Planning," *Independence Daily Reporter*, December 21, 1994, p. 1.
32. "Cessna Lands Here," *Independence Daily Reporter*, December 21, 1994, p. 1.
33. Cessna press release, July 12, 1996.
34. Pat Boyarski, interviewed by the author, February 6, 1997. Transcript, p. 7.
35. Michael Wright, interviewed by the author, February 7, 1997. Transcript, pp. 1, 7.
36. Program to the 48th Annual Wright Memorial Dinner, December 15, 1995, p. 6.
37. Dean Humphrey, interviewed by the author, April 17, 1997. Transcript, p. 12.
38. Frank Harris, interviewed by the author, February 19, 1997. Transcript, pp. 19-20.
39. Program to the 48th Annual Wright Memorial Dinner, p. 8.
40. *Ibid.*
41. Bob Knight, interviewed by the author, April 2, 1997. Transcript, p. 5.
42. Meyer interview, volume 4, p. 32.
43. Speech given by President Bill Clinton, November 17, 1997.
44. Speech given by Russ Meyer, November 17, 1997.
45. *Ibid.*
46. *Ibid.*
47. Treva West, interviewed by the author, February 19, 1997. Transcript, p. 5
48. Gary Hay, interviewed by the author, February 18, 1997. Transcript, p. 54.
49. Charlie Johnson, interviewed by the author, February 20, 1997. Transcript, p. 21.
50. Cessna press release, December 10, 1997.
51. *Ibid.*
52. Meyer interview, p. 105.
53. *Ibid.*
54. Notes supplied by Russ Meyer.

Chapter Nineteen Sidebar: FlightSafety

1. Al Ueltschi, interviewed by the author, July 17, 1997. Transcript, p. 6.
2. *Ibid.*, p. 13.
3. *Ibid.*, p. 5.
4. *Ibid.*, p. 21.
5. *Ibid.*, p. 23.

Chapter Nineteen Sidebar: 21st Street Project

1. John Moore, interviewed by the author, February 18, 1997. Transcript, p. 25.
2. Press Release, "Cessna Opens 21st Street Training and Subassembly Facility, November 29, 1990, published by Cessna.
3. "Payoff! Cessna Northeast Plant Comes Alive Through Community's Cooperation," *Wichita Eagle*, November 29, 1990.
4. Moore interview, p. 27.
5. Address by Russ Meyer, Center for Business and Government, John F. Kennedy School of Government. Harvard University, November 13, 1991.
6. Moore interview, p. 29.
7. Address by Meyer, November 13, 1991.

INDEX

W

XYZ

Cessna